OTHER A TO Z GUIDES FROM
THE SCARECROW PRESS, INC.

1. *The A to Z of Buddhism* by Charles S. Prebish, 2001.
2. *The A to Z of Catholicism* by William J. Collinge, 2001.
3. *The A to Z of Hinduism* by Bruce M. Sullivan, 2001.
4. *The A to Z of Islam* by Ludwig W. Adamec, 2002.
5. *The A to Z of Slavery & Abolition* by Martin A. Klein, 2002.
6. *Terrorism: Assassins to Zealots* by Sean Kendall Anderson and Stephen Sloan, 2003.
7. *The A to Z of the Korean War* by Paul M. Edwards, 2005.
8. *The A to Z of the Cold War* by Joseph Smith and Simon Davis, 2005.
9. *The A to Z of the Vietnam War* by Edwin E. Moise, 2005.
10. *The A to Z of Science Fiction Literature* by Brian Stableford, 2005.
11. *The A to Z of the Holocaust* by Jack R. Fischel, 2005.
12. *The A to Z of Washington, D.C.* by Robert Benedetto, Jane Donovan, and Kathleen DuVall, 2005.
13. *The A to Z of Taoism* by Julian F. Pas, 2006.
14. *The A to Z of the Renaissance* by Charles G. Nauert, 2006.
15. *The A to Z of Shinto* by Stuart D. B. Picken, 2006.
16. *The A to Z of Byzantium* by John H. Rosser, 2006.
17. *The A to Z of the Civil War* by Terry L. Jones, 2006.
18. *The A to Z of the Friends (Quakers)* by Margery Post Abbott, Mary Ellen Chijioke, Pink Dandelion, and John William Oliver Jr., 2006
19. *The A to Z of Feminism* by Janet K. Boles and Diane Long Hoeveler, 2006.
20. *The A to Z of New Religious Movements* by George D. Chryssides, 2006.
21. *The A to Z of Multinational Peacekeeping* by Terry M. Mays, 2006.
22. *The A to Z of Lutheranism* by Günther Gassmann with Duane H. Larson and Mark W. Oldenburg, 2007.
23. *The A to Z of the French Revolution* by Paul R. Hanson, 2007.
24. *The A to Z of the Persian Gulf War 1990–1991* by Clayton R. Newell, 2007.
25. *The A to Z of Revolutionary America* by Terry M. Mays, 2007.

The A to Z of the United States– Mexican War

Edward H. Moseley
Paul C. Clark Jr.

The A to Z Guide Series, No. 74

THE SCARECROW PRESS, INC.
Lanham • Toronto • Plymouth, UK
2009

Published by Scarecrow Press, Inc.
A wholly owned subsidary of
The Rowman & Littlefield Publishing Group, Inc.
4501 Forbes Boulevard, Suite 200, Lanham, Maryland 20706
http://www.scarecrowpress.com

Estover Road, Plymouth PL6 7PY, United Kingdom

British Library Cataloguing in Publication Information Available

Library of Congress Cataloging-in-Publication Data

The hardback version of this book was cataloged by the Library of Congress as
follows:

Moseley, Edward H., 1931–
  Historical dictionary of the United States–Mexican War / Edward H. Moseley
and Paul C. Clark, Jr.
    p. cm. — (Historical dictionaries of wars, revolution, and civil unrest ; v. 2)
  Includes bibliographical references (p.).
    1. Mexican War, 1846–1848—Dictionaries. I. Clark, Paul Coe. II. Title.
III. Series.
  E404.M84   1997   97-11302
  973.6'2'03—DC21   CIP

ISBN 978-0-8108-6861-8 (pbk. : alk. paper)
ISBN 978-0-8108-7024-6 (ebook)

⊖™ The paper used in this publication meets the minimum requirements of
American National Standard for Information Sciences—Permanence of Paper
for Printed Library Materials, ANSI/NISO Z39.48-1992.

Printed in the United States of America

To the West Point officers whose professionalism in battle
shortened the war with Mexico, saving thousands
of lives on both sides of the Rio del Norte

and

To the private soldiers from both countries who fought
in the war, gaining little glory and fortune, surviving
only with great luck the naked blade and dreaded
disease of that conflict
and, finally,
To the memory of Winfield Scott, who had the
vision to bring a cruel war to a quick end

GEN. WINFIELD SCOTT.

Contents

Maps

Illustrations

Editor's Foreword

It is understandable that the United States–Mexican War is so poorly known by the American people. It was overshadowed by bigger, bloodier wars such as the Civil War, which followed it by only 13 years, and, of course, by the world wars of this century and America's longest war, Vietnam. But there are strong reasons for remembrance. The United States war with Mexico was a war close to home; it was controversial, yet it aroused great patriotism in the land; and it was uniquely successful in expanding the nation's borders, however disquieting that fact may be today among those who view it as a war of pure aggression. Wars of conquest are not as popular today as they once were. Surely, that aspect of the war explains why it has not been forgotten in Mexico, a country that lost almost half of its national territory in the conflict. The war, along with subsequent military interventions by the United States, greatly intensified Mexico's distrust of its northern neighbor, a distrust that has perhaps subsided but not disappeared in the intervening century and a half.

It is hoped that this volume will assist those on both sides of the long, common border to better understand the conflict. A historical dictionary is particularly apt for such a task, since it is an analysis that neither voices praise nor apportions blame. It is not intended to be a history book to inflame passions but, rather, a straightforward reference work providing the essential facts, figures, and background. It includes numerous entries on participants, not only statesmen and generals but also ordinary persons who distinguished themselves in one way or another. It describes the lay of the land, the cities and states, the rivers and forts, and the many battles that determined the outcome of the war. It summarizes the origins and the conclusion of the war as well as the political and military positions of both sides during the conflict. Events are easier to follow because of the inclusion of a chronology; and those who wish to research further need merely consult the comprehensive if selective bibliography.

It would be hard to find a better team to recall this distant war. Both Paul Clark and Ed Moseley hold Ph.D.s in Latin American

xi

history. Clark teaches Latin American studies and U.S. strategic subjects at the Armed Forces Staff College. Moseley teaches history and directs international programs at the University of Alabama. Both authors are former army infantry officers who have lectured and written on the United States–Mexican War. They have recently retraced the campaign routes of the main armies of the war by extensive travel through the Southwest, California, and Mexico. This *Historical Dictionary of the United States–Mexican War* obviously benefits from that experience and interest and enhances our knowledge of the conflict.

Jon Woronoff
Series Editor

Maps

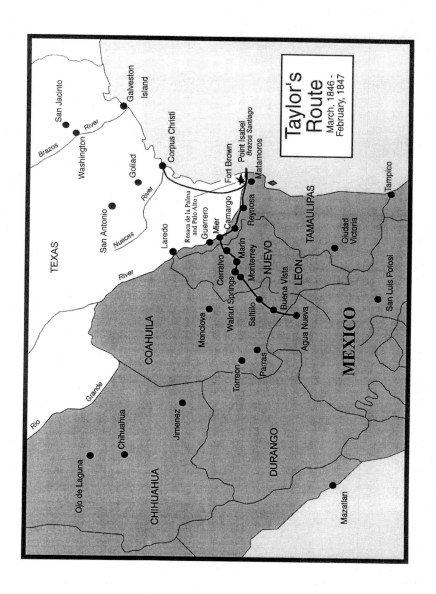

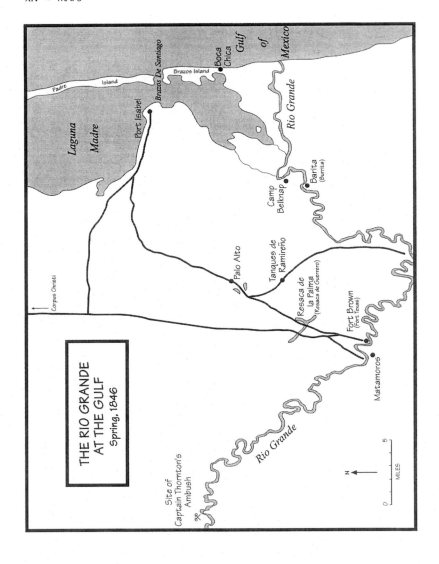

THE RIO GRANDE
AT THE GULF
Spring, 1846

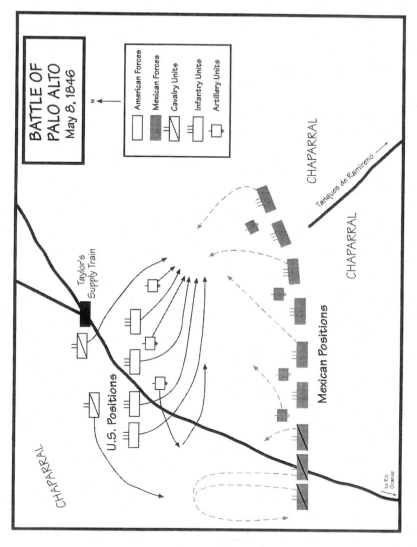

BATTLE OF
PALO ALTO
May 8, 1846

N

American Forces
Mexican Forces
Cavalry Units
Infantry Units
Artillery Units

CHAPARRAL

CHAPARRAL

Tanques de Ramireno

CHAPARRAL

Taylor's Supply Train

U.S. Positions

Mexican Positions

to Rio Grande

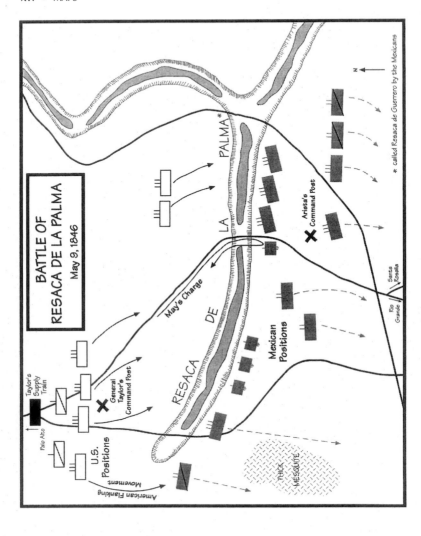

BATTLE OF
RESACA DE LA PALMA
May 9, 1846

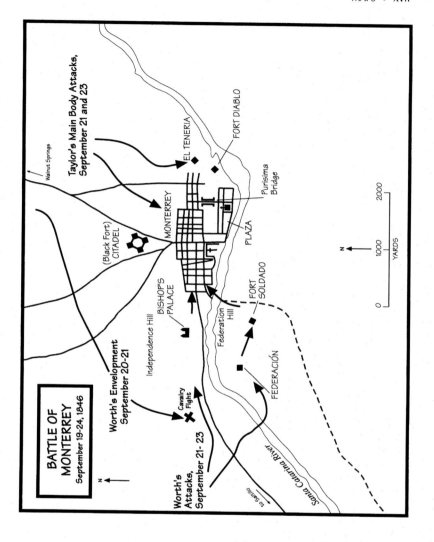

BATTLE OF
MONTERREY
September 19-24, 1846

Worth's Envelopment
September 20-21

Worth's
Attacks,
September 21- 23

Cavalry
Fight

Walnut Springs

Taylor's Main Body Attacks,
September 21 and 23

EL TENERIA

FORT DIABLO

MONTERREY

Purisima
Bridge

(Black Fort)
CITADEL

PLAZA

FORT
SOLDADO

BISHOP'S
PALACE

Independence Hill

Federation
Hill

FEDERACIÓN

to Saltillo

Santa Catarina River

0   1000   2000
        YARDS

N

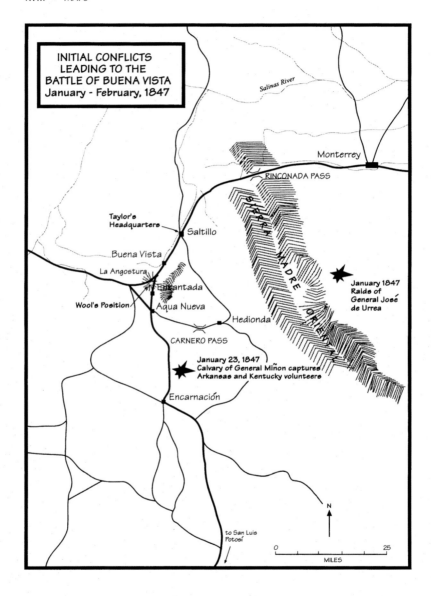

INITIAL CONFLICTS
LEADING TO THE
BATTLE OF BUENA VISTA
January - February, 1847

Salinas River

Monterrey

RINCONADA PASS

SIERRA MADRE ORIENTAL

Taylor's
Headquarters
Saltillo

Buena Vista

La Angostura

Encantada

Wool's Position

Aqua Nueva

Hedionda

CARNERO PASS

January 1847
Raids of
General José
de Urrea

January 23, 1847
Calvary of General Miñon captures
Arkansas and Kentucky volunteers

Encarnación

to San Luis
Potosí

N

0   25
MILES

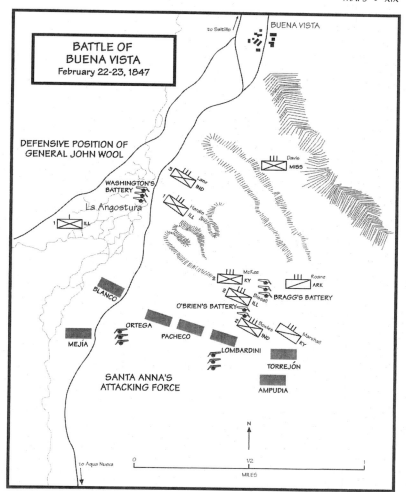

BATTLE OF
BUENA VISTA
February 22-23, 1847

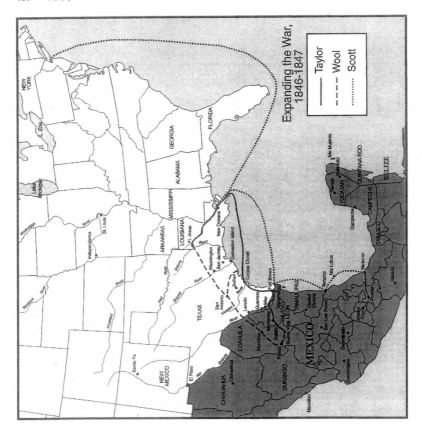

Expanding the War, 1846–1847

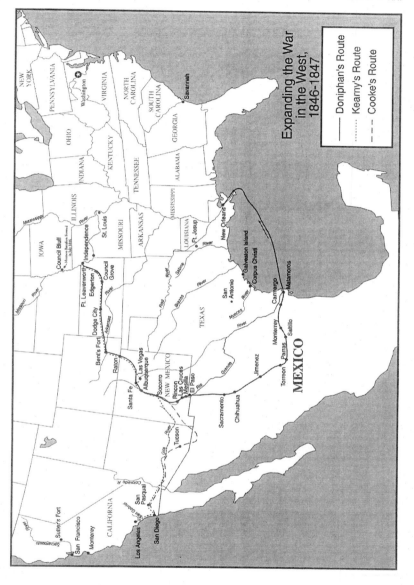

Expanding the War
in the West,
1846-1847

——— Doniphan's Route
·········· Kearny's Route
– – – Cooke's Route

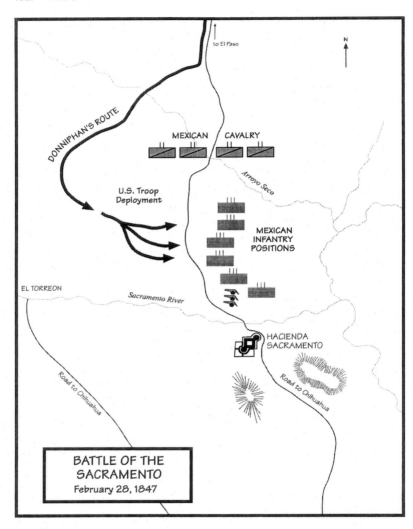

to El Paso

N

DONNIPHAN'S ROUTE

MEXICAN CAVALRY

U.S. Troop
Deployment

Arroyo Seco

MEXICAN
INFANTRY
POSITIONS

EL TORREON

Sacramento River

HACIENDA
SACRAMENTO

Road to Chihuahua

Road to Chihuahua

BATTLE OF THE
SACRAMENTO
February 28, 1847

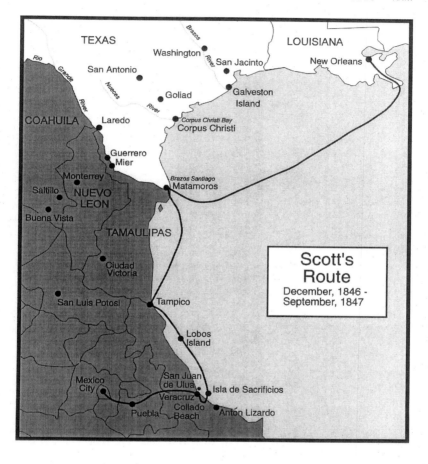

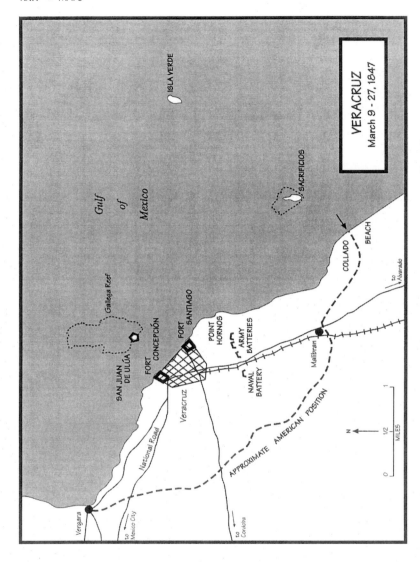

ISLA VERDE

Gulf
of
Mexico

SACRIFICIOS

COLLADO

BEACH

to
Alvarado

Gallega Reef

SAN JUAN
DE ULÚA

FORT
CONCEPCIÓN

FORT
SANTIAGO

POINT
HORNOS

ARMY
BATTERIES

NAVAL
BATTERY

Malibran

Veracruz

National Road

APPROXIMATE AMERICAN POSITION

to
Mexico City

to
Córdoba

Vergara

N

0   1/2   1
MILES

VERACRUZ
March 9 - 27, 1847

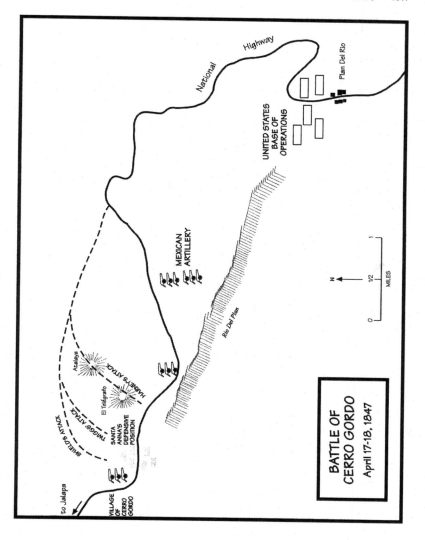

BATTLE OF
CERRO GORDO
April 17-18, 1847

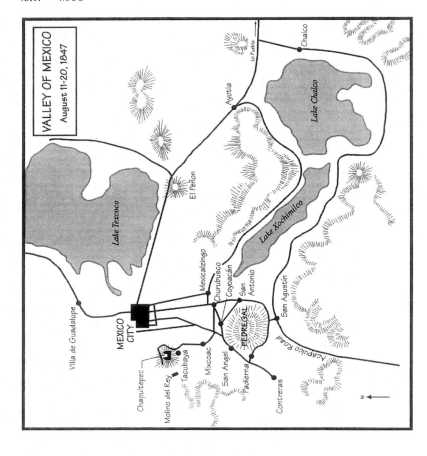

VALLEY OF MEXICO
August 11–20, 1847

Lake Texcoco

Lake Chalco

Lake Xochimilco

Chalco

to Puebla

Ayotla

El Peñón

Villa de Guadalupe

MEXICO CITY

Mexicaltzingo

Churubusco

Coyoacán

San Antonio

San Agustín

Acapulco Road

PEDREGAL

Chapultepec

Molino del Rey

Tacubaya

Mixcoac

San Ángel

Padierna

Contreras

N

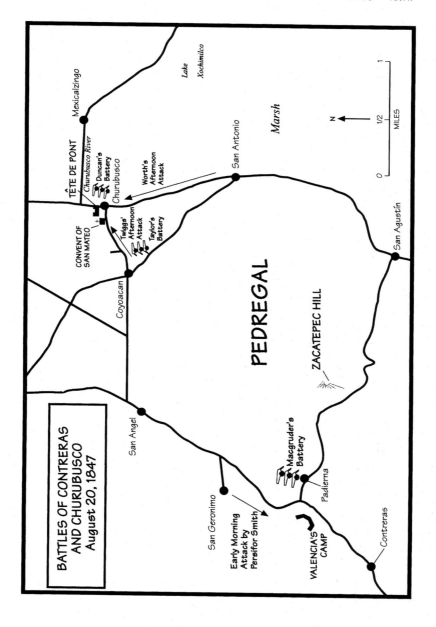

BATTLES OF CONTRERAS
AND CHURUBUSCO
August 20, 1847

Mexicalzingo

Lake
Xochimilco

TÊTE DE PONT

Churubusco River

Duncan's
Battery

Churubusco

Worth's
Afternoon
Attack

San Antonio

Marsh

N

1/2

MILES

0   1

San Agustín

CONVENT OF
SAN MATEO

Twiggs'
Afternoon
Attack

Taylor's
Battery

Coyoacan

PEDREGAL

ZACATEPEC HILL

San Angel

Macgruder's
Battery

Padierna

Contreras

San Geronimo

Early Morning
Attack by
Persifor Smith

VALENCIA'S
CAMP

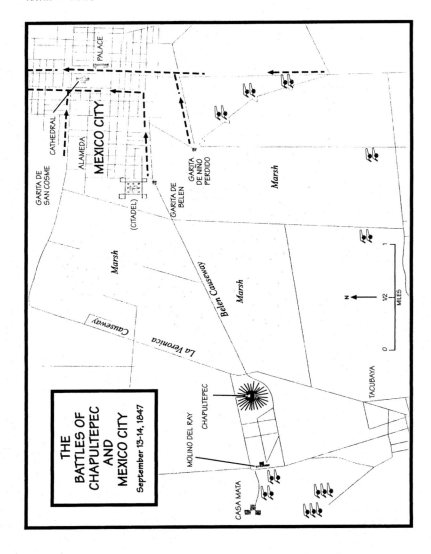

THE
BATTLES OF
CHAPULTEPEC
AND
MEXICO CITY
September 13-14, 1847

MEXICO CITY

PALACE

CATHEDRAL

ALAMEDA

GARITA DE
SAN COSME

(CITADEL)

GARITA DE
BELEN

GARITA
DE NIÑO
PERDIDO

Marsh

Marsh

Marsh

Marsh

Belen Causeway

La Verónica Causeway

Causeway

CHAPULTEPEC

MOLINO DEL RAY

CASA MATA

TACUBAYA

N

0   ½   1
         MILES

Preface

This work is not designed to be an interpretive history of the United States–Mexican War. Its purpose is to serve as a reference work—as near to the facts as possible—for scholars and others drawn to study the war on its 150th anniversary. This said, some interpretation had to be made as we sorted through and selected items from the vast amount of material we reviewed in libraries and private collections in the United States and Mexico.

We were attracted by the idea of a dictionary of the United States–Mexican War as we worked on a long-range project of revisiting all principal locations connected to the war, including campsites, routes of march, staging areas, and battlefields. Those visits gave us first-hand impressions of the geography and vast scope of the war and put us into contact with names and events, on-site descriptions and historical markers, that allowed us to sort through the often confusing material in primary and secondary sources. We believe that retracing the paths of generals Winfield Scott, Zachary Taylor, John Wool, and Stephen Kearny—over thousands of miles of terrain in Louisiana, Texas, Kansas, New Mexico, California, and three major campaign locations in Mexico—gave us a clearer idea of which figures and locations, among the thousands mentioned by historians, soldiers, and other chronologists, should be selected for inclusion in this reference work.

Grants from the University of Alabama provided assistance for our research trip to Mexico, some archival work, and conference presentations that formed the background for this project. The library at the Armed Forces Staff College, under the able directorship of Gail Nicula, provided us with considerable assistance, especially in the latter stages of research. Col. Charles "Chuck" Cornwall assisted with sound advice on technical aspects of the U.S. Army in the mid-19th century. The Gorgas Library and the W. S. Hoole Special Collections Library at the University of Alabama were outstanding sources throughout the project.

Many individuals have assisted in the preparation of the dictionary. Wayne C. Remington, supervisor of the cartographic laboratory of the University of Alabama, spent many hours preparing the maps for the volume. Without the technical advice and constant support of Sheila Rodenberry of the University of Alabama's Capstone International Program Center, the final manuscript could never have been completed. The expertise (and patience) of Brenda Griffith and Katherine Smith of the word processing division of the Armed Forces Staff College is very much appreciated. Finally, Mary Lynn Clark deserves special thanks as a full member of the research team throughout the entire project. She compiled lists of participants, dates, events, and other material and assembled significant primary and secondary sources that were crucial in constructing hundreds of dictionary entries. She also worked tirelessly on the chronology, organizing it into a format that logically integrated events from the various theaters of war. Her research included countless hours in the libraries of Old Dominion University and the College of William and Mary, as well as several visits to the Library of Congress. We are most grateful for her professional help on this project.

Chronology

EVENTS PRIOR TO 1846

1821 **February 19.** The U.S. Senate ratifies the Adams-Onís Treaty, acquiring Florida from Spain and establishing the Sabine River as the boundary between Spanish territory and the United States.

1833 **January.** Gen. Antonio López de Santa Anna's election as president of Mexico begins the "Age of Santa Anna" in that nation. In April of the following year, he assumes absolute power for the first of several tenures as dictator during the next two decades.

1836 **April 21.** The decisive victory of the Sam Houston-led Texans at San Jacinto establishes de facto Texas independence. Texas remains sovereign for the next nine years.

1837 **March 4.** The United States recognizes Texas independence.

1840 **August 20.** A tribunal is formed to arbitrate U.S. citizens' claims against Mexico. The following year, the tribunal awards over $2,000,000 to U.S. citizens. Mexico agrees to pay on an installment plan, makes several payments, and then defaults.

1842 **October 19.** Commo. Thomas ap Catesby Jones, under the mistaken impression that the United States and Mexico are on the verge of war, occupies the Mexican city of Monterey, provincial capital of California. On October 20, realizing his error, he returns control of Monterey to Mexican officials.

December 25. As part of a continuing border war between Texas and Mexico, a Mexican army under Gen. Pedro de Ampudia and Col. Antonio Canales defeats a force of Texans under Col. William Fisher at the town of Mier. Ampudia takes over 200 prisoners of the "Mier Expedition."

1843 **March 1.** Based on an order dispatched on this date by General Santa Anna, Mexican captors kill every 10th prisoner from the Mier Expedition in the "black bean" incident in Salado, Mexico.

December 30. Commo. David Conner is appointed to command the Home Squadron in the Gulf of Mexico.

1844 **November 12.** James K. Polk, a Democrat from Tennessee, is elected president on a platform that supports annexation of Texas.

1845 **March 3.** Outgoing President John Tyler sends a congressional resolution to Texas offering annexation to the United States.

March 4. James K. Polk is inaugurated as 11th president of the United States.

March 6. Mexican minister to Washington, Gen. Juan N. Amonte, sends a note to Secretary of State John C. Calhoun calling the attempt to annex Texas an act of aggression. In Mexico, the *Puro* political faction reaffirms its adamant position to pursue war rather than accept annexation.

March 24. Commodore John D. Sloat takes command of the Pacific Squadron in Callao, Peru.

June 3. Gen. Antonio López de Santa Anna, former strongman of Mexico, departs Veracruz for exile in Havana, one of many exiles during his career.

June 29. Gen. Zachary Taylor receives orders at Fort Jesup, Louisiana, to move his Army of Observation to a position near the Rio Grande in west Texas. His renamed Army of Occupation arrives at Corpus Christi, an alternate location chosen by Taylor, in early August.

July 4. The Texas convention accepts the U. S. annexation offer.

July 11. The Polk administration alerts Commodore Conner, commander of the Home Squadron, to the possibility of Mexican aggression. In the event of war, Conner is instructed to attack Mexican forces at any location east of the Rio Grande, to seize Tampico, and to take the fort of San Juan de Ulúa off Veracruz.

November 18. Commodore John D. Sloat arrives in Mazatlán.

November 30. John Slidell, President Polk's special diplomatic envoy, arrives in Mexico with instructions to negotiate a settlement between the two governments.

December 9. First Lt. John C. Frémont, known as the "Pathfinder" because of his explorations in the West, arrives with a small force at Sutter's Fort, California.

December 29. Texas officially becomes a state.

1846–1848

Mexico & U.S. Political and Diplomatic	Mexico & Texas Theater	New Mexico & California Theater
January 1846		Mid-January (California). Frémont moves from Sutter's Fort to Monterey.
4 (Mexico City). Gen. Mariano Paredes comes to power in Mexico. He vows to defend Texas to the Sabine River.	13 (Washington). Administration sends General Taylor orders to move to the Rio Grande.	
12 (Washington). News of the failure of Slidell's mission is received.	17 (Washington). Bancroft orders Conner to position all but the *Mississippi* and one other ship off Veracruz.	
February 1846		
	3 (Texas). Taylor receives orders to advance to the Rio Grande.	
March 1846		5 (California). Mexican authorities near Salinas order Frémont to leave California.
21 (Mexico). Slidell is given his passport and directed to return to the United States.	8 (Texas). Leading elements of Taylor's Army of Occupation depart Corpus Christi.	5 (California). Frémont refuses to leave, establishes a position on Gavilan Peak near Monterey, and hoists the U.S. flag. Gen. José María Castro places the location under siege.
21 (Mexico). President Paredes issues a manifesto calling for war.	19 (Texas). Advance elements of Taylor's army encounter Mexican force at the Arroyo Colorado. After threatening to oppose the American crossing, the Mexican troops withdraw without a fight.	
30 (Veracruz). Slidell sails from Mexico, ending the Polk administration's efforts to avoid war through diplomacy.		

Mexico & U.S. Political and Diplomatic	Mexico & Texas Theater	New Mexico & California Theater
	23 (Point Isabel). Both Taylor and U.S. naval ships arrive on this date.	
	28 (Texas). Taylor's army marches to a point across the Rio Grande from Matamoros, establishes camp in a cornfield, and raises the U.S. flag.	
	28 (Texas-Matamoros). General Worth is sent by Taylor to deliver a letter to General Mejía, assuring him that the move to the river is not a hostile act. Mejía refuses to see Worth but has Brig. Gen. Rómulo Díaz de la Vega meet with him. They communicate through officers on each side who speak French.	
April 1846		
23 (Mexico City). President Paredes declares a defensive war after hostilities break out along the Rio Grande.	4 (Mexico City). Minister of War, Gen. José María Tornel y Mendívil, orders Gen. Mariano Arista to take command of the Division of the North and attack the Americans.	
	10 (Rio Grande). Col. Trueman Cross, chief quartermaster of Taylor's army, is missing. His body would be found 11 days later.	

11 (Matamoros). Unaware that Arista has been appointed to replace him, Gen. Pedro de Ampudia arrives to take command of the Division of the North.

17 (mouth of the Rio Grande). The U.S. navy blockades Matamoros; Ampudia promptly protests, but the blockade continues.

24 (Matamoros). Brig. Gen. Anastasio Torrejón leads a force of 1,600 men across the Rio Grande.

25 (Rio Grande). An 80-man contingent commanded by Capt. Seth B. Thornton is ambushed at the Rancho de Carricitos. Thornton loses 11 killed and 6 wounded; most of the remaining men, including Thornton, are captured.

25 (Rio Grande). Gen. Mariano Arista arrives to take command of the Division of the North.

Mexico & U.S. Political and Diplomatic

May 1846

8 (Washington). John Slidell reaches Washington, reporting on his failed diplomatic mission in Mexico.

9 (Washington). President Polk discusses with his cabinet plans to declare war. At 1800, Polk receives Taylor's message of April 26, reporting the ambush of Thornton. At 1930, the cabinet supports the war bill, which is passed by the House on the 11th and the Senate on the 12th.

13 (Washington). Polk signs the war bill. Secretary of Navy Bancroft issues orders to Commodore Conner to blockade Mexican ports.

13–14 (Washington). Polk, Marcy, and Scott prepare plans to send three forces into Mexican territory (to northeastern Mexico, to Santa Fe, and to Chihuahua).

27 (Washington). Gen. John E. Wool is ordered to supervise raising of volunteers from Ohio, Indiana, Illinois, Kentucky, Tennessee, and Mississippi; he is not promised a command.

Mexico & Texas Theater

1 (Rio Grande). Taylor marches with most of his force to Point Isabel, leaving Maj. Jacob Brown in charge of Fort Texas.

3 (Rio Grande). Mexicans begin their attack on Fort Texas.

4 (Antón Lizardo). Commodore Conner, along with the bulk of the Home Squadron, sails for Brazos Santiago, arriving on the 8th.

6 (Rio Grande). Major Brown dies; Fort Texas is later renamed Fort Brown.

8 (Rio Grande). Battle of Palo Alto.

9 (Rio Grande). Battle of Resaca de la Palma.

11 (Rio Grande front). Taylor confers with Commodore David Conner at Point Isabel; they plan a joint operation to cross the Rio Grande near Barita.

14 (Gulf of Mexico). Commodore Conner issues blockade instructions for the Mexican ports along the Gulf of

New Mexico & California Theater

17 (California). Sloat receives word of Thornton ambush.

30 (Washington). General Scott orders Col. Stephen W. Kearny to gather an army at Fort Leavenworth and to prepare for a campaign in New Mexico.

Mexico. They declare the establishment of the blockade at Veracruz, Alvarado, Tampico, and Matamoros. Conner establishes his forward base of operations at Antón Lizardo, 12 miles south of Veracruz.

17 (Rio Grande). General Arista proposes an armistice. When Taylor rejects it, Arista evacuates the city of Matamoros.

18 (Rio Grande). Taylor leads his army across the Rio Grande to occupy Matamoros.

20 (Gulf of Mexico). The *St. Mary's* blockades Tampico, and the *Mississippi* blockades Veracruz.

June 1846

6 (Mexico City). The Mexican congress passes a measure authorizing President Paredes to repel the U.S. invading force.

12 (Washington). The U.S. Senate approves Oregon Treaty with Britain; it is signed on the 15th.

8 (Tampico). The port is bombarded by the *St. Mary's*.

11 (Washington). Gen. John E. Wool is ordered to take command of the Chihuahua expedition; his force is named the Centre Division.

June-July (Rio Grande). A supply point is established at Point Isabel, and a number of steam powered vessels move men and supplies up the Rio Grande.

17 (California). Sloat receives confirmation of battles of Palo Alto and Resaca de la Palma; this convinces him that he has authority to commence offensive operations.

22–28 (Leavenworth-Santa Fe). Forces of Colonel Doniphan depart Leavenworth for Bent's Fort (537 miles).

30 (Leavenworth-Santa Fe). Kearny and his staff, accompanied by artillery, depart Leavenworth. His Army of the West consists of 1,458 men; it would later be reinforced by 1,000 men.

Mexico & U.S. Political and Diplomatic

July 1846

1 (Mexico City). The Mexican congress formally declares war on the United States.

6–7 (Havana). Alexander Slidell Mackenzie opens discussions with Santa Anna relating to the return of the exiled Mexican leader to his country. An agreement is reached to allow Santa Anna to pass through the blockade.

End of July (Mexico City). Paredes is forced out of the presidency by Santa Anna loyalists.

Mexico & Texas Theater

14 (Carmago). Taylor occupies the town.

21 (Gulf of Mexico). Conner includes Soto la Marina, Tuxpán, Alvarado, and Tecoluto in the blockade.

31 (Mier). American forces occupy the town.

New Mexico & California Theater

2 (Monterey). Sloat arrives.

4 (Sonoma). Bear Flaggers hold a celebration and, influenced by Frémont, declare California's independence.

7 (Monterey). The U.S. Navy occupies this small port.

9 (San Francisco). Comdr. John Montgomery occupies San Francisco.

29 (California). Commodore Sloat transfers command of the Pacific Fleet to Commo. Robert F. Stockton.

29 (California). Frémont's force lands at San Diego to attack California forces in the southern region of the state.

August 1846

4 (Washington). Polk, encouraged by the reports from Mexico, sends a confidential message to the Senate, asking for a two million dollar appropriation for the settlement of the Texas boundary at the Rio Grande and the purchase of New Mexico and California.

6 (Mexico City). José Mariano Salas becomes Mexico's acting president, succeeding Paredes.

8 (Washington). Congressman David Wilmot of Pennsylvania introduces the "Wilmot Proviso" to prevent the expansion of slavery into territory that might be acquired from Mexico. It passes in the House of Representatives but fails in the Senate.

7 (Alvarado). U.S. ships attack the port but fail to take it.

12 (Washington). Matthew Perry is offered command of the *Mississippi*; he is to take command on October 6.

16 (Veracruz). Santa Anna is allowed to pass through the blockade and reenter Mexico; he quickly forgets promises to reach a settlement and places himself at the head of the army.

19–25 (Rio Grande). Taylor's army begins its march south. Worth leads the Second Division the 60 miles from Camargo to Cerralvo.

24–29 (San Antonio). Additional forces join the Centre Division of Gen. John Wool at Camp Crockett in San Antonio.

2–7 (Santa Fe). The Army of the West departs from Bent's Fort, crosses the Arkansas River, and moves through Raton Pass.

13 (Los Angeles). Stockton takes the city.

16 (Santa Fe). Governor Armijo, aware of the opposition of his troops to opposing the Americans, disbands the New Mexican army and flees toward Chihuahua.

18 (Santa Fe). Kearny and his troops peacefully occupy Santa Fe.

September 1846

9 (Washington). John Y. Mason replaces Bancroft as secretary of the navy.

14 (Mexico City). Santa Anna becomes commander in chief of the army.

4 (San Antonio). The last element of the Centre Division—a field battery from Carlisle Barracks, Pennsylvania commanded by Capt. John M. Washington—arrives to join General Wool at Camp Crockett.

2–11 (Santa Fe). Brigadier General Kearny's army moves down the Rio Grande from Santa Fe to Albuquerque.

9 (Mazatlán). Comdr. Joseph Hull blockades the port.

Mexico & U.S. Political and Diplomatic	Mexico & Texas Theater	New Mexico & California Theater
	9 (Rio Grande). Taylor and his staff arrive in Cerralvo.	22 (Santa Fe). General Kearny publishes a law code for the territory of New Mexico and appoints Charles Bent as territorial governor.
	11 (Rio Grande). The first units of Taylor's army leave Cerralvo for Monterrey.	23–30 (California). A fight begins between U.S. and California elements in Los Angeles; the city is evacuated by Captain Gillespie on September 30.
	14 (Rio Grande). The Texas Rangers and the Mexican cavalry skirmish at Ramos.	25 (Santa Fe). Kearny leaves Santa Fe for California with 300 dragoons and topographical engineers.
	19 (Monterrey). Taylor and the advanced guard arrive north of Monterrey, in view of the city. Mexican forces fire from the "Black Fort." Taylor establishes his HQ at Walnut Springs (Bosque de Santo Domingo).	29 (Los Angeles). The U. S. garrison surrenders.
	20 (Monterrey). General Worth's division initiates the attack against Monterrey.	
	20–24 (Monterrey). Battle of Monterrey.	
	23 (Gulf of Mexico). Commo. Matthew C. Perry, designated to assume command of the Home Squadron upon Conner's retirement, arrives at Antón Lizardo. Conner remains in command, however, and Perry commands the *Mississippi*.	

25 (Monterrey). Taylor and Ampudia conclude an armistice agreement providing for Mexican forces to evacuate within a week and retire beyond the Rinconada Pass-Linares-San Fernando de Parras line. The armistice is to last eight weeks.

25 (San Antonio). Wool leaves for Chihuahua.

28 (north of Mexico City). Santa Anna marches north toward San Luis Potosí.

30 (Saltillo). Ampudia moves to Saltillo where he will remain until leaving for San Luis Potosí on October 4.

October 1846

11–13 (Washington). Polk is angered by news of the Monterrey armistice. On October 13, Secretary of State Marcy sends an order to Taylor to end the armistice.

27 (Washington). Before the selection of a Veracruz commander, Gen. Winfield Scott presents to Secretary Marcy a paper entitled "Vera Cruz and Its Castle."

8 (San Luis Potosí). Santa Anna reaches San Luis Potosí and begins to build a large army.

9 (Rio Grande). Gen. John Wool and his men arrive at the Rio Grande opposite the Mexican town of Presidio del Rio Grande.

13 (Rio Grande). Wool and his men enter Presidio del Rio Grande unopposed; Wool receives word from Monterrey of the armistice.

6 (en route to California). Kearny's and Kit Carson's forces meet 10 miles below Socorro. Carson reports the seizure of California by Commo. Robert F. Stockton. Upon learning this, Kearny retains only two companies (100 men) for his march to California and returns the remainder of his force to Santa Fe. Carson goes back to California to accompany Kearny.

Mexico & U.S. Political and Diplomatic	Mexico & Texas Theater	New Mexico & California Theater
	13 (Rio Grande). Brig. Gen. James Shields arrives and becomes second in command to Wool.	19 (Santa Fe). Elements of the Mormon Battalion, commanded by Lt. Col. Philip St. George Cooke, move down the Rio Grande; on November 13, they move west over the Old Spanish Trail, marching south of Kearny's route into present-day Sonora and then north to Tucson.
	24–25 (Gulf of Mexico). Commo. Matthew C. Perry takes Tabasco but cannot hold it and retreats on the 30th to Antón Lizardo.	
	29 (Monclova). Wool occupies Monclova, establishes his HQ in the Governor's Palace, and uses the armistice period to prepare for his march to Chihuahua.	
	12 (Monterrey). Maj. Robert M. McLane arrives with instructions to halt the movement southward, but Taylor continues his plan to occupy Saltillo.	
	13 (Monterrey). Taylor sends word to the Mexicans that he will resume hostilities.	
November 1846		
17–19 (Washington). On the 17th, the cabinet unanimously approves the Veracruz landing; on the 19th, Polk appoints Scott commander in chief of the operation.	14 (Gulf of Mexico). A force under Commodore Conner occupies Tampico.	
23 (Washington). Scott leaves for New York; the following week he departs for New Orleans.	16 (Saltillo). Taylor arrives; he sends orders to Wool in Monclova to move his Centre Division south to Parras.	

December 1846

6 (Mexico City). Santa Anna is elected president, and Gómez Farías is elected vice president by the Mexican congress.

5 (Parras). After marching 181 miles from Monclova, Wool occupies the town.

17–21 (Rio Grande-Parras-Saltillo). On the 17th, Wool receives a report from Gen. William J. Worth in Saltillo of the move of Santa Anna's army from San Luis Potosí. Within two hours, Wool has his force in motion; they reach Agua Nueva on December 21.

27 (Rio Grande). General Scott reaches Brazos Santiago and departs for Camargo to meet General Taylor.

2 (California). Kearny and his men arrive at Warner's Ranch.

6–10 (California). On the 6th, Kearny suffers severe losses at the battle of San Pascual fighting Californians under Captain Andrés Pico. On the 7th, Pico attacks U.S. troops at Rancho San Bernardo and keeps them under siege until the 10th.

12 (San Diego). Kearny and his battle-weary men arrive after the long march from Leavenworth.

25 (Rio Grande). Doniphan's troops engage the Mexican forces at the battle of El Brazito; the Mexicans retreat.

27 (El Paso). Doniphan's force enters the town unopposed. His mission is to remain there until February 8, 1847, when artillery and additional supplies are to arrive from Santa Fe. Here Doniphan learns that Wool's march to Chihuahua has been aborted.

Mexico & U.S. Political and Diplomatic

January 1847

(Washington). The U.S. Senate's refusal to create a lieutenant generalcy thwarts Polk's plan to make Sen. Thomas H. Benton commanding general in Mexico.

11 (Mexico City). Mexican law is passed approving the sale of church property for the government's benefit.

13 (California). The Treaty of Cahuenga is signed between Capt. John C. Frémont and the Californians; Frémont arrives in Los Angeles the next day.

Mexico & Texas Theater

1st week (Rio Grande). General Scott travels up the Rio Grande, arriving in Camargo; Taylor does not show up for the meeting. On the 3rd, Scott sends an order to Taylor for troops for the Veracruz operation.

4 (Victoria). General Taylor arrives in Victoria, staying until the 14th when he departs to return to Monterrey.

9 (Saltillo). General Worth, responding to Scott's January 3 order, departs to join Scott's army; Worth arrives at Brazos Santiago on the 18th.

13 (Villa Gran). Lt. John A. Richey, en route to Victoria with Scott's January 3 order for troops, is murdered by Mexicans; the message is seized and sent to General Santa Anna.

24 (Monterrey). Taylor returns from Victoria.

27–28 (San Luis Potosí). Advance guard of Santa Anna's army departs for Saltillo, 250 miles to the north.

New Mexico & California Theater

8 (California). Mexicans retreat after the battle of San Gabriel, 12 miles south of Los Angeles.

9 (California). Battle of La Mesa.

10 (California). Commodore Stockton reoccupies Los Angeles.

14 (California). Frémont arrives in Los Angeles.

16 (California). Commodore Stockton makes Frémont governor of California; Kearny objects but acquiesces.

19 (New Mexico). Gov. Charles Bent is murdered during the Taos Rebellion; on the same day, in a coordinated uprising, additional Americans are murdered at Rio Colorado and Arroyo Hondo.

22 (California). Commo. W. Branford Shubrick assumes interim command of the Pacific Squadron from Commodore Stockton.

23 (California). General Kearny retires to San Diego and is joined by the Mormon Battalion under Lt. Col. Philip St. George Cooke.

February 1847

10 (Washington). Congress passes the "Ten Regiment Bill" to enlarge the army.

27 (Mexico City). Polko Rebellion breaks out.

2 (San Luis Potosí). Santa Anna and his main contingent depart for Saltillo.

5 (Saltillo). Taylor marches from Monterrey to join the forces he left at Saltillo. On the 5th, he establishes his headquarters at Agua Nueva, 20 miles south of the city, and by the 14th his forces had closed there.

15 (Brazos Santiago). Scott embarks for the Veracruz operation on the *Massachusetts*; he reaches Tampico on the 18th, Lobos Island on the 21st.

18–21 (30 miles south of Agua Nueva). Santa Anna's army closes on Encarnación.

19 (Tampico). General Scott implements martial law in this port city.

20 (Agua Nueva). General Wool convinces Taylor to pull back to Angostura Pass, 10 miles back toward Saltillo. At Wool's direction, new defenses are established at the pass on the 21st; Taylor sets up his command post at the Buena Vista Hacienda.

22–23. Battle of Buena Vista (or Angostura). On the 24th, Santa Anna begins his retreat through Agua Nueva toward San Luis Potosí. After the battle, Taylor reoccupies Agua Nueva.

3–5 (New Mexico). Col. Sterling Price subdues Taos Rebellion.

8 (El Paso). Col. Alexander Doniphan and the Missourians depart for Chihuahua.

28 (Chihuahua). Fifteen miles north of Chihuahua City, Doniphan defeats the Mexicans at the battle of Sacramento; he takes Chihuahua City on March 1 and occupies it until April 28 when the Missourians begin the long trek home.

Mexico & U.S. Political and Diplomatic	Mexico & Texas Theater	New Mexico & California Theater
March 1847	2 (Lobos Island). Scott departs for Veracruz, his forward units reach Antón Lizardo on the 4th, and the last of the 40 transports close the next day (March 5).	1 (California). Shubrick's proclamation, dated March 1 and released on the 4th, divides authority for land and port operations between army and navy officials. Shubrick recognizes Kearny as governor of California.
21 (Mexico City). Polko Rebellion ends.		
21 (Mexico City). Santa Anna resumes the presidency for a 10-day period.	6 (Veracruz). Scott and Commodore Conner, along with Scott's personal staff and senior commanders, make a reconnaissance of Veracruz aboard the *Petrita*.	1 or 2 (Chihuahua). Doniphan's troops take the town.
	9 (Veracruz). Scott conducts amphibious landing at Collado Beach, two miles south of the city. Siege of city and fort begins. Tattnall, on the *Spitfire*, makes a diversionary attack on the San Juan de Ulúa castle.	2 (California). Commo. James Biddle arrives to take command of the Pacific Squadron, a position he will hold until mid-July.
		30 (Baja California). San José surrenders to the U.S. Navy.
	21 (Veracruz). Commodore Perry replaces Conner as commander of the Home Squadron.	
	22 (Veracruz). Bombardment commences by Scott's forces on land and the navy offshore; a land-based naval battery joins in on the 24th.	

27 (Veracruz). General Landero surrenders city with its fort San Juan de Ulúa to Scott's army.

29 (Veracruz). Mexican troops leave; the town is occupied by U.S. forces.

31 (Alvarado). The port surrenders to the U.S. Navy.

April 1847

1 (Mexico City). Anaya becomes interim president of Mexico. Vice President Gómez Farías is ousted.

10–16 (Washington). President Polk appoints Department of State's Nicholas P. Trist as his diplomatic agent to Mexico and provides him with a draft peace treaty. Trist departs Washington on the 16th.

May 1847

6 (Veracruz). Nicholas Trist debarks and moves to Jalapa, arriving on the 14th. Contentious correspondence begins between Trist and Scott.

2 (Mexico City). Santa Anna reassumes the presidency of Mexico.

8 (Veracruz). Scott's advance guard under Twiggs initiates the march inland.

17–18 (near Jalapa). Scott fights battle of Cerro Gordo; occupies Jalapa on the 19th.

18 (Gulf Coast). Commodore Perry occupies Tuxpán and evacuates it on the 22d.

22. General Worth occupies Perote and its fort, San Carlos.

4 (Jalapa). Scott returns 12-month volunteers to the United States.

11 (Puebla). Santa Anna's army moves here to await Scott but abandons the town before Scott's arrival.

2 (Baja California). The U.S. Navy seizes San Lucas.

13 (Baja California). The U.S. Navy occupies La Paz.

31 (California). Kearny departs for St. Louis and takes Frémont, who faces a court martial, with him. Col. Richard B. Mason succeeds Kearny as governor of California.

Mexico & U.S. Political and Diplomatic

June 1847

10 (Mexico City). British Secretary of Legation Edward Thornton informs Trist that Santa Anna is willing to enter peace talks.

Mexico & Texas Theater

15 (Puebla). Worth occupies Puebla without a fight; Scott arrives on the 29th with the main body but leaves parts of his army garrisoning strong points from Veracruz to Puebla.

4 (Puebla). Scott decides to abandon all garrisons between the coast and Puebla, temporarily cutting his army's lifeline to the United States. The move prompts the Duke of Wellington to remark from England that "Scott is lost!"

16 (Gulf Coast). Commodore Perry's capture of Tabasco gives him last major Mexican port on the Gulf.

20 (Las Vigas). Samuel Walker and his Texas Rangers destroy a guerrilla base here. Mexican guerrilla attacks against American convoys, however, continue throughout the year.

New Mexico & California Theater

...(Mexico City). Mexican Congress refuses to authorize talks with Nicholas Trist.

17 (Puebla). Scott calls a meeting with his commanders to discuss offering money to Mexican officials to influence negotiations.

During July (Puebla). Scott and Trist end their feud and become allies.

August 1847

23 (southern outskirts of Mexico City). Scott and Mexican Foreign Minister J. R. Pacheco agree on the Armistice of Tacubaya, which goes into effect on the 24th.

25 (Mexico City). Trist notifies Pacheco that he desires to negotiate a more permanent peace; during succeeding days of negotiation, however, this goal is not achieved.

...(Puebla). The U.S. Navy evacuates the port.

...(California). Commodore Shubrick turns over command of the Pacific Squadron to Commodore Shubrick (who had previously commanded it from January 22 to March 2, 1847).

21 (Baja California). Lt. Col. Henry S. Burton's New York Volunteers occupy La Paz.

5 (Puebla). Scott orders his army to march on Mexico City.

6–8 (Puebla). Gen. Franklin Pierce arrives with 2,500 men after fighting his way along the guerrilla-infested National Highway from Veracruz (from which he departed on July 14); forces under Generals Pillow and Cadwalader also arrive, bringing Scott's strength to over 10,000.

7 (Puebla). Scott's army, led by Twiggs's division, departs for Mexico City; the divisions of Worth, Quitman, and Pillow follow at one-day intervals; by the 10th, the army has cleared Puebla. Colonel Thomas Childs is left to garrison Puebla.

11–12 (Valley of Mexico). Twiggs occupies Ayotla, 15 miles southeast of Mexico City; Scott arrives, and on the 12th Chalco and Chimalpa are occupied, setting the stage for the offensive against Mexico City.

6 (California). Shubrick calls for blockade of Mazatlán, San Blas, and Guaymas.

Mexico & U.S. Political and Diplomatic	Mexico & Texas Theater	New Mexico & California Theater
	15 (Valley of Mexico). Scott decides against a direct attack from the east; he orders the army to maneuver south along Lake Chalco and then turn west to gain a position from which to attack Mexico City from the south.	
	18 (Mexico City). Santa Anna orders General Valencia to fall back from Padierna. Valencia refuses, setting the stage for battle against Scott's approaching army.	
	20 (Valley of Mexico). Battles of Contreras (Padierna) and Churubusco.	
September 1847	8 (west of Mexico City). Battles of Molino del Rey and Casa Mata.	
6 (South of Mexico City). When negotiations fail, Scott announces the end of the Armistice of Tacubaya.	13 (west of Mexico City). Assault against Chapultepec Castle and the Belén and San Cosmé gates to Mexico City.	
16 (Mexico City). Santa Anna quits presidency.	14 (Mexico City). Scott occupies the capital of Mexico. Mexican forces under Gen. Joaquín Rea begin a siege of Puebla.	
16. Santa Anna marches toward Puebla with remnants of his army.		
26. Manuel Peña y Peña becomes president of Mexico.		

October 1847

7 (Querétaro). Querétaro becomes temporary capital of Mexico; Santa Anna removed as commander of the army.

13 (Mexico City). The Aztec Club, an American officers' club, is formed.

9 (Huamantla). Antiguerrilla raid by American forces under Gen. Joseph Lane results in death of Samuel Walker of the Texas Rangers.

12 (Puebla). General Lane's force arrives to lift the siege. Lane continues to conduct antiguerrilla operations in the area, capturing Atlixco on the 19th.

20 (California). Port of Guaymas captured by the U.S. Navy.

29 (California). Shubrick arrives at San José to begin a campaign in the Gulf of California.

November 1847

6 (Monterrey). General Taylor requests leave from occupation duty in Monterrey to return to the states. When the War Department gives its approval, Taylor turns over command in northern Mexico to General Wool and departs for the United States on the 25th. Taylor arrives in New Orleans on the 30th.

11 (Querétaro). Pedro María Anaya, favorable to peace negotiations, becomes president *ad interim* of Mexico.

16–22 (Mexico City). Scott's conflict with Worth and Pillow develops. Scott relieves both generals of their commands.

10–11 (west coast of Mexico). Commodore Shubrick attacks Mazatlán, occupying it on the 11th.

19 (Baja California). Siege of the garrison at San José is begun by Mexican troops; it ends on the 21st.

Mexico & U.S. Political and Diplomatic	Mexico & Texas Theater	New Mexico & California Theater
16 (Mexico City). Trist receives Polk's September 17 recall order.		
22 (Mexico City). Anaya appoints peace commissioners.		
December 1847		
4 (Mexico City). Based on advice from Scott and others, Trist decides to ignore Polk's recall order and continues peace efforts.	26 (Mexico City). Scott sends forces to occupy Pachuca, Toluca, and Cuernavaca.	
January 1848		
2 (Mexico City). Start of peace negotiations.		14 (Baja California). American reinforcements relieve naval detachment at San José.
8 (Querétaro). Replacing Anaya, Peña y Peña again assumes presidency of Mexico.		22 (Baja California). A second Mexican siege of the garrison at San José begins; it ends February 15.
13 (Washington). Polk orders Scott relieved of command. The decision is made to turn Scott's charges against Worth and Pillow (and Worth's countercharges) over to a board of inquiry.		
February 1848		
2 (Mexico City). The Treaty of Guadalupe Hidalgo is signed.		28 (California). Shubrick receives word of Treaty of Guadalupe Hidalgo.

18 (Mexico City). Polk's order relieving Scott of command arrives; Gen. William O. Butler assumes command.

23 (Washington). Polk submits the Treaty of Guadalupe Hidalgo to Congress for ratification.

29 (Mexico City). The two armies sign a military armistice.

March 1848

10 (Washington). With some changes, the U.S. Senate ratifies the Treaty of Guadalupe Hidalgo.

16 (Santa Cruz de Rosales, Chihuahua, Mexico). Gen. Sterling Price, although informed repeatedly by the Mexicans that a peace treaty has been signed in Mexico City, attacks Santa Cruz in the last significant battle of the war.

30 (Baja California). The last shots of the war are fired in a small engagement between Mexican troops and U.S. forces under Lt. Col. Henry Burton at Todos Santos in Baja California.

April 1848

5 (Veracruz). Santa Anna departs for exile in Havana, Cuba.

Mexico & U.S. Political and Diplomatic	Mexico & Texas Theater	New Mexico & California Theater
May 1848 25 (Querétaro). The Mexican Congress ratifies the Treaty of Guadalupe Hidalgo. 30 (Querétaro). Exchange of ratifications by Mexico and the United States. The Treaty of Guadalupe Hidalgo takes effect.		6 (west coast of Mexico). Commodore Thomas ap Catesby Jones, arriving at Mazatlán aboard the ship of the line *Ohio*, relieves Shubrick as commander of the Pacific Squadron.
June 1848	12 (Mexico City). American troops depart, ending occupation of the capital.	17 & 24 (west coast of Mexico). Commodore Jones returns Mazatlán to Mexican control on the 17th and Guaymas on the 24th.
July 1848	15 (Veracruz). The last contingent of U.S. troops departs Veracruz.	
August 1848		31 (Baja California). American forces return La Paz to Mexican authorities.
September 1848		6 (California). The U.S. ship *Ohio* embarks with a unit of New York volunteers, transporting them to Monterey. This ends the United States military intervention in Mexico

Introduction

Background to Conflict

As Mexico carried out its struggle for independence between 1810 and 1820, rebel leaders found sympathy for their cause in the United States, but the government in Washington maintained strict neutrality. Secretary of State John Quincy Adams was much more interested in territorial settlements in the East than in supporting a movement for independence south of the border. The United States surrendered to Spain its claim to territory between the Sabine and Rio Grande Rivers in exchange for Florida by the Adams-Onís Treaty of 1819. Shortly thereafter, Anglo-Americans migrated to Texas by Spanish invitation; in exchange for vast stretches of rich land along the coastal plain, Moses Austin and other *empresarios* not only pledged allegiance to the Spanish crown but also promised to respect the customs of their adopted country, including the authority of the Roman Catholic Church.

Between 1821 and 1823 the political climate in Mexico took an interesting turn; Agustín de Iturbide, a former royal officer, proclaimed independence and was crowned emperor of Mexico. The United States refused to recognize the New World monarchy but sent Joel Poinsett to interact with Iturbide's government. Stephen F. Austin arrived in San Antonio on August 10, 1821, taking up the lands that had been promised to his father. Although Mexican officials hesitated to recognize the grants issued by the former mother country, citizens on the northern frontier saw the new settlements as much-needed buffers against destructive Apache and Comanche raiders. In the following years, thousands of land-hungry families established farms in eastern Texas, especially in the Brazos and Colorado River basins. Often ignoring promises to respect Hispanic customs, they came with all of their cultural baggage, including Protestantism, the English language, and the institution of slavery. Farther north, Capt. William Becknell launched another form of peaceful penetration in 1822 as he led traders from St. Louis, Missouri, to Santa Fe, New Mexico, initiating a profitable commerce with that isolated region.

1

With the overthrow of Iturbide's short-lived empire, Mexican leaders embraced republicanism, modeling their constitution of 1824 upon that of the United States. Washington quickly granted recognition and appointed Joel Poinsett as its first representative in Mexico City. At first, relations were quite friendly, but within a short time conservatives accused Poinsett of injecting himself into the internal affairs of Mexico in support of liberal factions. Some officials were alarmed by the ever-increasing number of Anglo-Americans entering Texas; their concern seemed justified in 1826, when Haden Edwards proclaimed the "Fredonian Revolt" against Mexican authority. Austin and other loyal colonists denounced Edwards and renewed their pledge to abide by Mexican law, and in Washington secretary of state Henry Clay declared that the United States also opposed the rebel plots. It was clear to the Mexican envoy in the United States, however, that the Fredonian elements attracted widespread popular support in the United States, especially in the southern and western states. Some Mexicans were also concerned that the rapidly increasing trade between Missouri and Santa Fe posed a danger to their economic and political interests. From 1822 to 1828, the annual value of the commerce had increased from $15,000 to $150,000. In New Mexico and Chihuahua, however, there was widespread approval of the link which brought scarce goods to the people and increased revenues to local coffers.

After the presidential election of 1828, Mexican politics entered a new era of conflict and instability. Masonic lodges became nuclei for the emerging Conservative and Liberal parties, and in virtually every region of the country ambitious political leaders denounced efforts from Mexico City to exercise effective control. Increasing Anglo migration into Texas brought growing concerns, especially among the conservatives, and in 1830, the Mexican congress passed a decree prohibiting further colonization. Authorities were able to do little to enforce the measure and their clumsy attempts played into the hands of the more militant factions in Texas. Andrew Jackson's administration expressed its friendship toward Mexico, but flatly refused to restrict U.S. citizens wishing to cross the Sabine border. Anthony Butler, Poinsett's successor as ambassador to Mexico, was an outspoken expansionist and generated bitter Mexican criticism for his strident support of Texas dissidents.

In 1833, Antonio López de Santa Anna won the Mexican presidency as a champion of federalism. By late 1834, however, the caudillo reversed his position, proclaiming himself to be the protector of religion and order, and taking steps to consolidate power of the central government. His actions set off federalist revolts in Yucatán, Tamaulipas, Sonora, and many other regions, all demanding the return of states rights guaranteed in the constitution of 1824. Texans proclaimed their solidarity with other federalists, and on the surface their movement was simply a part of the general unrest throughout Mexico. A number of Hispanics, including Juan N. Seguín and Lorenzo de Zavala, supported the rebellion, but the vast majority who took up arms against the regime of Santa Anna in Texas was Anglo-American. By November of 1835, Texas had an army which was heavily armed and poised to fight. Its extensive border with the United States provided a ready link to additional resources, both financial and human. The struggle which soon erupted was much more than a regional rebellion, it was a cultural clash with far-reaching implications for U.S.–Mexican relations.

On December 11, 1835, the Texas army defeated Gen. Martín Perfecto de Cos, forcing him to retreat south of the Rio Grande. The victors called for a convention which met the following spring at Washington-on-the-Brazos. On March 2, 1836, the delegates proclaimed their separation from Mexico and the independence of the Republic of Texas. Santa Anna personally led an army from central Mexico against San Antonio and on March 6, 1836, crushed the small garrison at the Alamo, an event which furnished the most powerful symbol in Texas history. Santa Anna marched east and won another resounding victory at Goliad on March 27, increasing the Texans' hatred against him by ordering the execution of 445 captives. On April 21, 1836, however, the army of Gen. Sam Houston routed the Mexican force at San Jacinto, capturing Santa Anna in the process. The defeated general signed a treaty recognizing Texas independence, but it was immediately repudiated as news of events reached Mexico City.

U.S. Ambassador Powhatan Ellis arrived in Mexico City in May 1836, a month after San Jacinto. He attempted to convince the Mexicans that the Jackson administration was maintaining a position of neutrality in the dispute between Mexico and the Texas dissidents, but his claim fell on deaf ears. Minister of War José María Tornel y Mendívil denounced the United States for supporting the rebellion. His charge was strengthened when it became known that Gen. Edmund P. Gaines had led U.S. troops in the occupation of Nacogdoches during the course of the conflict. Furthermore, editors and politicians in many U.S. states had called for volunteers to join the Texans. A small minority in the United States, including former President John Quincy Adams, supported the Mexican charges, branding the events in Texas as a thinly veiled effort to expand slavery. Mexican ambassador to Washington Manuel Eduardo de Gorostiza denounced the Jackson administration for openly supporting war against his country and abandoned his post on the Potomac. Relations between Mexico and the United States were for all purposes ended when Ambassador Ellis departed from Mexico City on December 7, 1836. The riff deepened on March 3, 1837, when President Jackson officially recognized Texas independence on his last day in office.

After the defeat at San Jacinto and the end of Santa Anna's regime, Mexico experienced a glimmer of stability with the presidency of Anastasio Bustamante. In 1838, because of a financial claim, a French expedition blockaded Veracruz and seized the fortress of San Juan de Ulúa. Santa Anna's heroic opposition to that invasion paved the way for his later return to power but did nothing to solve Mexico's miserable financial conditions. In February 1840, dissident elements of Yucatán revolted once again, followed by federalist pronouncements in many other regions. These actions kept the government of President Bustamante off balance and thwarted all plans for the reconquest of Texas.

From the time of their declaration of independence many Texas leaders sought annexation by the United States. From 1837 to 1841, however, Pres. Martin Van Buren seemed to take his nation's declarations of neutrality more seriously than had the previous administration and in essence held the sister Anglo-American republic at arm's length. Many southerners denounced Van Buren for his lack of sympathy for Texas, but at the same time powerful political figures, including John Quincy Adams, denounced him for support of slave interests since the United States continued to serve Texas as a source of capital and provided a steady stream of emigrants. In Mexico City, former Ambassador Eduardo Gorostiza denounced all U.S. trade and interaction with Texas as evidence of support of the breakaway state and hostility to Mexico.

As Pres. William Henry Harrison took office in March 1841, there was a strong element within his Whig Party which opposed the annexation of Texas. This included secretary of state Daniel Webster, who placed very high priority on the settlement of boundary questions with Great Britain in the northeastern United States. With the death of Harrison after only one month in office, Vice Pres. John Tyler of Virginia brought a very different perspective to the White House. A former Jacksonian Democrat, Tyler was openly expansionist in his views and wished to work toward annexation. He faced hostility from powerful Whig elements, however, and Henry Clay led an effort to expel the president from the party. Aware of his weak political position and of the importance of Webster's negotiations over the boundary with Canada, Tyler allowed the question of Texas to be delayed. Meanwhile, the clash along the Rio Grande was renewed.

Santa Anna returned to power in October of 1841, following the overthrow of Bustamante. For the next three years the caudillo devoted much of his energy and an inordinate amount of the national budget to support an extravagant and highly ceremonial court life. Yet his attention was constantly demanded by the painful reminders of past humiliations and continuing threats from the Lone Star Republic. Texas president Mirabeau B. Lamar was not content to defend his borders, but formed an alliance with Yucatecan rebels and sent the small Texas navy to assist them in their defiance of Mexico. In June of 1841, Lamar sent a force of some 300 soldiers, merchants, and adventurers into New Mexico, inviting authorities in Santa Fe to join his Republic. The ill-planned invasion ended in defeat and humiliation, not only for Texas, but for secretary of state Daniel Webster as well since a number of U.S. citizens had accompanied the mission. When Sam Houston assumed the presidency of Texas for the second time in September 1841, he and Santa Anna stood toe to toe along the Rio Grande like two seasoned gladiators. Attacks and counterattacks continued throughout 1842; on September 10, a Mexican army captured San Antonio but soon after abandoned the prize. A Texas raid below the Rio Grande ended in disaster on Christmas Day in the little village of Mier. A number of U.S. citizens were among those captured and marched to Mexico City in chains. Although American participation in the raid was clearly a violation of the announced policy of neutrality, the treatment of captives led once again to an outcry throughout the United States against the cruelty of the dictatorial regime of Santa Anna.

Having successfully completed his negotiations with Great Britain, Daniel Webster resigned as secretary of state on May 8, 1843. As his successor, President Tyler chose Abel P. Upshur, an avowed expansionist. Although facing opposition from powerful Whig politicians, including Henry Clay, Upshur informed the Texas representative in Washington that the United States would come to the assistance of the Texas Republic in case of a Mexican invasion. Furthermore, he took energetic steps to counter a concerted effort on the part of Great Britain to play a dominant role in the internal politics of Texas. Those plans were interrupted on February 28, 1844, with the accidental death of Upshur, but Tyler continued the policy by selecting as secretary of state John C. Calhoun, an even more ardent supporter of expansion. Calhoun pushed for a treaty of annexation, assuring Texas of protection in case Mexico launched an attack.

By June of 1844, the question of the annexation of Texas emerged as the key issue in the United States presidential election. Henry Clay, the Whig nominee, refused to take an aggressive position on the Texas question. Former president Martin Van Buren also attempted to sidestep the issue as he sought the Democratic nomination. After bitter internal fighting the Democrats nominated James K. Polk of Tennessee and adopted a platform that clearly favored the annexation of Texas. Polk correctly judged the mood of the people in that decade of Manifest Destiny, and support for the controversial yet popular question carried him to the White House. After the election, President Tyler, reacting to the will of the people, signed a joint congressional resolution calling for the annexation of Texas. On the last day of his term, March 3, 1845, Tyler sent the offer to Texas. Texans responded cautiously, seeking assurance that Washington would furnish protection if Texas openly defied Mexico by entering the Union. In the following spring months of 1845 they debated the annexation proposal.

Texans claimed the Rio Grande as their southwestern border with Mexico. Mexicans, although never officially recognizing Texas independence, proclaimed the Nueces River their border with Texas. If the United States sent troops into Texas to secure the Texans' claim from Mexican incursions, military conflict would probably result. Nevertheless, President Polk, eager to show the flag and aware of angry reactions in Mexico to the possibility of the United States annexing Texas, alerted the navy to assemble the Home Squadron in Gulf waters off Mexican port towns along the Gulf coast.

The Northern Campaign of Zachary Taylor

As tensions increased, the administration sent a warning order to Bvt. Brig. Gen. Zachary Taylor to strengthen his Army of Observation at Fort Jesup in the Red River Valley of western Louisiana for possible duty in Texas. Taylor's force, consisting entirely of regulars, numbered about 3,000 troops. The 60-year-old Taylor, called "Old Rough and Ready" by his troops, was indeed a hard, tough soldier. In 1845, he had 37 years of active service, much of it on the frontier fighting Indians. Taylor had been stationed at Fort Jesup for over a year when Polk's War Department directed him in June 1845 to move his force, which was renamed the Army of Occupation, to the north bank of the Rio Grande. Taylor's mission was to move his army by ship across the Gulf of Mexico, to land in Texas once the Lone Star Republic had officially voted for annexation, and to repel any Mexican invasion of Texas. The Texas Congress voted to enter the Union on July 4, 1845.

Disregarding guidance from the administration, Taylor devised his own plan for transporting his troops into Texas: he sent his dragoons overland under the command of Col. David Twiggs; his infantry, which he accompanied, went by sea from the port of New Orleans. This initial troop movement marked the beginning of a long campaign that would take Taylor and his troops into the interior of Mexico to battle against forces which greatly outnumbered his army. Although the original destination of the American force was the Rio Grande, the river was too far from the army's supply bases. The Texans warned Taylor that the estuary of the Rio Grande was difficult to navigate and an unfortified camp along the river would dangerously expose his men to Mexican attacks by large forces in the vicinity. Taylor, based on the Texans' warning, which was reinforced by the recommendations of the American chargé d'affairs, Andrew Jackson Donelson, decided instead to choose a more friendly area near the mouth of the Nueces River as his initial staging base.

Corpus Christi

The *Alabama*, a steamer bearing Zachary Taylor and the vanguard of the Army of Occupation, left New Orleans on July 23 and arrived at Saint Joseph Island off the south Texas coast on the 25th. Since the draft of the large steamer was too deep to go into the bay, the troops disembarked on the barrier island. In the meantime, Taylor and his staff scouted for a suitable site for his new base of operations. He selected the small trading village of Corpus Christi, known also as "Kinney's Ranch," situated near the mouth of the Nueces. Because of the shallowness of the bay leading to the new site, the troops had to be transported to Corpus Christi by small fishing boats. With the arrival overland at the end of August of Twigg's dragoons, or mounted infantry, the entire army had closed on the new base. Taylor's force, now approximately 4,000 strong, was half of the standing U.S. Army at the time. Some one third of his army was immigrant—of Irish, German, English, French, or Polish birth. Many of the enlisted men spoke little English.

Taylor's main camp at Corpus Christi spread along a wide

stretch of beach in disputed territory just south of where the Nueces opens into the bay. The units were lined up on a level plain about a quarter of a mile wide; today this site is the northeastern section of the city of Corpus Christi. When Taylor's Army of Occupation arrived, the village consisted of a few wooden buildings and a small fort constructed by "Colonel" Henry Lawrence Kinney, an entrepreneur and rancher who survived on illegal trade between Mexicans and Americans passing through the region. Inhabitants of "Kinney's Ranch" were mostly the several dozen personal soldiers, traders, and cowboys who worked for Henry Kinney.

Zachary Taylor's army stayed in Corpus Christi for seven months, from August 1845 to March 1846. Conditions changed sharply from the pleasant atmosphere reported by the soldiers in late summer. "Northers," strong gales from the north, came in and changed the tropical climate to unpleasant conditions that made camp life both miserable and unhealthy. Disease, by far the largest killer in the coming war, began to take its toll: epidemics spread, morale plummeted and discipline fell apart. The troops were anxious to leave Corpus Christi at the end of the seven months.

While Taylor's army was at Corpus Christi, President Polk attempted, through diplomacy, to reach an agreement with Mexico on Texas annexation, to get Mexico to recognize the Rio Grande border, and to arrange for the purchase of California and the southwest territories. Mexico balked, and on December 2, 1845, Polk reported to Congress that negotiations had not succeeded and that diplomatic relations between the two nations had been suspended. Mexico threatened war against the United States, prompting Polk to declare that Taylor's army had been sent to Texas to protect citizens against the "menaced attack." In January, Polk won his cabinet's backing to increase the pressure on Mexico by ordering Zachary Taylor to move from Corpus Christi to the north bank of the Rio Grande. The order reached Taylor on February 3, 1846.

General Taylor took his time departing Corpus Christi. He had neither ordered reconnaissance of routes toward the border nor made detailed plans for the move, so he accomplished these tasks first. His army finally set out southwest for the Rio Grande on March 8, 1846; it was led overland by the dragoons and horse artillery and numbered about 3,000. After sending most of the army's supplies and heavy artillery by sea, Taylor departed on his horse, "Old Whitey," with the final elements on March 11. The remainder of the army's 800 to 1,000 soldiers were either too sick to deploy or were detailed to garrison the skeleton camp left at Corpus Christi.

The 20-day march to the Rio Grande crossed 190 miles of territory claimed by both Mexico and the United States. It was a generally flat land, although parts of it were rolling. Some of the prairie was completely open country, whereas other areas were covered with thick, impenetrable bush. The land from Corpus Christi to the Rio Grande was known on early Spanish maps and later by Texans as the "Wild Horse Desert," a name some still use today. After 13 days on the march, Taylor's vanguard reached a gorge and tidal stream called the Arroyo Colorado, 30 miles from the Mexican border. On March 20, a Mexican force appearing on the south bank sent a messenger to inform General Taylor that a crossing would be contested. Taylor's typically laconic reply was that his troops would cross immediately. A Mexican trumpet call stirred the air, indicating an assembly of forces; this soon proved a ruse as the American force crossed without a shot being fired by the retreating Mexican force. After crossing the Arroyo Colorado, Taylor waited three days for his supply trains to close before continuing south. Fifteen miles north of the Rio Grande, Taylor detoured east with a detachment to establish a supply base at Point Isabel, or *El Frontón de Isabela*, as the Mexicans called it, on Laguna Madre Sound. He planned for supplies to be ferried from Brazos Santiago, a Mexican port on Brazos Island, a small island off the southern end of Padre Island, across the shallow lagoon to Point Isabel; from there wagon trains would supply the army overland to his main camp along the river. In the year ahead, the Point Isabel base would be a critical conduit for supplies coming from New Orleans and other ports to sustain the army.

The Rio Grande Battles

Taylor rejoined the main body about 15 miles west of Point Isabel and continued south to establish bivouac in a corn field directly across the Rio Grande from the Mexican city of Matamoros. His first task was to order the engineers to build a fortified post, named Fort Texas (sometimes seen in records as Fort Taylor), at a crook of the Rio Grande within cannon range of Mexican artillery at Matamoros. They completed the fort by the end of the following month. The pentagonal fortress was constructed with earthen walls nine feet high and 15 feet thick. On April 24, Taylor sent a unit to the north to scout for Mexican cavalry that had reportedly crossed the river to threaten his position. Capt. Seth Thornton, leading a scouting force of two companies of dragoons, rode 20 miles above Fort Texas in an attempt to locate the Mexican force. Thornton ran into an ambush at Rancho Carricitos and lost 11 men killed and six wounded; he and the remainder of the officers and men were taken prisoner. Upon receiving Taylor's report of the ambush, President Polk interpreted the event as an act of war. In a message to Congress, Polk claimed that hostilities between the two nations had commenced with the Mexican attack. Mexico had crossed into the United States and "shed American blood upon the American soil," the president charged. Congress approved Polk's contention that a state of war already existed and authorized him to pursue war preparations.

Assured that Fort Texas could withstand an artillery attack from across the river, Taylor departed with the bulk of his army on May 1 to get supplies at Point Isabel, leaving Maj. Jacob Brown in command of a 500-man contingent consisting of the Seventh Infantry plus supporting artillery. After securing provisions, on May 7 Taylor began his return from Point Isabel with over 2,000 men and a train consisting of 300 wagons. Anticipating enemy action because of reports he received while on the coast, Taylor warned his men to expect close battle and to prepare to put "their main dependence on the bayonet." The warning was well-timed; the next day the Americans met a Mexican force of about 5,000 men under Gen. Mariano Arista blocking their route 10 miles short of Fort Texas. There, at a crossroads called Palo Alto, the first major battle of the war took place. Taylor's subsequent terse account of the Battle of Palo Alto stated that when he met the larger enemy army, "I did not hesitate to give him battle which continued until dark, when he was driven from his position." Later reports would show that Taylor's victory was due to the superb performance of his artillery. The effect of the light, horse-drawn "flying artillery" on the Mexican troops was devastating; it won the day at Palo Alto. This victory was followed the next day by another sharp engagement; this battle, called "Resaca de la Palma" by Americans and "Resaca de la Guerrero" by Mexicans, was primarily an infantry fight. It resulted in a complete rout of the Mexican forces as they fled across the Rio Grande. These two resounding victories stirred the nation to support Polk's expansionist policy and made Zachary Taylor a national figure.

During Taylor's absence, the Mexican force in Matamoros besieged Fort Texas. The small but solidly built fort held up well under the week-long exchange of artillery fire. Taylor had pledged upon leaving for Point Isabel that the fort would be re-named for the "first officer that falls here." That officer was the fort's commander, Major Brown, who had been killed during the siege. While at Fort Brown, Taylor encountered a problem in marked contrast to the situation that exists today in the Rio Grande border region. After the long march over hard country, many soldiers were sick of the discipline and deprivation of camp life. Some of them, motivated by their romantic view of Matamoros across the Rio Grande, elected to swim the river and defect to Mexico. They were undoubtedly lured by the excitement of the strange city and perhaps by the young Mexican women who would bathe nude on the opposite bank. Some may have defected to Catholic Mexico because they, too, were Catholic, whereas the majority of Taylor's troops were Protestant and openly anti-Cath-olic. Many, but certainly not all of the defectors, were foreign born, and a good part of these were from Ireland. The Irish turn-coats formed the nucleus of the famous "San Patricio Battalion" that participated in several battles against American forces. These defections became a serious problem for Taylor. On one night alone, 14 soldiers swam the river to desert in Mexico. Taylor had to issue an order for sentries to shoot defectors in the river if they refused to turn back. Several met this fate. Taylor's policy was apparently effective and the rate of desertions soon declined. He eliminated the problem for the time being when his army crossed the river and occupied the undefended city of Matamoros on May 18, 1846.

The events along the border in April and May of 1846 strength-ened President Polk's hand in pursuing the war. Congress appro-priated $10 million for military purposes and authorized Polk to increase the army by up to 50,000 twelve-month volunteers. Sec-retary of War William Marcy sent vague guidance to Zachary Tay-lor regarding methods to accomplish the administration's policy. The secretary let Taylor decide how to pursue the war; his in-structions to the field only referred to the need to "conquer a peace," although he did mention the possibility of Taylor attack-ing Monterrey, the largest city in northern Mexico situated in a high valley about 150 miles southwest of Matamoros. Taylor pur-sued this idea. His initial planning called for a campaign directly overland from Matamoros. After a reconnaissance indicated that route to have poor roads, he decided to take his force northwest on the Rio Grande to the town of Camargo on the San Juan River. From that base, the army would move overland to the southwest following the San Juan Valley to Monterrey.

Camargo, a "Yawning Graveyard"

The Army began departing Matamoros for Camargo on July 6. Some troops went overland through the dry, harsh country west of the Rio Grande. Others traveled by steamboat and closed on the small port town by the middle of August 1846. On August 18, Taylor ordered his regular army troops to stage a dress parade. The entire force in the parade, now over 6,000 troops after the arrival of numerous volunteer units, may have made it, at that point in time, the largest review in the history of the American army.

Although Taylor and most of his army would remain in Camargo only a few weeks, the town continued to be of critical importance as a resupply base and replacement depot for his campaign in northern Mexico. Especially for those soldiers who remained in Camargo for an extended period, the town came to be a true hellhole. A spring flood had covered the town, rendering it, according to reports of many of the soldiers, ugly, unpleasant, and above all, extremely unhealthy. The atmosphere was stifling, with intolerable heat, high humidity, and a lack of breeze to stir the air. The San Juan River was described by one soldier as "the nastiest river in the world." The river became at once a sewer and the only source of drinking water. Camargo became, in the words of one historian, a "yawning graveyard." It became a killing field for an unfortunate number of the 12,000 American soldiers who would eventually pass through or bivouac near the town. The strange diseases of the day were rampant and largely untreatable. Yellow fever (called *el vómito* in Mexico at that time), cholera, smallpox, malaria, and dysentery spread death among the officers and men of Taylor's army. Often dozens died in one day. Material for coffins ran out and men were buried in their blankets. Causes of the death tolls were many: miserable climate; tainted, fetid water; and foul camp conditions, particularly the unsanitary conditions of undisciplined volunteer forces. The death figures for Taylor's army at Camargo were astounding. Approximately 15 percent, some 1,500 of the soldiers who came to Camargo in 1846–1847, were buried there. That figure is about equal to the total number of soldiers killed in combat action during the war with Mexico. In a real sense Camargo was the preeminent battlefield of the war.

Monterrey

For the fortunate majority of Taylor's troops, Camargo was left behind when the army began its march toward Monterrey after the review on August 18. The route took the army up the San Juan valley and through the towns of Mier, Punta Aguada (today named General Treviño), Agualeguas, Cerralvo, Ramos (the present-day Dr. Gonzalez), and finally Marín, the last town before Monterrey. At first the men found the terrain as harsh and the march as difficult as the trek to Camargo. As the route turned southwest at Mier, impressions of the land became more favorable as elevation increased, climate moderated, and the Sierra Madre mountains came into view. Cerralvo was the most impressive town along the route. Taylor reported the beautiful vista of the "high mountains" there and of his tent's location in a shaded area "amidst large brooks of clear, cool water running in torrents from them." Some of the major units stayed in Cerralvo for over two weeks during the march to Monterrey. The town later became an intermediate depot for the Camargo-to-Monterrey route and would be occupied by American troops for over a year.

In 1846, Monterrey was a heavily fortified city of between 10,000 and 15,000 civilians and a strong military garrison. In September, when Zachary Taylor's army approached from the east, it was defended by 10,000 cavalry and infantry troops and 38 pieces of artillery. On Saturday morning, September 19, Taylor moved his army of 6,500 men from Marín into the northern part of Monterrey and established his command post in a grove of trees called Walnut Springs. Despite the disparity in the size of the forces and the fortified positions of the Mexicans, Taylor went on the attack and took the city in a series of fierce battles over a four-day span beginning on September 21. On September 25, the Mexican general in command of Monterrey, Pedro de Ampudia, surrendered the city. In contrast to other battles in the war, artillery did not play a decisive role in the battle. The battle for Monterrey was won through dogged, close combat actions and desperate infantry assaults against solid, strongly defended structures—assaults often ending in use of the bayonet. After the Mexican capitulation, Taylor agreed to a truce which restricted his army from going on the offensive for six weeks.

Saltillo

Although the American public looked on Monterrey as a great victory for Zachary Taylor, President Polk, fearing a political threat from the general if he became too popular, refused to properly recognize Taylor's achievement. Polk ordered Gen. Winfield Scott, the General in Chief of the army, to prepare a major invasion of Mexico from the Gulf coast and gave him authority to draw units from Taylor's army. The army, which Taylor had begun to reconstitute after the battle for Monterrey, would again be drawn down. Its fighting strength was fewer than 5,000 men, and most of these were volunteer troops. Polk, incensed by Taylor's independently arranging a truce, canceled the agreement; at first the War Department ordered Taylor to resume the offensive but within a short period reversed this decision, ordering him instead to establish a defensive line running through Monterrey to the coast. Taylor was told not to advance south to Saltillo. After reviewing the potential strategic points for a defensive line in his theater of operations, Taylor disregarded the administration's order regarding Saltillo. Seeking advantageous terrain from which to confront a reportedly 20,000-man Mexican army advancing from San Luis Potosí, Taylor decided to occupy a line running from Saltillo northeastward to Monterrey, then to Victoria, and finally to the coast at Tampico. Taylor's line would be about 500 miles long. In November 1846, he marched out and occupied the undefended city of Saltillo, 60 miles southwest of Monterrey, on the 16th. He left Gen. William Worth there with a force of 1,200 men and returned to his Walnut Springs camp at Monterrey to plan his defensive campaign. For the next two months, Taylor moved between his key defensive locations of Tampico, Monterrey, and Saltillo, deploying his forces and preparing for a continually rumored Mexican attack. During this time he also continued to detach units to the gathering army being formed under the command of Gen. Winfield Scott.

Wool's Expedition

As Taylor established his line of defense in late 1846, the administration was preparing to send another expedition into his theater. In late May 1846, weeks after Taylor's battles along the Rio Grande, Secretary of War Marcy had called Brig. Gen. John E. Wool, the third-ranking officer in the army, to Washington to give him instructions for organizing and training a force which would later be sent to the war zone. Marcy informed Wool that the administration was concerned about the northern Mexican city of Chihuahua, a regional center south of New Mexico that was reported to be strongly garrisoned. Like Santa Fe, Chihuahua was an important trading center with ties to St. Louis. Wool's mission was to train volunteers from several states in preparation for an expedition against Chihuahua. Despite Wool's reputation as the most professional senior officer in the army, after Winfield Scott, he was, like Scott, politically suspect. At his first meeting with Marcy, Wool was not officially given the active, war zone command he had hoped for. On June 11, however, he received orders to command the Chihuahua expedition. His force, the Centre Division (sometimes called the Army of the Center), would come under the command of Taylor's Army of Occupation. Wool's division would consist mostly of volunteer units but would have a leavening of regular troops. The division's staging and training base would be at San Antonio de Bexar. Sending his cavalry overland, Wool took his main body by ship from New Orleans to Port Lavaca on Matagorda Bay along the coast of Texas. From there he rode the 150 miles overland to San Antonio, arriving in mid-August. For the next six weeks, units marched in, some arriving overland from the east, others by sea through Port Lavaca. Wool established a post he named Camp Crockett, located several miles from the Alamo where the Texans had been annihilated 10 years before. Although Wool had problems at San Antonio with his volunteer officers and men (which would plague him throughout the coming campaign), the stern disciplinarian, professional to the core, continuously trained his troops until he marched south for the Rio Grande on September 25.

The division, 2,000 strong, reached the river two weeks later. On October 12, using a pontoon bridge constructed under the supervision of Engineer Captains William Fraser and Robert E. Lee, the division crossed the river at Presidio del Rio Grande (presently Eagle Pass, Texas). After marching unmolested through Santa Rosa, Mexico, on the 24th, Wool's division reached Monclova on the 29th. At Monclova, where he headquartered in the Governor's Palace, Wool halted his advance after receiving news of the Monterrey truce. During the next month, Wool grew increasingly restless because of behavioral problems with his volunteer troops. Both officers and enlisted men grew dissatisfied under his discipline; mutiny threatened. Wool sent out patrols and learned that Chihuahua's defenses had been drawn down by General Santa Anna at San Luis Potosí. He decided to request that Taylor allow him to abandon Chihuahua as an objective and proceed instead to Parras. After several requests, Taylor finally agreed that Chihuahua was no longer vital and ordered Wool to proceed to Parras.

Wool led his division out of Monclova on November 24. Marching his troops 181 miles in 12 days, he arrived in Parras on December 5, 1846. Taylor's defensive line was now extended west by 100 miles. Wool occupied Taylor's right flank and the U.S.

Navy, which had taken Tampico, anchored his left. Twelve days later, as Taylor was enroute from Monterrey to Victoria, General Worth received intelligence that a large Mexican army under General Santa Anna was marching north from San Luis Potosí on Worth's small garrison at Saltillo. Worth, greatly alarmed, sent a request on December 17 to Wool in Parras and Maj. Gen. William Butler in Monterrey to reinforce Saltillo. Within two hours after the arrival of Worth's message, Wool's well-trained troops were on the march. After pushing his division (with its trains of 300 wagons) over 100 miles in four days, the hard-charging division commander arrived at Encantada, a point on the road from Saltillo to San Luis Potosí. Wool's troops were now in a position to intercept any Mexican force marching from the south. Reinforcements also came in from Monterrey when General Butler arrived with his reserves. Taylor, in the meantime, had received the same alarm from Worth as he marched on Victoria. He turned briefly back toward Monterrey but soon resumed his march to Victoria after being informed that the report concerning Santa Anna's army was a false alarm. By the end of the year, however, Taylor's line was established. When new reports came in regarding Santa Anna's threatening Saltillo, Taylor's army, though greatly reduced, would be in a defensive position chosen by his new second-in-command, Brig. Gen. John Wool.

Buena Vista

Initially Wool deployed most of his forces at Agua Nueva, an open position on a high plateau 20 miles south of Saltillo. When scouting reports indicated that Santa Anna's army of 20,000 men was actually approaching from San Luis Potosí in February 1847, both Taylor and Wool realized the position at Agua Nueva was vulnerable to envelopment and they pulled the American forces back near the Hacienda Buena Vista, eight miles below Saltillo. The critical point of the new position was established at *La Angostura,* or the Narrows, located in a cut in the mountains two miles south of the hacienda house where Taylor set up his headquarters. Angostura was a scarcely passable choke point in a valley on the main road from Saltillo to San Luis Potosí. To the west of the road, a series of gullies made an attack from that direction nearly impossible; to the east, extended ridges and several large ravines ran down from the higher mountain range across a plateau. Although a Mexican attack against the American left flank would be possible across this plateau, Taylor thought it nevertheless good defensive terrain which would limit, and possibly channelize, an enemy attack. His army met Santa Anna's on this field on February 22 and 23, 1847. On February 22, the engagement was cautionary, mostly probing by the Mexican cavalry of the American left flank. Combat began at mid-afternoon and lasted until it ceased at dusk. Taylor, concerned about his defenses in his trains area, left the battlefield with an escort and returned to Saltillo for the night.

The serious fighting at Buena Vista took place on February 23. Santa Anna made a furious attack against the American left, turning it in places and causing some U.S. volunteer units to flee the field. Taylor arrived from Saltillo at midmorning, and under his and Wool's battlefield leadership, the tide was held. The Mexican attack was repulsed by timely, effective, and daring employment of the "flying artillery," and by fearless counterattacks by Col. Jefferson Davis's Mississippi Rifles and other units. At the close of the second day of fighting, both sides, badly hurt, rested for another day of combat. After literally sleeping on their guns for the second consecutive night, Taylor's mostly volunteer army awoke on the 24th to discover that Santa Anna had used the darkness to withdraw from the field. The battle, called "Buena Vista" by the Americans and "Angostura" by the Mexicans, was essentially a draw. Both sides suffered heavily, but Taylor's small army, by percentage, paid the dearest price. When the media reported the battle back in the United States, however, Buena Vista was a great American victory; after all, Taylor had held the field of battle.

The American victory at Buena Vista surpassed all others in the war in terms of its impact on the American public. It enhanced Zachary Taylor's already strong national stature. He became the war's looming national hero. This fame would the next year carry the general to the White House. After the battle, Taylor fell back to Monterrey and Walnut Springs; this was his last battle in the war—indeed, the last of his long career as a soldier. Buena Vista ended the northern campaign of the American forces in Mexico. Taylor's army would continue to occupy his defensive lines, as well as the positions along the Rio Grande, for the remainder of the war. With the exception of counterguerrilla operations, the Army of Occupation's battles in Mexico were over. The general himself left the war zone in the autumn of 1847, returning to the United States as a national hero. The Polk administration's strategy would now focus on a new theater in southern Mexico, where Gen. Winfield Scott was preparing to launch a campaign to end the war. Long before that strike to the heart of Mexico was launched, however, the conflict took on far-reaching dimensions.

The United States Expands the Struggle

The clash along the lower Rio Grande in the spring of 1846 not only led to the invasion of northeastern Mexico but also expanded the war into a conflict of truly continental proportions. The size of the U.S. regular army was increased, but the primary growth in military power came from the formation of volunteer units. In Mississippi, Louisiana, Illinois, and Tennessee, young men rushed to join the colors. Despite northern opposition to Polk's policy, troops were levied in Pennsylvania, Massachusetts, New Hampshire, and New York. The state of Missouri was especially important as a source for recruits. Politicians extolled the virtues of expanding Anglo-Saxon institutions, and Protestant ministers proclaimed the invasion to be a justified opportunity to spread "true Christianity" into a godless land. Walt Whitman and countless less-talented poets expressed enthusiasm for the war against Mexico.

During the spring and summer of 1846, volunteers boarded steamboats on the Ohio and Mississippi Rivers or gathered at hundreds of other staging areas throughout the nation. Dragoons and infantrymen pushed cross-country from Little Rock, Arkansas, and Shreveport, Louisiana, to San Antonio, Texas. The Missouri volunteers, along with a small regular force, marched from Fort Leavenworth, Kansas, to Santa Fe, New Mexico, a distance of 800 miles. Some of them, along with the "Mormon Battalion," continued across the desert of Arizona and southern California to the Pacific coast. The most challenging marathon, however, was the Missouri regiment led by Col. Alexander Doniphan, which moved from Fort Leavenworth to Santa Fe, Chihuahua, and eventually the mouth of the Rio Grande, a march of over 2,000 miles.

Naval operations in the Atlantic and Gulf of Mexico extended from New York to Pensacola, New Orleans, Veracruz, and the coast of Yucatán. The secretary of the navy ordered an effective blockade of Mexican ports and support of the invading armies by the Gulf Squadron. In the Pacific, naval commanders focused primarily on California; after U.S. annexation of that vast and sparsely populated region, sailors were ordered ashore to garrison key towns and to fight as infantry. Other operations extended down the entire Pacific coast of Mexico and even to South

America. The final campaign of the war, directed by Gen. Winfield Scott, entailed the coordination of land and sea transportation, an amphibious landing at the fortified city of Veracruz, and a march of over 250 miles to the heart of the Mexican nation by an army that never numbered more than 15,000 effective men.

The logistical challenges posed by the war were overwhelming. At times equipment and supplies were woefully inadequate, in part due to poor planning by commanders in the field, but also because of the sheer distances involved and the lack of adequate production and distribution systems. In general, the U.S. Quartermaster Corps, under the direction of Thomas S. Jesup, met the challenges; wagons were constructed, weapons supplied, and thousands of items procured. Horses, mules, and oxen had to be fed and watered in regions of few streams and inadequate pastures. The navy shared many of the logistical difficulties that plagued the army; aboard ship food grew stale and at times drinking water had to be transported from Pensacola to Veracruz.

Mexico at War

In Mexico there was also an immediate reaction to the clash of arms on the Rio Grande in the spring of 1846. Political leaders in Mexico City and throughout the far-flung provinces denounced the aggression of the Yankee army and called for a patriotic expulsion of the invader. This sentiment was echoed by clergymen, writers, and many of the more educated citizens. The nation boasted a professional officer corps and a sizeable federal army, supplemented by militia units which were organized in the various states. Even after the defeat of General Ampudia at Monterrey, Mexico retained armies in the field. It was with the return of Antonio López de Santa Anna in August 1846, however, that larger military forces were massed. By December of that year the Mexican army at San Luis Potosí numbered more than 20,000 men, with substantial artillery support. Other troops were mustered in New Mexico, Chihuahua, California, and Veracruz to meet the threat from the United States.

Mexico had the advantage of interior lines of communication and supply. That "advantage," however, was more theoretical than real; the initial clash in the spring of 1846 was far removed from the major population centers and from the traditionally centralized military and political commands. The army raised by Santa Anna in San Luis Potosí by February 1847 had to march to Coahuila over a cold and desolate high-desert landscape, with little water and only a small ration of parched corn carried by the soldiers. The logistical support was far inferior to that of the invading army and Santa Anna was constantly plagued by a lack of funds to support his campaigns.

Santa Fe, El Paso, and even Chihuahua were more closely linked commercially with St. Louis, Missouri, than with Mexico City and Veracruz. California was over 2,000 miles from the capital, and despite a sea link via Acapulco, the deplorable state of the Mexican navy left that distant territory in splendid isolation. Small garrisons in desolate towns such as Tucson and Los Angeles were neglected by bickering factions in Mexico City. Furthermore, local elites and ambitious politicians in important provincial cities such as Zacatecas, Guadalajara, and Mérida had little loyalty to the central government. Factionalism was also rife in the capital city where coups and rumors of coups constantly disrupted military planning and effective logistical support. At the very time Santa Anna faced General Taylor at Buena Vista, factions in Mexico City plotted to overthrow acting president Valentín Gómez Farías.

American Technology and Military Professionalism

The United States not only had the advantage of political stability and more efficient logistical support in the course of the struggle with Mexico, it also enjoyed an important technological edge. The conflict came on the edge of the age of steam: the railroad, so important in the American Civil War 13 years after the conflict, did not enter into the plans of either side between 1846 and 1848. On the high seas, however, steamships such as the *Mississippi*, the *Alabama*, and the *Massachusetts* took their places alongside the traditional sailing vessels. Small, light-draft steamers pushed across sandbars on the Rio Grande and other rivers flowing into the Gulf of Mexico. Matthew C. Perry, replacing Commodore Conner on the very day of the successful landing at Veracruz, represented the generation of steam ship officers which would come to rule the U.S. Navy. Although most elements of communication had changed little since the time of Napoleon, the magnetic telegraph appeared during the war. Probably the most significant technological advantage enjoyed by the United States, however, was that of superior artillery support for operations. In the 20 years prior to the conflict, an effort was undertaken to improve the ordnance, both for siege guns and tactical artillery to support armies in the field. The "light" or "flying" artillery played an important role in many United States victories; this was due to the light six pounders employed and to the training of the officers who directed the emplacement of the guns and the men who drove the horses and mules which pulled them. In the operation against Veracruz the howitzers and mortars of the army were supplemented by the fire of naval guns which were brought ashore. Mexican artillery, although at times greater in number and heavier, were never as effective in battle, in part because of a lack of training of the gunners but also due to inferior ammunition.

The Yankees enjoyed the advantage of an effective and highly professional officer corps. Gen. Winfield Scott, although never having received a professional military education, was one of the brilliant military minds of the century. Other general officers, such as Stephen W. Kearny, John Wool, and William Worth, proved to be highly effective on the field of battle. More important, the Military Academy at West Point provided well-trained 2and highly motivated professional officers in company and field grade positions, essential engineering skills, and invaluable staff support for the armies which pushed into Mexico.

War in the Far West: California

As James Polk took office in 1845, he did not hide his interest in acquiring territory on the Pacific coast. Secretary of the Navy George Bancroft instructed Commo. John D. Sloat, naval commander in the Pacific, to seize key California ports in case of the outbreak of war. Thomas O. Larkin, U.S. consul in Monterey, on the other hand, hoped for a peaceful settlement with the California citizens who had long considered themselves to be neglected and even abused by Mexico City. Conditions were further complicated by the arrival of Lt. John C. Frémont at Sutter's Fort in the Sacramento Valley in December 1845. In early January 1846, Frémont and his small band of adventurers moved to the coast and voiced vague threats. Marine Lt. Archibald H. Gillespie arrived in April of that year with letters for Frémont which possibly encouraged revolt.

Commodore Sloat, though aware of the early clash between Taylor and Arista on the Rio Grande, would not take action before knowing that there was a formal declaration of war. On June 10, a group of Anglo-American settlers north of San Francisco Bay denounced Mexican authorities, raised the "Bear Flag," and declared an independent republic. Two weeks later, with support from Frémont and Gillespie, they clashed with the troops of Gen. José María Castro. On July 4, 1846, at Sonoma, the rebels celebrated the independence of the Bear Flag Republic and placed their "army" of 224 men under the command of Frémont.

Commodore Sloat, having finally learned of the declaration of war, seized Monterey in the name of the United States on July 6, 1846, and occupied San Francisco three days later. In Sonoma, the Bear Flag was replaced by the Stars and Stripes but was to be retained as a symbol of the state of California. By the end of July, Sloat turned over his command to Commo. Robert Stockton, a much more energetic and ambitious officer. The new commander sought an alliance with Frémont and Gillespie, recognizing their force as a legitimate army. Frémont moved south to San Diego in an effort to crush the remaining Mexican loyalists under General Castro. In order to support that effort, Stockton sent a naval force to San Pedro, his ships arriving on August 6, 1846. Castro, bitter against Stockton, abandoned California, taking the remnants of his army south to Sonora. By September the vast region of Upper California, from San Diego to San Francisco, and east to Sutter's Fort, seemed to be firmly in the hands of the small American garrison. Stockton planned to extend that control to Baja California, and eventually to Acapulco, with long-range dreams of marching against Mexico City. Events in Los Angeles, however, interrupted Stockton's ambitious plans. The Mexican population of that town resented the high-handed actions of Gillespie. On September 24, 1846, Capt. José María Flores led an uprising, which forced the Americans to evacuate Los Angeles. In the following two months Flores seized many other settlements in southern California. Stockton shifted his headquarters to San Diego, and Frémont, now commanding some 400 men, fortified his position at Monterey. By early December, Stockton was engaged in plans to attack Flores when he learned of the arrival of an American force from New Mexico under the command of Gen. Stephen W. Kearny. The war in California was thus merged with events which had their beginning six months earlier.

Out the Santa Fe Trail to New Mexico and Beyond

As early as 1822, Anglo-American traders pushed from St. Louis, Missouri, to Santa Fe; by 1846, a generation of New Mexican officials had grown accustomed to the profits which had come with the rapidly increasing trade. Those officials were not surprised to learn that the region was a target of Yankee expansion. At the same time he persuaded Congress to declare war on Mexico, President Polk ordered Col. Stephen W. Kearny to march with the First Dragoons from Fort Leavenworth, Kansas, to Santa Fe. Kearny's official mission was to protect the civilian caravan already on its way to New Mexico, but it was understood that he would also acquire the region for the United States.

In addition to the small regular force, a thousand men rushed to the colors of the First Missouri Mounted Volunteers commanded by Col. Alexander Doniphan. Within weeks, Kearny's "Army of the West" numbered some 1,500 men, and in the coming months other units were to be added. Lead elements of Kearny's force left Leavenworth on June 5, 1846; although the Santa Fe Trail was well known, the sparse grass and water supply was a major test for an army of 1,500 men, with over 19,000 horses, mules, and cattle. They moved unopposed along the Arkansas River, for over five hundred miles, reaching Bent's Fort in present-day eastern Colorado on July 29, 1846. After only a brief stop, the army marched south on August 2 and passed through the rugged Raton Pass five days later. Kearny attempted to convince the people of New Mexico that his mission was one of peace and that the United States would guarantee property and religious liberties. He was informed, however, that New Mexico Governor Manuel Armijo was establishing a strong defensive position at Apache Canyon, just 12 miles southeast of Santa Fe. Kearny, having just received his commission to brigadier general, seized the two small towns of Las Vegas and San Miguel, making it clear that any opposition to his mission would be severely punished. On August 16, Governor Armijo, realizing that the citizens of New Mexico did not intend to fight, disbanded his military force and fled south to Chihuahua. The Army of the West entered Santa Fe without opposition on August 18, 1846, having marched over 850 miles in less than two months.

In the following weeks General Kearny consolidated his position, constructed a fortress on a hill outside Santa Fe, and sent patrols throughout the Rio Grande Valley to demonstrate the strength of his command. Col. Alexander Doniphan prepared a code of law which went into effect on September 22, and Kearny appointed Charles Bent as territorial governor.

Two additional military units were on their way to New Mexico: the Second Missouri Regiment of Volunteers under Col. Sterling Price and the "Mormon Battalion," composed of volunteers from the Iowa territory. Anticipating those reinforcements, Kearny prepared two separate expeditions to further extend U.S. control. The first, under his personal command, was to march from the Rio Grande across Arizona to California. The second, to be led by Colonel Doniphan, was to move directly south into Chihuahua. On September 25, 1846, although Price's regiment had not arrived, Kearny departed with some 300 dragoons. On October 6, near the village of Socorro, he met Kit Carson who reported that California had already been secured by Commodore Stockton. With this news, Kearny sent most of his troops back to Santa Fe and continued the march west with only 100 men, guided by Carson. On October 20 they reached the Gila River, following that stream through extremely rugged territory. After a march of 450 miles, Kearny reached the Colorado River near present-day Yuma, Arizona, in late November. The force then crossed into the harsh desert of southern California. After a short rest at "Warner's Ranch," located at a pleasant spring, the general struck out for San Diego. On December 6, at San Pascual, a California force commanded by Capt. Andrés Pico struck the small army, inflicting heavy casualties, including 18 dead; Kearny was among the wounded. The remnants of the Army of the West staggered into San Diego on December 12, 1846.

In January, Kearny and Stockton met and combined forces. The army troops, naval bluecoats and marines, numbering just over 600 men, moved north from San Diego, and on January 8, 1847, defeated the Californians under Captain Flores at the San Gabriel River. Two days later the United States flag was raised once again in Los Angeles. Frémont forced the surrender of the remnants of Flores's army, and by January 12, 1847, California was in American hands. That position was further strengthened with the arrival in San Diego of the Mormon Battalion under Col. Philip St. George Cooke at the end of January. Their march, having gone farther south than that of Kearny, helped to set the later claim for additional territory in southern Arizona. The Mormon expedition prepared the way for a wagon road and eventually the Southern Pacific Railroad. To further strengthen the Anglo-American hold on the Pacific, most of the 500 members of the battalion remained in California following the end of their enlistment.

On January 16, 1847, a new clash emerged, this one between U.S. officials. Commodore Stockton named John C. Frémont governor of California, an action which was immediately rejected by General Kearny, who had orders from President Polk giving him political authority over the territory. The intraservice conflict was soon ended, however, with the arrival of Commo. W. Branford Shubrick in Monterey. Shubrick replaced Stockton and recognized Kearny's authority. Exercising civil power, Kearny ordered Frémont to discharge his battalion; when the captain refused,

Kearny pressed charges against him, leading to a court-martial and bitter political fight with far-reaching consequences.

The March to Chihuahua

General Kearny had planned an expedition to Chihuahua prior his departure from Santa Fe and appointed Col. Alexander Doniphan as its commander. Before he could set out, however, Doniphan had to put down potential uprisings among the Pueblos, and in the fall of 1846, he led a successful expedition into Navajo country. On December 14, Doniphan formed his column of 856 men at Valverde on the Rio Grande and set out for Chihuahua, unaware that General Wool had abandoned his plan to march to that distant city from San Antonio. In order to shorten his route, the colonel left the river and crossed the "Jornada del Muerto," harsh desert terrain 90 miles wide. He was accompanied by a caravan of traders, intent upon profiting from the long-established commercial links with Chihuahua.

On Christmas Day, at a location some 30 miles north of El Paso called Brazito, Doniphan encountered a Mexican force of some 500 men, commanded by Maj. Antonio Ponce de León. The Missouri volunteers waited until Ponce's troops came in range of their defensive position, then opened fire; within 30 minutes the Mexican force was dispersed. Two days later Doniphan entered El Paso without opposition. He remained there for a month, awaiting the arrival of an artillery battery commanded by Maj. Meriwether Lewis Clark. After Clark's arrival, the volunteers moved south from El Paso on February 8, 1847, their ranks having swollen to 1,200 soldiers and civilians. Despite having learned that Wool would not meet him in Chihuahua, Doniphan pressed ahead on the march of almost 250 miles, equally desolate as the route from Valverde to El Paso and deep in the heart of enemy territory.

Fifteen miles north of Chihuahua, near the Sacramento River, Gen. José A. Heredia established a strong defensive position. His army, numbering 3,000 men and supported by 12 artillery pieces, was entrenched on a mesa south of the river. Early on the morning of February 28, Doniphan advanced toward the Mexican position, with his infantry, cavalry and artillery, accompanied by four columns of wagons. As he approached the mesa, Doniphan turned his entire force 90 degrees. Before Heredia's cavalry could attack, the Americans mounted a seemingly impassable bluff, some 50 feet high, and used the wagons to construct a "fort."

With that protection, Clark's artillery was effectively employed against the advancing lancers. In less than four hours the battle was over; only one American was killed and eight wounded, whereas Doniphan estimated that Heredia suffered 300 killed, 300 wounded, and 40 captured.

On March 2, 1847, Gov. Angel Trías Alvarez abandoned Chihuahua, and the Missouri volunteers entered the city of some 14,000 inhabitants. Rumors circulated that a large Mexican army was approaching from Durango or Zacatecas, while the closest American allies were at Saltillo, some 500 miles to the east. Unaware of the outcome of the battle of Buena Vista, Doniphan felt isolated and vulnerable. Anglo traders found ready markets and excellent prices for their goods, but the dragoons showed little respect for local citizens and their property.

On April 25, having received orders from General Wool, Doniphan and his men set out for Parras, Saltillo, and eventually, Monterrey. By the time of their arrival at the headquarters of General Taylor, the war in northern Mexico had ended. With the end of their enlistments rapidly approaching, the Missourians marched to the Rio Grande, and on June 10, 1847, set out for New Orleans. They eventually returned to Missouri and a hero's welcome, having carried out one of the most difficult campaigns of the entire war. Meanwhile, the last military operation of the conflict was underway.

Landing at Veracruz

The idea of a strike at the Gulf Coast of Mexico was considered as early as August 1846. After the capture of Monterrey, there was brief discussion of Taylor's army marching overland to the central Valley of Mexico, but that idea was soon abandoned because of the great distances and the desolate nature of the land. Tampico was briefly considered as a landing point for a thrust to the interior. By October 1846, however, President Polk was convinced that the principal landing should be at Veracruz, the most important Mexican port on the Gulf. Gen. Winfield Scott drew up two very detailed and thoughtful plans, stressing the absolute necessity of moving rapidly into the interior after a landing to avoid the dreaded "vómito" (yellow fever). He called for an army of 10,000 men, supported by strong naval forces, specially designed landing craft, and massive supplies necessary to complete the task. Details relating to the coast and off-shore area were furnished by Commodore Conner and the former U.S. consul general of Veracruz.

The president was convinced of the practicality of Scott's plan but hesitated to give the Whig general command of the mission. Polk schemed to create the position of lieutenant general and to bestow that rank upon the powerful Democratic senator from Missouri, Thomas Hart Benton. With the failure of that plot, the president reluctantly appointed Scott to the command. The general worked with great energy to fill out the details of his plan, hoping to land at Veracruz by February 1, 1847. Despite effective leadership in the Quartermaster Corps and in many of the supporting services, the monumental problems of logistics and distances delayed the timetable. Scott insisted that some 5,000 men, mostly seasoned regulars, be furnished from Taylor's forces. "Old Rough and Ready" resented having his army stripped of its finest units and lashed out against President Polk. On March 2, 1847, despite the fact that many supplies and some troops had still not been assembled, General Scott moved from the Rio Grande to Lobos Island, then reached the coast off Veracruz three days later. Eyewitnesses were overwhelmed by the massive flotilla as it arrived before the city walls. In the days after the arrival, joint planning was carried out by the top commanders of the army and navy. Although briefly delayed by weather, on March 9, 1847, Scott gave the signal to land on Collado Beach. The navy provided invaluable assistance, not only with supporting fire, but in supervising transport of the troops, and manning the landing crafts which put 8,600 men ashore before midnight without a single casualty. This was accomplished primarily because the Mexican defenders offered no opposition.

In the following days a siege line was established in a half-moon around the walled city. Artillery batteries were emplaced; ammunition and other supplies were ferried ashore, then hauled through the deep sand to key locations along the strengthened line. Although some of his officers wished to assault the city walls, Scott decided to take the city by siege and bombardment rather than suffer the inevitable high casualties of an attack. In addition to fire by field artillery and mortars, naval ships kept up a constant bombardment against the city and the fortress of San Juan de Ulúa. One naval battery was brought ashore, giving effective support to the army's efforts. Few Americans were killed or wounded, but destruction and casualties in Veracruz were heavy. Morale was low among the defenders, and on March 25 Brig. Gen. José Juan Landero informed General Scott that he would surrender the city. Firing ended, and a formal surrender was carried out on March 29, 1847. In less than three weeks the strongest point on the Mexican coast had been captured and it was time for the Americans to march to the interior.

March on Mexico City

Gen. David E. Twiggs led his division out of Veracruz on April 8, taking the National Highway that led to Jalapa, Perote, and eventually Puebla. The rest of Scott's army followed, moving from the hot coastal sands into a more pleasant region of foothills, meeting only light opposition from scattered Mexican units. On April 11, Twiggs's lead division reached the village of Plan del Rio, just below a sharp rise in the National Highway, and found a sizable Mexican army blocking the way. It was commanded by General Santa Anna, who had retreated to Mexico City after the battle of Buena Vista and now had gathered some 12,000 men, with strong artillery support. He established a defensive position on hills near the village of Cerro Gordo, just west of General Twiggs's camp. The Mexican commander was aware that if the Americans were halted at Cerro Gordo they would be forced to remain in the unhealthy hot country as the yellow fever season rapidly approached. His position was a formidable one, protected by a steep cliff on the right and thickly wooded arroyos on the left. Twiggs prepared for a frontal assault on April 14, but action was delayed until the arrival of General Scott. Lt. P. G. T. Beauregard and Capt. Robert E. Lee discovered a route on the Mexican left which would allow a flanking attack, and Scott approved the approach. Early on the morning of April 17, 1847, the Americans advanced, meeting formidable rifle and artillery fire. Casualties were heavy on both sides and by the end of the day neither army had a major advantage. The battle continued on the following morning; Scott's army flanked the Mexican position and secured the National Highway behind the defensive line. Santa Anna's forces fled the field of battle in complete disorder, and the commander himself barely escaped capture. Now there was no organized Mexican force between Scott's army and the national capital.

Cerro Gordo was a glorious victory for Winfield Scott and his small invading army. Scott next moved to the beautiful and healthy city of Jalapa, established hospitals for the wounded, and prepared for further advance. Those plans had to be delayed, however, due to the expiration of the one-year enlistment of many of the volunteers in the army. Most of the men had no intention of remaining beyond their promised period of service. Although Congress approved President Polk's call for additional regular and volunteer units, there was a long delay in getting them trained and to the Mexican front. Ammunition and supplies were short, as were wagons and draft animals. General Scott denounced the inefficiency of the system, which was bogged down in partisan politics. Despite the precarious position, Gen. William Worth pushed 60 miles farther west to Puebla, the second largest city of Mexico, and found that many of the leaders of that conservative stronghold were supportive of the American cause. By early June, Scott advanced his entire army (now barely 7,000 men) to that city, temporarily cutting off his supply line to the coast. The commander's problems were compounded by personal clashes with Nicholas Trist, who had been sent by Polk to open negotiations with the Mexican government.

After a period of uneasy waiting, reinforcements arrived in Puebla in July and August, including a contingent of over 2,000 men under Brig. Gen. Franklin Pierce. With an effective force of approximately 11,000, divided into three divisions, Scott initiated his march to the Valley of Mexico on August 7, 1847. On August 12, lead elements reached the village of Ayotla, only 12 miles from the capital. Just beyond Ayotla, Santa Anna had established a strong defensive position at El Peñón, blocking the eastern entrance into the city. Approaches were restricted by three lakes and extensive marshlands, which severely limited movement of artillery and supply wagons. With advice from his engineers, Scott moved his army along the eastern edge of Lake Chalco and approached his objective from the south.

Rather than move directly against the village of Churubusco, which blocked one of the southern gates of the city, the Americans moved across the pedregal, a rugged volcanic field, and struck Gen. Gabriel Valencia's army at Padierna. The battle, fought early in the morning of August 20, was an American victory primarily because of the decisive action of Brig. Gen. Persifor F. Smith. On the heels of the panicked retreat of Valencia, General Scott ordered a concentrated attack against the Mexican position at Churubusco, defended in part by the San Patricio Battalion, made up of deserters from the U.S. Army. Casualties on both sides were heavy, much of the fighting having been done at close quarters, but eventually the strong points at Churubusco fell to Scott's army.

Mexico City seemed open after Churubusco, but General Scott felt that to seize that prize might actually jeopardize the opportunity for a negotiated peace. He accepted overtures from Santa

Anna for a truce, worked out by a commission on August 22. Scott asked Nicholas Trist to enter into negotiations to bring about an end to the war, but it soon became clear that Santa Anna had no intention of accepting the terms offered by the U.S. envoy. By September 6 it became clear that efforts to reach a permanent peace treaty would not succeed, and Scott informed Santa Anna that he would end the truce. Two days later, General Worth launched an assault against two fortified positions west of Mexico City. Known as the Battle of Molino del Rey, this action was extremely costly to the attacking American force, with a loss of 116 killed and over 600 wounded. It set the stage, however, for the final phase of the war in the Valley of Mexico.

After considering alternative approaches to Mexico City, General Scott announced on September 11 that the primary attack would be concentrated on Chapultepec, an imposing hill and fortress just west of the capital. Early on the morning of September 12, the action was initiated with an artillery bombardment. The following day (September 13, 1847) an infantry assault was launched from the west and from the south. With ladders, the attackers mounted the wall of Chapultepec Castle and succeeded in seizing it from the small Mexican detachment. The divisions of Worth and Quitman pushed along the causeways and through the city gates. Some fighting continued the next day, but by noon General Scott rode into the Zócalo, the principal plaza of the Mexican capital, and observed the Stars and Stripes raised over the National Palace.

Scattered fighting, mostly against guerrilla forces, continued in the following months; the small American garrison at Puebla was almost captured by Santa Anna, but the attack was repulsed by Col. C. F. Childs. After the fall of Mexico City, primary attention was focused on the efforts of Nicholas Trist to negotiate a treaty with the remnants of the defeated Mexican government. The Treaty of Guadalupe Hidalgo, signed February 2, 1848, provided for the end of the war and for the evacuation of Mexican territory by U.S. armed forces. In return, Mexico was to surrender vast stretches of its northern territory to the victor. There was strong opposition to the treaty on the part of various Mexican political leaders, but the nation's will to resist seemed to have been exhausted. In the United States, news of the settlement produced bitter disputes, based to a large degree upon sectional and party politics. The Treaty of Guadalupe Hidalgo was eventually ratified, but the legacy of the war was to contribute to the nation's most tragic era.

The Dictionary

A

ABERDEEN, FOURTH EARL OF (GEORGE HAMILTON GOR-DON) (1784–1860). British foreign secretary at the time the United States considered the annexation of Texas, the Earl of Aberdeen attempted to influence Texas officials to remain as an independent republic and to gain the support of Mexico for that independence. His efforts to create a buffer state in Texas failed, in part because of British opposition to slavery but also because of Mexico's rejection of the plan. He was also involved in other aspects of diplomatic relations between the United States and Mexico before the declaration of war. *See also* OREGON.

ABERT, JOHN JAMES (1788–1863). Col. John J. Abert was chief of the topographical engineers who in 1845 complied with the efforts of Sen. Thomas Hart Benton (q.v.) to have his son-in-law John C. Frémont (q.v.) carry out his third expedition into western North America, including California.

ABOLITIONISTS. The forces that advocated the abolition of slavery in the United States, especially its expansion into western territories being added to the union, generally opposed the war with Mexico. They charged that the struggle was a conspiracy for the expansion of slavery. *See also* AMERICAN PEACE SOCIETY.

ACAPULCO, GUERRERO. Acapulco was an important Mexican port on the Pacific Ocean and a base for Mexican privateer forces throughout the war. Commo. Robert F. Stockton (q.v.) made plans to seize the port in 1846 but had to abandon the effort because of a lack of adequate forces and because of uprisings in California against American control.

ACAPULCO ROAD. The Acapulco Road, leading from the Pacific port to Mexico City through the towns of San Agustín (q.v.) and San Antonio (q.v.), became the avenue of approach for the army of Gen. Winfield Scott (q.v.) following his move around Lake Chalco (q.v.) in August 1847.

ADAMS, HENRY. Comdr. Henry Adams led a U.S. naval force to Yucatán (q.v.) in September 1847 and negotiated with regional leaders on neutrality for that area.

ADAMS, JOHN QUINCY (1767–1848). President of the United States from 1825 to 1829, by the outbreak of the war with Mexico, John Quincy Adams had been elected to the House of Representatives and led Whig opposition to the declaration of war in May 1846. Throughout the struggle, the former president denounced the conflict as a scheme to expand slavery.

AGUA CALIENTE, CALIFORNIA. The Agua Caliente Valley is to the west of the Coastal Range in California, so named for the hot spring found there. When Gen. Stephen Kearny (q.v.) and his small force arrived there December 2, 1846, on their way to San Diego (q.v.), they took refuge at the ranch of American Jonathan Trumbull Warner and gained strength before meeting the forces of the Californios in the battle of San Pascual (q.v.) on December 6, 1846. *See also* WARNER'S RANCH.

AGUA NUEVA, COAHUILA. Agua Nueva is a village in the southern region of the state of Coahuila (q.v.), on the road from Saltillo (q.v.) to San Luis Potosí (q.v.). Gen. John Wool (q.v.) occupied the settlement in December 1846 but withdrew with the approach of the force of Santa Anna in February 1847. *See also* BUENA VISTA, BATTLE OF.

AGUIRRE, JOSE MARIA DE. José María de Aguirre was governor of the state of Coahuila (q.v.) at the time of its occupation, November 16, 1846, by U.S. forces under Gen. William Worth (q.v.).

ALABAMA. The steamship USS *Alabama* transported Gen. Zachary Taylor (q.v.) from New Orleans to Aransas Pass (Corpus Christi Bay), July 24–29, 1845. *See also* CORPUS CHRISTI.

ALAMO. A small Franciscan mission in the heart of present-day San Antonio, Texas, the Alamo was the site of the victory of

Gen. Antonio López de Santa Anna (q.v.) over the Texas force, March 6, 1836. Its fall created a symbol of anti-Mexican feeling among Anglo-American Texans and the rallying cry that continued throughout the war, "Remember the Alamo."

ALBANY. The *Albany* (along with the *Germantown*) was a sloop of war completed shortly before the declaration of war with Mexico.

ALBUQUERQUE, NEW MEXICO. In 1847 Albuquerque was a small village in New Mexico south of Santa Fe, occupied by the army of Gen. Stephen W. Kearny (q.v.) in the course of his march to California. Today it is the largest city in New Mexico.

ALCARAZ, RAMON (1823–1886). A poet, dramatist, and journalist, Ramón Alcaraz fought against the U.S. invasion of Mexico. Later he edited a collection of essays that illustrated Mexican concepts and interpretations of the war. It was edited and translated into English by Albert C. Ramsey (q.v.) under the title *The Other Side: Notes for the History of the War between Mexico and the United States.*

ALCORTA, LINO JOSE (d. 1854). Brig. Gen. Lino José Alcorta fought in the battle of Cerro Gordo (q.v.) and was later appointed minister of war and navy by Antonio López de Santa Anna (q.v.) at the time of the fall of Mexico City to Gen. Winfield Scott (q.v.) in September 1847.

ALEXANDER, EDMUND B. (1803–1888). Capt. Edmund B. Alexander participated in many battles throughout the campaign for central Mexico, including the siege of Veracruz (q.v.) and the battle of Cerro Gordo (q.v.). As commander of the Third Infantry, Alexander led the charge against the convent of San Mateo (q.v.) in the battle of Churubusco (q.v.), August 20, 1847. He was brevetted major for Cerro Gordo and lieutenant colonel for Contreras (q.v.) and Churubusco.

"ALL OF MEXICO" MOVEMENT. With the defeat of Mexico by the Army of Invasion under Gen. Winfield Scott (q.v.), a growing sentiment among a small but vocal element in the United States advocated the annexation of all Mexican territory. Prominent Whigs, including John Quincy Adams (q.v.), denounced their efforts. Although supported by a number of prominent leaders, especially in the Democratic Party, the signing of the

Treaty of Guadalupe Hidalgo (q.v.) in February 1848 ended that effort. *See also* MANIFEST DESTINY.

ALLEN, GEORGE W. (d. 1848). Capt. George W. Allen commanded the Fourth Infantry in the battle of Palo Alto (q.v.), May 8, 1846.

ALLEN, JAMES (1806–1846). Capt. James Allen organized the Mormon Battalion (q.v.) at Council Bluffs, Iowa, July 16, 1846, and was appointed to command it as a lieutenant colonel. His force became a part of General Kearny's Army of the West (q.v.). Following Allen's death, command of the battalion was assigned to Philip St. George Cooke (q.v.).

ALLEN, ROBERT (1811–1886). A graduate of the West Point class of 1832, at the time of the outbreak of the war with Mexico, Capt. Robert Allen served as assistant quartermaster in the Kentucky Cavalry during its march to Monterrey, Nuevo León (q.v.). He participated in the siege of Veracruz (q.v.) under the command of Gen. David Twiggs (q.v.). He was brevetted Major for his role in the battle of Cerro Gordo (q.v.) and fought in a number of battles in the Valley of Mexico (q.v.). During the Civil War Allen was brevetted major general for meritorious service in the U.S. Army.

ALLEN, WILLIAM (1803–1879). Sen. William Allen of Ohio was chairman of the Senate Committee on Foreign Relations at the time of the outbreak of the war with Mexico. He was a strong supporter of efforts to win major territorial concessions.

ALMONTE, JUAN NEPOMUCENO (1803–1869). The natural son of José María Morelos, hero of the movement for Mexican independence, Juan N. Almonte fought in the rebellion against Spain at an early age. He was educated in New Orleans, Louisiana, and upon his return to Mexico warned of the dangers of Anglo-American colonization in Texas. With the revolt in Texas, Almonte fought with Santa Anna at the Alamo (q.v.) and in the battle of San Jacinto. As Mexican ambassador to the United States from 1842 to 1845, he denounced the Tyler administration's efforts to annex Texas and acquire additional Mexican territory. When the U.S. Congress approved of Texas annexation in February 1845, Almonte branded it "an act of aggression," demanded his passport, and departed for home.

On his return to Mexico, he became a supporter of Antonio López de Santa Anna (q.v.).

ALVARADO, VERACRUZ. At the beginning of the war in the spring of 1846, the town of Alvarado, south of the port of Veracruz (q.v.), was one of the targets of the U.S. Navy's blockading (q.v.) tactics. Located on a shallow river of the same name, Alvarado was the objective of several abortive attacks by the naval force under the command of Commo. David Conner (q.v.), in July, August, and October 1846. Following the surrender of Veracruz (q.v.), Alvarado was taken by a force commanded by Gen. John A. Quitman (q.v.) and Commo. Matthew C. Perry (q.v.).

ALVAREZ, JUAN (1790–1867). Juan Alvarez fought for Mexican independence and became a powerful regional leader in the area southwest of Mexico City. Rising to the rank of major general, by 1842, Alvarez was a regional caudillo in what is today the state of Guerrero, west of Mexico City, commanding the Army of the South, which numbered some 2,500 men. He later was appointed commander of cavalry operating against the communication lines of Gen. Winfield Scott (q.v.) during the latter's move into the Valley of Mexico. Alvarez also commanded a cavalry force of 4,000 men during the American attacks at Casa Mata (q.v.) and Molino del Rey (q.v.), but his troops retired without major damage to the attackers. Following the war, Alvarez continued to play a significant role in Mexican politics and was one of the primary leaders in the Revolution of Ayutla against Santa Anna in 1853. With the eventual triumph of that revolt, Alvarez was chosen provisional president in October 1855 by the liberal faction and served until September 15, 1856. Alvarez continued to play a role in the War of the Reform and against French intervention.

AMERICAN EAGLE. The *American Eagle* was an English-language newspaper established in Veracruz (q.v.) shortly after the fall of that city in April 1847. *See also* NEWSPAPERS.

AMERICAN FLAG. The *American Flag* was an English-language newspaper established in Matamoros (q.v.) following that city's occupation by the army of Gen. Zachary Taylor (q.v.). *See also* NEWSPAPERS.

AMERICAN PEACE SOCIETY. The American Peace Society was an organization opposed to the war with Mexico, denouncing the conflict as an effort to expand slavery. *See also* ABOLITIONISTS.

AMERICAN STAR. The *American Star*, an English-language newspaper for distribution in the American army, was established following the occupation of Jalapa (q.v.) by Gen. Winfield Scott (q.v.), April 1847. With the fall of Mexico City, the *Star* was transferred to that city and published with a Spanish-language section under the title *Estrella Americana.* The publishers were John H. Peoples and James R. Barnard. *See also* NEWSPAPERS.

AMOZOC, PUEBLA. Amozoc (or Amozoque) was a village in the state of Puebla, about 10 miles east of the capital and along the American route of march from Jalapa (q.v.). A light skirmish took place there in May 1847 between the force of Santa Anna (q.v.) and the army of Gen. William Worth (q.v.).

AMPUDIA, PEDRO DE (1805–1868). Born in Havana, Cuba, Pedro de Ampudia arrived in Mexico in 1821 as a member of the Spanish military force sent to put down rebellion. In a short time, the young officer deserted the Spanish and embraced Mexican independence. He fought in Texas in the troubled times between 1840 and 1842, rising to the rank of colonel. At the beginning of hostilities with the United States, Ampudia was a major general and commanded the Mexican Army of the North (q.v.). He moved from Monterrey (q.v.) to Matamoros (q.v.), arriving at the latter point on April 11, 1846, and demanded that Gen. Zachary Taylor (q.v.) retire north of the Nueces River (q.v.). Shortly after that time, Ampudia was replaced as commander of the division by Gen. Mariano Arista (q.v.), but the former commander continued to play a role in the siege of Fort Texas (q.v.) and the battles of Palo Alto (q.v.) and Resaca de la Palma (q.v.). Following the fall of Matamoros, Ampudia was restored to command and established his fortified position at Monterrey (q.v.). There he was defeated by General Taylor, but on September 26, 1846, he was allowed to evacuate the city, moving his force to Saltillo (q.v.) and eventually to San Luis Potosí (q.v.). General Ampudia commanded a unit in the battle of Buena Vista (q.v.), February 22–23, 1847, and then marched with his brigade to face Gen. Winfield Scott's (q.v.) army at Cerro Gordo (q.v.). For a short time he served as governor of Nuevo León; with the outbreak of civil war in Mexico, he took the side of the liberals.

ANAYA, PEDRO MARIA DE (1794–1854). Following his defeat at Buena Vista (q.v.), Antonio López de Santa Anna (q.v.) returned to Mexico City to take control of the government. Within a short time, however, he organized an army to oppose the march of Gen. Winfield Scott (q.v.) from Veracruz (q.v.) and appointed Gen. Pedro María de Anaya as interim chief of state. After the battle of Cerro Gordo (q.v.), Anaya declared Mexico City to be in a state of siege and announced that Santa Anna would serve as commanding general of the Federal District. He defended the Convent of San Mateo (q.v.) during the battle of Churubusco (q.v.) and was taken prisoner in that action by Gen. David Twiggs (q.v.). After the surrender of Mexico City to the American force, Anaya, then considered a moderate, was elected interim president by the Mexican Legislative Assembly and appointed a commission to meet with Nicholas Trist (q.v.) to discuss peace terms. These efforts led to the signing of the Treaty of Guadalupe Hidalgo (q.v.) in February 1848.

ANDREWS, TIMOTHY PATRICK (d. 1868). Col. Timothy Patrick Andrews was the Irish-born commander of the U.S. Voltigeur Regiment (q.v.), which played a prominent role in the attacks against Casa Mata (q.v.), Molino del Rey (q.v.), and Chapultepec (q.v.). He was brevetted brigadier general for the latter action.

ANGNEY, WILLIAM Z. Capt. William Z. Angney was commander of a Missouri infantry battalion in the campaign to win New Mexico.

ANGOSTURA, BATTLE OF. *La Angostura* ("the narrows"), in the United States–Mexican War, refers to a narrow valley on the road between Saltillo (q.v.) and San Luis Potosí (q.v.), south of the hacienda of Buena Vista (q.v.). The position was selected by Gen. John E. Wool (q.v.) as the site of a major battle between the armies of generals Zachary Taylor (q.v.) and Antonio López de Santa Anna (q.v.), February 22–23, 1847. U.S. historians came to call it the battle of Buena Vista, but Mexican sources refer to the clash as the battle of Angostura. *See also* BUENA VISTA, BATTLE OF.

ANSALDO RANCH. A farm near the village of Padierna (q.v.) in the Valley of Mexico, the Rancho Ansaldo was involved with the clash on August 19–20, 1847, called the battle of Contreras (q.v.) by the U.S. authorities but the battle of Padierna by the Mexicans.

ANTON LIZARDO, VERACRUZ. Antón Lizardo is a prominent geographic feature approximately 12 miles south of Veracruz (q.v.) protected from storms by a number of barrier islands and reefs. In 1846, Commo. David Conner (q.v.) chose that location as the primary anchorage for the Home Squadron (q.v.) of the U.S. Navy. Antón Lizardo played an important role in the expedition of Gen. Winfield Scott (q.v.) against Veracruz (q.v.) in March 1847. *See also* VERACRUZ, VERACRUZ.

APACHE CANYON. Apache Canyon was a strong position on the Pecos River, some 12 miles south of Santa Fe, New Mexico (q.v.), fortified by Gov. Manuel Armijo (q.v.) but then abandoned before the arrival of the forces of Gen. Stephen Kearny (q.v.), in August 1846. Passing through the position without opposition, Kearny and his army occupied Santa Fe.

APACHES. The Apaches are one of the important members of the Athabascan linguistic stock which settled in the American Southwest, especially in the region of present-day Arizona and New Mexico. The Navajos (q.v.) and Eutaws were in part subdued by the army of Col. Alexander Doniphan (q.v.) in late 1846. Gen. Stephen W. Kearny (q.v.), during his march from the Rio Grande to California, encountered several Apache groups in present-day southern Arizona.

ARANSAS PASS, TEXAS. Aransas Pass, at the entrance to Corpus Christi Bay (q.v.), figured prominently in the landing of the army of Gen. Zachary Taylor (q.v.) in late July and early August 1845.

ARCHULETA, DIEGO. Col. Diego Archuleta was lieutenant governor of New Mexico at the time of the invasion by the army of Gen. Stephen Kearny (q.v.). He was involved with an anti-American uprising on January 19, 1847, that resulted in the murder of Gov. Charles Bent (q.v.) and a general rebellion that was put down by Brig. Gen. Sterling Price (q.v.).

ARISTA, MARIANO (1802–1855). Maj. Gen. Mariano Arista was the Mexican commander on the lower Rio Grande in the vicinity of Matamoros (q.v.) before the outbreak of hostilities. He opposed Texas independence and in 1842 insisted that Mexican authority be recognized. In early 1846, Arista was proposed by northern Mexican leaders to head a revolt against the central government of Mexico City, but the rebellion did not materialize. On April 4, 1846, he was once again placed in command of the Army of the North (q.v.), replacing Gen. Pedro de Ampudia (q.v.). On May 3, 1846, Arista sent some 5,000 men north of the Rio Grande, challenging Gen. Zachary Taylor (q.v.) in the battles of Palo Alto (q.v.) and Resaca de la Palma (q.v.). With those defeats, the general retreated across the Rio Grande to Matamoros and surrendered his command to Ampudia. After returning to Mexico City, Arista faced a court-martial and in July 1846 was dismissed from the army. In 1851, he once again gained the presidency but 18 months later was deposed by Santa Anna (q.v.) in 1853 and died in European exile.

ARMIJO, MANUEL. Manuel Armijo was a prosperous and ambitious political leader in New Mexico. His wealth, centered in Albuquerque (q.v.), was derived in part from his participation in the trade between Santa Fe (q.v.) and St. Louis, Missouri. Governor of New Mexico at the time of the outbreak of hostilities with the United States, Armijo called upon the citizens of New Mexico to resist the invasion of Gen. Stephen Kearny (q.v.). He established a defensive position at Apache Canyon (q.v.), but, gaining little support for his proclamation, Governor Armijo abandoned the position and fled south to Chihuahua (q.v.), leaving Santa Fe open to the invading force.

ARMSTRONG, WILLIAM (1815–1847). Following his graduation from West Point in 1837, Lt. William Armstrong joined the Second Artillery. He participated in the siege of Veracruz (q.v.) and then the battle of Cerro Gordo (q.v.). Being promoted to captain in August 1847, he fought at Churubusco (q.v.) and was then killed in the battle of Molino del Rey (q.v.).

ARMY OF CHIHUAHUA. This army, organized by Gen. John E. Wool (q.v.) in San Antonio, Texas (q.v.), was officially designated as the Centre Division but came to be referred to as the Army of Chihuahua, since that provincial capital was its planned destination. With a force of some 1,500 men, Wool marched from San Antonio in late September 1846, crossed the Rio Grande at present-day Eagle Pass, Texas, and occupied Monclova (q.v.) in the state of Coahuila (q.v.). Although originally ordered to occupy Chihuahua City, Wool asked for a change in his mission, and in early 1847, he was ordered by

Gen. Zachary Taylor (q.v.) to move to Parras, Coahuila (q.v.). Wool's army played an important role in the battle of Buena Vista (q.v.). *See also* BUENA VISTA, BATTLE OF.

ARMY OF OBSERVATION. The force under the command of Brevet Brig. Gen. Zachary Taylor (q.v.) at Fort Jesup, Louisiana (q.v.), in 1844–1845 was called the Army of Observation or Corps of Observation. With the acceptance of annexation to the United States by the Republic of Texas (July 4, 1845), Pres. James K. Polk (q.v.) ordered Taylor to shift his force to a position near the Texas boundary with Mexico. Taylor chose to establish his camp at the mouth of the Nueces River (q.v.) and changed the name of the force to the Army of Occupation.

ARMY OF OCCUPATION. After moving to Corpus Christi (q.v.) in July 1845, Gen. Zachary Taylor (q.v.) changed the name of his force from the Army of Observation to the Army of Occupation. That concentration of some 3,500 men moved from the Nueces River (q.v.) on March 8, 1846, to take up a position on the Rio Grande (q.v.), across from Matamoros (q.v.). It was involved in the initial clashes with the Mexican army.

ARMY OF THE EAST (*Ejercito del Oriente*). With the landing of the U.S. forces at Veracruz (q.v.) in March 1847 Gen. Antonio López de Santa Anna (q.v.) dispatched the *Ejercito del Oriente* to Jalapa (q.v.) under Gen. Valentín Canalizo (q.v.). Santa Anna took personal command of this army in the battle of Cerro Gordo (q.v.), April 17–18, 1847. *See also* CERRO GORDO, BATTLE OF.

ARMY OF THE NORTH (*Ejercito del Norte*). This Mexican army commanded by Gen. Mariano Arista (q.v.) is referred to in U.S. sources as the Army of the North or Division of the North. It was later assigned to Gen. Gabriel Valencia (q.v.), who on August 17, 1847, occupied a position at San Angel (q.v.), then advanced to Padierna (q.v.) in spite of orders from Santa Anna to remain in a defensive posture. In the battle of Contreras (q.v.), August 20, 1847, the Army of the North was virtually destroyed. *See also* CONTRERAS AND CHURUBUSCO, BATTLES OF.

ARMY OF THE WEST. The Army of the West, organized at Fort Leavenworth, Kansas (q.v.), soon after the outbreak of hostilities on the Rio Grande (q.v.), was composed of the First Dragoons commanded by Col. Stephen Watts Kearny (q.v.) and the First Regiment of Missouri Mounted Volunteers, which elected Col. Alexander W. Doniphan (q.v.) as its commander. With the addition of other units, the force of some 1,700 men set out for Santa Fe, New Mexico (q.v.), in late June 1846. Despite severe logistical problems, the army moved some 800 miles to Bent's Fort (q.v.) and eventually into Santa Fe. It occupied the New Mexican capital without firing a shot on August 18, 1846. The force was later strengthened by the Mormon Battalion (q.v.), numbering some 500 men, and the Second Missouri Regiment commanded by Col. Sterling Price (q.v.). Following the occupation of New Mexico, Kearny continued to California, and Doniphan led a remarkable march with his 1,000 Missouri volunteers to Chihuahua.

ARROYO. *Arroyo* is a Spanish term for a stream or creek, often a dry streambed, which is filled with water only during periods of heavy rainfall.

ARROYO COLORADO. The Arroyo Colorado is a small stream that runs through present-day Harlingen, Texas, approximately 30 miles north of Brownsville (q.v.). On March 19, 1846, Mexican dragoons under Gen. Francisco Mejía (q.v.) challenged the advance of Gen. Zachary Taylor (q.v.) at the arroyo, but on the following day, Taylor moved across the stream without opposition and continued his march to the Rio Grande (q.v.).

ARROYO HONDO. At the time of the Taos rebellion (q.v.) against the authority of Gov. Charles Bent (q.v.) in New Mexico, a force of Indians at Arroyo Hondo murdered Simeon Turley and six other Americans.

ARROYO SECO, CHIHUAHUA. A small dry streambed north of the Mexican position along the Sacramento River some 15 miles from Chihuahua City (q.v.), the Arroyo Seco played an important role in the battle of Sacramento (q.v.) between Col. Alexander Doniphan (q.v.) and Gen. José María García Condé (q.v.), February 28, 1847.

ARROYO, MIGUEL. Miguel Arroyo, secretary of the Mexican peace commission at the end of the war, was possibly involved with a bribe paid by Gen. Winfield Scott (q.v.) relating to the signing of an acceptable treaty. *See also* BRIBERY SCHEME.

ARTILLERY. Joel Poinsett, the first U.S. minister to Mexico (1825–1829), was later appointed as secretary of war in the cabinet of Pres. Martin Van Buren (1837–1841). One of his most important actions was to send a commission to Europe to make an inspection of the latest developments in artillery and then to apply them in the U.S. arsenal. As a result, by the time of the war with Mexico, the United States had developed an artillery arm that was the equivalent of any belonging to other armies at the time. The basic field piece was the six-pounder gun, an artillery weapon that weighed 880 pounds, had a range of 1,500 yards, and fired a shell weighing six pounds. The development of tactics was as important as the ordnance. Before the outbreak of hostilities, Capt. Samuel Ringgold (q.v.) played an important role in the development of light or "flying artillery," so-called because of the rapid movement of the guns in support of infantry units on the field of battle. Artillerymen of the battery were mounted on horses rather than on the limbers which were utilized to transport the guns. The U.S. Congress authorized the organization of one of these horse-drawn batteries for each of the four artillery regiments of the regular army and Poinsett supervised their formation prior to the outbreak of war with Mexico. Ringgold's light artillery played a decisive role at Palo Alto (q.v.), but in the course of that battle the young officer was mortally wounded. The bold use of artillery, however, continued to play a significant part in many later actions, including Col. Doniphan's (q.v.) victory in the battle of Sacramento (q.v.), February 28, 1847. By comparison, Mexican artillery tactics were not so well developed, and Mexican ammunition was often inferior.

Heavier artillery weapons were also developed for the U.S. arsenal, including 8-inch howitzers and 8 and 10-inch mortars used primarily as siege guns. The principal test for these weapons came during the operations against Veracruz (q.v.), March 9–27, 1847. Four batteries of army artillery were brought into action against the walls of the city. In addition, Gen. Winfield Scott (q.v.) accepted Commo. David Conner's (q.v.) offer to bring heavy naval guns into the siege operation. These included three French Paixhans, an eight-inch gun that fired a 68-pound exploding shell at a high velocity. The bombardment caused heavy damage and many casualties in Veracruz and resulted in the surrender of the city within a short time. The heavy Mexican guns of San Juan de Ulúa (q.v.), with defective ammunition and lacking mobility, were never effective in the defense of the city. Some scholars of the war have concluded that U.S. superiority in artillery was one of the primary factors in the outcome of the war with Mexico.

ARTISTS. A number of artists from the United States, both professional and amateur, recorded their impressions of Mexico throughout the war in visual images. The most popular form of reproduction was the lithograph; several outstanding artists sent sketches or elaborate drawings from Mexico that were published in newspapers, magazines, and books throughout the United States. Two of the most prominent were Nathaniel Currier and Carl Nebel. One of the most interesting collections of sketches are those prepared by Samuel Chamberlain (q.v.), many published in *Life* magazine (1957). *See also* the Bibliographical Essay.

ATALAYA. The mountain known as Atalaya is located on the National Highway between Veracruz (q.v.) and Jalapa (q.v.), one-half mile northeast of a hill called El Telégrafo (q.v.). Much of the action in the battle of Cerro Gordo (q.v.), April 17–18, 1847, took place on Atalaya. *See also* CERRO GORDO, BATTLE OF.

ATLISCO, PUEBLA. Atlisco (Atlixo), a small town south of Puebla (q.v.), was the site of a skirmish between Brig. Gen. Joseph Lane (q.v.) and Gen. Joaquín Rea (q.v.) on October 19, 1847.

ATOCHA, ALEJANDRO JOSE. Col. Alejandro José Atocha, a confidential agent of Antonio López de Santa Anna (q.v.), approached Pres. James K. Polk (q.v.) on February 13, 1846. Atocha suggested that if the exiled Santa Anna (then in Havana, Cuba) were allowed to return to Mexico, he might be able to arrange for an end to hostilities with the United States. According to the envoy, Santa Anna advised President Polk to send strong land and naval forces to Mexico to convince political leaders to come to terms. Atocha later played a minor role in the negotiations that led to the Treaty of Guadalupe Hidalgo (q.v.).

ATRISTAIN, MIGUEL. Miguel Atristáin was a member of the Mexican negotiating team at the end of the war involved with the negotiation of the Treaty of Guadalupe Hidalgo (q.v.).

ATZCAPUZALCO, FEDERAL DISTRICT. Atzcapuzalco is a town in the Federal District of Mexico where the Mexican commissioners met with Nicholas Trist (q.v.) on August 27, 1846. The discussions were soon after moved to Casa Colorado near Tacubaya (q.v.) but were discontinued when no agreement was reached.

AULICK, JOHN H. Capt. John H. Aulick was in command of the U.S. naval force at the mouth of the Rio Grande (q.v.) in May 1846. In early August, he participated in an unsuccessful attempt by Commo. David Conner (q.v.) to take the city of Alvarado (q.v.). At the time of the invasion of Veracruz (q.v.), Aulick was second in command of the Home Squadron (q.v.) and on March 23, 1847, took personal command of the naval battery that played an important part in the siege of Veracruz.

AYOTLA. Ayotla is a small village in the Federal District of Mexico, 15 miles east of the capital on the road from Puebla (q.v.). Gen. Winfield Scott (q.v.) reached that town in August 1846. Rather than proceed directly against the fortified position at El Peñón (q.v.), Scott moved his army south from Ayotla and around the eastern shore of Lake Chalco (q.v.), setting the stage for his campaign in the Valley of Mexico. Gen. David E. Twiggs (q.v.) remained at Ayotla as a threat to El Peñón during that maneuver.

AZTEC CLUB OF 1847. The Aztec Club of 1847 was a U.S. officer's club established on October 13, 1847, following the surrender of Mexico City. It was open to all officers who had served in the war against Mexico after the landing at Veracruz, and Gen. John A. Quitman (q.v.) was its first president.

B

BACA, TOMAS. Tomás Baca was a Pueblo Indian leader implicated in the murder of Gov. Charles Bent (q.v.) of New Mexico on January 19, 1847, during the Pueblo Revolt. *See also* TAOS REBELLION.

BACKUS, ELECTUS (1804–1862). Capt. Electus Backus of the First U.S. Infantry participated in key actions of the battle of Monterrey (q.v.), especially during the assault against La Tenería (q.v.), and was brevetted major for that action. He also participated in the siege of Veracruz (q.v.) and commanded the Castle of San Juan de Ulúa (q.v.). *See also* MONTERREY, BATTLE OF.

BACON, JOHN D. (1818–1847). Following his graduation from West Point in 1849, Lt. John D. Bacon joined the Second Infantry. He served in the Florida War from 1840 to 1842 and then carried out a number of assignments on the western frontier. Promoted to first lieutenant in 1846, Bacon was assigned to the Sixth Infantry. He joined the army of Gen. Winfield Scott (q.v.) in the campaign for the Valley of Mexico (q.v.) and was mortally wounded during the battle of Churubusco (q.v.).

BAGBY, ARTHUR P. (1794–1858). Arthur P. Bagby was a senator from Alabama who supported the Jacksonian faction in the national government and came to be a close ally of Sen. Thomas Hart Benton (q.v.) during the war with Mexico.

BAILEY, THEODORUS (1805–1877). Lt. Theodorus Bailey commanded the storeship *Lexington*, which supplied the U.S. operations against California and transported the New York troops of Lt. Col. Henry S. Burton (q.v.) in the invasion of La Paz, Baja California (q.v.), July 4, 1847.

BAJA CALIFORNIA. Baja California is a peninsula on the western side of Mexico, bounded on the west by the Pacific Ocean and on the east by the Gulf of California. At the time of the United States–Mexican War, it was a part of the administrative region of California and very sparsely populated. With the occupation of San Diego (q.v.) by the forces of Commo. Robert F. Stockton (q.v.), Baja California was a source of supplies. On August 19, 1846, Stockton proclaimed a blockade (q.v.) of the Pacific Coast of Mexico, including the peninsula, but Mexican trade continued. In September 1846, the village of La Paz (q.v.), capital of Baja California, was attacked, and efforts were made to neutralize the region. On July 21, 1847, two companies of New York volunteers under the command of Lt. Col. Henry S. Burton (q.v.) occupied La Paz. Later there was an active effort on the part of Commo. W. Branford Shubrick (q.v.) to acquire the region for the United States, a plan that won the support of a number of the natives of the region. Mexican Capt. Manuel Pineda attacked La Paz and San José del Cabo (q.v.) in November 1847 but was defeated. These operations did, however, help disrupt Shubrick's plans. Pineda mounted another attack against San José del Cabo in January 1848, but it failed with the arrival of U.S. reinforcements under Comdr. Samuel F. DuPont (q.v.). Additional reinforcements made it possible for Colonel

Burton to gain control over the entire region by the end of March 1848.

When Nicholas Trist (q.v.) was dispatched to Mexico, his instructions were to acquire all of California, including the lower peninsula, but in the final treaty it remained a territory of Mexico, as did the mouth of the Colorado River. A number of the citizens who had supported U.S. efforts went into exile. Today the peninsula is divided into the two Mexican states of Baja California Norte and Baja California Sur.

BAKER, EDWARD DICKINSON (1811–1861). Col. Edward D. Baker was commander of the Fourth Illinois Volunteer Regiment, appointed by Secretary of War William Marcy (q.v.). His troops clashed with Georgia volunteers during the occupation of the Rio Grande Valley. Later Baker played a key role in the battle of Cerro Gordo (q.v.).

BALDERAS, LUCAS (1797–1847). Col. Lucas Balderas was an officer in the *Batallón de Mina* and was killed at the battle of Molino del Rey (q.v.).

BANCROFT, GEORGE (1800–1891). George Bancroft was appointed secretary of the navy by Pres. James K. Polk (q.v.) in 1845. Hoping that a conflict with Mexico might be avoided, Bancroft was the lone member of Polk's cabinet who opposed the declaration of war before reports of the clash on the Rio Grande. With the declaration, Secretary Bancroft immediately ordered Commo. David Conner (q.v.) to establish a blockade of the Mexican coast in the Gulf and strengthened naval forces in that region. Even before the outbreak of hostilities, Bancroft instructed Commo. John D. Sloat (q.v.) to take possession of San Francisco (q.v.) and to occupy or blockade other points along the Pacific Coast in case of a declaration of war.

With the retirement of Louis McLane as head of the U.S. mission in London, the president offered that diplomatic post to Bancroft, and the secretary accepted. He was replaced in the Navy Department on September 9, 1846, by John Y. Mason (q.v.). Bancroft is best remembered as an outstanding historian and author of *A History of the United States*. *See also* BLOCKADE.

BANGS, SAMUEL. Samuel Bangs was a printer who initiated the publication of the Corpus Christi *Gazette* in early 1846, after the arrival there of the forces of Gen. Zachary Taylor (q.v.).

BANKHEAD, CHARLES. Charles Bankhead was the British minister to Mexico at the time the Texas Republic was considering joining the United States. Working with British Minister to Texas Charles Elliot (q.v.), Bankhead attempted to convince Mexican leaders to accept the loss of Texas with the assurance that the new republic would not join the United States. With the failure of that effort and the acceptance of annexation by Texas, war became inevitable. In June 1847, Bankhead initiated an effort to work for a negotiated settlement between Mexican authorities and the U.S. representative Nicholas Trist (q.v.), but once again he failed in his diplomatic effort. Following Gen. Winfield Scott's (q.v.) victory at Churubusco (q.v.), August 20, 1847, Foreign Minister Francisco Pacheco (q.v.) of Mexico appealed to Bankhead to help negotiate a peace. The British minister forwarded a letter to Trist from the Mexican authorities and also expressed his hope for peace. A truce was arranged, but within a short time the final assault against Mexico City was launched by General Scott.

BARANDA, MANUEL (b. 1789). Having served as governor of the state of Guanajuato, by 1843 Manuel Baranda was active in Mexican national politics. He served as minister of justice from July 17, 1843, to December 6, 1844, and was foreign minister at the time of the march of the U.S. Army against Mexico City. He favored negotiation with Nicholas Trist (q.v.) but resigned under pressure from the Mexican War Party.

BARBACHANO Y TARRAZO, MIGUEL (1807–1859). Born in the city of Campeche, Miguel Barbachano was recognized as an outstanding orator. He entered politics in the state of Yucatán with strong seperatist views and sought assistance for his cause from Texas and the United States. Barbachano served as governor of Yucatán on two occasions, 1844–1846 and 1847–1853. He declared neutrality in the struggle between the United States and Mexico and sought assistance from both in the Mayan uprising called the Caste War. See also CASTE WAR OF YUCATAN.

BARBOUR, PHILIP NORBOURNE (1813–1846). A graduate of West Point in 1834, Capt. Philip Norbourne Barbour fought in the battle of Palo Alto and played a key role in the defeat of Mexican forces in the battle of Resaca de la Palma (q.v.), for which he was brevetted major. Barbour was killed during the battle of Monterrey (q.v.). His journal is a valuable and interesting source of information relating to the northern campaigns.

BARITA, TAMAULIPAS. Barita was a small settlement on the Rio Grande (q.v.) used in the supply activities of Gen. Zachary Taylor's (q.v.) army following the battle of Resaca de la Palma (q.v.).

BARNARD, JOHN GROSS (1815–1882). A graduate of the West Point class of 1833, Lt. John G. Barnard received his commission in the Corps of Engineers. Having risen to the rank of captain, Barnard oversaw the construction of the defense of the port of Tampico (q.v.) in 1846 and 1847. In 1848, he was brevetted major for meritorious service in the Valley of Mexico (q.v.). Following the war, Barnard served as chief engineer of the Tehuantepec Railroad and rose to the rank of brigadier general in the U.S. Army during the Civil War.

BARNBURNERS. The Barnburners were a faction in the Democratic Party of New York that supported Pres. Martin Van Buren.

BARNES, JOSEPH K. (d. 1883). Capt. Joseph K. Barnes served as an assistant surgeon during the war with Mexico. In 1863, Barnes was appointed as surgeon general of the United States with the dismissal of Surgeon General William A. Hammond.

BARRAGAN, JOSE. A staff officer in the army of Gen. Francisco Mejía (q.v.), Capt. José Barragán delivered a warning to Gen. Zachary Taylor (q.v.) as he prepared to cross the Arroyo Colorado (q.v.) on March 20, 1846. When Taylor ignored the threat, Barragan withdrew to the south, allowing the American army to cross uncontested.

BAXTER, CHARLES (d. 1847). With the wounding of Col. Ward Burnett (q.v.) at the battle of Churubusco, Lt. Col. Charles Baxter took command of the New York volunteer regiment, serving under Gen. James Shields (q.v.). In the battle of Chapultepec (q.v.), Baxter was himself mortally wounded.

BEACH, MOSES Y. (1800–1868). Moses Y. Beach was editor of the New York *Sun* and a prominent Roman Catholic leader in the United States. He was appointed as a confidential agent by Secretary of State James Buchanan (q.v.) to attempt to negotiate a peace settlement with Mexico in January 1847. Beach was involved with the Roman Catholic-supported revolt against Vice President Valentín Gómez Farías (q.v.), setting the stage for the return to power of Antonio López de Santa Anna (q.v.) after the battle of Buena Vista (q.v.). In June 1847, following the U.S. landing at Veracruz (q.v.) and advance toward Mexico City, Beach reported that the Catholic leaders would accept U.S. dominance in Mexico if they could be assured that church property would be protected. His advice was followed, and many clerical leaders, especially in the important city of Puebla, accepted U.S. rule.

BEALE, EDWARD FITZGERALD (1822–1893). Naval lieutenant Edward Beale participated in the battle of San Pascual (q.v.), December 6, 1846, and was chosen by Gen. Stephen Kearny (q.v.) to accompany Kit Carson (q.v.) in a dangerous mission to San Diego (q.v.) to seek assistance. Marching 35 miles without shoes, Beale arrived in San Diego, only to learn that Commodore Stockton (q.v.) had already dispatched a force to rescue Kearny's small army.

BEAR FLAG REVOLT. In June 1846 U.S. citizens in the Napa and Sacramento River valleys of California revolted against Mexican authority and found support from Capt. John Charles Frémont (q.v.). They declared independence in Sonoma on July 4, 1846, and William B. Ide (q.v.) of Vermont was selected commander in chief of the California Republic. The rebels raised a flag with the picture of a bear, thus gaining the name Bear Flag Republic. Within a short time, however, the banner was replaced with that of the United States. Today the state flag of California includes the image of a bear.

BEAUREGARD, PIERRE GUSTAVE TOUTANT (1818–1893). A native of Louisiana and graduate of the U.S. Military Academy in 1838, Lt. P. G. T. Beauregard was commissioned in the Corps of Engineers. In late 1846, he was assigned to strengthen the defenses of the recently captured port of Tampico. Beauregard later joined the force of Gen. Winfield Scott (q.v.) in the Veracruz invasion (q.v.). Following that successful operation, the lieutenant was involved in the location of artillery emplacements during the siege of the city. Beauregard also contributed to the preparation of an attack route during the battle of Cerro Gordo (q.v.) that allowed Scott's army to flank the Mexican defenses. Beauregard continued to render important service in the invasion of the Valley of Mexico, especially in the battle of Chapultepec (q.v.). Though brevetted captain for the battles of Contreras and Churubusco (q.v.) and major for Chapultepec, the young officer was extremely critical of his superior officers for failing to give him appropriate recognition for his valuable services. In 1861, he resigned his commission in the U.S. Army and joined the Confederacy, serving as commander of southern forces in Charleston, South Carolina, at the beginning of the Civil War.

BECKNELL, WILLIAM (1790–1832). In 1821, Capt. William Becknell led a group of U.S. traders from St. Louis, Missouri, to Santa Fe, New Mexico (q.v.), initiating commerce to that important Mexican outpost. Becknell has thus been credited with having established the Santa Fe Trail. Gen. Stephen W. Kearny (q.v.) used the route in the course of the war for his successful operation against New Mexico.

BELEN, GATE. The Belén Gate, or Garita de Belén, was one of the principal entrances into Mexico City. Located on the southwest corner of the city, it was a key defensive position taken by the forces of Gen. John A. Quitman (q.v.) after the fall of Chapultepec Castle (q.v.), September 13, 1847. The capture of the *garita* opened the way to the capital for Gen. Winfield Scott's (q.v.) army.

BELKNAP, WILLIAM G. (d. 1851). Following his move to the Rio Grande (q.v.) and the establishment of Fort Texas (q.v.) opposite the city of Matamoros (q.v.), Gen. Zachary Taylor (q.v.) divided his forces into two brigades, one under the command of Brevet Lt. Col. William G. Belknap (q.v.), of the Eighth Infantry. Belknap commanded that regiment at the battles of Palo Alto (q.v.) and Resaca de la Palma (q.v.), and in the latter he was instrumental in the capture of Brig. Gen. Rómulo Díaz de la Vega (q.v.). He participated in further engagements in the northern campaign, including the battle of Buena Vista (q.v.).

BELTON, FRANCIS S. (d. 1861). Lt. Col. Francis S. Belton of the Third Artillery Regiment commanded a force of 450 men in the occupation of Tampico (q.v.) following its capture on November 14, 1847. He was brevetted colonel for the battles of Contreras and Churubusco (q.v.).

BENHAM, TIMOTHY. Lt. Timothy Benham was commander of the USS *Bonita* as a part of the Home Squadron (q.v.) based at Antón Lizardo (q.v.).

BENJAMIN, CALVIN (d. 1847). A graduate of the West Point class of 1842, Lt. Calvin Benjamin served as an artillery officer in the battles of Palo Alto (q.v.), Resaca de la Palma (q.v.), and Monterrey (q.v.). He then joined the invasion force of Gen. Winfield Scott (q.v.) and fought at Veracruz (q.v.), Cerro Gordo (q.v.), and in various actions in the Valley of Mexico (q.v.). In September 1847, Benjamin was involved in a crucial decision to place howitzers along the Belén Causeway and shortly thereafter was killed.

BENT, CHARLES (1799–1847). Charles Bent moved from St. Louis, Missouri, to New Mexico in 1826 and with his brother William established a very successful trading post near the present-day town of Las Animas, Colorado. That well-fortified position came to be known as Bent's Fort (q.v.) and played an important role in the march of General Kearny (q.v.) from Fort Leavenworth to Santa Fe (q.v.). Following the surrender of the Mexican authorities in New Mexico, Kearny appointed Bent as territorial governor, September 22, 1846. By early 1847, following the departure of Kearny for California, there was an uprising of disgruntled New Mexican elements. Governor Bent was killed by revolting Pueblo Indians at his home in Taos (q.v.) on January 19, 1847.

BENTON, THOMAS HART (1782–1858). Sen. Thomas Hart Benton of Missouri favored westward expansion but in 1844 opposed Pres. John Tyler and Secretary of State John C. Calhoun in their efforts to annex Texas. He proposed an alternate bill that would have brought annexation through negotiation with Mexico. In the long run, the issue was resolved by a compromise producing a joint resolution for annexation by both branches of Congress.

When President Polk (q.v.) called for a declaration of war against Mexico, Benton was one of his most outspoken opponents in the Senate. He eventually gave in to political pressures, however, and supported the president. Polk, distrustful of Winfield Scott (q.v.) because of his connections with the Whig Party, sought military advice from Benton and even supported a scheme to appoint the senator as a lieutenant general, a rank above that of Scott and all other military officers. The scheme was defeated in Congress, but Benton remained a strong critic of the Whig generals who occupied many of the top positions in the army. His relations with Polk became strained, in part because of the senator's unbounded ego and political ambition but also because of charges brought against his son-in-law John C. Frémont. *See also* FREMONT, JOHN CHARLES.

BENT'S FORT. Brothers Charles and William Bent established a trading post in the southeastern region of the present-day state of Colorado. Located on a strategic point along the Santa Fe Trail (q.v.), it came to be known as Bent's Fort. It played an important role in the march of the U.S. forces under Gen. Stephen Kearny (q.v.) in his move from Fort Leavenworth (q.v.) to New Mexico. *See also* KEARNY, STEPHEN WATTS.

BERRA, FRANCISCO DE. At the time of the attack against Monterrey (q.v.) by the army of Gen. Zachary Taylor (q.v.), the Obispado (q.v.) was a fortified position on the western outskirts of the city, defended by Lt. Col. Francisco de Berra. Berra's position fell to an attack by Gen. William J. Worth (q.v.). *See also* MONTERREY, BATTLE OF.

BIDDLE, JAMES (1783–1848). Commo. James Biddle was in the Pacific at the time of the outbreak of the war with Mexico. He arrived in California on March 2, 1847, and became involved with the conflicts surrounding Gen. Stephen Kearny (q.v.) and John C. Frémont (q.v.).

BIGLOW PAPERS. James Russell Lowell published a number of articles denouncing the war policy of Pres. James K. Polk (q.v.). These were published in Boston in 1848 under the title *Biglow Papers*. *See also* ABOLITIONISTS.

BISHOP'S PALACE. The Bishop's Palace (Obispado) was a large ecclesiastical residence on Independence Hill (q.v.), overlooking the city of Monterrey, Nuevo León (q.v.). During the attack by General Taylor's (q.v.) army, the palace was defended by Lt. Col. Francisco de Berra (q.v.) but fell to the assault commanded by Gen. William Worth (q.v.), September 22, 1846. Today the restored building houses a regional historical museum. *See also* MONTERREY, BATTLE OF.

BISSELL, WILLIAM H. (1811–1860). Col. William H. Bissell was commander of the Second Illinois Volunteer Infantry. As a part of the command of Gen. John E. Wool (q.v.), he moved from San Antonio, Texas (q.v.), to the Rio Grande (q.v.), October 2–12, 1846, and continued to Monclova (q.v.) and Parras (q.v.), vacating the latter place by December 5, 1846. Bissell and other volunteer officers became quite alienated against General Wool in the course of the campaign. The Second Illinois was involved in the battle of Buena Vista (q.v.), February 22, 1847, came under heavy attack by the Mexican force, but withdrew in good order. Following the war, Bissell returned to civilian life and was elected to the U.S. House of Representatives, and later, governor of Illinois.

BLACK, JOHN. John Black was U.S. consul in Mexico City in 1845, at the time of the annexation of Texas by the United States, and predicted that Mexico would not go to war over that action. He tried to convince Pres. José Joaquín de Herrera (q.v.) to receive John Slidell (q.v.) as a commissioner, but the proposal was rejected. With the outbreak of hostilities, Consul Black remained at his post in Mexico City, continuing in his efforts to negotiate a settlement. The consul also played a part in the decision by the James K. Polk (q.v.) administration to allow Antonio López de Santa Anna (q.v.) to return from exile, a move that produced further problems for the United States.

BLACK FORT. As the army of Gen. Zachary Taylor (q.v.) approached Monterrey, Nuevo León (q.v.), September 1846, Gen. Pedro de Ampudia (q.v.) carried out the fortification of an area north of the city known as the *ciudadela* (citadel). Because of its dark color, the American invaders soon christened the position the Black Fort. Taylor's assaulting troops suffered severe casualties in their attempt to seize the position, and it managed to hold out until the surrender by General Ampudia on September 25, 1846. *See also* MONTERREY, BATTLE OF.

BLAIR, FRANCIS PRESTON, JR. (1791–1876). Francis Preston Blair was editor of the Washington *Globe*, national organ of the Democratic Party, and a staunch supporter of both Andrew Jackson and Martin Van Buren. Never a strong advocate of James K. Polk (q.v.), Blair agreed in 1845 to step aside and turn the *Globe* over to other individuals. Polk later blocked an attempt by Secretary of State Buchanan (q.v.) and other Democrats to reinstate Blair.

BLAKE, JACOB E. (1812–1846). Lt. Jacob E. Blake was a member of the topographical engineers and played an important role in the reconnaissance before the battle of Palo Alto (q.v.). He was accidentally killed by a shot from his own pistol.

BLANCHARD, ALBERT GALLATIN (1810–1891). Capt. Albert G. Blanchard commanded the Phoenix Company of Louisiana volunteers. Many units left General Zachary Taylor's Army of Occupation (q.v.) in the summer of 1846 when their enlistments expired, but the captain and his company elected to stay. They played an important role in the battle of Monterrey (q.v.), especially in the attack against the Bishop's Palace (q.v.). During the Civil War, he served as a brigadier general in the army of the Confederacy.

BLANCO, MIGUEL (1816–1900). Miguel Blanco was a prominent citizen of the state of Coahuila (q.v.) and owner of one of the largest haciendas of northern Mexico. On the arrival of the force under the command of Gen. John E. Wool (q.v.), Blanco extended hospitality to the invaders.

BLANCO, SANTIAGO (1815–1883). Born in Campeche, Santiago Blanco was a cadet in Mexico City, specializing in artillery and engineering. Following the completion of his training, he returned to Campeche where he worked to strengthen the city's fortifications. He traveled to the United States, where he studied the emerging railroad system. In 1842, after his return to Mexico, he fought on the northern frontier against Anglo-American filibusters. Blanco was made commander of the Corps of Engineers in Mexico City in 1846 and promoted to general during the battle of Buena Vista (q.v.), February 22–24, 1847, where he commanded one of Santa Anna's (q.v.) divisions. Returning to central Mexico, he was gravely wounded in the battle of Contreras (q.v.).

BLISS, WILLIAM WALLACE SMITH (1815–1853). Graduating from the U.S. Military Academy at 18, William W. S. Bliss was commissioned in the infantry. With a strong interest in academics, he taught mathematics at West Point and devoted much of his time to the study of languages and classical literature. Before the outbreak of war with Mexico, Gen. Winfield Scott (q.v.) assigned Bliss, at that time a captain, as adjutant general and chief of staff to Gen. Zachary Taylor (q.v.). Bliss, later promoted to the rank of major, remained with Taylor throughout the campaigns in Texas and northern Mexico. A highly intelligent and well-trained officer, he was a valuable assistant to Taylor and wrote most of his orders and reports. Bliss was very likely the chief architect of the campaign against Monterrey (q.v.) and played a prominent part in the battle of

Buena Vista (q.v.), being brevetted lieutenant colonel in that action. Eventually he married General Taylor's daughter Betty, and when "Old Rough and Ready" assumed the presidency, Bliss served as his private secretary. He died of yellow fever at age 38 in 1853.

BLOCKADE. With the approach of war with Mexico, Secretary of the Navy George Bancroft (q.v.) ordered naval forces in the Gulf of Mexico to establish an effective blockade against all of the Mexican ports. With his base at Antón Lizardo (q.v.), Commo. David Conner (q.v.) carried out this order, virtually halting commerce in the major locations and restricting it throughout the region. At the same time, Bancroft ordered Commo. John D. Sloat (q.v.) to set up blockading operations along the coast of California and western Mexico. Although the sailors found blockading duties to be extremely boring, the operation was most effective. Never seriously challenged by the Mexican navy, the United States squadron often sent landing parties up rivers and against key locations such as Tampico (q.v.), Veracruz (q.v.), and Monterey, California (q.v.).

BOCANEGRA, JOSE MARIA DE (1787–1862). José María de Bocanegra was twice Mexican minister of foreign affairs (1837 and 1841–1844). He denounced U.S. support to the Texas rebels and the violation of Mexican territory by U.S. citizens, charging that such moves had the approval of Washington officials and political leaders at the state and local level throughout the country.

BONHAM, MILLEDGE LUKE (1813–1890). Lt. Col. Milledge L. Bonham was a battalion commander in the Twelfth Infantry and played a prominent role in the battle of Contreras (q.v.). During the American Civil War, Bonham rose to the rank of brigadier general in the Confederate army.

BONITA. The Bonita was one of three 59-foot schooners (along with the USS Petrel and USS Reefer) purchased by the U.S. Navy on May 25, 1846. Mounting a single 32-pounder carronade, these schooners played a very important role in naval operations in the Gulf of Mexico. The Bonita was commanded by Lt. Timothy Benham (q.v.).

BONNEVILLE, BENJAMIN L. E. (1796–1878). A graduate of the U.S. Military Academy in 1815, Maj. Benjamin L. E. Bonneville was commander of a battalion of regular infantry in the army of Gen. John E. Wool (q.v.) in northern Mexico. He later accompanied Gen. Winfield Scott (q.v.) in the occupation of Veracruz (q.v.) and the invasion of the Valley of Mexico. Bonneville played an important role in the key battle of Churubusco (q.v.) and was wounded in that action.

BORGINNIS, SARAH. Sarah Borginnis (or Bourdett) was a large, strong, and blustery camp follower with the army of Gen. Zachary Taylor (q.v.). Given the name "the Great Western," she carried out many services for the troops, including care for the wounded, and became an important part of western lore.

BORLAND, SOLON (1808–1864). Maj. Solon Borland commanded an Arkansas volunteer scouting party that in January 1847 occupied Encarnación (q.v.), south of Saltillo (q.v.). Disregarding instructions from Gen. John Wool (q.v.), Borland and his small force of some 71 officers and men were captured by Col. Miguel Andrade.

BOSTON. The sloop of war USS *Boston*, commanded by Comdr. George F. Pearson, wrecked in the Bahamas on November 15, 1846.

BOWLES, WILLIAM A. Col. William A. Bowles was commander of the Second Indiana Volunteer Infantry and served under Brig. Gen. Joseph Lane (q.v.) at the battle of Buena Vista (q.v.). During a critical moment in the battle, Bowles misunderstood a command from Lane and ordered his unit to retreat. Many men broke and fled the field of battle, but Bowles was able to bring order to a part of his command, preventing a complete rout.

BRAGG, BRAXTON (1817–1876). Lt. Braxton Bragg (later promoted to captain), commanded a field artillery battery assigned to the defense of Fort Texas (q.v.) in early May 1846, under the command of Maj. Jacob Brown (q.v.). He also saw action in the battle for Monterrey (q.v.) and at Buena Vista (q.v.). In the latter battle, Bragg's artillery stopped the Mexican advance at a crucial time in the conflict. He was brevetted lieutenant colonel for that battle. During the Civil War, Bragg served as a general officer in the Confederacy.

BRANNAN, SAMUEL (1819–1889). In February 1846, Samuel Brannan sailed from New York to California with 238 Mormon settlers, reaching San Francisco in July. By that time, Commo. John D. Sloat (q.v.) had declared the region to be a part of U.S. territory, and the Mormons became an important element in the region.

BRAVO, NICOLAS (1776–1854). One of the major leaders in the movement for Mexican independence, Gen. Nicolás Bravo served as president briefly in 1843. He reassumed the office later on the abdication of Mariano Paredes (q.v.) in July 1846 but, again, only for a short time. Returning to the army, Bravo commanded the defensive position at Mexicalzingo (q.v.) as Gen. Winfield Scott (q.v.) approached the capital. On August 20, 1847, Bravo was unsuccessful in his attempt to halt the advancing American forces south of Churubusco (q.v.) and fell back in confusion. He later commanded a force of some 1,000 men in the defense of Chapultepec Castle (q.v.) but was forced to surrender the position to Lt. Charles B. Browder (q.v.) of the New York volunteers and was taken prisoner. After the war, Bravo continued to play a role in his nation's political intrigues.

BRAZITO, BATTLE OF (December 25, 1846). Brazito (called Temascolitos by the Mexicans) was a location on the Rio Grande (q.v.), approximately 30 miles north of El Paso (q.v.). On Christmas Day 1846, Col. Alexander Doniphan's (q.v.) Missouri volunteers clashed with the Mexican army of Maj. Antonio Ponce de León in the battle of Brazito. Capt. Rafael Carabajal, having replaced the wounded Ponce, withdrew from the battlefield, allowing Doniphan to occupy El Paso on December 27, 1846.

BRAZOS ISLAND. A sandy peninsula south of the Brazos Santiago (q.v.) at the mouth of the Rio Grande (q.v.) was known as Brazos Island (also called Brazos Santiago Island). Although not a true island, this low-lying and wind-swept area served as a rendezvous point for arriving U.S. volunteers and as a supply depot for Gen. Zachary Taylor's (q.v.) army before the occupation of Matamoros (q.v.). At times the entire area—including the south end of Padre Island, Brazos Island, and Point Isabel (q.v.)—was called "The Brazos." It continued to play an important logistical role in the campaign of Gen. Winfield Scott (q.v.) as he carried out the amphibious operation against Veracruz (q.v.).

BRAZOS RIVER. The Brazos River played an important role in the early history of Anglo-American settlement of Texas. Washington-on-the-Brazos was the site of the declaration of Texas independence on March 2, 1836, and served as the first capital of the Texas Republic.

BRAZOS SANTIAGO. The Brazos Santiago is a channel between South Padre Island and Brazos Island (q.v.) and served as a supply route to Point Isabel (q.v.) for the army of Gen. Zachary Taylor (q.v.) during his campaign in the Rio Grande Valley. It was also utilized briefly as the headquarters of the Home Fleet (q.v.) by Commo. David Conner (q.v.) before the shifting of that command to Antón Lizardo (q.v.). As Gen. Winfield Scott (q.v.) prepared the Veracruz (q.v.) landing in late 1846 and early 1847, the Brazos Santiago again was used as an important staging area for troops and supplies.

BREESE, SAMUEL L. In 1847, Navy Capt. Samuel L. Breese, along with Comdr. Alexander Slidell Mackenzie (q.v.), was dispatched by Commo. Matthew C. Perry (q.v.) to confer with officials in Yucatán (q.v.). The talks helped to produce a declaration of neutrality by that state in the war between Mexico and the United States.

BRIBERY SCHEME. In June 1847, after the army of Gen. Winfield Scott (q.v.) had occupied Puebla (q.v.), Nicholas Trist (q.v.) of the Department of State suggested to the commander the payment of a bribe to Mexican officials in exchange for their support of a peace treaty favorable to the United States. Under this plan, an initial payment of $10,000 would be made and an additional $1 million would be supplied when the treaty was concluded. Scott conferred with his commanders and eventually agreed to the scheme. By July 13, 1847, the plan was rejected by Mexican authorities, although they seemed to have taken the initial $10,000 payment. Soon after the collapse of those negotiations, the invasion of the Valley of Mexico was initiated. When Pres. James K. Polk (q.v.) learned of the proposed bribery efforts he denounced both General Scott and Trist, thus further driving a wedge between the president and his representatives in Mexico. *See also* THORNTON, EDWARD.

BRIGGS, GEORGE N. (1796–1861). Governor of Massachusetts George N. Briggs supported the antiwar faction in his state. He refused to issue commissions to officers chosen for the regiment organized by Brig. Gen. Caleb Cushing (q.v.).

BRONAUTH, ROBERT. On September 21, 1846, Gen. Zachary Taylor (q.v.) ordered Capt. Robert Bronauth and his Baltimore Battalion to guard his headquarters at Walnut Springs while most of his army moved against the Mexican position at Monterrey (q.v.). Bronauth bitterly denounced the assignment, insisting that his unit had come to Mexico to fight and not to guard supplies.

BROOKE, GEORGE M. On June 2, 1845, when Gen. Edmund P. Gaines (q.v.) was dismissed as commander of the Western Division of the U.S. Army, Brig. Gen. George M. Brooke was appointed to that position. Brooke continued in administrative duties at New Orleans throughout the war and in November 1847 was appointed president of the court-martial that tried John C. Frémont (q.v.) for insubordination.

BROOKS, WILLIAM (1821–1870). Lt. William Brooks graduated in the West Point class of 1841 and fought in the battles of Palo Alto (q.v.), Resaca de la Palma (q.v.), and Monterrey (q.v.). He participated in the siege of Veracruz (q.v.) and served as an aide to Gen. David E. Twiggs (q.v.) during the march from Veracruz (q.v.) to the Valley of Mexico. On April 13, 1847, Brooks discovered a path that led to the left flank of the Mexican position at Cerro Gordo (q.v.) and then assisted Lt. P. G. T. Beauregard (q.v.) in the further reconnaisance of that route. This resulted in an important flanking movement that contributed to General Scott's (q.v.) victory in the battle of Cerro Gordo (q.v.). Brooks was brevetted major for the battles of Contreras and Churubusco (q.v.).

BROWDER, CHARLES B. Lt. Charles B. Browder of the New York volunteers received the surrender of Gen. Nicolás Bravo (q.v.) to end the battle of Chapultepec (q.v.), September 13, 1847.

BROWN, JACOB (d. 1846). On May 1, 1846, Gen. Zachary Taylor (q.v.) assigned command of Fort Texas (q.v.), on the Rio Grande (q.v.) opposite Matamoros (q.v.), to Maj. Jacob Brown of the Seventh Infantry. The position held out against the attacks of Gen. Pedro de Ampudia (q.v.), but on May 6, Major Brown was mortally wounded. General Taylor returned to the area following the battles of Palo Alto (q.v.) and Resaca de la Palma (q.v.) and renamed the fortification Fort Brown (q.v.) in honor of the fallen defender. Jacob Brown was also honored by the community that grew up around the fort, the city of Brownsville, Texas (q.v.).

BROWN, JUAN "FLACO." On the night of September 24–25, 1846, Juan "Flaco" Brown rode out of Los Angeles, California (q.v.), avoided the Californio forces, and carried word to Commo. Robert Stockton (q.v.) of an uprising against U.S. authority. He arrived in San Francisco (q.v.) on October 1, after a five-day ordeal.

BROWNSVILLE, TEXAS. The city of Brownsville, Texas, was established on the site of Fort Brown (q.v.), opposite Matamoros (q.v.) on the Rio Grande (q.v.), and was named in honor of Maj. Jacob Brown (q.v.).

BUCHANAN, FRANKLIN (1800–1874). Comdr. Franklin Buchanan was the first superintendent of the Naval Academy at Annapolis. He left that post to join the Home Squadron (q.v.) in the Gulf of Mexico. Buchanan commanded the lead boats in a successful attack against the port of Tuxpan (q.v.) under Commo. Matthew C. Perry (q.v.). With the secession of the Southern states, Buchanan was given the rank of admiral and appointed commander of the Confederate navy.

BUCHANAN, JAMES (1791–1868). A prominent Democratic politician from Pennsylvania, James Buchanan was appointed secretary of state by Pres. James K. Polk (q.v.) and served in that position for Polk's entire term (1845–1849). He favored the vigorous pressing of claims against Mexico and felt that negotiations with Pres. José Joaquín de Herrera (q.v.) would persuade him to sell California for the settlement of Mexico's outstanding debt. After the failure of those negotiations, however, Buchanan wished to deny any intention to annex California as a part of the war aims, a position rejected by President Polk. The secretary later sent Nicholas Trist (q.v.) to negotiate with Mexico, continuing to be a moderate on the issue of expansion. In 1856, Buchanan was elected president of the United States as the Democratic candidate and served in that office from 1857 to 1861, an era of bitter sectional dispute that had emerged in part from the war with Mexico.

BUCHANAN, ROBERT C. (1811–1878). A graduate of the West Point class of 1830, Capt. Robert C. Buchanan of the Fourth Infantry played an important role in the battles of Palo Alto (q.v.),

Resaca de la Palma (q.v.), and Monterrey (q.v.), being brevetted major for the first two of those actions. He later joined the army of Gen. Winfield Scott (q.v.) in its invasion of central Mexico, participating in a number of battles and skirmishes, and served with special distinction at the battle of Molino del Rey (q.v.).

BUENA VISTA, BATTLE OF (February 22–23, 1847). One of the most celebrated battles of the war, the battle of Buena Vista (called "Angostura" by the Mexicans) was fought February 22–23, 1847, between the armies of Gen. Zachary Taylor (q.v.) and Gen. Antonio López de Santa Anna (q.v.). Ironically, it was fought by a U.S. army that had been stripped of its seasoned regiments to strengthen the newly formed invasion force being directed against Veracruz (q.v.). The narrowly won American victory propelled Zachary Taylor into the White House.

With the end of the armistice following the capture of Monterrey (q.v.) by American forces, General Santa Anna took precautions to thwart any attempt by General Taylor to march south. "Old Rough and Ready" did not, however, have any intention of setting out into the rugged elevated desert, convinced that such a campaign would require a minimum of 20,000 well-trained men. He was, nevertheless, quite miffed upon receiving instructions from the Polk (q.v.) administration to establish a defensive line between Tampico (q.v.) and Monterrey; the general extended it another 60 miles west to Saltillo (q.v.), capital of Coahuila. Taylor's position was strengthened by the arrival of Gen. John Wool's Army of Chihuahua (q.v.) from the nearby village of Parras (q.v.).

By November 1846, Santa Anna took steps to build up a massive force in San Luis Potosí (q.v.), some 250 miles south of Saltillo. He was encouraged in his plan to attack Saltillo by learning that a sizable portion of the American army was marching to Tampico (q.v.) on the coast of the Gulf of Mexico. At several times during December 1846, the U.S. forces were alarmed by reports of an impending attack from the south. Taylor initiated a march to Saltillo but then turned back toward Tampico as Santa Anna's threat seemed to have disappeared. Gen. William O. Butler (q.v.), in command of the area around Saltillo in the absence of Taylor, ordered a concentration of forces at Encantada (q.v.), just south of the rugged narrow valley known as La Angostura (q.v.). In early January 1847, the seasoned regiments of Gen. William Worth (q.v.) were transferred from that front to the mouth of the Rio Grande to form a part of the invasion force against Veracruz (q.v.). Santa Anna learned of this shift when Gen. Winfield Scott's (q.v.) plans were taken from the body of ambushed Lt. John A. Richey (q.v.), and he marched from San Luis Potosí with some 21,000 men and 21 pieces of artillery. His target was Saltillo, but his major objective was to destroy Taylor's army or drive it north of the Rio Grande. Gen. José de Urrea (q.v.) was assigned the task of raiding to the east of the Sierra Madre Oriental and disrupting the American lines of communication.

As rumors of the approach of Santa Anna circulated in Saltillo, Generals Butler and Wool sent out a number of patrols. Early on the morning of January 23, 1847, Mexican lancers from Gen. José Vicente Miñón's (q.v.) cavalry command surrounded a patrol of Arkansas and Kentucky volunteers at Encarnación (q.v.), forcing their surrender without a fight. It was clear by the end of the month that the Mexican force was moving in strength toward an encounter. On the advice of Gen. Wool, Taylor established his defensive position at the rugged valley of Angostura, five miles south of Saltillo and just below the imposing hacienda of Buena Vista (q.v.). Wool, assigned to the task of commanding the field, anchored his left wing on the steep sides of the Sierra Madre and his right on a series of deep arroyos. Capt. John M. Washington's (q.v.) artillery battery was set up at a strategic point on the road that entered the narrow valley from the south, considered to be the most likely avenue of approach for the Mexican army. On each side of the five artillery pieces, volunteer units were placed in a blocking position across the valley: the First Illinois, commanded by Col. John J. Hardin (q.v.); the Second Kentucky of Col. William McKee (q.v.); the Second Illinois, commanded by Col. William H. Bissell (q.v.); and the Second and Third Regiments of Gen. Joseph Lane's (q.v.) Indiana Brigade. Kentucky and Arkansas volunteer cavalry guarded the left flank of the line, anchored on the side of the mountain. Texas volunteers and the regular dragoons formed the reserve. General Taylor established his headquarters in Saltillo, guarded by the Mississippi Rifles (q.v.) under Col. Jefferson Davis (q.v.), the dragoons of Lt. Charles A. May (q.v.), and two artillery batteries.

On the morning of February 22, 1847, Santa Anna moved toward Wool's position, his army having been reduced by the severity of the march but still numbering over 15,000 men. At 1100 hours he demanded that the Americans surrender, but Taylor, having just arrived from Saltillo, rebuffed the message. Brig. Gen. Francisco Mejía (q.v.) led his brigade against the American right, an area where the gullies were especially deep and rugged, but he was unable to penetrate. The primary Mexican attack, led by Gen. Pedro de Ampudia (q.v.), was directed against the left flank of Wool's defensive position, along the edge of the mountains. At 1530 hours Ampudia's infantry advanced against the Kentucky volunteer cavalry of Col. Humphrey Marshall (q.v.), supported by artillery emplaced above their position on the side of the mountain. The fighting continued for the rest of the afternoon; with nightfall both armies ceased fire but retained their positions. Early on the morning of February 23, General Ampudia, supported by additional heavy artillery, renewed pressure against the American right and pushed Marshall back. Santa Anna then launched a major thrust at the center of the field with two divisions commanded by Maj. Gen. Manuel María Lombardini (q.v.) and Maj. Gen. Francisco Pacheco (q.v.). They struck head-on against the Second Indiana and the Second Illinois, breaking the defensive line and causing some American troops to retreat from the field in disorder. The road to Buena Vista seemed open to the Mexican cavalry of Brig. Gen. Julián Juvera (q.v.), but Taylor was able to bring up reinforcements, highlighted by the accurate marksmanship of the Mississippi Rifles under Col. Jefferson Davis and the effective artillery fire of Lt. Braxton Bragg's (q.v.) battery. Juvera was turned back, and the American lines were restored, though badly split. At 1700 hours, Santa Anna called up his reserves and reorganized elements of the shattered divisions under Gen. Francisco Pérez (q.v.). As Pérez pushed forward, his men engaged the Illinois and Kentucky volunteers in hand-to-hand combat. Among the Americans killed was Lt. Col. Henry Clay, Jr. (q.v.), son of the famous Kentucky political leader.

Artillery directed by Capt. John M. Washington, Capt. John P. J. O'Brien (q.v.), Lt. Braxton Bragg, and Lt. George H. Thomas (q.v.) was crucial in bringing a halt to Santa Anna's thrust. Despite very heavy casualties (272 killed and 387 wounded), Taylor held his postition at the end of the day. Santa Anna's losses were greater (591 killed, 1,048 wounded, and 1,894 missing), but he retained a much larger force in the field. General Taylor expected the Mexican assault to be renewed on February 24, but at dawn on that day it was realized that the Mexican army had retreated from Angostura, moving in disarray back to San Luis Potosí.

The battle of Buena Vista was the last important battle in the northeastern theater, as action shifted to the Gulf of Mexico and the campaign of General Scott for Mexico City. The narrow victory at Buena Vista, however, had far-reaching political implications, leading in 1848 to the presidential victory of Zachary Taylor.

BUENA VISTA, COAHUILA. The Hacienda San Juan de la Buena Vista is approximately eight miles south of Saltillo, Coahuila (q.v.), just north of a narrow pass on the road to San Luis Potosí (q.v.) known as La Angostura (q.v.). The battle of Buena Vista (q.v.) was fought primarily to the south of the hacienda. Today the main house of the hacienda and surrounding lands serve as an agricultural university for the state of Coahuila.

BURGWIN, JOHN H. K. (1811–1847). Capt. John H. K. Burgwin commanded a company of dragoons in the Missouri volunteers of Col. Sterling Price (q.v.) in New Mexico. He died of wounds suffered on February 4, 1847, at the battle for the Pueblo of Taos (q.v.), a part of the New Mexican uprising against U.S. authority.

BURNETT, WARD B. (1810–1884). A graduate of West Point in 1832, Col. Ward B. Burnett participated in the landing at Veracruz (q.v.) and the battle of Cerro Gordo (q.v.). As commander of a regiment of New York volunteers, Burnett was wounded in the battle of Churubusco (q.v.) and turned over his command to Lt. Col. Charles Baxter (q.v.).

BURNHAM, JAMES C. Maj. James C. Burnham was commander of a New York volunteer regiment and played an important role in the placement of an eight-inch howitzer at a crucial moment in the battle of Cerro Gordo (q.v.), April 17, 1847.

BURTON, E. H. A surgeon during the siege of Veracruz (q.v.), Dr. E. H. Burton reported the use of ether during the amputation of a teamster's leg.

BURTON, HENRY S. (1818–1869). Henry S. Burton graduated from the U.S. Military Academy in 1839 and during the war with Mexico was assigned to the action in the Pacific coastal region. As a lieutenant colonel, Burton commanded two companies of New York volunteers that sailed from California on July 4, 1847, and occupied La Paz, Baja California (q.v.), on July 21. He also played an important role in the skirmish at Todos Santos (q.v.).

BUSTAMANTE, ANASTASIO (1780–1853). Gen. Anastasio Bustamante was president of Mexico briefly between 1830 and 1832. A moderate conservative, he was forced to resign in 1832 by the federalist faction, thus preparing the way for rule by Antonio López de Santa Anna (q.v.). Bustamante returned to power by election from 1837 to 1841 but once again was forced from power. He attempted to maintain stability in the nation but failed in that effort. Following the Treaty of Guadalupe Hidalgo (q.v.), Bustamante once again took a role in Mexican national affairs.

BUTLER, ANTHONY. Appointed U.S. minister to Mexico by Pres. Andrew Jackson, Anthony Butler followed Joel Poinsett in that position, serving from 1829 to 1836. Warned to refrain from meddling in the internal affairs of Mexico, Butler disregarded instructions from Secretary of State Martin Van Buren and became deeply involved in a series of schemes to influence the state of affairs in the host nation. An avid supporter of the annexation of Texas, he created strong hostility against himself and against his country among influential Mexican political leaders. This helped to set a tone of suspicion against the United States that would continue to the outbreak of war in 1846.

BUTLER, EDWARD G. W. (1800–1888). Having graduated from West Point in 1820, Col. Edward G. W. Butler commanded the District of the Upper Rio Grande (q.v.) from September 23, 1847, to June 30, 1848. He was a member of the court of inquiry appointed by Secretary of War William Marcy (q.v.) on January 13, 1848, to investigate the charges against Gen. Winfield Scott (q.v.). During the Civil War, Butler resigned his commission and served in the army of the Confederacy.

BUTLER, WILLIAM ORLANDO (1791–1880). William O. Butler was a Kentucky politician who had seen military service in the War of 1812 with Andrew Jackson at New Orleans, then served in the U.S. House of Representatives. Following the declaration of war against Mexico, Butler was appointed by President James K. Polk (q.v.) as major general in command of the First Division of Volunteers, composed of troops from Kentucky, Ohio, and Indiana. He joined the army of Gen. Zachary Taylor (q.v.) on the Rio Grande (q.v.) and fought in the battle of Monterrey (q.v.), being wounded on September 22, 1846. Following his recovery, however, the general continued to serve in northern Mexico, including action in the battle of Buena Vista (q.v.). In August 1847, President Polk ordered Butler to join the army of Gen. Winfield Scott (q.v.), with instructions to take command in case Scott should become incapacitated. When a dispute broke out between Scott and several of his senior officers, including Generals Pillow and Worth, Polk recalled the general in chief on January 8, 1848, and placed General Butler in charge. The Kentuckian retained command of the American forces during the completion of the negotiations of the Treaty of Guadalupe Hidalgo (q.v.) and its ratification by the Mexican government, February–May 1848. He then supervised the evacuation of the U.S. forces from Mexico and left Veracruz (q.v.) himself on June 20, 1848.

C

CADWALADER, GEORGE (1803–1879). In March 1847, Brig. Gen. George Cadwalader, a native of Pennsylvania, led a relief force to Brazos Santiago (q.v.) to strengthen the American position in the lower Rio Grande Valley. He then shifted his brigade to Veracruz (q.v.) and in June 1847 carried out a successful operation along the National Highway (q.v.) to Jalapa (q.v.). After combating Mexican guerrilla (q.v.) forces to the west of Jalapa, he joined Gen. Gideon Pillow (q.v.) in his march to Puebla (q.v.), thus bringing much needed replacement troops to Gen. Winfield Scott (q.v.). During the operations in the Valley of Mexico, Cadwalader's brigade played important roles in the battles of Contreras and Churubusco (q.v.) and the battle of Molino del Rey (q.v.). The general also participated in the move against the center of Mexico City following the capture of Chapultepec Castle (q.v.).

CAHUENGA, CONVENTION OF. A document was signed at Rancho Cahuenga, California, on December 13, 1846, whereby the Californio (q.v.) forces surrendered to Lt. John C. Frémont (q.v.). This document came to be known as the Convention of Cahuenga.

CALDERON DE LA BARCA, MARQUESA DE (1806–1882). Frances Erskine Inglis was born in Scotland, grew up in Boston, Massachusetts, and married the Spanish diplomat Angel Calderón de la Barca, who was appointed ambassador to Mexico. Known as "Fanny," Mme. Calderón de la Barca traveled with her husband to Mexico in late 1839 and remained until 1842; her keen observations serve as a most useful background to events leading to war between Mexico and the United States.

CALHOUN, JOHN C. (1782–1850). Sen. John C. Calhoun of South Carolina was a strong advocate of states' rights and author of the doctrine of nullification. As secretary of state in the administration of Pres. John Tyler, Calhoun played a significant role in the annexation of Texas to the United States, being accused of doing so for the expansion of slavery. When James K. Polk (q.v.) came to the presidency, Calhoun, although a member of the Democratic party, was often in opposition to the administration. He attempted to delay the declaration of war, opposed the invasion of central Mexico, and spoke against the annexation of territory in which cultural and racial compositions were markedly different from those in the United States.

CALIFORNIA. Many of the proponents of Manifest Destiny saw in California the primary target for U.S. expansion. President Polk (q.v.) made its annexation one of the objectives of his administration, and in the Treaty of Guadalupe Hidalgo (q.v.), the vast region on the Pacific coast was ceded to the United States by Mexico. The area of Baja California (q.v.), however, remained in Mexico's possession.

CALIFORNIOS. The residents of California at the time of the war between the United States and Mexico were highly independent and aloof from the controls of Mexico City. They were known as Californios.

CALLENDAR, FRANKLIN D. (1816–1882). Lt. Franklin D. Callendar was an artillery officer under the command of Gen. Gideon J. Pillow (q.v.), who saw important action in the battle of Contreras (q.v.) and was wounded in the course of the battle.

CAMARGO, TAMAULIPAS. Camargo, located on the right bank of the San Juan River, just above its confluence with the Rio Grande (q.v.), had approximately 3,000 inhabitants in 1846. Largely because of its accessibility to shallow-draft steamers, the town was selected by Gen. Zachary Taylor (q.v.) as the key supply point in his campaign against Monterrey (q.v.). Gen. William Worth (q.v.) occupied the town on July 14 and 15, 1846, and Taylor shifted his headquarters there on August 8. By the beginning of the campaign against Monterrey, over 6,000 men were camped in the hot and unhealthy region, plagued by bugs, ants and other "critters." Continuing as an important supply depot along the line of communication from the mouth of the Rio Grande to Monterrey, Camargo came to be recognized as a "graveyard" for many of the Americans who stopped there.

CAMPBELL, REUBEN C. Lt. Reuben C. Campbell of the Second Dragoons was ambushed by a Mexican guerrilla (q.v.) force under Mucho Martinos on November 2, 1847, at Agua Fria, near Marín (q.v.) on the Rio Grande (q.v.).

CAMPBELL, ROBERT B. Robert B. Campbell was U.S. consul in Havana during the war and sent reports to Pres. James K. Polk (q.v.) relating to the scheme of Antonio López de Santa Anna (q.v.) to pass through the blockade (q.v.) to return to power in Mexico.

CAMPBELL, WILLIAM BOWEN (1807–1867). Col. William B. Campbell was commander of the First Tennessee Volunteer Regiment during the battle of Monterrey (q.v.) and carried out an effective attack against the Mexican position known as La Tenería. He was a staunch defender of the volunteers, denouncing those who gave all credit in the war to regular forces.

CAMPUZANO, ANTONIO (1810–1866). Antonio Campuzano fought with Mexico against the Texas revolt, and as a major he was assigned to Sinaloa and Sonora in 1841. Promoted to colonel, Campuzano was the Mexican commandant at Guaymas (q.v.) on the coast of Sonora at the time of the attack against that city by Commo. Samuel F. DuPont (q.v.) on October 7, 1846. Because of the continuing pressure of the American blockade (q.v.), Campuzano eventually abandoned his position in April 1848.

CANAL Y CASTILLO, MANUEL DE LA. Gen. Manuel de la Canal y Castillo took command of the port of Mazatlán (q.v.) on June 13, 1848, following the ratification of the Treaty of Guadalupe Hidalgo (q.v.).

CANALES, ANTONIO (d. 1852). In 1839, Antonio Canales initiated a revolt against central Mexican authority in the state of Tamaulipas, recruiting an army including both Mexicans and Anglo-Americans. In 1840, Canales controlled much of the region of northeastern Mexico, proclaiming it to be the Republic of Rio Grande. Later that year, he came to terms with Pres. Anastasio Bustamante (q.v.), thus ending the dream of a separate republic. After the annexation of Texas by the United States, however, the caudillo negotiated with Gen. Zachary Taylor (q.v.)—then at Corpus Christi—relating to the establishment of a separate nation in northern Mexico, but the American commander rejected this proposal. With the outbreak of the war, Canales assumed the title of brigadier general over an irregular cavalry force that operated throughout much of 1846 and 1847 between Matamoros (q.v.) and Point Isabel (q.v.). His guerrilla operations along the Rio Grande continued after the fall of Monterrey (q.v.) and the battle of Buena Vista (q.v.), constantly threatening the supply line of General Taylor's army. After the war, Canales renewed his separatist and regional schemes in the northeastern region of Mexico. In 1851, he was governor of Tamaulipas and continued to play a role in regional politics until his death the following year.

CANALIZO, VALENTIN (1794–1850). Having served briefly as president of Mexico in 1844, Maj. Gen. Valentín Canalizo was appointed minister of war and marine in 1846–1847. As Gen. Winfield Scott (q.v.) marched inland from Veracruz (q.v.), Gen. Antonio López de Santa Anna (q.v.) named Canalizo commander of the Mexican Army of the East (q.v.), with headquarters at Jalapa (q.v.). The general was placed in overall command of the defensive position at Cerro Gordo (q.v.) but was replaced after the arrival of Santa Anna on the scene of battle. Canalizo did, however, remain in command of the Mexican cavalry forces for that action.

CANO Y CANO, JUAN CRISOSTOMO (1815–1847). Juan Crisóstomo Cano y Cano was born in Yucatán but at age three was sent to New York to be educated. He returned to Mexico as a military engineer and worked on a number of fortifications throughout the country. As a lieutenant colonel, he advised Antonio López de Santa Anna (q.v.) relating to the defensive position at Cerro Gordo (q.v.), warning that the general must take precaution to protect his left flank. Cano y Cano later prepared fortifications at El Piñón, Churubusco (q.v.), and Chapultepec (q.v.). He participated in the battles of Molino del Rey (q.v.) and Chapultepec (q.v.), being killed in the latter action.

CARABAJAL, JOSE MARIA. A Mexican political leader and military officer educated in the United States, Col. José María Carabajal was involved in schemes to separate northeastern Mexico from the central government. On several occasions he attempted to reach an independent settlement with the United States, thus weakening the efforts of Mexican federal authorities.

CARABAJAL, RAFAEL. After Maj. Antonio Ponce de León was wounded at the battle of Brazito (q.v.) (December 25, 1846), Capt. Rafael Carabajal took command of the Mexican force against Col. Alexander Doniphan (q.v.) and led his army in retreat.

CARMEN, CAMPECHE. The port of Carmen, in the Gulf Coast state of Campeche, was neutralized at the beginning of the war by a movement in Yucatán (q.v.) against the central Mexican government. It became an important source of fresh fruits and vegetables for the American blockading squadron. On December 21, 1846, Commo. Matthew C. Perry (q.v.) seized Carmen to prevent trade with Mexican ports to the west but later withdrew. With the resumption of that trade, Commodore Perry once again took possession of the town on May 17, 1847, and established a military government to control contraband.

CARNERO PASS. Carnero Pass is some six miles south of Buena Vista (q.v.), on the road from San Luis Potosí (q.v.) to Saltillo (q.v.). It was used by Gen. Antonio López de Santa Anna (q.v.) as his last staging area before the attack against the army of Gen. Zachary Taylor (q.v.) at Angostura (q.v.) on February 22, 1847. *See also* BUENA VISTA, BATTLE OF.

CARPENDER, EDWARD W. Edward W. Carpender, commander of the brig USS *Truxtun* that grounded on a reef off the Mexican port of Tuxpan (q.v.), was forced to surrender to Mexican authorities on August 17, 1846. He and members of his crew were later exchanged for Mexican prisoners of war who had been captured at Resaca de la Palma (q.v.).

CARRASCO, JOSE MARIA (1813–1851). Col. José María Carrasco was commander of the Mexican Second Regiment at the battles of Palo Alto (q.v.) and Resaca de la Palma (q.v.). He then commanded the Querétaro Battalion during the battle of Monterrey (q.v.). After the Treaty of Guadalupe Hidalgo (q.v.), Carrasco was prominent in the wars against Indian groups in northwestern Mexico.

CARRICITOS, RANCHO DE. On April 25, 1846, the small force of Capt. Seth B. Thornton (q.v.) was ambushed at the Rancho de Carricitos on the north bank of the Rio Grande (q.v.). Eleven Americans were killed, 6 wounded, and 46 captured, including Thornton himself. Pres. James K. Polk (q.v.) used this event in his call for a declaration of war against Mexico "for the spilling of American blood on American soil."

CARSON, CHRISTOPHER (KIT) (1809–1868). The famous frontier scout and Indian fighter Kit Carson assisted Lt. John C. Frémont (q.v.) in his mysterious expedition in California. He later served as a guide for Gen. Stephen W. Kearny (q.v.) in his march from New Mexico to California, beginning October 6, 1846.

CASA MATA. The Casa Mata, a large stone building some 500 yards west of the Molino del Rey (q.v.), was heavily defended against the American attacking army on September 8, 1847. Gen. William Worth's (q.v.) division attacked the position after only a short artillery bombardment. Although successful in seizing the position, Worth's army suffered extensive casualties: 116 dead and 671 wounded. The action at Casa Mata was a part of the battle of Molino del Rey. See also MOLINO DEL REY, BATTLE OF.

CASEY, SILAS (1807–1882). Capt. Silas Casey was the leader of a storming party of 265 men during the battle of Chapultepec (q.v.).

CASS, LEWIS (1782–1866). A Democratic senator from Michigan, Lewis Cass was very influential with Pres. James K. Polk (q.v.) and supported the annexation of extensive territory in the course of the war with Mexico. In 1848, Cass received the Democratic nomination for president but was defeated by the Whig candidate, Gen. Zachary Taylor (q.v.).

CASTE WAR OF YUCATAN. In December 1846 an adventurer named Juan Vázquez raised an army of Mayan Indians in southern Yucatán (q.v.) and on January 15, 1847, assaulted the town of Valladolid, killing many of the white citizens. Mayan leaders such as Cecilio Chi (q.v.) and Jacinto Pat called for a war of extermination against all Europeans, and by May 1848, the Indians occupied four-fifths of the peninsula in an uprising called the Caste War. Gov. Miguel Barbachano (q.v.) prepared to abandon Mérida, and Yucatecan agent Justo Sierra suggested to Pres. James K. Polk (q.v.) that the United States annex his state. The offer was refused. *See also* "ALL OF MEXICO" MOVEMENT.

CASTILLO Y LANZAS, JOAQUIN M. DE (1801–1878). Born in Jalapa, Veracruz, educated in England and Spain, Joaquín M. de Castillo y Lanzas served as Mexican minister to the United States at the time of the Texas revolt. He was later foreign minister at the time of the mission of John Slidell (q.v.) to Mexico. On March 12, 1846, Castillo y Lanzas notified Slidell that he would not be received by the Mexican government. This failure of diplomatic efforts led directly to the outbreak of armed conflict on the Rio Grande (q.v.) and the formal declaration of war. Castillo y Lanzas was also an accomplished poet and made the first translation in Mexico of the works of Lord Byron.

CASTRO, JOSE MARIA. At the beginning of 1846, Brig. Gen. José María Castro was the Mexican commander in California. Controlling the port of Monterey (q.v.) and surrounding territory, he virtually ignored the authority of Gov. Pío Pico (q.v.) in Los Angeles (q.v.). In March 1846, Castro forced Lt. John C. Frémont (q.v.) to retire to Oregon (q.v.). With news of the declaration of war between the United States and Mexico and the uprising of pro-American forces in Sonoma, however, General Castro abandoned Monterey and joined Governor Pico at Los Angeles. Commo. Robert F. Stockton (q.v.) moved against Castro, demanding that his army surrender to U.S. controls. Castro declared his intention to oppose the demand on August 10, 1846, but, aware of the superior force against him, abandoned southern Upper California for Sonora, accompanied by Governor Pico.

CASTRO, MAURICIO. When Gov. Francisco Palacio Mirranda took steps to surrender to the United States in February 1847, Mauricio Castro headed a rebellion in Baja California (q.v.), which rejected that move. In April of 1848, however, Castro's small force was defeated by Lt. Col. Henry S. Burton (q.v.).

CATANA, MASSACRE OF (February 10, 1847). The Catana Massacre took place near Agua Nueva (q.v.) when elements of the Arkansas volunteers opened fire on Mexican civilians suspected of being involved in the murder of one of their comrades. Following the event, Gen. Zachary Taylor (q.v.) ordered the two companies involved to return to the mouth of the Rio Grande, but that order was later canceled.

CEBOLLETA, NEW MEXICO. Cebolleta was a settlement on the northern frontier of New Mexico where Gen. Stephen W. Kearny (q.v.) met with Navajo (q.v.) leaders in October 1846 in an effort to bring an end to fighting. Kearny's efforts were successful, at least in the short run.

CENOBIO, MARIANO. Col. Mariano Cenobio headed Mexican guerrilla forces in the state of Veracruz (q.v.) following the landing by Gen. Winfield Scott (q.v.) in March 1847. Based at his hacienda of San Juan, Cenobio disrupted the American lines of communication, but his effectiveness was hampered by his quarrel with Celedonio Dómeco Jarauta (q.v.), a Roman Catholic priest who commanded another guerrilla army in the same region.

CENTRALISTS. Following Mexican independence in 1821, a major problem arose between those elements that favored a highly centralized government based in Mexico City (q.v.) and factions that insisted upon a federalized structure along the lines of the United States. Although many centralists were conservative and favored a close alliance with the Roman Catholic Church, the situation was made more complex by the presence of many specific interest groups, including the professional military officers. Mexican efforts to oppose the U.S. invasion were often disrupted by the constant internal bickering, in part due to the conflict between centralists and federalists. See also *MODERADOS* and *PUROS*.

CENTRE DIVISION. On June 11, 1846, Brig. Gen. John E. Wool (q.v.) was ordered by Secretary of War William Marcy (q.v.) to organize a military force to move against the important Mexican city of Chihuahua (q.v.). Designated as the Centre Division but called the Army of Chihuahua, it was separate from Gen. Zachary Taylor's (q.v.) Army of Occupation (q.v.) and was formed in San Antonio, Texas (q.v.), during the summer of 1846. Although its original objective was Chihuahua, Wool soon realized that it was not practical to march over the very difficult desert region to that location. He requested permission to move to Parras, Coahuila (q.v.), and the Centre Division became an important part of the American force that met Gen. Antonio López de Santa Anna (q.v.) at the battle of Buena Vista (q.v.) in late February 1847. *See also* ARMY OF CHIHUAHUA, BUENA VISTA, BATTLE OF.

CERRALVO, NUEVO LEON. The division of Brig. Gen. William J. Worth (q.v.) occupied Cerralvo, a settlement of 1,800 inhabitants on the route from Camargo (q.v.) to Monterrey (q.v.), on August 25, 1846. A well-watered town with a delightful climate, Cerralvo served as an important station during the march of Gen. Zachary Taylor (q.v.) from Camargo to Monterrey. Taylor departed the attractive little town on September 11, 1846, but it continued to be important in the supply route between the Rio Grande (q.v.) and Monterrey.

CERRO FRIJOLES, CHIHUAHUA. Cerro Frijoles ("Bean Hill") was the site of a Mexican fortification just south of the Sacramento River in Chihuahua and was one of the positions attacked by Col. Alexander Doniphan (q.v.) in the course of the battle of Sacramento (q.v.) (February 28, 1847).

CERRO GORDO, VERACRUZ. The village of Cerro Gordo is a small settlement on the National Highway (q.v.) between Veracruz (q.v.) and Jalapa (q.v.), near the hacienda of El Encero (q.v.). El Telégrafo (q.v.), a prominent mountain just east of the town, also called "Cerro Gordo," was selected by Gen. Antonio López de Santa Anna (q.v.) as the primary defensive position against the invading army of Gen. Winfield Scott (q.v.) in April 1847. *See also* CERRO GORDO, BATTLE OF.

CERRO GORDO, BATTLE OF (April 17–18, 1847). Anxious to escape the unhealthy coastal region following the capture of Veracruz (q.v.), Gen. Winfield Scott (q.v.) initiated his march along the National Highway (q.v.) to the interior of Mexico on April 2, 1847. By April 11, his lead division, commanded by Brig. Gen. David Twiggs (q.v.), reached the small settlement of Plan del Rio (q.v.) at the foot of a steep incline that led to the village of Cerro Gordo (q.v.), five miles to the west. Twiggs made immediate preparations to attack the Mexican force blocking his path.

Gen. Antonio López de Santa Anna's (q.v.) Army of the East (q.v.), with approximately 12,000 men and 19 artillery pieces, established its primary defensive position on Telegraph Hill (q.v.) (called Cerro Gordo by most U.S. accounts). The position was extremely strong; Lt. Col. Manuel M. Robles (q.v.) fortified several positions on El Telégrafo and nearby Atalaya (q.v.) and placed artillery batteries to guard the road from Plan del Rio. Although Santa Anna expressed optimism, the Mexican troops were ill trained, and their morale was very low.

Lt. P. G. T. Beauregard (q.v.) suggested a flanking attack against Atalaya, but General Twiggs prepared to make a frontal assault against the primary Mexican position early on the morning of April 13. He delayed the movement to give the newly arrived units time to rest before the attack. Then Maj. Gen. Robert Patterson (q.v.) ordered a further delay, awaiting the arrival of General Scott. Scott reached Plan del Rio on April 14 and ordered additional reconnaissance of the enemy position. This was carried out by the engineers under the supervision of Capt. Robert E. Lee (q.v.), who used the previous intelligence of Beauregard, then explored a path to the Mexican left that would give access to Atalaya, allowing El Telégrafo to be flanked. Scott accepted that recommendation and on April 17, 1847, launched the attack. General Twiggs pushed along the path that had been marked by Lee and then sent a brigade under Lt. Col. William S. Harney (q.v.) against the Mexican position on Atalaya; some of Harney's men reached El Telégrafo but were forced back by heavy Mexican fire. At the end of the day Santa Anna, pleased that his guns had repelled the American attack, sent reinforcements to strengthen the center of his line. At the same time, Twiggs ordered artillery emplacements to be prepared on Atalaya, anticipating a continuation of the battle on the following day.

On the second day of the battle (April 18) at 0700 hours, General Harney's brigade moved from Atalaya against the defensive emplacements on El Telégrafo, this time with success. In the close fighting, Brig. Gen. Ciriaco Vásquez (q.v.), one of Santa Anna's most able officers, was killed, and many of his troops retreated in disorder. By 1000 hours, additional fresh troops under Brig. Gen. James Shields (q.v.) and Brig. Gen. Bennet Riley (q.v.) pushed to the rear of Atalaya and Telégrafo and struck Santa Anna's camp at the village of Cerro Gordo, also taking control of the National Road that ran west to Jalapa. With the exception of a blow against a Mexican artillery position well in front of El Telégrafo that was badly mismanaged by Maj. Gen. Gideon Pillow (q.v.), the attack went according to plan; within three hours Santa Anna's army was in flight. The Mexican Army of the East was completely routed, and Santa Anna barely missed being captured before escaping to Orizaba (q.v.). Losses for the American army were 63 killed and 368 wounded, many of them among Pillow's Tennessee volunteers.

Scott's victory at Cerro Gordo was a significant one, not only because it shattered the Mexican army but also because it allowed the American force to move to Jalapa, a beautiful city with food and water, located well above the dreaded coastal zone of yellow fever (q.v.).

CHALCO, LAKE. Lake Chalco was one of three large, shallow lakes in the Valley of Mexico (q.v.) at the time of the war, though today much of the area is no longer under water. In August 1847, Gen. Winfield Scott (q.v.) decided to avoid a frontal assault against the strong position of Santa Anna at El Peñón (q.v.) and moved east, then south around Lakes Chalco and Xochimilco (q.v.) to attack Mexico City from the south.

CHALCO, STATE OF MEXICO. Chalco was a small village to the east of Lake Chalco (q.v.), on the route selected by Gen. Winfield Scott (q.v.) on August 15, 1847, for a flanking movement to the south of Mexico City (q.v.).

CHAMBERLAIN, SAMUEL EMERY (1829–1908). Samuel Chamberlain was an enlisted participant in the war who served with Gen. John Wool's Army of Chihuahua (q.v.) and participated in the battle of Buena Vista (q.v.). He is best known for his very colorful commentary on the war, its participants, and especially the beautiful señoritas he seemed to find at every town and ranch. His *Confessions*, published long after the end of the struggle, is often questioned by the serious historian, but Chamberlain's social commentary and the delightful illustrations, published in *Life* magazine in 1957, have been widely circulated.

CHAPITA. Chapita was a Mexican spy employed by Gen. Zachary Taylor (q.v.) during his occupation of Corpus Christi (q.v.) in August and September 1845.

CHAPLAINS, ROMAN CATHOLIC. Secretary of War William Marcy (q.v.) arranged for the appointment of several Roman Catholic chaplains to accompany the U.S. invasion forces in Mexico. This was in part to counter the charges of militant Protestantism being made by the Mexican government against the policy of Pres. James K. Polk (q.v.).

CHAPULTEPEC, BATTLE OF (September 13, 1847). During the truce after the battle of Churubusco (q.v.), Gen. Winfield Scott (q.v.) and his staff studied the various approaches to Mexico City (q.v.). The American army could strike from the south along one of the four causeways or could attack Chapultepec, thought to be a formidable defensive position to the west of the city. The castle, commanded by Maj. Gen. Nicolás Bravo (q.v.), had a force of only about 1,000 men, including a number of young cadets who refused to go home in the face of the enemy. Its defenses were further weakened when Gen. Antonio López de Santa Anna (q.v.) shifted some of the artillery from the castle to other positions along his line.

After the battles of Casa Mata (q.v.) and Molino del Rey (q.v.) (September 8, 1847), a number of reconnaissances were carried out by Scott's engineers. On September 11, 1847, the General in Chief convened a council of war to discuss the plan of action. Although most of the general officers spoke in favor of an attack from the south against the San Antonio Gate (q.v.), Lt. P. G. T. Beauregard (q.v.) strongly advocated the western approach, which included an attack on Chapultepec. General Scott, having earlier spoken in favor of such a plan, decided that Chapultepec would be the next key objective. To confuse Santa Anna, Gen. John Quitman's (q.v.) troops advanced along the southern route against the village of Piedad but then moved under cover of darkness to Tacubaya (q.v.), just south of Chapultepec.

On September 12, 1847, General Scott directed an artillery bombardment against the castle, causing considerable destruction and inflicting heavy casualties on the small force commanded by General Nicolás Bravo (q.v.). Among the defenders were some 50 young cadets who refused to abandon the position. Santa Anna hesitated to send reinforcements, however, still expecting the primary attack to come along the southern causeways. On the following day, September 13, 1847, the assault was launched; Gen. Gideon Pillow's (q.v.) volunteers, led by the brigade of Franklin Pierce (q.v.), moved from Molino del Rey (q.v.), through the swampy cyprus grove, and against the western side of Chapultepec. At the same time, forces under the command of General Quitman attacked from the south. Despite delays in providing the scaling ladders, the American troops, including a small detachment of Marines, mounted the walls and seized the castle.

The fall of Chapultepec opened the way for Scott's forces to push into the Mexican capital. More than any other single action in the war, this battle at the "Halls of Montezuma," came to be identified with the U.S. victory. At the same time, the bravery of the young cadets at Chapultepec, the *niños héroes* (q.v.), provided a symbol for Mexican national pride and, in the long run, a step toward national unity.

CHAPULTEPEC, CASTLE OF. Chapultepec ("Place of the Grasshopper") is a fortified castle located on an imposing hill, approximately 200 feet above the valley floor, west of Mexico City. This wooded hill was occupied in the time of the Aztec Empire and later served as a residence for the viceroys of New Spain. At the time of the U.S. invasion, the castle was utilized as a military academy and dominated the western approaches to the city. It became the site of one of the key battles in the campaign of Gen. Winfield Scott (q.v.) in the Valley of Mexico. *See also* CHAPULTEPEC, BATTLE OF.

CHASE, ANNA. Anna Chase, a British citizen and wife of Franklin Chase, U.S. consul at Tampico (q.v.), remained at the port city following the departure of her husband. On October 27–28, 1846, she informed Commo. David Conner (q.v.) that Mexican forces had abandoned the port. As American troops occupied Tampico, they were greeted by the Stars and Stripes hoisted by Mrs. Chase.

CHASE, FRANKLIN. Franklin Chase was U.S. consul at Tampico (q.v.) at the time of the outbreak of hostilities and left his post at that time.

CHAVEZ, PABLO (d. 1847). Pablo Chávez was one of the principal organizers of the rebellion in Taos, New Mexico (q.v.), against the authority of the United States. This uprising was crushed February 3, 1847, and Chávez was killed during the fighting.

CHI, CECILIO. Cecilio Chi, leader of a militant Maya faction in Yucatán (q.v.), was involved in the outbreak of the Caste War (q.v.) against Yucatecan state authorities in 1847. *See also* CASTE WAR OF YUCATAN.

CHIHUAHUA, ARMY OF. Gen. John Wool (q.v.) organized a military force at San Antonio, Texas (q.v.), in the summer of 1846. The primary objective at that time was the capture of Chihuahua (q.v.), and Wool's came to be called the Army of Chihuahua. The original mission was abandoned, however, and Wool joined Gen. Zachary Taylor (q.v.) in time to play an important part in the battle of Buena Vista (q.v.).

CHIHUAHUA, CHIHUAHUA. Chihuahua is the capital city of the northwestern Mexican state of the same name, located 200 miles south of El Paso, Texas (q.v.). In 1846, it had a population of 14,000 and had an important trade connection with St. Louis, Missouri, via the Camino Real and Santa Fe Trail (q.v.). An expedition to capture Chihuahua, considered to be an important military objective, was organized under the command of Gen. John E. Wool (q.v.) in June 1846. That army was diverted to the region of Saltillo (q.v.), however, and played an important role in the battle of Buena Vista (q.v.). The city was occupied by Col. Alexander Doniphan (q.v.) on March 1, 1847, following the battle of Sacramento (q.v.). Doniphan left, but in March 1848, another regiment of Missouri volunteers marched from El Paso under Col. Sterling Price (q.v.), occupying Chihuahua for a second time.

CHILDS, THOMAS (1796–1853). Lt. Col. Thomas Childs commanded an artillery battalion in the first brigade at the battle of Palo Alto (q.v.). His troops, known as the red-legged infantry because of the red stripes on their trousers, played an important role in the battle for Monterrey (q.v.), especially in the capture of Independence Hill (q.v.). Childs later served with Gen. Winfield Scott (q.v.), commanding the garrison at Jalapa (q.v.), and then that at Puebla (q.v.) during the course of the American campaign in the Valley of Mexico. Following the surrender of Mexico City (q.v.), General Santa Anna (q.v.) attacked Puebla, placing the small force commanded by Colonel Childs under siege from September 13 to October 12, 1847. The Mexican commander, Brig. Gen. Joaquín Rea (q.v.), demanded the surrender of the city, but Childs refused, thus holding control of that strategic point until reinforced by Gen. Joseph Lane (q.v.).

CHINA, NUEVO LEON. A small village east of Monterrey, Nuevo León (q.v.), China served as a base for Mexican guerrilla (q.v.) operations throughout much of the war.

CHURCHILL, SYLVESTER (d. 1862). Col. Sylvester Churchill was commander of two Illinois regiments at San Antonio (q.v.) following the departure of Gen. John Wool (q.v.) for the Rio Grande (q.v.) in August 1846. He joined Wool in the march to Monclova (q.v.), Parras (q.v.), and eventually the region of Saltillo (q.v.). Churchill played an effective role during the battle of Buena Vista (q.v.). He was also a member of the court-martial panel that tried Capt. John C. Frémont (q.v.) in November 1847.

CHURCHILL, WILLIAM H. (1819–1847). Lt. William H. Churchill was an artillery officer under Capt. Samuel Ringgold (q.v.) and provided significant supporting fire for Gen. Zachary Taylor's (q.v.) army during the battle of Palo Alto (q.v.).

CHURUBUSCO, BATTLE OF. See CONTRERAS AND CHURUBUSCO, BATTLES OF.

CHURUBUSCO, DISTRITO FEDERAL. In 1847, Churubusco was a small settlement south of Mexico City (q.v.) located on the Churubusco River, a sluggish stream flowing into the western end of Lake Xochimilco (q.v.). At the time of the American invasion, it was dominated by the Franciscan Convent of San Mateo (q.v.), occupied by some 1,500 men, including the San Patricio Battalion (q.v.). Today Churubusco is a part of the urban region of Mexico City, and the river has been covered by a wide avenue. The convent has been converted into a museum displaying a number of items related to foreign intervention in Mexico.

CIMARRON CUTOFF. The Cimarron Cutoff was a branch of the Santa Fe Trail (q.v.) that turned southwest from the Arkansas River near the present town of Cimarron, Kansas, to the Cimarron River, and eventually to Las Vegas, New Mexico. It was shorter and less mountainous, but Col. Stephen W. Kearny (q.v.) chose the longer route to Bent's Fort (q.v.) because it had better forage and water for his army and the many accompanying animals.

CITADEL (Mexico City). Following the capture of Chapultepec Castle (q.v.) Gen. John A. Quitman (q.v.) pushed forward to the Belén Gate (q.v.), facing heavy fire from the troops of General Andrés Terrés (q.v.). As Quitman's men reached the *garita* (q.v.), their progress was blocked by very heavy fire from a fortified position to the northeast known as the *ciudadela* (citadel). Quitman did not seize that fortified position, but on the following day it was surrendered as a part of the general surrender of the city to Gen. Winfield Scott (q.v.). The citadel played an important role in the era of the Mexican Revolution after 1910 and today is utilized as a museum and library.

CITADEL (Monterrey, Nuevo León). As Gen. Zachary Taylor (q.v.) initiated the battle of Monterrey (q.v.), one of the most important obstacles was a fortification that had been constructed on the foundation of an old church, just to the north of the city. Known as the *ciudadela* by the Mexican defenders, it came to be called the Black Fort (q.v.) because of its dark color. On September 21, 1846, General Taylor directed an attack against the position as a part of a general movement on the eastern area of Monterrey, in part to distract the attention of Gen. Pedro de Ampudia (q.v.) from the attack by Gen. William Worth (q.v.) to the west of the city. Although other strong points were taken by the American assault, the citadel did not fall. With the general surrender of Monterrey on September 23, 1846, however, the Mexican flag over the strong point was lowered. *See also* MONTERREY, BATTLE OF.

CLARK, MERIWETHER LEWIS (1809–1881). Maj. Meriwether Lewis Clark was commander of the Missouri volunteer artillery in Gen. Stephen Kearny's (q.v.) Army of the West (q.v.). In February 1847, Clark joined Col. Alexander Doniphan (q.v.) in his march from El Paso (q.v.) to Chihuahua (q.v.). His artillery force played a key role in the victory over the Mexican army in the battle of Sacramento (q.v.), February 28, 1847.

CLARKE, JAMES FREEMAN (1810–1888). James Freeman Clarke was an abolitionist clergyman who spoke at an antiwar rally at Faneuil Hall in Boston, February 1847, along with Charles Sumner. *See also* ABOLITIONISTS.

CLARKE, NEWMAN S. (d. 1860). Following the fall of Veracruz (q.v.) on March 29, 1847, Gen. Winfield Scott (q.v.) reorganized his army. Col. Newman S. Clarke was assigned command of one of the two brigades in the regular division of Gen. William Worth (q.v.). During the battle of Churubusco (q.v.) he led his brigade from San Agustín (q.v.) to San Antonio and then assaulted the bridgehead over the Churubusco River, suffering very heavy casualties. Clarke also played a major role in the attack on the Casa Mata (q.v.), again with the loss of many of his men. He led an attack against Chapultepec Castle (q.v.) and into Mexico City (q.v.) via the San Cosmé Gate (q.v.).

CLAY, CASSIUS MARCELLUS (1810–1903). Capt. Cassius Marcellus Clay commanded a Kentucky cavalry unit that carried out a scouting mission south of Agua Nueva (q.v.) and Encarnación (q.v.) before the battle of Buena Vista (q.v.). Joining the force of Maj. Solon Borland (q.v.), Clay and his men were captured by Col. Miguel Andrade.

CLAY, HENRY (1777–1852). Henry Clay, distinguished senator from Kentucky, held many top offices in the U.S. government and was for many years leader of the Whig Party. He clashed with Pres. John Tyler over a number of issues, including policy toward Mexico and the annexation of Texas. When the Whigs nominated Clay for president in the election of 1844, he took a moderate position relating to the Texas question and was defeated by the Democratic candidate James K. Polk (q.v.). During the war with Mexico, Clay continued to serve in the Senate and was one of the harshest critics of President Polk, opposing extensive annexation of Mexican territory. In 1848, he lost the Whig presidential nomination to Gen. Zachary Taylor (q.v.) but continued to play an important role in national politics.

CLAY, HENRY JR. (1811–1847). Lt. Col. Henry Clay, Jr., son of Sen. Henry Clay (q.v.), was the deputy commander of the Second Kentucky Volunteer Regiment in the campaign of northern Mexico and was killed in the battle of Buena Vista (q.v.).

CLAYTON, THOMAS (1777–1854). Thomas Clayton was a Whig senator from Delaware who cast one of the two votes against Pres. James K. Polk's (q.v.) War Bill on May 13, 1846.

CLIFFORD, NATHAN (1803–1881). Nathan Clifford, attorney general in the cabinet of Pres. James K. Polk (q.v.), favored the annexation of an extensive part of Mexican territory. Clifford was a member of the commission sent to Mexico to seek ratification of the Treaty of Guadalupe Hidalgo (q.v.) after it had been passed by the U.S. Senate. The commissions exchanged official ratification on May 30, 1848, in Querétaro (q.v.).

COAHUILA. The state of Coahuila in north-central Mexico was combined with Texas during the Spanish rule and the early period of Mexican independence into the single state of Coahuila y Tejas. Disputes relating to the capital of the combined state influenced the Anglo-American rebellion in Texas that resulted in its independence (1836). When Gen. Zachary Taylor (q.v.) invaded northern Mexico, the capital of Coahuila was Saltillo (q.v.), some 60 miles west of Monterrey (q.v.). The battle of

Buena Vista (q.v.), a key event in the struggle for northern Mexico, was fought south of Saltillo (February 22–23, 1847).

COLEGIO MILITAR. At the time of the invasion of the Valley of Mexico (q.v.) by the army of Gen. Winfield Scott (q.v.), the Castle of Chapultepec (q.v.) served as a military school, the Colegio Militar. Among the defenders of the position were a number of young cadets, and, according to some accounts, six leaped to their deaths rather than surrender to the Americans. They came to be known as the *niños héroes* (q.v.).

COLLADO BEACH. Collado Beach, some two and one-half miles south of the city of Veracruz (q.v.), was recommended by Commo. David Conner (q.v.) as the best landing point for the invading army of Gen. Winfield Scott (q.v.). *See also* VERACRUZ, VERACRUZ.

COLLINGWOOD. The British flagship HMS *Collingwood* departed from the Mexican port of Mazatlán (q.v.) on May 20, 1846, under the command of Rear Adm. Sir George F. Seymour (1787–1870). When he reached Monterey, California (q.v.), on July 23, Seymour made no attempt to block U.S. efforts to take control of that port and other positions along the Pacific coast.

COLLINS, JOHN L. John L. Collins, a Chihuahua trader who led a small party from that city to Saltillo (q.v.), delivered Col. Alexander Doniphan's (q.v.) message to Gen. John Wool (q.v.) indicating that his Missouri volunteer force was available to assist in the campaign for northern Mexico. Collins carried out the 1,000-mile journey to Saltillo and back to Chihuahua (q.v.) in 32 days.

CONCEPCION, FORT. *See* FORT CONCEPCION.

CONDOR. The Mexican vessel *Condor* was destroyed in the port of Guaymas (q.v.) on October 6, 1846, by Comdr. Samuel F. DuPont (q.v.).

CONGRESS. Commo. Robert F. Stockton (q.v.) arrived in Monterey Bay, California (q.v.), on July 15, 1846, aboard the flagship USS *Congress*. The ship was involved in the military action along the California coast in the following months, supplying a number of landing parties to carry out operations ashore. In the fall of 1847, at the time of the capture of Mexico City, the

Congress and other U.S. vessels occupied key ports on the Pacific coast, including Guaymas (q.v.) and Mazatlán (q.v.). *See also* BLOCKADE.

CONNER, DAVID E. (1792–1856). Commo. David E. Conner, commander of the Home Squadron (q.v.), was at Veracruz (q.v.) on May 3, 1846, when he received word of the declaration of a defensive war by the Mexican government. He moved with most of his vessels to Point Isabel (q.v.), near the mouth of the Rio Grande (q.v.). Reaching that point on May 8, 1846, Conner supported Gen. Zachary Taylor (q.v.) along the Rio Grande line and cooperated with the army to cross into Mexico at Barita (q.v.).

Within a short time, Conner turned his major attention to the blockade (q.v.) of the Mexican coast from the Rio Grande to Yucatán (q.v.). Establishing his base at Antón Lizardo (q.v.), 12 miles south of Veracruz, the commodore blocked the major ports of entry throughout the Gulf. He was continually aware of dangers from sudden northers (q.v.) that threatened the ships and tropical diseases that plagued the men during the warm season. To break the monotony of the boring blockading duties, Conner conducted a number of raids against port cities, using light draft steamers to cross the shoals. Most of these efforts were unsuccessful, but, on November 14, 1846, he seized the port of Tampico (q.v.). Even before that move, he had advised Pres. James K. Polk (q.v.) that it would be possible to seize Veracruz and use it as a base to attack Mexico City. In early 1847, Conner and his naval force cooperated with Gen. Winfield Scott (q.v.) in organizing the invasion force against Veracruz and San Juan de Ulúa (q.v.). The landing of some 8,600 men at Collado Beach (q.v.) on March 9, 1847, has been recognized as one of the most successful amphibious operations in history, being carried out without the loss of a single life. Throughout the landing, Commodore Conner played a significant role. Ironically, he was replaced in command of the Home Squadron by Commo. Matthew C. Perry (q.v.) shortly after the successful operation. This was not due to any dissatisfaction with his role in the naval operations of the war but had been planned for several months before the actual change of command.

CONTRERAS, DISTRITO FEDERAL. In 1847, Contreras was a small village southwest of Mexico City, just to the west of the pedregal (q.v.). The battle fought at Padierna (q.v.), about a mile to the north, on August 20, 1847, was labeled by American soldiers and writers as the "Battle of Contreras," though no action in the battle touched the settlement. Today Contreras retains some of the characteristics of a small Mexican town but is greatly affected by the urban expansion from the national capital. *See also* CONTRERAS AND CHURUBUSCO, BATTLES OF.

CONTRERAS AND CHURUBUSCO, BATTLES OF (August 20, 1847). The two intertwined battles that took place on August 20, 1847, marked the initial clash between Gen. Antonio López de Santa Anna (q.v.) and Gen. Winfield Scott (q.v.) in the Valley of Mexico (q.v.). The first action, taking place early in the morning, was actually fought at Padierna (q.v.) and given that name by Mexican authorities, but it came to be called Contreras in the United States owing to a mistake related to the location of the village approximately two miles south of the struggle.

Following his victory over Santa Anna at Cerro Gordo (q.v.), General Scott advanced to Puebla (q.v.) but was then forced to delay his movement to Mexico City (q.v.) because many of his volunteers returned home at the end of their one-year enlistment. By August 7, 1847, however, new recruits increased the American army to over 10,000 men, and on that day Gen. David Twiggs (q.v.) led his division from Puebla, followed by Gen. William Worth (q.v.), Gen. John Quitman (q.v.), and Gen. Gideon Pillow (q.v.). Passing in the shadow of the magnificent Popocatépetl volcano and into the Valley of Anahuac without opposition, Scott's army reached the village of Ayotla (q.v.), 25 miles from the heart of Mexico City (q.v.), on August 11.

Santa Anna returned to Mexico City after his crushing defeat at Cerro Gordo and was able to pull together a new force of some 30,000 to defend the capital, though many men were poorly trained and some officers were unreliable. Mexico City seemed ideally suited for a defensive stand; located in an elevated valley, it was guarded on the east and south by three large shallow lakes, Texcoco (q.v.), Chalco (q.v.), and Xochimilco (q.v.). Much of the rest of the surrounding terrain was soft, wet, and marshy. A series of causeways led through the lakes and across the marshlands, channeling any opposing force into a few narrow gateways, or *garitas* (q.v.). Santa Anna assumed that Scott would take the road northwest from Ayotla, that being the most direct route into the capital, and centered his defense on El Peñón (q.v.), a hill rising 450 feet out of the marshlands south of Texcoco. Gen. Nicolás Bravo (q.v.) concentrated a second force at Mexicalzingo (q.v.). Between those two strong points, Santa Anna placed the Army of the North (q.v.), commanded by his bitter rival, Gen. Gabriel Valencia (q.v.). The cavalry, for all practical purposes the personal army of Gen. Juan Alvarez (q.v.), was poised to strike Scott's column on the march and to cut its communications.

With his army backed up along the road into Ayotla, General Scott was aware that he was in a vulnerable position. His engineers, led by Capt. James L. Mason (q.v.) and Capt. Robert E. Lee (q.v.), examined the route to El Peñón and reported that the road would support the advancing army but that an assault would most likely be very costly. The road from Ayotla to Mexicalzingo was also considered but dismissed. Scott wished to avoid a direct assault on either of the strongly held positions, realizing that his artillery and wagons would be confined to the narrow roadways. The General in Chief sought detailed reports on the route that cut south to the village of Chalco (q.v.), skirted Lakes Chalco and Xochimilco to the south, and joined the Acapulco Road (q.v.) at the village of San Agustín (q.v.). On August 14, Col. James Duncan (q.v.) of General Worth's division examined the route and reported that the road was quite good and that there did not seem to be any major defensive barriers. With this report, Scott was ready to act; on the following day (August 15), he ordered Worth to initiate the move, and by August 16, the covering force at Ayotla, commanded by General Twiggs, pulled out of its blocking position and joined the march to the south, facing only light opposition from the cavalry of General Alvarez. This maneuver shifted the focus of Scott's army to the village of San Agustín, some 10 miles south of the capital on the road to Acapulco.

Santa Anna was reluctant to abandon the magnificent fortifications at El Peñón but realized that he would have to shift his force of some 20,000 men to meet the challenge. On August 17, he moved his headquarters to the village of Churubusco and advanced Gen. Nicolás Bravo (q.v.) south to San Antonio (q.v.), about halfway between Churubusco and the American position at San Agustín. Gen. Francisco Pérez (q.v.) established his new position at Coyoacán (q.v.), a half-mile southwest of Churubusco. Santa Anna instructed General Valencia to center his army of some 6,000 men on the western end of the defensive line, near the town of San Angel (q.v.). On the 18th, Valencia advanced south from San Angel, establishing a strong position at Padierna (q.v.), protected by a steep ravine. Santa Anna ordered him to pull back, but the intrepid commander refused to listen. The Mexican defensive position, spread out to the south of Mexico City, was further strengthened by natural barriers; not only were the marshlands to the east of the Acapulco Road (q.v.) a special problem for the movement of the American army, but the pedregal (q.v.), an oval-shaped field of lava considered to be virtually impenetrable, seemed to prevent any flanking movements to the west of the approach from San Agustín.

On the morning of August 18, General Worth dispatched the dragoons of Col. William S. Harney (q.v.) north toward San Antonio, accompanied by members of the engineers. They not only encountered heavy fire but also reported that the marshes east of the road and the pedregal to the west would severely limit their ability to bring force to bear on the objective. Scott halted the advance. At about the same time, another probe was carried out to the west of San Agustín under Capt. Robert E. Lee and Lt. P. G. T. Beauregard (q.v.). From Zacatepec Mountain (q.v.), near the western edge of the pedregal, they observed Valencia's troops around San Gerónimo (q.v.). Lee reported that the pedregal was very rugged, but with effort a road could be prepared to support the movement of both infantry and artillery.

On August 19, Scott instructed Gen. Gideon J. Pillow (q.v.) to advance to the west, supported by Gen. David Twiggs (q.v.). Lee and his engineers supervised a work detail to prepare a road across the southern edge of the pedregal, Pillow occupied Padierna and set up an artillery battery commanded by Capt. John B. Magruder (q.v.). The battery opened fire but then was forced to retreat by the heavier and more numerous guns of the Army of the North (q.v.). Pillow prepared to attack Valencia's position; he ordered Brig. Gen. Persifor Smith (q.v.) to launch a frontal assault across the ravine at the middle of the Mexican defensive line and despatched Brig. Gen. Bennet Riley (q.v.) of Twiggs's division to occupy the village of San Gerónimo. Riley advanced, encountering light opposition from Santa Anna's forces, which had shifted to San Angel. Gen. Persifor Smith was unable to advance, shifted north and also moved toward San Gerónimo. With three brigades at the rear of Valencia's position, Pillow was in a vulnerable position as Santa Anna moved with some 5,000 men to San Angel on the afternoon of the 19th. Valencia felt that he would be able to crush the Americans and initiated a premature celebration, at the same time failing to post adequate security.

During the night, General Riley informed General Smith of a ravine that would allow his troops to move to the rear of

Valencia's position without detection. Smith issued orders to move at 0300 hours the following morning and requested that General Scott provide a diversionary attack against Valencia's front.

In the dark hours of the early morning of August 20, Smith directed General Riley and Brig. Gen. George Cadwalader (q.v.) to move south, leaving Brig. Gen. James Shields (q.v.) near San Gerónimo to guard against an attack by Santa Anna. At 0500 hours, the men under Brig. Gen. Franklin Pierce (q.v.) opened fire from the western edge of the Pedregal against Valencia's front. By the time Riley and Cadwalader arrived at his rear, the sun had risen; they were not detected, however, until General Smith's men rushed with fixed bayonets against the rear of the Mexican defensive position. In only 17 minutes, Valencia's army fled in panic, rushing north toward San Angel; they were subject to flanking fire from General Shields's brigade near San Gerónimo. Valencia lost 700 men killed and 850 captured, along with most of his artillery and supplies. By contrast, the attacking force of Persifor Smith lost only 60 killed and wounded.

The battle of Contreras was an overwhelming American victory; the way seemed open for a strike at the gates of the Mexican capital. Scott, though elated, was aware that he must not rush directly toward Tacubaya (q.v.), leaving General Worth's division and his supply train at San Agustín exposed to the 20,000-man army that Santa Anna might still be able to amass. The General in Chief did not wish to allow the moment of Mexican confusion to go unexploited, however, and turned his attention on Churubusco, destined to be the scene of the second major battle of that very long day.

At midmorning, with the taste of victory still strong, General Scott decided to converge on his objective from two directions. He ordered General Worth to move from San Agustín, up the Acapulco Road against San Antonio, and then toward the bridge over the Churubusco River. At the same time, Scott would personally direct the victorious troops of Persifor Smith and David Twiggs in an advance through Coyoacán to Churubusco. Uncharacteristically, the General in Chief did not make a careful study of the targeted area and was unaware of the defensive forces being massed there.

Santa Anna, aware of the negative impact of the defeat of Valencia, moved quickly to reposition his remaining units. He ordered Brig. Gen. Francisco Pérez (q.v.) to strengthen the fortification (*tête de pont*) at the bridge across the Churubusco River.

The second concentration at Churubusco was at the ancient Franciscan Convent of San Mateo (q.v.), where some 1,600 men with seven artillery pieces were commanded by Maj. Gen. Manuel Rincón (q.v.). One of the most seasoned units in the convent was the San Patricio Battalion (q.v.), made up in large part of deserters from the U.S. ranks. To further concentrate his strength, Santa Anna instructed Gen. Nicolás Bravo (q.v.) to pull back from San Antonio and ordered Gen. Antonio Gaona (q.v.) to shift his troops from Mexicalzingo (q.v.) to a position closer to Churubusco.

At about 1100 hours, General Worth sent Col. John Garland (q.v.) from San Agustín toward San Antonio, accompanied by the artillery battery of Col. James Duncan (q.v.). At the same time, he ordered Col. Newman S. Clarke (q.v.) to lead his brigade through the eastern edge of the pedregal to approach San Antonio from the flank. General Bravo had already initiated his withdrawal toward Churubusco when Garland entered San Antonio; the narrow, muddy road over which the Mexican army retreated was very crowded, creating chaos and confusion. Garland and Clarke joined forces and struck them before they could reach the *tête de pont*, scattering many of Bravo's troops. The general was able, however, to reach the fortified position with a sizable percentage of his men, strengthening the position of General Pérez. General Worth posted Colonel Clarke's brigade directly in front of the fortified bridgehead, then ordered the elite Sixth Infantry Regiment, commanded by Maj. Benjamin L. E. Bonneville (q.v.), to assault the position. Colonel Duncan attempted to support the attack, but his flying artillery was severely limited by the muddy road and surrounding marshlands. Bonneville's initial thrust was repulsed, but after protracted hand-to-hand fighting and heavy casualties on both sides, the defenders began to retreat. The withdrawal was brought about in part by an attack led by Brig. Gen. James Shields (q.v.) from Coyoacán across the Churubusco River, to the rear of the Mexican defensive positions. That diversion created confusion in Mexican ranks and weakened the *tête de pont*. By 1600 hours, Garland and Lt. Col. C. F. Smith (q.v.) were able to cross the river and turn the Mexican line. Worth's division suffered heavy casualties but by the end of the day could claim a victory.

The second central thrust against Churubusco was also initiated around 1100 hours on the morning of August 20. General Scott led the victorious forces that had routed Valencia at Padierna and marched to Coyoacán, arriving around 1200 hours.

At that position the General in Chief was informed of the struggle by Worth and his forces at the bridgehead. He assumed that the convent was not strongly defended and ordered General Twiggs to assault the position, with Persifor Smith's brigade in the lead, supported by Capt. Francis Taylor's (q.v.) artillery battery; the attack got under way at about 1300 hours. General Riley advanced with the Second and Seventh Infantries against the right of the convent, supported by Captain Taylor's battery. Rincón's defense was highly disciplined and tenacious; his men held their fire until the Americans were within musket range and then opened with great effect. Twiggs fell back with heavy casualties.

The dash by General Shields from Coyoacán across the Churubusco River to the rear of the Mexican position that had assisted Worth in his fight for the bridgehead was equally important for Twiggs to the west. Rincón was called upon to shift some of his forces to meet the threat, weakening his defensive perimeter. Twiggs ordered Capt. E. B. Alexander (q.v.) of the Third Infantry to assault San Mateo from the south. He was able to push the weakened Mexican defenders to the inner building of the convent. Worth's success at the *tête de pont* enabled General Scott to call upon Col. Duncan to direct his battery's fire against the convent. After additional close combat, Rincón surrendered. The Americans took 1,259 prisoners, including 85 members of the San Patricio Battalion.

With the fall of both the bridgehead and the convent, the way into Mexico City seemed open; Colonel Harney pushed up the causeway, and Capt. Philip Kearny (q.v.) dashed against a Mexican battery at the Garita de San Antonio (q.v.). General Scott decided, however, that it would be best to halt his troops short of the city gates. His losses had been severe, with 133 killed and 865 wounded (nearly 12 percent of the American force that had been engaged). Santa Anna lost about 10,000 men in the two battles, which greatly weakened his ability to continue an active campaign. An uneasy truce was arranged, lasting until the following month when the final assault was to be launched by Scott and the invading army.

COOKE, PHILIP ST. GEORGE (1809–1895). Lt. Col. Philip St. George Cooke was involved with events in New Mexico as early as 1829 and joined the Army of the West (q.v.) to assist Gen. Stephen W. Kearny (q.v.) as a guide and adviser as well as a commander of dragoons (q.v.). As Kearny's army pushed into New Mexico, Cooke, with an escort of 12 dragoons, accompanied James W. Magoffin (q.v.) to Santa Fe (q.v.). Reaching that city on August 12, 1846, Cooke delivered a letter from General Kearny to Gov. Manuel Armijo (q.v.), advising the New Mexican official against violence.

Cooke was later assigned the task of leading the Mormon Battalion (q.v.) to California and cutting a road on the way. He set out on October 19, 1846, and reached San Diego, California (q.v.), at the end of January 1847. He came to play an important role in the confused state of affairs in that region. Cooke later served as a major general in the U.S. Army during the Civil War.

CORCORAN, WILLIAM W. (1798–1888). William W. Corcoran was a Washington banker who convinced Quartermaster Gen. Thomas S. Jesup (q.v.) to transfer $2 million to New Orleans for military purchases relating to the war. Corcoran used a part of those funds for stock speculation.

CORONA, ANTONIO. Gen. Antonio Corona was chief of artillery in the army of Gen. Antonio López de Santa Anna (q.v.) during the campaign in Coahuila (q.v.), including the battle of Buena Vista (q.v.) in February 1847.

CORPS OF ENGINEERS. See ENGINEERS.

CORPS OF TOPOGRAPHICAL ENGINEERS. See ENGINEERS.

CORPUS CHRISTI, TEXAS. Established in 1838 as a ranch and trading post by Col. Henry L. Kinney (q.v.), Corpus Christi by 1845 was a small settlement on the southern shore of the Nueces River (q.v.), near its mouth. Although claimed as a part of Texas territory, Mexico considered the settlement below the Nueces to be a rightful part of the state of Tamaulipas. Gen. Zachary Taylor (q.v.) reached the town in late July 1845 and used it as a training base for his Army of Occupation (q.v.), a force of some 4,000 men. The town itself grew to a population of around 1,000 to meet the needs of the troops. On March 8, 1846, the army set out from Corpus Christi for the Rio Grande (q.v.), some 150 miles to the south.

CORWIN, THOMAS (1794–1865). Thomas Corwin was a Whig senator from Ohio who opposed the annexation of major regions of Mexican territory and bitterly attacked the Polk (q.v.) administration for its unwarranted invasion of Mexico. He continued to oppose the annexation of major regions of Mexican territory.

COS, MARTIN PERFECTO DE (1800–1854). In 1835, Brig. Gen. Martín Perfecto de Cos commanded an army sent by the central Mexican government to subdue the Texas rebellion. Besieged by the Texans and forced to surrender, Cos agreed to withdraw to the right bank of the Rio Grande (q.v.), thereby giving credence to the Texans' claim that the river marked their border with Mexico. During the war with the United States, General Cos surfaced in the spring of 1847 as the commander at Tuxpán (q.v.) at the time Commo. Matthew C. Perry (q.v.) led a force against that port. Overwhelmed by the assault, Cos withdrew his troops, and the river port fell to the Americans.

COUNCIL GROVE, KANSAS. The last stand of hardwood trees on the Santa Fe Trail (q.v.) for those moving west was on the Neosho River at the site of present-day Council Grove, Kansas. It was an important stop for Gen. Stephen W. Kearny (q.v.) as he moved along the trail in 1846, the first stage of his campaign for New Mexico (q.v.).

COUTO, JOSE BERNARDO (1803–1862). A prominent Mexican lawyer, José Bernardo Couto was a member of the commission appointed to negotiate a peace settlement with U.S. agent Nicholas Trist (q.v.). The talks eventually led to the signing of the Treaty of Guadalupe Hidalgo (q.v.). Following the war, Couto had a distinguished career as an author and promoter of the arts.

COYOACAN, DISTRITO FEDERAL. In 1847, Coyoacán was a small settlement in the Valley of Mexico on the road between San Antonio (q.v.) and Tacubaya (q.v.), north of the pedregal (q.v.). As the American army approached Mexico City, Coyoacán was defended by Gen. Francisco Pérez (q.v.) with 3,500 men, a situation that influenced conditions during the battles of Contreras and Churubusco (q.v.). Following the fall of Churubusco, Gen. Winfield Scott (q.v.) moved his headquarters to Coyoacán in preparation for the next phase of the attack against Mexico City.

CRIOLLA. The Criolla was a Mexican schooner involved with blockade running from the port of Veracruz (q.v.) and also engaged in spy activity under the guidance of Commo. David

Conner (q.v.). The *Criolla* was burned on November 26, 1846, by the brig USS *Somers*.

CRITTENDEN, JOHN JORDAN (1787–1863). John J. Crittenden was a Whig (q.v.) senator from Kentucky who in 1842 pressured the Tyler administration to take action against Mexico following the arrest of his son, who had participated in a Texas raid against the town of Mier (q.v.). The incident led to a deterioration of relations between the two countries. In the course of the war, however, Crittenden adhered to a policy of limiting the territorial acquisitions that might be gained in the settlement with Mexico.

CRITTENDEN, THOMAS LEONIDAS (1819–1893). Following the capture of Monterrey (q.v.) in September 1846, Gen. Zachary Taylor (q.v.) was concerned that a supply link be retained between that forward position and Camargo (q.v.) on the San Juan River. Thomas L. Crittenden, a civilian volunteer, played an important role in keeping that line of communication open.

CROCKETT, DAVID (1786–1836). Raised in the frontier country of eastern Tennessee, David ("Davy") Crockett won fame as a hunter, Indian fighter, and friend of the common man. He fought in the Creek Wars and rose to the rank of colonel in the militia. Elected to the U.S. House of Representatives despite a lack of formal education, Crockett opposed Pres. Andrew Jackson's policy of Indian removal. Defeated for reelection to Congress in 1835, he moved to Texas just as its movement for independence was under way. With the invasion of the new republic by Gen. Antonio López de Santa Anna (q.v.) in 1836, Crockett moved to San Antonio (q.v.) to join a small band of defenders at the Alamo (q.v.). He was killed in the course of the battle, thus adding to the many legends surrounding his career.

CROSS, OSBORN (1803–1876). Maj. Osborn Cross was U.S. quartermaster in Veracruz (q.v.) at the time of the Treaty of Guadalupe Hidalgo (q.v.). He played a key role in organizing the evacuation of troops and equipment.

CROSS, TRUEMAN (d. 1846). By early 1846, Col. Trueman Cross was chief quartermaster in charge of supplies of the Army of Occupation (q.v.) at Corpus Christi (q.v.). On April 10, 1846, Cross was killed during a horseback ride on the north bank of the Rio Grande (q.v.), leading to increased tensions with Mexican elements along the river. In the search for his body Lt. Theodoric Porter's patrol was ambushed and Porter himself killed. These incidents helped to increase tensions on both sides in the weeks leading up to the outbreak of war.

CUEVAS, LUIS GONZAGO (1800–1867). Luis G. Cuevas was Mexican foreign minister under the government of Pres. José Joaquín Herrera (q.v.). In 1845, he negotiated with British envoy Charles Elliot (q.v.) relating to the independence of Texas, but that scheme fell through. On February 2, 1848, Cuevas met with Nicholas Trist (q.v.) at Guadalupe Hidalgo (q.v.) to sign the preliminary agreement to end the war.

CULLUM, GEORGE W. A graduate of West Point in 1833, Lt. George W. Cullum rose to the rank of captain in the engineers (q.v.) by 1838. During the war with Mexico, he was at West Point involved with the training of cadets in the field of engineering. During the American Civil War, he was brevetted brigadier general in the U.S. Volunteers, and was brevetted major general in 1865 for meritorious service. Retiring in 1874 at age 62, Cullum prepared the *Biographical Register of the Officers and Graduates of the U.S. Military Academy* in 1891.

CUMBERLAND. The USS *Cumberland* was the flagship of Commo. David Conner (q.v.) that, on July 28, 1846, ran aground off Antón Lizardo (q.v.), which brought the cancellation of plans to attack the Mexican port of Alvarado (q.v.). Commo. Matthew C. Perry (q.v.) later used the *Cumberland* as his flagship.

CURTIS, SAMUEL RYAN (1805–1866). A graduate of the West Point class of 1826, Samuel R. Curtis was appointed adjutant general for Ohio and organized three volunteer infantry regiments. As a colonel, Curtis took command of the Third Ohio Regiment and departed for Mexico on July 3, 1846. After reaching the Rio Grande (q.v.), his regiment did not join the forces of Gen. Zachary Taylor (q.v.) moving against Monterrey (q.v.) but remained in Matamoros (q.v.) and later Camargo (q.v.), guarding the line of supply and attempting to maintain order over the highly volatile civilian and military population. In February 1847, Curtis expressed fear that General Taylor had been defeated by the superior force of Antonio López de Santa Anna (q.v.) and appealed to the governor of Texas to raise additional forces to meet the threat. The voice of alarm sounded by Curtis was criticized by many political leaders, including President Polk (q.v.), and has remained a stigma against the Ohio officer.

CUSHING, CALEB (1800–1879). Caleb Cushing, a political leader in Massachusetts at the time of the outbreak of the war with Mexico, raised a regiment in spite of strong political opposition to the conflict in his state. Promoted to the rank of brigadier general, he served under Gen. John E. Wool (q.v.) in Coahuila (q.v.) and was later transferred to Mexico City (q.v.) after the fall of that capital. Cushing was appointed as a member of the Court of Inquiry in the dispute between Gen. Winfield Scott (q.v.) and his subordinates, including Gen. William Worth (q.v.) and Gen. Gideon Pillow (q.v.), which met in Mexico City April 13–22, 1848.

CUYLTI, GAVINO. Col. Gavino Cuylti was commander of the Mexican military force in El Paso (q.v.) at the time of the approach of the American army under Col. Alexander Doniphan (q.v.) in December 1846. Cuylti turned over command to Lt. Col. Luis Vidal, however, and fled to Chihuahua (q.v.). Doniphan marched into El Paso without opposition.

CYANE. The sloop of war USS Cyane, commanded by Capt. William Mervine (q.v.), moved from Mazatlán (q.v.) February 22, 1846, and became involved with the complex operations along the coast of California. Later, under the command of Comdr. Samuel F. DuPont (q.v.), the Cyane was involved in the efforts to expel Brig. Gen. José María Castro (q.v.) from southern California. Gen. Stephen Kearny (q.v.) also used the sloop in January 1847 in his California campaigns.

D

DALE. The USS Dale was a ship involved in Pacific blockading operations (q.v.) under Comdr. T. A. Selfridge (q.v.) between November 1847 and April 1848. Selfridge carried out a series of assaults near Guaymas (q.v.), forcing the abandonment of Mexican bases near that port.

DALLAS, GEORGE M. (1792–1864). George M. Dallas was elected vice president in 1844 on the Democratic ticket with James K. Polk (q.v.). Although attending most cabinet meetings, the vice president seemed to have little influence on policy in the course of the war with Mexico. In late 1847, however, Dallas expressed support for the annexation of extensive Mexican territory by the United States.

DAVENPORT, WILLIAM (d. 1858). On July 23, 1848, following the end of hostilities between the United States and Mexico, Col. William Davenport assumed command of the Army of Occupation (q.v.) from Gen. John Wool (q.v.) near the Rio Grande (q.v.). He transferred the headquarters from Mexico to Fort Brown (q.v.), an important step in the formation of the Texas city of Brownsville (q.v.).

DAVIDSON, JOHN W. (1823–1881). Upon his graduation from West Point in 1845, Lt. John W. Davidson joined the First Dragoons and was assigned to duty at Fort Leavenworth, Kansas (q.v.). As a member of the Army of the West (q.v.), he marched with Gen. Stephen W. Kearny (q.v.) to California, participating in the skirmishes at San Pascual (q.v.) and San Gabriel (q.v.). Following the Treaty of Guadalupe Hidalgo (q.v.), Davidson remained in California, carrying out a variety of military duties in the western United States. During the American Civil War, he rose to the rank of brigadier general in the U.S. Army and fought in a number of engagements, primarily in the western theater of the war.

DAVIS, GARRETT (1801–1872). Garrett Davis was a Whig (q.v.) member of the House of Representatives from Kentucky who rejected Pres. James K. Polk's (q.v.) claim that the Rio Grande (q.v.) was the historic boundary between Mexico and the United States. He voted against the declaration of war with Mexico, and denounced moves by the United States into California and New Mexico.

DAVIS, JEFFERSON (1808–1889). Jefferson Davis was a native of Mississippi, a graduate of the U.S. Military Academy, and son-in-law of Gen. Zachary Taylor (q.v.). As commander of the Mississippi Rifles, Colonel Davis saw limited action during the battle of Monterrey (q.v.), but at the battle of Buena Vista (q.v.) his regiment was praised for its discipline and effective fire, and Davis gained a reputation for bravery and leadership. Following the war he entered politics, was elected U.S. senator from Mississippi, and later served as secretary of war under Pres.

Franklin Pierce. Following the secession of the southern states, Davis was elected president of the Confederacy.

DAVIS, JOHN (1787–1854). John Davis was a Whig senator from Massachusetts, and on May 13, 1846, cast one of the two votes against the War Message of President James K. Polk (q.v.). He also filibustered against the military appropriations bill that same year.

DEAS, EDWARD (1812–1849). Lt. Edward Deas, a graduate of the West Point class of 1832, conducted a dangerous mission in the course of the battle for Monterrey (q.v.). With a detachment of some 50 artillerymen, he carried a dismantled 12-pound howitzer up Independence Hill (q.v.) and used it against the Mexican position at the Bishop's Palace (q.v.). On May 16, 1849, he drowned in the Rio Grande (q.v.).

DE CASTRO, BERMUDEZ. Bermudez de Castro was Spanish minister to Mexico at the time of the invasion of that country by the U.S. army. Following the battle of Churubusco (q.v.), Antonio López de Santa Anna (q.v.) attempted to get him to help establish a truce with Gen. Winfield Scott (q.v.), but the minister refused.

DE LA ROSA, LUIS. Luis de la Rosa was minister of foreign relations in the Mexican government of interim president Manuel de la Peña y Peña (q.v.) after the fall of Mexico City (q.v.) to the United States. Nicholas Trist (q.v.) carried out negotiations with de la Rosa, which eventually led to the Treaty of Guadalupe Hidalgo (q.v.).

DE LA VEGA, ROMULO DIAZ. See DIAZ DE LA VEGA, ROMULO.

DERUSSY, LEWIS G. Col. Lewis G. DeRussy commanded some 300 Louisiana volunteers whose transport grounded on February 1, 1847, about 40 miles south of Tampico (q.v.). DeRussy escaped by setting campfires and marching off under cover of darkness. Later he led an unsuccessful attempt to free American captives at the town of Huejutla, near Tampico.

DESERTERS. At the beginning of the war with Mexico, some of the United States forces deserted their units. Many were recent immigrants to the United States, and most seemed to have been

Roman Catholics, though not a majority were Irish, as has often been charged. The most famous deserters joined the Mexican army as members of the San Patricio Battalion (q.v.). They fought bravely for Mexico in a number of battles. Many members of the battalion were taken prisoner at the battle of Churubusco (q.v.) and tried by military court, and several were executed. According to official statistics, 9,207 men deserted the U.S. ranks during the course of the war (5,331 regulars and 3,876 volunteers).

DIABLO. *See* FORT DIABLO.

DIAZ DE LA VEGA, ROMULO (1804–1877). Brig. Gen. Rómulo Díaz de la Vega fought at the Alamo (q.v.) against the Texas rebellion and in 1838 opposed the French attack on Veracruz. As Gen. Zachary Taylor (q.v.) marched south from Corpus Christi (q.v.), Díaz was second in command to Brig. Gen. Francisco Mejía (q.v.) in Matamoros (q.v.). He initiated talks with Gen. William Worth (q.v.) before the outbreak of hostilities, but with no positive result. The general commanded a brigade in the battles of Palo Alto (q.v.) and Resaca de la Palma (q.v.), being captured in the latter conflict, along with members of his staff. Later released in an exchange of prisoners, General Díaz joined the force of General Santa Anna (q.v.) opposing the invasion from Veracruz (q.v.) and commanded an artillery battery at the battle of Cerro Gordo (q.v.). He was again captured and placed in San Juan de Ulúa (q.v.) and later the fortress at Perote (q.v.). Díaz later fought in Yucatán against the Mayan uprising known as the Caste War (q.v.). Following the French intervention, he supported the empire of Maximilian.

DIAZ MIRON, PEDRO. Pedro Díaz Mirón was a naval commander (*capitán de fragata*) in August 1846 at Alvarado (q.v.) when that port was attacked by Commo. David Conner (q.v.).

DICKINSON, DANIEL S. (1800–1866). Daniel S. Dickinson, a Democratic senator from New York, was a strong supporter of the annexation of extensive Mexican territory.

DICKINSON, JOHN P. (d. 1847). Lt. Col. John P. Dickinson of the South Carolina volunteers (Palmetto Regiment) was killed in the battle of Churubusco (q.v.), August 20, 1847.

DIMICK, JUSTIN (1800–1871). Maj. Justin Dimick, West Point class of 1819, participated in the battles of Palo Alto (q.v.) and

Resaca de la Palma (q.v.). He then shifted to the army of Gen. Winfield Scott (q.v.) and was placed temporarily in command of the brigade of Gen. Persifor Smith (q.v.) during the battle of Contreras (q.v.). Dimick continued to play an important role at Churubusco (q.v.) and was wounded at Chapultepec (q.v.). He commanded the garrison at Veracruz (q.v.) in 1847 and 1848.

DIMOND, FRANCIS M. Francis M. Dimond, a native of Rhode Island, was U.S. consul in Veracruz (q.v.) at the time of the mission to Mexico by John Slidell (q.v.) and sent a warning to Pres. James K. Polk (q.v.) that the envoy would most likely be rejected by Mexican authorities. With the declaration of war, Dimond left Veracruz and supplied valuable information on the port and its facilities before the expedition under Gen. Winfield Scott (q.v.). Later Scott sent Dimond to Havana to assist in the recruiting of agents for intelligence work in Mexico.

DOBBINS, STEPHEN D. Lt. Stephen D. Dobbins was involved with early scouting action along the Rio Grande (q.v.) before the outbreak of hostilities. At the battle of Resaca de la Palma (q.v.), Dobbins performed heroically, drawing enemy fire to locate gun emplacements.

DODSON, JACOB. Jacob Dodson was an African-American servant of Capt. John C. Frémont (q.v.) who in March 1847 accompanied the pathfinder on a 400-mile journey from Los Angeles to Monterey, California (q.v.), in less than three and one-half days.

DOMINGUEZ, MANUEL. Manuel Dominguez was the Mexican commander of a spy company in the U.S. Army. At the end of the war, he and a number of his followers settled in New Orleans.

DONA ANA, NEW MEXICO. Doña Ana is a small settlement on the Rio Grande (q.v.), north of the present-day city of Las Cruces, New Mexico. In December 1846, it was a rendezvous point for the army of Col. Alexander Doniphan (q.v.) after it crossed the *Jornada del Muerto* (q.v.), on the way to El Paso (q.v.).

DONELSON, ANDREW JACKSON (1799–1871). Andrew Jackson ("Jack") Donelson was a nephew of Pres. Andrew Jackson and a friend of Texas president Sam Houston (q.v.). He was appointed U.S. chargé to the Republic of Texas and worked to gain the approval of that republic's annexation to the United States by President Anson Jones (q.v.) in March 1845. Although facing strong efforts by British chargé Charles Elliot (q.v.) to block the plan, the Texas congress supported annexation, and it was finalized by the action of a convention on July 4, 1845.

DONIPHAN, ALEXANDER WILLIAM (1808–1887). A lawyer by training, Col. Alexander Doniphan was chosen commander of the First Missouri Mounted Volunteers, a part of Kearny's Army of the West (q.v.). His force set out from Fort Leavenworth (q.v.) in late June 1846, marched over 850 miles, and reached Santa Fe (q.v.) on August 18. Doniphan helped draft a code of law for the newly acquired territory of New Mexico and carried out a series of campaigns into Navajo country. In December 1846, he brought his volunteers together at Valverde, New Mexico, and initiated a march to El Paso (q.v.) and eventually to Chihuahua City (q.v.). He defeated a Mexican force at Brazito (q.v.) on Christmas Day of 1846 and occupied El Paso two days later. On February 8, 1847, Doniphan resumed his march south and, following a victory over a superior Mexican force in the battle of Sacramento (q.v.), February 28, 1847, occupied Chihuahua. The Missourians eventually traveled overland to Monterrey, Nuevo León (q.v.), and then to the mouth of the Rio Grande (q.v.), having marched some 2,000 miles over very rugged territory. They embarked for New Orleans and eventually reached Missouri in June 1847.

DOYLE, PERCY W. Percy W. Doyle was appointed British minister to Mexico in 1847. He arrived in the war-torn capital in December, advising Pres. Antonio Peña y Peña (q.v.) to name a commission to treat with the U.S. envoy Nicholas Trist (q.v.).

DRAGOONS. Dragoons, or mounted infantry, played an important part in many phases of the war between the United States and Mexico. Sometimes lacking the romantic flair of cavalry units, which were more mobile, the dragoons often fought on foot and utilized their horses or mules as both personal mounts and draft animals.

DRUM, SIMON H. (1807–1847). Capt. Simon Drum participated in the siege of Veracruz (q.v.) and the battle of Cerro Gordo (q.v.). He was a member of the Fourth Artillery at the battle of Contreras (q.v.) and, during that battle, assisted in the recapture of two artillery pieces that had been taken by the Mexicans at Buena Vista (q.v.). Captain Drum employed those two guns effectively during the battle of Molino del Rey (q.v.), September 8, 1847. He also played an important role during the assault on Mexico City (q.v.) following the capture of Chapultepec (q.v.), but he was killed during the advance into Mexico City near the Belén Gate (q.v.).

DUNCAN, JAMES (1813–1849). A West Point graduate in the class of 1834, Capt. James Duncan was an artillery commander with the army of Gen. Zachary Taylor (q.v.) that moved from Corpus Christi (q.v.) to the Rio Grande (q.v.) in March 1846. Duncan's light artillery battery was especially effective in the battle of Palo Alto (q.v.), May 8, 1846, and, along with that of Maj. Samuel Ringgold (q.v.), was largely responsible for the American victory. Duncan continued to provide outstanding support fire at Resaca de la Palma (q.v.), during Taylor's march against Monterrey (q.v.), and then in the battle for that key city. In March 1847, having been promoted to lieutenant colonel, Duncan joined Gen. Winfield Scott (q.v.) in the landing at Veracruz (q.v.) and the march on Mexico City (q.v.). He fought at Cerro Gordo (q.v.) and played an important role in the campaign for the Valley of Mexico, especially in the battles of Churubusco (q.v.) and Molino del Rey (q.v.). Following the American occupation of Mexico City, Colonel Duncan joined with Gen. Gideon Pillow (q.v.) and Gen. William Worth (q.v.) in their denunciation of Gen. Winfield Scott and was placed under arrest.

DUPONT, SAMUEL FRANCIS (1803–1865). Comdr. Samuel F. DuPont was in command of the USS *Cyane* (q.v.) off the coast of California in the summer of 1846. He transferred the small force of John C. Frémont (q.v.) to San Diego (q.v.) in July of that year to attack the army of Brig. Gen. José María Castro (q.v.). In August and September, Dupont commanded the *Cyane* in operations in the Gulf of California and along the coast of Sonora. In February 1847, he led a landing party at San José del Cabo, Baja California (q.v.), rescuing an American force that had been under siege there. He continued to carry out blockading activities (q.v.) in the Pacific area in the latter months of the conflict. DuPont was promoted to the rank of rear admiral of the U.S. Navy during the Civil War.

E

EARLY, JUBAL ANDERSON (1816–1894). Maj. Jubal Early, a graduate of the West Point class of 1837, served with the First Virginia Volunteers in the Army of Chihuahua (q.v.) under Gen. John Wool (q.v.). From May to June 1847, Early served as acting governor of Monterrey (q.v.) and also as acting inspector-general in the brigade of Gen. Caleb Cushing (q.v.). In July 1848, he brought charges against his superior, Col. John F. Hamtramck, charging that he had abandoned his post without authorization. During the American Civil War, Early became a general officer of the Confederacy.

EASTON, ALTON R. Col. Alton R. Easton commanded a St. Louis volunteer unit that joined Gen. Zachary Taylor (q.v.) on the lower Rio Grande (q.v.) in the spring of 1846.

EATON, JOSEPH H. (1816–1896). Capt. Joseph H. Eaton fought in the battles of Palo Alto (q.v.), Resaca de la Palma (q.v.), and Monterrey (q.v.). Following the last of those encounters, Eaton carried the message from Gen. Zachary Taylor (q.v.) to Pres. James K. Polk (q.v.) relating the capture of the city, arriving in Washington, D.C., on October 11, 1846. Returning to northern Mexico, Eaton fought in the battle of Buena Vista, being brevetted lieutenant colonel for that action.

ECHAGARAY, DOMINGO (1803–1854). Col. Domingo Echagaray was Mexican commander of Tabasco (q.v.) on June 15, 1847, when it was attacked by an American force commanded by Commo. Matthew C. Perry (q.v.). He withdrew upstream to Tamulté, thus leaving Tabasco in control of the U.S. naval force. Following the war, Echagaray was named governor and commanding general of the state of Michoacán by Santa Anna (q.v.). He was killed in 1854 during an attack against the governor's palace.

ECHEAGARAY, MIGUEL MARIA (1816–1891). Lt. Col. Miguel María Echeagaray commanded the Third Light Infantry of the Mexican army. He led a counterattack from Chapultepec (q.v.) during the battle of Molino del Rey (q.v.), inflicting major losses on the column of Maj. George Wright (q.v.).

EDSON, ALVIN. Capt. Alvin Edson commanded a detachment of 180 U.S. Marines in the landing at Veracruz (q.v.).

EDWARDS, JOHN C. At the outbreak of the war with Mexico, Gov. John C. Edwards of Missouri acted quickly to add a force of 1,000 mounted volunteers to the army of Gen. Stephen F. Kearny (q.v.). He continued to support the war effort by sending Missouri troops to serve in the struggle.

EL BOSQUE DE SANTO DOMINGO. On his arrival on the northern outskirts of Monterrey (q.v.), September 1846, Gen. Zachary Taylor (q.v.) established his camp at the Bosque de Santo Domingo, a location that came to be called Walnut Springs by the Americans. *See also* MONTERREY, BATTLE OF.

EL ECO DEL COMERCIO. The Spanish-language newspaper *El Eco del Comercio,* published in Mexico City (q.v.) during the occupation by the army of Gen. Winfield Scott (q.v.), was strongly in favor of a peaceful settlement between the two warring nations.

EL ENCERO, VERACRUZ. El Encero (or Lincero) is a beautiful hacienda on the eastern outskirts of Jalapa, Veracruz (q.v.), on the National Highway (q.v.) to Cerro Gordo (q.v.). Established during the 16th century by Spanish conquistadors, by 1847 the hacienda had been acquired by Gen. Antonio López de Santa Anna (q.v.) who used it as a personal retreat before the battle of Cerro Gordo (q.v.). Following the battle, U.S. troops occupied the hacienda and found a considerable treasure, along with the wooden leg of the defeated Mexican commander.

EL PASO, CHIHUAHUA (TEXAS). In 1846, El Paso was a town of some 10,000 inhabitants, located on the south side of the Rio Grande (q.v.) in the present-day Mexican state of Chihuahua (q.v.). Following the battle of Brazito (q.v.), the volunteers of Col. Alexander Doniphan (q.v.) marched into El Paso on December 27, 1846, finding the inhabitants friendly and the supply of food and wine abundant. Doniphan remained there until early February 1847, at which time he resumed his march south toward Chihuahua (q.v.) City. Later in the war, El Paso was the site of additional operations by Col. Sterling Price (q.v.). In the Treaty of Guadalupe Hidalgo (q.v.), Mexico retained the city, but within a short time the United States established a settlement on the north side of the river. The Mexican town was eventually renamed Ciudad Juárez, and the name El Paso was retained by the Texas city.

EL PENON, DISTRITO FEDERAL. El Peñón ("the craggy rock") was an abrupt hill jutting out of the flat marshlands of the Valley of Mexico, north of Lake Chalco (q.v.). On August 10, 1847, General Santa Anna (q.v.) established his headquarters there and assigned command of the strong point to Gen. Pedro María de Anaya (q.v.) of the national guard. After hearing reports from his engineers and discussing the situation with his staff, Gen. Winfield Scott (q.v.) chose to avoid El Peñón and moved around Lake Chalco to attack Mexico City from the south. Presently called Peñón Viejo, the hill is on the eastern outskirts of Mexico City.

EL SOLDADO. El Soldado was a fortified position on the eastern end of Federation Hill (q.v.), south of the Santa Catarina River, a part of the defensive system guarding the city of Monterrey, Nuevo León (q.v.), at the time of Gen. Zachary Taylor's (q.v.) attack against that town. On September 21, 1846, elements of Gen. William Worth's (q.v.) Second Division overran the position, thus leading to the capture of Independence Hill (q.v.), north of the Santa Catarina River. See also MONTERREY, BATTLE OF.

EL TELEGRAFO. see TELEGRAPH HILL.

ELLIOT, CHARLES (1801–1875). When Great Britain extended diplomatic recognition to the Republic of Texas in 1841, Capt. Charles Elliot was appointed as chargé d'affaires to the new government. From the time of his arrival on August 23, 1842, Elliot attempted to convince the Texas authorities to reject annexation by the United States, making every effort to persuade the Mexican government to extend recognition to Texas, with the stipulation that the republic would remain independent. Elliot seemed to have considerable influence with Texas president Anson Jones (q.v.) who was inaugurated December 9, 1844, but when the Mexican government refused to embrace his plan, the Texans accepted the offer from Washington, thus defeating Elliot's persistent efforts.

EMORY, WILLIAM HEMSLEY (1811–1887). A graduate of West Point in 1831, Lt. William H. Emory commanded a small unit of topographical engineers that accompanied Gen. Stephen W. Kearny (q.v.) on his march from Fort Leavenworth (q.v.) to New Mexico (q.v.) and eventually to California (q.v.). He served as assistant adjutant general to Kearny and participated in the battle of San Pascual (q.v.) and other skirmishes in California. Emory's notes serve as one of the important sources of information on that phase of the war. He later headed the commission established to survey the boundary between the United States and Mexico.

ENCANTADA, COAHUILA. On receiving reports in late December 1846 that the Mexican army of General Santa Anna (q.v.) was marching north from San Luis Potosí (q.v.), Gen. John E. Wool (q.v.) occupied the small village of Encantada. Wool eventually withdrew north to the area of Angostura Pass (q.v.) to await the Mexican attack. *See also* BUENA VISTA, BATTLE OF.

ENCARNACION, COAHUILA. On January 22, 1847, a cavalry unit of some 50 Arkansas volunteers under Maj. Solon Borland (q.v.) and a small patrol of Kentucky horsemen occupied the hacienda of Encarnación, approximately 30 miles south of Angostura (q.v.) Pass in Coahuila. Failing to post a guard during the night, Borland and his men were surprised the following morning by a large Mexican army and were forced to surrender. Following the battle of Buena Vista (q.v.), the hacienda was used by the retreating force of Santa Anna (q.v.) as a station for the care of the wounded.

ENGINEERS. The engineers were the most prestigious branch of the U.S. Army at the time of the Mexican-American War. Top graduates from West Point, including Robert E. Lee (q.v.), P. G. T. Beauregard (q.v.), George McClellan (q.v.), and George G. Meade (q.v.), entered that field. The Corps of Engineers had the mission of constructing fortifications and building bridges; these duties were carried out by units of sappers, miners, and pontoniers (q.v.). Topographical engineers, called "topogs," were primarily responsible for conducting surveys and preparing maps, but they were also construction engineers, working primarily on civil projects rather than military fortifications. Congress created an independent Corps of Topographical Engineers in 1838, appointing Col. John James Abert (q.v.) as its head. Both the Corps of Engineers and the Corps of Topographical Engineers came under the chief engineer, who was a member of the executive staff of the secretary of war. The Engineer Department also had the responsibility of administering the U.S. Military Academy.

    With the declaration of war with Mexico, Congress created a company of "engineer soldiers" to be a part of the Corps of

Engineers, consisting of 10 sergeants, 10 corporals, 2 musicians, and 78 privates. This company was assigned to Gen. Zachary Taylor (q.v) in northeastern Mexico but was later shifted to the command of Gen. Winfield Scott (q.v.). Throughout the campaigns from Veracruz (q.v.) to the Valley of Mexico (q.v.), the engineers made valuable contributions. Officers of both the Corps of Engineers and the Corps of Topographical Engineers performed reconnaissance missions and on several occasions led units into combat. The actions of Capt. Robert E. Lee were singled out for the highest praise by General Scott. The engineers made a significant contribution to the success of the armies of the United States. *See also* ABERT, JOHN JAMES; SMITH, GUSTAVUS WOODSON; SWIFT, ALEXANDER J.

ENGLE, FREDERICK. Comdr. Frederick Engle commanded the steamer USS *Princeton*, which was assigned to the Home Squadron (q.v.) in the Gulf of Mexico (q.v.), serving under Commo. David Conner (q.v.).

ENTERPRISE. The steamer USS *Enterprise* transported the Seventh Infantry, commanded by Capt. Dixon Miles (q.v.), the first U.S. forces to move from Matamoros (q.v.) to Camargo (q.v.) in the early stages of the campaign against Monterrey, Nuevo León (q.v.). The ship departed on July 6, 1846, reaching Camargo (q.v.) eight days later.

EWELL, RICHARD STODDERT (1817–1872). A graduate of West Point in 1840, Lt. Richard S. Ewell served in the dragoons (q.v.) of Col. William S. Harney (q.v.). He fought in the siege of Veracruz (q.v.), the battle of Cerro Gordo (q.v.) and in the various actions in the Valley of Mexico (q.v.). Following the battle of Churubusco (q.v.), Ewell accompanied Capt. Philip Kearny (q.v.) to the walls of Mexico City and was brevetted captain following that action. During the American Civil War, Ewell commanded a corps in Gen. Robert E. Lee's Army of Northern Virginia.

F

FALCON, BLAS. Blas Falcón was a guerrilla leader in the region of northeastern Mexico who disrupted the supply lines of Gen. Zachary Taylor (q.v.) during his move from the Rio Grande (q.v.) to Monterrey (q.v.). Falcón was also accused of the murder of Col. Trueman Cross (q.v.) in April 1846, an event that set the stage for the declaration of war.

FALCON, MANUEL. Col. Manuel Falcón was a guerrilla leader in the region between Puebla (q.v.) and Mexico City (q.v.). On February 8, 1848, he clashed with the American force of Gen. Joseph Lane (q.v.).

FALMOUTH. The USS *Falmouth* was a sloop of war operating in the Gulf of Mexico, commanded by Comdr. Joseph R. Jarvis (q.v.) in the early days of the war. It played an important role in the establishment of the blockade against Veracruz (q.v.) and Alvarado (q.v.).

FARIAS, VALENTIN GOMEZ. *See* GOMEZ FARIAS, VALENTIN.

FAUNTLEROY, DAINGERFIELD. On July 8, 1846, Daingerfield Fauntleroy, purser with the U.S. naval force in California, organized a company to patrol the region around Monterey, California (q.v.). He marched to San Juan Bautista on July 16, 1846, to join the force of Lt. John C. Frémont (q.v.).

FEDERATION HILL. Federation Hill is a long rocky ridge to the south of the Santa Catarina River, just west of Monterrey, Nuevo León (q.v.). Gen. Pedro de Ampudia (q.v.) fortified the position, but it was taken on September 21, 1846, by the forces of Gen. William Worth (q.v.), opening the way for the fall of Monterrey to Gen. Zachary Taylor (q.v.). *See also* MONTERREY, BATTLE OF.

FERRO, JOSE. Lt. Col. José Ferro commanded the *Activos* unit of Aguascalientes, in the defense of Monterrey, Nuevo León (q.v.), against the American invasion in September 1846. His unit defended a position at the Purísima Bridge, one of the most effective actions in the Mexican plan. *See also* MONTE-RREY, BATTLE OF.

FISCHER, WALDEMAR. At the outbreak of the war with Mexico, Capt. Waldemar Fischer was selected as commander of a battery of light artillery in St. Louis, Missouri. Consisting of two companies, one "American" and the other "German," Fischer's battery moved from Fort Leavenworth, Kansas (q.v.). in June 1846 as a part of Gen. Stephen W. Kearny's Army of the West (q.v.).

FITZHUGH, ANDREW. At the beginning of the outbreak of hostilities with Mexico in the spring of 1846, Capt. Andrew Fitzhugh commanded the USS *Mississippi* in the Gulf of Mexico. On May 20, 1846, he proclaimed the blockade of Veracruz (q.v.) and Alvarado (q.v.).

FITZPATRICK, TOM. On October 6, 1846, near Socorro, New Mexico, Gen. Stephen W. Kearny (q.v.) met the famous guide Christopher "Kit" Carson (q.v.) returning from California to his home in New Mexico. Kearny persuaded Carson to guide him to California, while Tom Fitzpatrick, a member of the Army of the West (q.v.), turned back to Santa Fe (q.v.) with dispatches relating to events in California.

FLORES, JOSE MARIA (1818–1866). On September 24, 1846, Capt. José María Flores took command of the Californio (q.v.) forces at La Mesa (q.v.) and attacked the U.S. position in Los Angeles (q.v.). Successful in that effort, Flores then defeated other American forces in southern California and carried out raids throughout the rest of the year. On January 6, 1847, he ambushed the small force of Commo. Robert Stockton (q.v.) on the San Gabriel River, but the battle of San Gabriel (q.v.) ended in a victory for Stockton, opening the way for his occupation of Los Angeles. Following these events, Flores resigned his post and moved south to Sonora. In 1851, he led a military force into the Gila River (q.v.) region to expel U.S. intruders, and opposed the filibuster raids of William Walker in northwestern Mexico in 1854.

FOREST, FRENCH (1796–1866). Capt. French Forest commanded the USS *Cumberland*, flagship of Commo. David Conner (q.v.), in the Home Squadron (q.v.) based at Antón Lizardo (q.v.). His ship ran aground in one of the early attempts to capture Alvarado (q.v.), thus aborting that mission. On October 16, 1846, Captain Forest led a landing party of 253 men from the anchorage at Antón Lizardo against Tabasco (q.v.). After a short while, however, the commander withdrew on orders of Commo. Matthew C. Perry (q.v.). On March 9, 1847, Captain Forest, commanding the frigate USS *Raritan*, supervised the ship-to-shore movement of Gen. Winfield Scott's (q.v.) invading army at Collado Beach (q.v.).

FORT BROWN. As Gen. Zachary Taylor (q.v.) moved to the north bank of the Rio Grande (q.v.) in late March 1846, he ordered

the construction of an earthen fortress opposite the city of Matamoros (q.v.). Designed by Capt. Joseph K. F. Mansfield (q.v.),
it was christened Fort Texas but also called Fort Taylor. When
General Taylor moved with most of his army to Point Isabel
(q.v.), he assigned Maj. Jacob Brown (q.v.) as commander of
the position. The fortress was almost complete when it was
brought under siege on May 1, 1846, by Gen. Mariano Arista
(q.v.). On May 3, Arista sent Gen. Pedro de Ampudia (q.v.).
against the position. Major Brown and his small garrison continued to hold their ground as the main American army under
Taylor returned from the coast to engage Arista at Palo Alto
(q.v.) and Resaca de la Palma (q.v.). In the course of the siege,
however, Major Brown was killed. On his return, General Taylor decreed that the position would be renamed Fort Brown in
honor of the fallen commander. Following the war, the city of
Brownsville, Texas (q.v.), grew up around the fort and developed into one of the most important commercial and cultural
towns along the newly established border.

FORT CONCEPCION. Fort Concepción formed a part of the fortifications guarding the city of Veracruz (q.v.). It was on the
north side of the city opposite San Juan de Ulúa (q.v.).

FORT DIABLO. Fort Diablo (Devil's Fort) was one of two fortifications constructed at the eastern side of Monterrey, Nuevo
León (q.v.), by Gen. Pedro de Ampudia (q.v.). The initial attack
against the position by the division of Col. John Garland (q.v.),
September 21, 1846, was repulsed by the defenders. On the following day, however, General Ampudia abandoned Fort Diablo, setting the stage for the final phase of the battle of
Monterrey. *See also* MONTERREY, BATTLE OF.

FORT JESUP, LOUISIANA. Established to guard the disputed
area west of the Sabine River (q.v.), Fort Jesup served as a training base for the army of Brig. Gen. Zachary Taylor (q.v.). Taylor's Army of Observation (q.v.) left Fort Jesup in June 1845 to
take up a forward position at Corpus Christi, Texas (q.v.).

FORT LEAVENWORTH, KANSAS. A fortified post on the west
bank of the Missouri River, Fort Leavenworth became the training ground and point of departure for most of the U.S. forces
that marched west to New Mexico (q.v.). This included the
Army of the West (q.v.) commanded by Col. Stephen W.

Kearny (q.v.), which departed from Leavenworth in June and July 1846.

FORT MARCY. Following the occupation of Santa Fe (q.v.), August 18, 1846, Gen. Stephen W. Kearny (q.v.) established a fortification on a hill overlooking the city, naming it Fort Marcy in honor of the secretary of war.

FORT PAREDES. As the army of Gen. Zachary Taylor (q.v.) took up its position along the Rio Grande (q.v.) opposite the city of Matamoros (q.v.), March 28, 1846, Gen. Pedro de Ampudia (q.v.) initiated construction of an earthen fortress, naming it Fort Paredes in honor of President Mariano Paredes y Arrillaga (q.v.) of Mexico.

FORT POLK, TEXAS. When Gen. Zachary Taylor (q.v.) reached Point Isabel (q.v.), north of the mouth of the Rio Grande (q.v.), he established a supply depot and ordered the construction of an earthen fortress for its defense. This position was named Fort Polk in honor of Pres. James K. Polk (q.v.).

FORT SAN JUAN DE ULUA. See SAN JUAN DE ULUA.

FORT SANTIAGO. Fort Santiago, located on the south side of Veracruz (q.v.), was one of the strong points in the defensive wall around that city.

FORT SOLDADO. See EL SOLDADO.

FORT TAYLOR, TEXAS. See FORT BROWN.

FORT TEXAS, TEXAS. See FORT BROWN.

FOSTER, JOHN GRAY (1823–1874). Lt. John G. Foster commanded a party of pioneers that assisted Capt. Robert E. Lee (q.v.) in cutting a path to the east of the Mexican position at Cerro Gordo (q.v.) on April 15, 1847. This set the stage for the victory of the army of Gen. Winfield Scott (q.v.) over Santa Anna (q.v.) in the battle of Cerro Gordo (q.v.).

FRANKLIN, WILLIAM BUEL (1823–1903). A graduate of the West Point class of 1843, Lt. William B. Franklin was an engineer with the Army of Chihuahua (q.v.), commanded by Gen. John Wool (q.v.). He played an important part in the crossing of the Rio Grande (q.v.) near the town of Presidio, October 12, 1846, and the march to Saltillo (q.v.). He was brevetted first lieutenant for his role in the battle of Buena Vista (q.v.).

FREANER, JAMES L. James L. Freaner was a correspondent who covered the Mexican War for the New Orleans *Delta*. He helped expose the exaggerated claims made by Gen. Gideon Pillow (q.v.) regarding his role in the battles in the Valley of Mexico. As a friend of Nicholas Trist (q.v.), Freaner was entrusted with taking the Treaty of Guadalupe Hidalgo (q.v.) to Washington, reaching the capital on February 19, 1848.

FREMONT, JESSIE BENTON (1824–1902). Jessie Benton, daughter of Sen. Thomas Hart Benton (q.v.), married Lt. John C. Frémont (q.v.) and became involved in a number of the clashes between her husband and the administration of Pres. James K. Polk (q.v.).

FREMONT, JOHN CHARLES (1813–1890). As a member of the Army Corps of Topographical Engineers, Lt. John C. Frémont was a flamboyant explorer who gained great popularity as the "Pathfinder." An advocate of Manifest Destiny (q.v.) and son-in-law of powerful Sen. Thomas Hart Benton (q.v.) of Missouri, Frémont enjoyed great political and popular appeal. Commissioned to explore the Arkansas and Red Rivers before the outbreak of war with Mexico, Frémont led a small force of men to Sutter's Fort, California (q.v.), arriving on December 9, 1845. Defying Mexican authority, he raised the U.S. flag near Monterey (q.v.) but, in the face of a superior force, retreated toward Oregon in March 1846. He returned to California within a few months, joining an insurrection near San Francisco known as the Bear Flag Revolt (q.v.) and declaring the independence of California on July 4, 1846. The Bear Flag was soon replaced by the Stars and Stripes. Commanding the California Battalion with the rank of captain, Frémont carried out a number of military engagements against Mexican authorities in cooperation with the naval force of Commo. Robert Stockton (q.v.). They succeeded in gaining control over much of the vast region of Upper California. On January 16, 1847, Stockton named Frémont as governor of California, an action that placed the intrepid captain in the middle of a dispute between Stockton and Gen. Stephen Kearny (q.v.). After Stockton was replaced by Commo. William Branford Shubrick (q.v.), Kearny brought charges against Frémont. Despite strong political influence by

Senator Benton, President Polk (q.v.) carried out the court-martial against Frémont in November 1847; the captain was found guilty of disobedience and misconduct and dismissed from the service. The sentence was set aside by the president, but Frémont resigned his commission in early 1848. He continued to play an important role in national politics, and was nominated as the first Republican candidate for president in 1856.

FRONTERA, TABASCO. The small village of Frontera, located near the mouth of the Usumacinta River, was occupied on October 23, 1846, by a naval force led by Commo. Matthew C. Perry (q.v.), opening the way to the city of Villahermosa (called Tabasco by some U.S. sources). Frontera was later abandoned by Perry but on June 14, 1847, was taken for a second time and held, which thus closed Tabasco (q.v.) to Mexican commerce.

FRONTON DE SANTA ISABEL. Frontón de Santa Isabel (called Point Isabel by the U.S. forces) was burned by Mexican authorities in March 1846, on the approach of Gen. Zachary Taylor's Army of Occupation (q.v.). With the arrival of that force, Point Isabel became a major supply depot for the U.S. campaign into northeastern Mexico.

G

GAINES, EDMUND PENDLETON (1777–1849). Before the outbreak of war with Mexico, Brig. Gen. Edmund P. Gaines was commander of the U.S. Western Division, with headquarters in New Orleans. Concerned by the growing Mexican threat, Gaines issued a request for six-month volunteers from Louisiana and surrounding states. Secretary of War William L. Marcy (q.v.) canceled the order, but not before some of the short-term volunteers had gone to Texas to join Gen. Zachary Taylor (q.v.). These short-term recruits were of little assistance to Taylor and a great burden from a logistical standpoint. Gaines further complicated matters by advocating a call for 250 battalions of mounted men to be sent to Texas by November 1845, with himself in command. Following the outbreak of hostilities along the Rio Grande (q.v.), Gaines once again raised volunteers, some being sent to Point Isabel (q.v.) in May 1846. As in his previous action, no adequate preparation was made to take care of the supply and training of the troops. On June 2, 1846, Gaines was dismissed as commander of the Western Division, eventually found guilty of exceeding his authority by a court of inquiry. Meanwhile, he was reassigned as commander of the Eastern Division, centered in New York, and had no further involvement in the war with Mexico.

GAINES, JOHN P. (1795–1857). During the late days of January 1847, Maj. John P. Gaines joined Maj. Solon Borland (q.v.) in a reconnaissance action near Encarnación, Coahuila (q.v.). Gaines and Borland, with all their men, were surprised by a Mexican army and forced to surrender on January 23, 1847. This was one of the incidents that helped to warn Gen. Zachary Taylor (q.v.) of the growing threat from the army of General Santa Anna (q.v.) which was moving north from San Luis Potosí (q.v.). *See also* BUENA VISTA, BATTLE OF.

GALAXRA PASS. Galaxra Pass, near the city of Puebla (q.v.), was the scene of a clash between the American force of Brig. Gen. Joseph Lane (q.v.) and the Mexican guerrilla leader Gen. Joaquín Rea (q.v.) in November 1847.

GALLATIN, ALBERT (1761–1849). Albert Gallatin was a Democratic political leader who was strongly against the expansion of slavery, and therefore opposed to much of the Mexican policy of Pres. James K. Polk (q.v.).

GANDARA DE GORTARI, MANUEL MARIA (1801–1878). A son of Spanish parents who were expelled from Mexico after the movement for independence, Manuel María Gándara de Gortari remained in the northwestern region of Sonora, where he controlled the family hacienda and other properties. He became involved in the struggle against the Apache (q.v.) and other Indian groups and also played a role in the Mexican struggle between centralists and federalists. At the time of the U.S. push into northern Mexico in the fall of 1846, Gándara was governor of Sonora and organized the national guard in an effort to defend the state. At the time of the march of the Mormon Battalion (q.v.), however, there was no open hostility as the American force occupied Tucson. Gándara de Gortari continued in Mexican political affairs after the war and, during the empire, became an official under Maximilian. With the triumph of Benito Juárez, he was imprisoned but released in 1870.

GAONA, ANTONIO (1793–1848). Born in Havana, Cuba, Antonio Gaona went to Mexico as a Spanish soldier to oppose the movement for independence. In 1821, he joined the ranks of Agustín de Iturbide, however, and became the commander of San Juan de Ulúa (q.v.). Promoted to the rank of brigadier general, Gaona was in command of the force at Mexicalzingo (q.v.) at the time of the arrival of the army of Gen. Winfield Scott (q.v.) in the Valley of Mexico. *See also* CONTRERAS AND CHURUBUSCO, BATTLES OF.

GARCIA CONDE, JOSE MARIA (1801–1878). During the battle of Monterrey (q.v.), Brig. Gen. José María García Conde commanded two regiments of Mexican cavalry and was heavily involved in the fighting around the Purísima Bridge (q.v.). With the end of the battle, he served as one of the Mexican commissioners appointed by Gen. Pedro de Ampudia (q.v.) to negotiate the terms. In February 1847 García Conde was a cavalry commander in the army of General Santa Anna (q.v.) during the battle of Buena Vista (q.v.).

GARCIA CONDE, PEDRO (1806–1851). A native of Sonora, Pedro García Conde received his commission in Mexico City (q.v), then returned to fight against Indian uprisings in Chihuahua (q.v.). Rising to the rank of colonel by 1838, he served for six years as director of the national military college. As a brigadier general, García Conde was military commander in Chihuahua at the time of the march into that region by Col. Alexander Doniphan (q.v.). His army was defeated in the battle of Sacramento (q.v.), February 28, 1847, 15 miles north of the city of Chihuahua. With the defeat, García Conde fled the state. After the war, he served on the commission to define the boundary between the United States and Mexico and died while carrying out that duty.

GARITA. The Spanish term *garita* is usually translated into English as "sentry box." The Aztec city of Tenochtitlán was built on a low-lying island near the center of the Valley of Mexico (q.v.) and could be entered by a number of raised causeways. In Spanish colonial times, some of the marshlands were drained and certain lands recaptured from the lake, but most of the causeways continued to be utilized. *Garitas* (toll collection points) were established at key entrance points, thus also called "gates." Some were fortified and in effect a part of the defensive structure of the city. The most important *garitas* relating to the invasion by the army of the United States were San Cosmé (q.v.), Belén (q.v.), Niño Perdido (q.v.), and San Antonio (q.v.).

GARLAND, JOHN (d. 1861). Lt. Col. John Garland fought at Palo Alto (q.v.) and Resaca de la Palma (q.v.) and then served as a member of the army that occupied Matamoros (q.v.) in May 1846. He commanded a force of dragoons (q.v.) and Texas Rangers (q.v.) that fought against the Mexican army of Gen. Mariano Arista (q.v.). During the battle of Monterrey (q.v.), Garland assumed temporary command of Gen. David Twiggs's (q.v.) division but had little success in the assault against the city. Promoted to the rank of brevet colonel, Garland commanded a brigade during the march from Veracruz (q.v.) to Mexico City (q.v.) and was especially involved at the battles of Churubusco (q.v.) and Chapultepec (q.v.). During the occupation of Mexico City, he was severely wounded by fire from irregular elements in the city. See also CONTRERAS AND CHURUBUSCO, BATTLES OF.

GATES, WILLIAM (1788–1868). Col. William Gates was among the first cadets to enter the U.S. Military Academy and was commissioned in the artillery in 1806. He served in a number of campaigns during the War of 1812 and rose to the rank of lieutenant colonel while participating in the campaigns against Indians of the southeastern United States and on the western frontier between 1815 and 1845. During the war with Mexico, Colonel Gates commanded the Third Artillery and was appointed governor of the port of Tampico (q.v.).

GEARY, JOHN W. (1819–1873). Lt. Col. John W. Geary commanded the Second Pennsylvania Volunteers during the assault against Chapultepec (q.v.) and was wounded in that battle.

GENTRY, MEREDITH P. Meredith P. Gentry was a Whig (q.v.) member of the House of Representatives from Tennessee and bitterly attacked the efforts of Pres. James K. Polk (q.v.) to promote war with Mexico.

GIBSON, GEORGE (d. 1861). Col. George Gibson was U.S. commissary general in the Polk (q.v.) administration. The president harshly criticized Gibson for the inefficient operation of his department during preparation for the march from Veracruz (q.v.) to Mexico City (q.v.).

GIDDINGS, JOSHUA R. (1795–1864). Rep. Joshua Giddings, Whig (q.v.) congressman from Ohio, was one of the major opponents of war with Mexico, constantly opposing the claim by President Polk (q.v.) that the Rio Grande (q.v.) was the rightful boundary between the United States and Mexico. After the war, Giddings continued as one of the strongest abolitionists in the House of Representatives.

GIDDINGS, LUTHER. Maj. Luther Giddings commanded a force of the Second Ohio Volunteers in the successful operation of the supply line between Monterrey (q.v.) and the Rio Grande (q.v.), thus assuring Gen. Zachary Taylor (q.v.) of adequate supplies following the capture of Monterrey (q.v.). *See also* MONTERREY, BATTLE OF.

GILA RIVER. The Gila River is one of the principal streams in southern Arizona and a tributary of the Colorado, entering that stream near present-day Yuma, Arizona. During his march from New Mexico (q.v.) to California (q.v.), Gen. Stephen W. Kearny (q.v.) followed the Gila throughout much of his journey in Arizona, as did Lt. Col. Philip St. George Cooke (q.v.). The stream served as a portion of the boundary established by the Treaty of Guadalupe Hidalgo (q.v.). In the Gadsden Treaty of 1853, however, territory south of the Gila, to the present-day southern boundary of Arizona, was added to the United States. The stream is significant as a source of water for irrigation and other purposes in southern Arizona today.

GILLESPIE, ARCHIBALD H. In October 1845, marine captain Archibald H. Gillespie was commissioned by President Polk (q.v.) and Secretary of the Navy George Bancroft (q.v.) to convey memorized instructions to U.S. Consul Thomas O. Larkin (q.v.) in Monterey, California (q.v.). In addition, Gillespie carried letters from Sen. Thomas Hart Benton (q.v.) to his son-in-law John C. Frémont (q.v.) and possibly secret instructions to Frémont from the president. Passing through Mexico to the port of Mazatlán (q.v.) in February 1846, Gillespie conferred with Commo. John D. Sloat (q.v.), then traveled to California via the Sandwich Islands (Hawaii), arriving in Monterey (q.v.) on April 17, 1846. The captain took part in the Bear Flag revolt (q.v.) and, after California's annexation to the United States, commanded Los Angeles (q.v.) but was forced to surrender the city on September 28, 1846. The following December, Gillespie assisted Gen. Stephen Kearny (q.v.) in his march to San Diego (q.v.) and was wounded in both the battles of San Pascual (q.v.), December 6, 1846, and San Gabriel (q.v.), January 8, 1847.

His role in the acquisition of California, like that of the more famous John C. Frémont, is one of mystery and contradictions.

GILMER, JEREMY FRANCIS (1818–1883). Lt. Jeremy Gilmer accompanied Gen. Stephen W. Kearny (q.v.) in his expedition to New Mexico (q.v.) and was appointed as chief engineer of the Army of the West (q.v.). Following the occupation of Santa Fe (q.v.), he supervised the construction of Fort Marcy (q.v.). During the Civil War, Gilmer served as a major general and chief of engineers for the Confederacy.

GILPIN, WILLIAM (1813–1894). Maj. William Gilpin served under Col. Alexander Doniphan (q.v.) in the New Mexico (q.v.) campaign. On October 22, 1846, he led a force of some 200 men into southern Colorado, contacted Navajo (q.v.) leaders, and persuaded them to enter into negotiations. Gilpin commanded a detachment of approximately 300 men in Doniphan's march from Santa Fe (q.v.) to Chihuahua (q.v.), and, after the war, he was appointed as territorial governor of Colorado.

GLADDEN, ADLEY HOGAN (1810–1862). Maj. Adley H. Gladden took command of the South Carolina volunteers in the battle of Churubusco (q.v.) following the deaths of Col. Pierce Butler and Lt. Col. John P. Dickinson. He participated in other battles in the campaign for Mexico City (q.v.) and was wounded in action at the citadel (q.v.) following the capture of Chapultepec (q.v.), September 13, 1847. Gladden was later to serve as a general in the Confederacy.

GODEY, ALEXIS. Alexis Godey was one of the mountain men of California who supported the efforts of Lt. John C. Frémont (q.v.). Following the battle of San Pascual (q.v.), December 6, 1846, Godey traveled to San Diego (q.v.) to bring back reinforcements to the small army of Gen. Stephen W. Kearny (q.v.). Although successful in that mission, Godey was captured by Mexican authorities during his return.

GOMEZ FARIAS, VALENTIN (1781–1858). Born in Guadalajara, Valentín Gómez Farías studied medicine in Mexico City and initiated practice in 1807 in Aguascalientes. Shortly after that time, he entered politics and was elected to the Cortes after the adoption of the constitution of 1812. Following Mexican independence, Gómez Farías became a leading member of the radical wing of the Mexican Liberal Party, the *Puros* (q.v.). During the 1830s, Valentín Gómez Farías took action to secularize the California missions and other property of the Roman Catholic Church. A staunch opponent of Texas independence, he refused to compromise on that issue. Although a long-time opponent of Santa Anna (q.v.), he was elected as that caudillo's vice president on December 6, 1846, and exercised control of the government as Santa Anna marched to meet General Taylor at Buena Vista (q.v.). The acting president faced a proclerical rebellion, the *Polkos* uprising (q.v.) in early 1847, and was ousted from office by Santa Anna and his newly found conservative allies. Following the Treaty of Guadalupe Hidalgo (q.v.), Gómez Farías continued to play a prominent role in the liberal faction of Mexican politics, especially in the formation of the constitution of 1857.

GOMEZ PEDRAZA, MANUEL (1789–1851). Manuel Gómez Pedraza was a professional military officer who fought with the Spanish during the early phase of Mexico's war for independence but changed sides after 1820 to support the revolt of Agustín Iturbide. In 1828, Gómez Pedraza was elected president of Mexico as a *Moderado* (q.v.) but was not allowed to take office by the more radical liberal faction. In and out of high office for the next two decades, Gómez Pedraza remained embroiled in the chaotic political life of Mexico and the struggles between the federalists and centralists. He played a minor role in the failed peace negotiations just before the final American assault on Mexico City in 1847. In 1850, he was once again candidate for the presidency but was defeated by Gen. Mariano Arista (q.v.).

GORDON, GEORGE HAMILTON. *See* ABERDEEN, FOURTH EARL OF.

GORGAS, JOSIAH (1818–1883). A graduate of West Point in 1841, Lt. Josiah Gorgas entered the Ordnance Corps. During 1845 and 1846, he traveled to Europe to observe developments in a number of armies, returning to the United States on the eve of the war with Mexico. Gorgas joined the army of Gen. Winfield Scott (q.v.) and participated in the siege of Veracruz (q.v.). Scott appointed him as chief of ordnance at the rank of first lieutenant in the supply depot at Veracruz, thus Gorgas contributed to the supply of the American army during its invasion of the Valley of Mexico (q.v.). In 1861, Gorgas resigned his commission in the U.S. Army and was appointed by Confederate President Jefferson Davis (q.v.) as chief of ordnance in the Confederate army.

GORMAN, WILLIS A. (1816–1876). Maj. Willis A. Gorman commanded four companies of Indiana volunteers in the battle of Buena Vista (q.v.), playing a key role in protecting the left flank of the American position.

GRAHAM, JAMES D. (1799–1865). Maj. James D. Graham was sent by Secretary of War William Marcy (q.v.) with instructions to Gen. Zachary Taylor (q.v.) ordering an end to the armistice that had followed the surrender of Monterrey (q.v.). Graham reached Monterrey on November 2, 1846, and the following day Taylor announced his intention to resume hostilities on November 13. In 1848, Graham was a member of the military court which tried Capt. John C. Frémont (q.v.).

GRAHAM, WILLIAM MONTROSE (1798–1847). A graduate of the West Point class of 1817, Lt. Col. William M. Graham fought at Palo Alto (q.v.) and Resaca de la Palma (q.v.). He then joined the forces of Gen. Winfield Scott (q.v.) in the campaign for the Valley of Mexico (q.v.). Graham commanded the 11th Infantry during the battles of Contreras and Churubusco (q.v.). His regiment played a key role in the assault against Molino del Rey (q.v.), and Graham was killed in that action, September 8, 1847.

GRANT, ULYSSES S. (1822–1885). Lt. Ulysses S. Grant, a graduate of West Point, was an artillery officer in the Army of Observation (q.v.) that occupied Corpus Christi, Texas (q.v.), in the summer of 1845. He followed Gen. Zachary Taylor (q.v.) on his march to the Rio Grande (q.v.) in February 1846 and was among the forces shifted to the Veracruz campaign (q.v.) in early 1847. Although involved with a number of actions, including the battle of Cerro Gordo (q.v.) and the marches to Puebla (q.v.) and Mexico City (q.v.), Grant tended to remain out of the spotlight. Following the fall of Chapultepec Castle (q.v.), however, as an artillery officer in the Fourth Infantry, Grant played an important role in the movement into the city of Mexico and was cited for bravery by his commander. Although he did not gain any major distinction in the course of the war with Mexico, Grant's experience in that conflict undoubtedly played a role in preparing him for command of the Union forces in the American Civil War. He was elected president of the United States on the Republican ticket in 1868 and again in 1872, serving two complete terms.

GRAY, ANDREW V. F. Lt. Andrew V. F. Gray commanded the relief force that was sent by Commo. Robert Stockton (q.v.) on December 8–11, 1846, to rescue the small army of Gen. Stephen Kearny (q.v.) and escort it to San Diego, California (q.v.).

GRAYSON, JOHN B. (1806–1861). A native of Kentucky, Lt. John B. Grayson received his commission in 1826, having completed his education at the U.S. Military Academy. From 1838 to 1846, he served as a captain in the Second Artillery. In 1847, he joined Gen. Winfield Scott (q.v.) in the attack against Veracruz (q.v.). He participated in the battle of Cerro Gordo (q.v.) and was brevetted major for meritorious conduct in the battles of Contreras and Churubusco (q.v.). Grayson also fought at Molino del Rey (q.v.) and Chapultepec (q.v.), being brevetted to lieutenant colonel for the latter action.

GREGG, JOSIAH (1806–1850). Josiah Gregg, author of an influential book, *Commerce of the Prairies*, accompanied the Arkansas volunteers in their march to San Antonio (q.v.) and then continued with them as a part of the Army of Chihuahua (q.v.), commanded by Gen. John Wool (q.v.), into northern Mexico. His journal and letters are a valuable source of information on this phase of U.S. operations during the war with Mexico. Following the Treaty of Guadalupe Hidalgo (q.v.), Gregg traveled to California and continued to play an important role in describing the western region of the North American continent.

GREGORY, FRANCIS H. Naval captain Francis H. Gregory led a force of 500 sailors and marines to reinforce the U.S. position at Point Isabel (q.v.) in April 1846, following the outbreak of hostilities along the Rio Grande (q.v.). Later in that same year, as commander of the frigate USS *Raritan*, Gregory was involved in other operations in the Gulf of Mexico.

GRIFFIN, JOHN S. John S. Griffin served as assistant surgeon with the small force that accompanied Gen. Stephen W. Kearny (q.v.) in his march from Santa Fe (q.v.) to California (q.v.).

GRIFFIN, WILLIAM P. Naval lieutenant William P. Griffin commanded the USS *Tampico* during operations against Veracruz (q.v.) in March 1847.

GRIJALVA, RIO. The Grijalva River, called the Tabasco by many U.S. sources, is the principal stream in the state of Tabasco (q.v.), flowing generally from west to east. It is joined by the Usumacinta, which rises in Guatemala and serves as the boundary between that country and Mexico. Villahermosa, the capital of Tabasco, is located along the Grijalva, approximately 40 miles from the coast and the town of Frontera (q.v.) that guards the entrance from the sea. During the war, a number of U.S. naval operations centered in this region were commanded by Commo. Matthew C. Perry (q.v.).

GRINGO. The word *gringo*, a pejorative term referring to Anglo-Americans in Mexico, is alleged to have originated during the war. Some of the soldiers in the invading armies were heard singing a verse from a poem by Robert Burns:
    Green grow the rashes, O;
    Green grow the rashes, O;
    The sweetest hours that e'er I spend
    Are spent among the lasses, O!

GUADALUPE. The steamer *Guadalupe* was one of two important Mexican naval vessels (along with the *Moctezuma*) transferred to private British interests at the beginning of the war.

GUADALUPE HIDALGO, DISTRITO FEDERAL. The village of Guadalupe Hidalgo (Villa de Guadalupe), presently on the northern edge of Mexico City, contains the most sacred relic of the Mexican Catholic Church, the image of the Virgin of Guadalupe. In the course of the war against the United States, the village became one of the principal sites for diplomatic discussions and eventually the site of the signing of the treaty that ended the war.

GUADALUPE HIDALGO, TREATY OF (February 2, 1848). The Treaty of Guadalupe Hidalgo was signed at the Villa de Guadalupe on February 2, 1848. Proclaiming the end to the war, the treaty provided for a boundary line that left the United States in control of a vast region, approximately one-half the previous national territory of Mexico. The United States was to pay Mexico $15 million and to absorb all of the outstanding claims that had been cited as a justification for the struggle. Although Pres. James K. Polk (q.v.) had serious doubts relating to the negotiations that Nicholas Trist (q.v.) had carried out, he submitted the document to the U.S. Senate and that body ratified it on March 10, 1848. The Mexican Congress delayed in its ratification process but finally approved the document in mid-May. The final exchange of official ratifications took place at Querétaro (q.v.) on May 30, 1848. The exact boundary was to be determined by a mixed commission, and various other details were to be worked out in the coming years.

GUADALUPE VALLEJO, MARIANO. Gen. Mariano Guadalupe Vallejo was an influential citizen of Sonoma, California. A friend of Thomas Larkin (q.v.), U.S. consul in Monterey (q.v.), he favored the peaceful annexation of California by the United States. In the course of the Bear Flag revolt (q.v.), however, the Anglo-American rebels treated Guadalupe Vallejo quite harshly, placing him under arrest. Despite this treatment, he continued to support annexation.

GUAYMAS, SONORA. The Sonoran port of Guaymas, located on the Gulf of California, was one of the targets of the U.S. Pacific blockading squadron at the time of the outbreak of war. On October 6, 1847, Commo. Samuel F. DuPont (q.v.) attacked the city, destroying several ships and other property. Additional U.S. naval attacks came in late 1847 and early 1848, weakening Mexican power on the Pacific coast. In the course of those moves U.S. naval forces occupied Guaymas and did not evacuate it until June 24, 1848, almost a month after the ratification of the Treaty of Guadalupe Hidalgo (q.v.).

GUERRILLAS. Throughout the war against the United States, Mexican guerrilla forces played an important role. Following the capture of Monterrey, Nuevo León (q.v.), by Gen. Zachary Taylor (q.v.) the irregulars of Gen. José Urrea (q.v.) disrupted communications and supply lines between that city and Camargo (q.v.). The guerrillas were often supported by the Mexican population that suffered acts of violence and theft at the hands of U.S. troops, especially members of volunteer units. In the fall of 1847, General Taylor granted Gen. John Wool (q.v.) authority to try in military courts any Mexican accused of murder or other crimes against Americans. Armed with this decree, Wool carried out a plan to move against all citizens who supported the guerrillas.

  Gen. Winfield Scott (q.v.) also faced the menace of irregular bands as his supply lines stretched from Veracruz (q.v.) to Jalapa (q.v.), Puebla (q.v.) and eventually the Valley of Mexico (q.v.). After the battle of Cerro Gordo (q.v.), guerrilla activities increased under the leadership of an audacious priest, Padre Caledonio Domeco de Jarauta (q.v.), who commanded a band of some 700 men. Capt. Samuel Walker (q.v.) led a Texas cavalry force against him, scattering his army and destroying the town of Las Vigas, one of the principal centers of guerrilla activity. Another important irregular leader, especially after the death of Padre Jarauta, was Col. Mariano Cenobio (q.v.), who operated in the region west of Veracruz (q.v.). One of the most effective forces against these elements was the Texas Ranger (q.v.) company under Col. Francis M. Wynkoop (q.v.). Guerrilla factions were also important in many other regions of Mexican territory, including California, but eventually they tended to lose much of the support from local citizens when U.S. commanders enacted a policy to punish crimes by the invading armies.

GULF SQUADRON. See HOME SQUADRON.

GUTIERREZ, PATRICIO. Lt. Col. Patricio Gutierrez, with some 300 men, commanded the strong point at Purísima Bridge (q.v.) against the attacking force of Gen. Zachary Taylor (q.v.) in the battle of Monterrey (q.v.)

GUTIERREZ VILLANUEVA, JOSE. Col. José Gutierrez Villanueva was named by Gen. Juan José Landero (q.v.) as one of three commissioners to negotiate the surrender of Veracruz (q.v.) to Gen. Winfield Scott (q.v.) on March 27, 1847.

GUZMAN, LUIS. Maj. Gen. Luis Guzman was in command of two Mexican brigades that marched from San Luis Potosí (q.v.) on January 31, 1847. He joined the army of Gen. Antonio López de Santa Anna (q.v.) as that leader prepared to engage the American army of General Taylor (q.v.) in the battle of Buena Vista (q.v.), February 22–23, 1847.

H

HALE, JOHN P. (1806–1873). John P. Hale served as a member of the U.S. House of Representatives from New Hampshire during the course of the war with Mexico. A member of Pres. James K. Polk's (q.v.) Democratic Party, he nevertheless took a strong antislavery position and opposed many of the president's policies.

HALL, WILLARD P. (1820–1882). Pvt. Willard P. Hall, a lawyer in the Army of the West (q.v.) under Gen. Stephen W. Kearny (q.v.), joined Col. Alexander Doniphan (q.v.) in preparing a code of law for New Mexico (q.v.) following its occupation by the United States.

HALLECK, HENRY WAGER (1815–1872). Lt. Henry W. Halleck, an 1839 graduate of the U.S. Military Academy, was commissioned in the Corps of Engineers (q.v.). From October 16, 1847, to June 28, 1848, he was aide-de-camp to Commo. William B. Shubrick (q.v.), and established the fortifications at Mazatlán (q.v.) following its capture by Shubrick in November 1847. Later promoted to captain, Halleck continued to serve in Baja California (q.v.) and northwestern Mexico. During the Civil War, Halleck served as Pres. Abraham Lincoln's chief of staff.

HAMER, THOMAS L. (1800–1846). Ohio Democratic congressman Thomas L. Hamer was appointed as brigadier general in the volunteer forces of his state. He led his brigade in the battle of Monterrey (q.v.), being involved especially with action around the Purísima Bridge (q.v.) and the Tenería (q.v.). General Hamer died in Monterrey (December 1846), an event much lamented by Gen. Zachary Taylor (q.v.).

HAMMOND, THOMAS C. (1821–1846). A graduate of West Point, class of 1842, Lt. Thomas C. Hammond joined the Army of the West (q.v.) and led the advance guard of that force into Santa Fe (q.v.) on August 18, 1846, facing no opposition from the Mexican authorities. Hammond, commanding a small force of dragoons (q.v.), accompanied Gen. Stephen W. Kearny (q.v.) in his march to California (q.v.) and was killed in the battle of San Pascual (q.v.), December 6, 1846.

HANNEGAN, EDWARD A. (1807–1859). Edward Hannegan, U.S. senator from Indiana, was a leader in the movement to annex extensive territory from Mexico and opposed the efforts of John Quincy Adams (q.v.) and others who denounced the Polk (q.v.) administration for initiating the war. *See also* "ALL OF MEXICO" MOVEMENT.

HARDEE, WILLIAM JOSEPH (1815–1873). Capt. William J. Hardee, second in command to Capt. Seth B. Thornton (q.v.), was among those captured at Rancho de Carricitos (q.v.), April 24, 1846. During the Civil War, he was commissioned as a lieutenant general of the Confederacy and commanded a corps of the Army of Tennessee.

HARDIN, JOHN J. (1810–1847). Col. John J. Hardin, former Whig (q.v.) congressman from Illinois, commanded the First Illinois Volunteers that moved from New Orleans (q.v.) to Port Lavaca in July 1846 and formed a part of the Army of Chihuahua (q.v.) under Gen. John E. Wool (q.v.). Departing from San Antonio (q.v.) on October 2, Hardin arrived at the Rio Grande (q.v.) on the 12th and continued south. He and Wool had a series of disputes during the march from Monclova (q.v.) to Parras (q.v.). Colonel Hardin commanded the First Illinois in the battle of Buena Vista (q.v.) and was killed while leading a counterattack against a Mexican position. His papers, located at the Chicago Historical Society, are a valuable source relating to the war and especially the campaign in the northern region of Mexico.

HARNEY, WILLIAM SELBY (1800–1889). At San Antonio, Texas (q.v.), Lt. Col. William S. Harney commanded the Second Dragoons, a part of the Army of Chihuahua (q.v.) under Brig. Gen. John E. Wool (q.v.). In July 1846, without authorization from his commander, Harney led a small force from San Antonio to the Rio Grande (q.v.) and was placed under arrest by Wool. After his release, the colonel was placed in charge of the army as it marched from San Antonio to the Rio Grande and crossed that river near Eagle Pass, Texas, October 9, 1846. Harney requested a transfer from Wool's command after additional clashes. He later accompanied Gen. Winfield Scott (q.v.) in his landing at Veracruz (q.v.), commanding a force of dragoons during the siege of that port. He then led the march from Veracruz to Cerro Gordo (q.v.), April 2, 1847. During the battle of Cerro Gordo (q.v.), Harney temporarily commanded the brigade of Gen. Persifor Smith (q.v.) and led a successful attack against the key Mexican position on Telegraph Hill (q.v.). He saw further action in the Valley of Mexico (q.v.) and, following the battle of Churubusco (q.v.), led his dragoons in pursuit of the defeated Mexican army, reaching almost to the walls of Mexico City. Following the battle of Chapultepec (q.v.), Harney and his dragoons escorted General Scott and his staff into the Zocalo, the central plaza of the Mexican capital. The colonel was also placed in command of the first convoy (some 400 wagons) to move to Veracruz following the end of hostilities.

HARRIS, JOHN (1795–1864). Maj. John Harris commanded a battalion of marines initially scheduled to attack the Isthmus of Tehuantepec (q.v.). By the time he arrived in Mexico, however, the war had ended, and Harris and his troops garrisoned the port of Alvarado (q.v.) in early 1848. In 1855, he was appointed as commandant of the U.S. Marine Corps and continued in that position through the first three years of the Civil War.

HASKELL, WILLIAM. Col. William Haskell commanded the Second Tennessee Volunteers under Gen. Gideon Pillow (q.v.). Haskell's regiment was the lead unit in the attack against Mexican artillery batteries in the battle of Cerro Gordo (q.v.) and suffered the heaviest losses of any American regiments in the course of that battle.

HAWKINS, EDGAR S. (1801–1865). Capt. Edgar S. Hawkins, West Point class of 1820, assumed command of Fort Texas (q.v.) on the Rio Grande (q.v.) following the death of Maj. Jacob Brown (q.v.) on May 6, 1846. He refused to accept the Mexican demand for the surrender of the position and succeeded in withstanding attacks until the arrival of reinforcements under Gen. Zachary Taylor (q.v.). Hawkins was brevetted major for that action.

HAYS, JOHN COFFEE (1817–1883). Col. John C. ("Jack") Hays commanded a regiment of Texas volunteer cavalry, Texas Rangers (q.v.), which formed a part of the army of Gen. Zachary Taylor (q.v.). In the battle of Monterrey (q.v.), Hays served under the command of Gen. William Worth (q.v.). He was ordered to shift his regiment to Veracruz (q.v.) with the objective of combating Mexican guerrilla (q.v.) forces on the National Highway (q.v.). Hays and his Texas Rangers were effective against the guerrilla leader Col. Mariano Cenobio (q.v.) and in protecting American forces in the region of Puebla (q.v.), Perote (q.v.), and Jalapa (q.v.).

HAZARD, SAMUEL F. (1784–1870). Lt. Samuel F. Hazard of the U.S. Navy, commanded the schooner USS *Nonata* during the campaign along the coast from the Coatzacoalcos River to Isla Carmen (q.v.) in the Gulf of Mexico (q.v.), October 1846.

HEADY, WILLIAM J. Capt. William J. Heady was a cavalry commander in the Kentucky volunteers operating south of Saltillo (q.v.). His patrol was captured without a fight near Encarnación (q.v.) on the morning of January 27, 1847. This, along with the capture of a larger force under Maj. Solon Borland (q.v.), was an indication of the increased strength of the Mexican force approaching Buena Vista (q.v.).

HEINTZLEMAN, SAMUEL PETER (1805–1880). Capt. Samuel P. Heintzleman commanded a battalion of regulars that had been raised to reinforce the army of Gen. Winfield Scott (q.v.) following the enlistment termination of many one-year volunteers after the battle of Cerro Gordo (q.v.). Heintzleman was commissioned as a major general in the U.S. Army during the Civil War and commanded a division in the Army of the Potomac.

HENDERSON, JAMES PINCKNEY (1808–1858). Texas president Sam Houston (q.v.) named J. Pinckney Henderson as an agent to the United States. Following annexation, Henderson was elected governor of Texas but resigned to take command of the "Texas Division" (two mounted regiments), in the army of Gen. Zachary Taylor (q.v.) as a major general. He participated in the battle for Monterrey (q.v.) and, following the fall of that city, was appointed by Taylor as a member of the commission to negotiate with Gen. Pedro de Ampudia (q.v.).

HENDLEY, ISRAEL R. (d. 1846). Capt. Israel R. Hendley formed a part of the army of Col. Sterling Price (q.v.) in New Mexico (q.v.) following the departure of Gen. Stephen W. Kearny (q.v.) for California. Facing rebellious forces, Hendley occupied the settlement of Las Vegas, New Mexico (q.v.), and on December 24, 1846, was killed during an encounter at the town of Mora.

HENRY, THOMAS. Sgt. Thomas Henry of the Seventh Infantry raised the U.S. flag to celebrate Gen. Winfield Scott's (q.v.) victory at Cerro Gordo (q.v.).

HENRY, WILLIAM SEATON (1817–1851). Capt. William S. Henry graduated from West Point in the class of 1835. As a member of the Third Infantry, he was involved in a number of actions in the course of the war, including Palo Alto (q.v.), Resaca de la Palma (q.v.), Monterrey (q.v.), and Veracruz (q.v.). His account of the war was published in 1847 as *Campaign Sketches of the War with Mexico*, a work that became one of the most popular accounts of the war.

HEREDIA, JOSE ANTONIO (b. 1800). In early 1847, Chihuahua governor Angel Trías Alvarez (q.v.) appointed Brig. Gen. José

A. Heredia as commander of the army defending that state. Heredia was defeated in the battle of Sacramento (q.v.), February 28, 1847, by Col. Alexander Doniphan (q.v.), opening the way for the occupation of Chihuahua (q.v.) City by the Americans.

HERNDON, W. L. (1813–1857). Lt. Comdr. W. L. Herndon commanded the steamer USS *Iris* (q.v.) in the Gulf of Mexico during the war. He was ordered by Commo. Matthew C. Perry (q.v.) to assist refugees from the town of Valladolid, Yucatán, after it had been overrun by Mayan rebels. *See also* CASTE WAR OF YUCATAN.

HERRERA, JOSE JOAQUIN DE (1792–1854). Gen. José Joaquín de Herrera was a member of the moderate wing of the Mexican Liberal Party, *Moderados* (q.v.), in the 1840s and tended to oppose elements demanding a war with the United States. As he was selected as president in early 1845, there was an expression of hope in the United States that Herrera would seek a negotiated settlement relating to the annexation of Texas and other outstanding questions. When Pres. James K. Polk (q.v.) sent John Slidell (q.v.) to discuss the issues, however, the Mexican president was unwilling to take the political risk of opening negotiations with the envoy. Despite this, Herrera was overthrown by a military uprising headed by Maj. Gen. Mariano Paredes y Arrillaga (q.v.) in December 1845. Herrera continued to reside in Mexico and participated in several actions following the fall of Mexico City (q.v.) to the American forces. He was a member of the commission appointed to negotiate with Nicholas Trist (q.v.). The Mexican Congress selected Herrera as president of the nation once again in April 1848, and he took office the following month, presiding over the initial days in the aftermath of the Mexican defeat.

HERRERA, JOSE MARIA. Lt. Col. José María Herrera commanded a military force from the state of Querétaro (q.v.) that was stationed at the Purísima Bridge (q.v.) during the battle of Monterrey (q.v.), September 19, 1846.

HERRERA, PEDRO MIGUEL. Brig. Gen. Juan José Landero (q.v.) appointed Col. Pedro Miguel Herrera on March 26, 1847, as one of the members of a negotiating team to work out a settlement with the United States commissioners for the surrender of Veracruz (q.v.).

HERRON, JOHN. Capt. John Herron led a company of Pennsylvania volunteers in defending Puebla (q.v.) during October 1847, at the time that city was under siege.

HEYWOOD, CHARLES. Lt. Charles Heywood commanded a small garrison of U.S. Marines in San José del Cabo, Baja California (q.v.). Despite attacks by Mexican forces during November 19–21, 1847, and again in January and February 1848, the marines held out until relieved by two whaling vessels.

HIDALGO, CLARO. Col. Claro Hidalgo commanded the fortress of Acachapán, Tabasco. As the force of Commo. Matthew C. Perry (q.v.) attacked the position on July 16, 1847, Hidalgo's troops fled, opening the way for the occupation of Tabasco (q.v.) by the Americans.

HIGGINS, EUGENE. Midshipman Eugene Higgins, along with William P. Toler, raised the Stars and Stripes over the customs house at Monterey, California (q.v.), on July 7, 1846, following the proclamation of its annexation to the United States by Commo. John D. Sloat (q.v.).

HILL, AMBROSE P. (d. 1865). A graduate of West Point, Lt. Ambrose P. Hill was commissioned on July 1, 1847, in the First Artillery. He joined the army of Gen. Winfield Scott (q.v.) following the capture of Veracruz (q.v.) and the battle of Cerro Gordo (q.v.). He did see action, however, in the battles of Huamantla (q.v.) and Atlisco (q.v.). Hill rose to the rank of general in the army of the Confederacy and was killed on April 2, 1865.

HILL, DANIEL HARVEY (1821–1889). Lt. D. H. Hill was an artillery officer in the invading army of Gen. Winfield Scott (q.v.) and was in the storming party of Capt. Gabriel Paul against the Castle of Chapultepec (q.v.). During the Civil War, Hill joined the Confederacy and commanded a corps in the Army of Northern Virginia.

HITCHCOCK, ETHAN ALLEN (1798–1870). Lt. Col. Ethan A. Hitchcock, a graduate of the West Point class of 1817, commanded the Third Infantry, the leading unit in the move of the Army of Occupation (q.v.) from New Orleans (q.v.) to Corpus Christi (q.v.), July 24, 1845. At Corpus Christi he played an important role in the training of Gen. Zachary Taylor's (q.v.) forces, insisting that his West Point education was of major importance in the proper conduct of military preparation. At the same time, Hitchcock became involved with disputes relating to the determination of seniority within the army, creating a variety of problems for General Taylor. As Gen. Winfield Scott (q.v.) initiated the campaign against Veracruz (q.v.), he appointed Hitchcock to his "little cabinet," (q.v.), an inner circle on which he depended for advice. Hitchcock saw action during the siege of Veracruz and participated in the battle of Cerro Gordo (q.v.). He was also appointed as inspector general for the army and played an important role in the system of security and communication during the campaign for Mexico City (q.v.). In the Valley of Mexico (q.v.), he continued to advise Scott in a staff capacity and fought in the battles of Churubusco (q.v.), Molino del Rey (q.v.), and Chapultepec (q.v.). Hitchcock's account of the war was published in his *Fifty Years in Camp and Field*, which offers an interesting interpretation of events.

HOLZINGER, SEBASTIAN. Mexican Marine Lt. Sebastián Holzinger, along with Francisco A. Velez, carried out an heroic act during the siege of Veracruz (q.v.). As the Mexican flag was cut from its position by artillery fire, the two officers rescued it and displayed it on the stump of the flagpole.

HOME SQUADRON. The naval squadron under the command of Commo. David Conner (q.v.), which was charged with operations in the Gulf of Mexico at the time of the outbreak of war with Mexico, was officially designated as the Home Squadron but was also called the Gulf Squadron. Its primary responsibility was to establish an effective blockade of the east coast of Mexico. In the early days of the war, Conner commanded only 13 ships, including two steamers, but by the time of the landing at Veracruz (q.v.) in March 1847, some 50 vessels made up the squadron. At first stationed off the Brazos Santiago (q.v.), Conner decided that the most effective base of operation would be at Antón Lizardo (q.v.), just 20 miles south of the Mexican port city of Veracruz (q.v.). The boredom of the blockading duties was broken from time to time by raids against coastal cities, including Tampico and Tabasco (q.v.). The Home Squadron furnished invaluable assistance to Gen. Winfield Scott (q.v.) in his landing at Veracruz, including one naval battery that was placed ashore to help reduce the city walls. *See also* CONNER, DAVID E.; NAVY, U.S., AND NAVAL OPERATIONS.

HOOKER, JOSEPH (1814–1879). Lt. Joseph Hooker was brevetted captain for his outstanding service in the battle of Monterrey (q.v.). Under the command of Gen. George Cadwalader (q.v.), Hooker moved from Veracruz (q.v.) to Puebla (q.v.) in June 1847. During that march he fought off attacks at the Puente Nacional (q.v.), June 11, 1847, an action that won him a brevet to major. He saw further action in the Valley of Mexico (q.v.), being brevetted to lieutenant colonel at the battle of Chapultepec (q.v.). Hooker, given the name "Fighting Joe" for his activities in the American Civil War, was appointed commander of the Army of the Potomac. He was defeated at the battle of Chancellorsville by the forces of Gen. Robert E. Lee (q.v.).

HOUSTON, SAM (1793–1863). Gen. Sam Houston was the victor over Antonio López de Santa Anna (q.v.) at the battle of San Jacinto (April 20–21, 1836), assuring Texas independence. As president of Texas, Houston negotiated with the United States regarding annexation but also maintained links with Great Britain. Following annexation, Houston was elected U.S. senator from Texas, and throughout the war with Mexico, he strongly supported the efforts of U.S. military forces.

HOWARD, GEORGE T. George T. Howard was an experienced trader on the Santa Fe trail (q.v.) who was used by the James K. Polk (q.v.) administration to warn traders of the outbreak of war with Mexico. Howard traveled to Santa Fe in May 1846 in an effort to initiate negotiations with Governor Manuel Armijo (q.v.) of New Mexico and to persuade the citizens of the region to accept U.S. rule with the arrival of the Army of the West (q.v.).

HOWARD, W. A. (1813–1880). Capt. W. A. Howard commanded the Revenue Steamer *McLane*, a shallow-draft vessel that joined the U.S. force in the Gulf of Mexico in October 1846, which made it possible to carry out operations across the shallow bars and into the rivers along the coast. He continued to play an important role in operations under Commo. Matthew C. Perry (q.v.) during the late months of the war.

HUAMANTLA, BATTLE OF (October 8, 1847). In September 1847, an American force under Gen. Joseph Lane (q.v.) marched to raise the siege of Puebla (q.v.). When Gen. Antonio López de Santa Anna (q.v.) concentrated his force at Huamantla to ambush Lane, that position was assaulted by the cavalry force of Maj. Samuel H. Walker (q.v.). Huamantla was captured on October 8, but in a counterattack Walker and several of his men were killed. When Lane's army arrived on the scene, his soldiers were allowed to carry out a plundering of the town, the only such action approved by a major U.S. commander.

HUDSON, THOMAS B. Capt. Thomas B. Hudson commanded a volunteer force of 95 men called the Chihuahua Rangers, a portion of the Missouri volunteer regiment of Col. Sterling Price (q.v.). In December 1846, Captain Hudson joined Col. Alexander Doniphan (q.v.) in his move from Santa Fe (q.v.) to El Paso (q.v) and eventually to Chihuahua (q.v.).

HUGER, BENJAMIN (1805–1877). A graduate of the U.S. Military Academy in 1825, Capt. Benjamin Huger was chief of ordnance in the army of Gen. Winfield Scott (q.v.). In charge of the siege train during the operation against Veracruz (q.v.), Huger was brevetted for his part in that action. He was equally effective in the battle of Cerro Gordo (q.v.) and during the bombardment of the Molino del Rey (q.v.), September 8, 1847, was brevetted lieutenant colonel. Huger then played a key role in the placement of artillery for the bombardment of Chapultepec (q.v.) and the approaches to Mexico City (q.v.) along the San Cosmé causeway. During the Civil War, Huger served as a general, commanding a division in the Confederate army.

HUGHES, GEORGE WURTZ (1806–1870). Capt. George W. Hughes joined the Army of Chihuahua (q.v.) in San Antonio, Texas (q.v.) and served as chief engineer on the staff of Gen. John Wool (q.v.). In 1847, he joined the division of Gen. William Worth (q.v.) and saw important action at the National Bridge (q.v.). He was brevetted major at the battle of Cerro Gordo (q.v.) and later carried out a series of important intelligence operations directed at combating the guerrilla (q.v.) forces. In late 1847, Hughes commanded the garrison at Jalapa (q.v.) and later the fortress at Perote (q.v.). Following the war, he became chief engineer of the Panama railroad.

HUGHES, JOHN (1797–1864). Bishop John Hughes of New York assisted Pres. James Polk (q.v.) in finding Roman Catholic priests to accompany the U.S. forces that entered Mexico in the course of the war. This was considered to be of importance in combating the religious propaganda against the American army on the part of pro-Catholic elements in Mexico.

HUGHES, JOHN TAYLOR (1817–1862). John T. Hughes was a Missouri volunteer in the First Missouri Cavalry who participated in a number of expeditions in New Mexico (q.v.). He wrote an account of the Doniphan (q.v.) expedition and other aspects of the war in the West. His is one of the most valuable firsthand accounts of that phase of the conflict.

HULL, JOSEPH B. Comdr. Joseph B. Hull commanded the USS sloop of war *Warren* in the Pacific Squadron (q.v.) of the U.S. Navy. On September 9, 1846, he succeeded in closing the port of Mazatlán (q.v.) but was unable to hold the position.

HUNT, HENRY JACKSON (1819–1889). Lt. Henry J. Hunt graduated from the U.S. Military Academy in 1839. He served as an artillery officer in the battery of Col. James Duncan (q.v.), participating in the battles of Veracruz (q.v.), Cerro Gordo (q.v.), Contreras, and Churubusco (q.v.). He was wounded twice at Molino del Rey (q.v.) but was able to assist in the bombardment of Chapultepec (q.v.), where he was brevetted major. Hunt played a significant role in the assault along the San Cosmé Causeway into Mexico City (q.v.). During the Civil War, Hunt was appointed brigadier general and brevet major general, serving as chief of artillery in the Army of the Potomac.

HUNT, THOMAS F. (d. 1856). Lt. Col. Thomas F. Hunt served as army quartermaster at New Orleans (q.v.) and obtained supplies for the forces of Gen. Zachary Taylor (q.v.) during his move to the Rio Grande (q.v.) and into northern Mexico.

HUNT, WILLIAM E. Lt. William E. Hunt was commander of the USS *Porpoise*, a ship that served as a part of the blockade force in the Gulf of Mexico. In 1846, Hunt succeeded in capturing the Mexican merchant schooner *Nonata*.

HUNTER, BUSHROD. Lt. Bushrod Hunter was a member of the crew of the brig USS *Truxtun*, commanded by Comdr. Edward W. Carpender (q.v.), which grounded at the mouth of the Tuxpan River on August 15, 1846. Most of the members of the crew were captured, but Hunter and Lt. Otway Berryman escaped and made their way to Antón Lizardo (q.v.).

HUNTER, CHARLES G. Lt. Charles G. Hunter commanded the steamer USS *Scourge* during the blockade (q.v.) of Gulf of Mexico ports. On March 30, 1847, he fired on Alvarado (q.v.), the fortress guarding the mouth of the Madellin River, thus alerting the Mexican force that an attack was under way. This warning allowed the Mexican commander to destroy most of the supplies that had been the objective of Gen. John A. Quitman (q.v.) and Commo. Matthew C. Perry (q.v.). Perry denounced Hunter's action as irresponsible and placed him under arrest.

I

IBARRA, DOMINGO (1804–1850). Domingo Ibarra served as Mexican foreign minister following the fall of Mexico City to the army of Gen. Winfield Scott (q.v.). He favored negotiating with Nicholas Trist (q.v.) but was forced to resign by the Mexican War Party.

IDE, WILLIAM B. William B. Ide was a member of the Anglo-American group that was led by Ezekiel Merritt (q.v.) in the seizure of Sonoma, California (q.v.), on June 14, 1846. As Merritt took prisoners to Sutter's Fort (q.v.), Ide remained in Sonoma to proclaim the Bear Flag Republic.

INDEPENDENCE. The USS *Independence* was a razee that served in the Pacific Squadron (q.v.) and was the flagship of Commo. W. Branford Shubrick (q.v.) when he arrived in Monterey, California (q.v.), in January 1847. The ship carried out blockading duties along the coast of California and northern Mexico.

INDEPENDENCE BATTALION. The *Batallón de Independencia* was a national guard unit of the Mexican army stationed in the national capital. When Vice President Valentín Gómez Farías (q.v.) ordered it to march to Veracruz (q.v.) to oppose the landing of the U.S. invasion force, the officers refused, issuing a pronouncement against the vice president. This was the onset of the *Polko* Rebellion (q.v.), which succeeded in forcing Gómez Farías from office and preparing the way for the return of Antonio López de Santa Anna (q.v.) as the hero of the conservative faction. During the invasion of the Valley of Mexico (q.v.), the Independence Battalion, commanded by General Manuel Rincón (q.v.), defended the Convent of San Mateo (q.v.) in the battle of Churubusco (q.v.).

INDEPENDENCE HILL. *La Independencia* (Independence Hill) is a low mountain to the west of the city of Monterrey, Nuevo

León (q.v.). At the time of the attack against the city by Gen. Zachary Taylor (q.v.), it was strongly fortified, especially at its eastern end where the Bishop's Palace (Obispado) (q.v.) was located. In the course of the battle, the division of Gen. William Worth (q.v.) seized the hill (September 22, 1846), an important step leading to the fall of Monterrey.

INGRAHAM, DUNCAN N. (1802–1891). Comdr. Duncan N. Ingraham commanded the USS *Somers* in the Gulf of Mexico. In May 1846, he carried out an intelligence mission to Campeche, Yucatán (q.v.), reporting that the authorities in that port city showed a determination to retain their independence from Mexico.

IRIS. The steamer USS *Iris*, commanded by Lt. Comdr. W. L. Herndon (q.v.), was sent to assist refugees in Valladolid, Yucatán, after that city had been occupied by Mayan Indians in the spring of 1847. *See also* CASTE WAR OF YUCATAN.

IRVIN, WILLIAM (1819–1852). Lt. Col. William Irvin, a graduate of the West Point class of 1839, commanded three companies of the Second Ohio Volunteers at Marín, Tamaulipas, following the battle of Monterrey (q.v.). On February 22, 1847, Col. José Urrea (q.v.) and Gen. Antonio Canales (q.v.) moved against the position, but Irvin held off the assault until February 25, when he received reinforcements from Monterrey. He continued to clash with the irregular forces of Urrea in the area of northeastern Mexico. *See also* GUERRILLAS.

ISLA VERDE. Isla Verde (Green Island) is a small island approximately five miles from the port of Veracruz (q.v.). In March 1847, Commo. David Conner (q.v.) used the island as a base of operations to guide ships transporting the army of Gen. Winfield Scott (q.v.) in preparation for the landing at Collado Beach (q.v.).

J

JACKSON, CONGREVE. Lt. Col. Congreve Jackson commanded a force of some 200 Missouri volunteers, who marched from Valverde, New Mexico, on December 16, 1846, and formed a part of the army under Col. Alexander Doniphan (q.v.) in the expedition to El Paso (q.v.) and Chihuahua (q.v.).

JACKSON, SAMUEL. Seaman Samuel Jackson served on blockade (q.v.) duty in the Gulf of Mexico aboard the USS *St. Mary's*. He was court-martialed for a number of infractions, including the striking of an officer, convicted and executed on September 17, 1846. This action was an indication of the disciplinary policy of Commo. David E. Conner (q.v.).

JACKSON, THOMAS JONATHAN (1824–1863). Lt. Thomas J. Jackson, a graduate of the class of 1846 at West Point, participated in the siege of Veracruz (q.v.) and fought in the battle of Cerro Gordo (q.v.). He served as an artillery officer in the Valley of Mexico (q.v.), seeing action at Contreras and Churubusco (q.v.), Molino del Rey (q.v.), and Chapultepec (q.v.). He was brevetted captain at Contreras and Churubusco and major at Chapultepec. Jackson was one of the most outstanding Confederate commanders in the American Civil War and was given the name "Stonewall Jackson."

JALAPA, VERACRUZ. Jalapa, the capital of the Mexican state of Veracruz, played an important role in Gen. Winfield Scott's (q.v.) invasion of Mexico. Located 74 miles from the seacoast in the temperate zone (4,680 feet above sea level), Jalapa was well away from the fever-ridden coastal plain. Following the battle of Cerro Gordo (q.v.), American forces occupied the city (April 19, 1847) and used it as a staging area for the next phase of the campaign. Although most of the army of General Scott marched to Puebla (q.v.) and eventually the Valley of Mexico (q.v.), Jalapa continued as an important position on the line of communication between Veracruz (q.v.) and Mexico City (q.v.).

JARARO, JOSE MARIA. Brig. Gen. José María Jararo was one of the commanders who served under Gen. Antonio López de Santa Anna (q.v.) in the battle of Cerro Gordo (q.v.).

JARAUTA, CALEDONIO DOMECO DE (1814–1848). A Spanish-born Franciscan priest, Celedonio Dómeco Jarauta led a band of some 700 guerrillas (q.v.) in an attempt to ambush U.S. forces at La Joya Pass (q.v.) in June 1847. Padre Jarauta was defeated by Col. Francis M. Wynkoop (q.v.), and his forces were scattered. In the following August, Jarauta gathered another guerrilla force of some 1,200 men and attacked an American wagon train near the Paso de Ovejas (q.v.). Although failing to capture the rumored payroll of one million dollars, he did disrupt Gen. Winfield Scott's (q.v.) communications.

Despite clashes with rival guerrilla leaders, Padre Jarauta continued to carry out irregular operations in a wide arc around Puebla (q.v.) and Mexico City (q.v.). He was finally defeated by Gen. Joseph Lane (q.v.) at Sequalteplán, near Pachuca, on February 25, 1848, effectively bringing an end to guerrilla warfare in central Mexico.

JARVIS, JOSEPH R. Comdr. Joseph R. Jarvis was in charge of the sloop of war USS *Falmouth* that formed a part of the blockading force (q.v.) under Commo. David Conner (q.v.) in the Gulf of Mexico.

JESUP, THOMAS SIDNEY (1788–1860). Brig. Gen. Thomas S. Jesup served as quartermaster general of the United States during the war with Mexico. Responsible for supplies to the armies in the field, Jesup was under constant pressure and criticism. Gen. Zachary Taylor (q.v.) denounced the shortage of wagons and other supplies during his march to the Rio Grande (q.v.) in the spring of 1847 and throughout most of his campaign in northern Mexico. "Old Rough and Ready" blamed the quartermaster corps and Jesup personally. In turn, Jesup pointed out that Taylor did not plan adequately for transportation and supplies and requested wagons when pack mules would have been much more practical.

General Jesup faced additional pressures in late 1846 and early 1847, as he worked to furnish transportation, weapons, and supplies for the landing at Veracruz (q.v.). Despite the quartermaster general's energetic efforts, he was denounced by Gen. Winfield Scott (q.v.) when all supplies did not arrive in the time requested. Although never sufficient to meet the demands of the commanders in the field, Jesup's record in the course of the war was impressive. Despite shortages of supplies and delays in their delivery, Jesup and his department carried out an effective operation over great distances. Superior logistics played a significant role in the U.S. victory over Mexico. *See also* QUARTERMASTER DEPARTMENT.

JOHN ADAMS. The brig USS *John Adams*, commanded by William J. McCluney, served with the blockading (q.v.) squadron in the Gulf of Mexico during the early part of the war. In May 1847, under Comdr. Henry Adams (q.v.), the ship played a role in Commo. David Conner's (q.v.) efforts to assure the neutrality of Yucatán (q.v.).

JOHNSON, CAVE (1793–1866). Cave Johnson, a Tennessee Democrat, was appointed postmaster general by Pres. James K. Polk (q.v.). Throughout the war with Mexico, he remained a close friend and adviser to the president.

JOHNSON, ISAAC. With the outbreak of hostilities on the Rio Grande (q.v.) in April 1846, Gen. Zachary Taylor (q.v.) called on Gov. Isaac Johnson of Louisiana to supply volunteers for his army. Although there was at first a rush to arms, the governor had difficulty persuading citizens to join the cause but eventually raised some 4,500 men.

JOHNSTON, ABRAHAM R. (1815–1846). Capt. Abraham R. Johnston, West Point class of 1835, commanded a force of dragoons (q.v.) and was aide-de-camp to Gen. Stephen W. Kearny (q.v.), marching from New Mexico (q.v.) to California (q.v.). On December 6, 1846, he led a small squadron against the defensive position held by Pio Pico (q.v.) in the battle of San Pascual (q.v.). In the course of the struggle Johnston and 17 other men were killed, most by skilled Californio (q.v.) lancers.

JOHNSTON, ALBERT SIDNEY (1803–1862). Col. Albert Sidney Johnston commanded a regiment of Texas riflemen in Gen. Zachary Taylor's (q.v.) Army of Occupation (q.v.). Most of the members of his unit left Mexico before the battle of Monterrey (q.v.) because of the expiration of their enlistments. Johnston remained, however, and was appointed inspector general in the volunteer division of Maj. Gen. William O. Butler (q.v.). In the Civil War, Johnston was commissioned as a general and became one of the major commanders of the Confederate forces.

JOHNSTON, JOSEPH EGGLESTON (1807–1891). Capt. Joseph E. Johnston, West Point class of 1829, was commissioned in the artillery (q.v.) but later switched to the Corps of Topographical Engineers (q.v.). He was a member of the force that landed at Veracruz (q.v.) in March 1847. Promoted to lieutenant colonel just before the battle of Cerro Gordo (q.v.), Johnston was seriously wounded in that action. Following his recovery, he participated in several battles in the Valley of Mexico (q.v.) and was brevetted colonel for his role as commander of the Voltigeurs (q.v.) in the attack against Chapultepec (q.v.). Although wounded again in that action, Johnston continued to serve in the region between Veracruz and Mexico City. He was one of the major commanders of the Confederacy during the American Civil War.

JONES, ANSON (1798–1858). Anson Jones served as a representative of the Republic of Texas (q.v.) to the United States in 1838 and 1839. On September 2, 1844, Jones was elected president of the Republic and, despite charges of being pro-British, took steps to call a convention on July 4, 1845, which resulted in the annexation of Texas by the United States. That action set the stage for the outbreak of war between the United States and Mexico.

JONES, ROGER. Brig. Gen. Roger Jones served as adjutant general in the U.S. Army at the beginning of the hostilities with Mexico and continued in that capacity throughout the war. Jones had responsibility for the assignment of troops to the armies in the field, a major task due to the far-flung lines of communication.

JONES, THOMAS AP CATESBY (1790–1858). On October 19, 1842, assuming that war with Mexico had been declared, Commo. Thomas ap Catesby Jones occupied the Mexican port city of Monterey, California (q.v.). On discovering his error, Jones abandoned the city and issued an apology. The incident increased Mexican suspicion of the motives of its North American neighbor and at the same time illustrated the vulnerable position of California to invasion.

JORNADA DEL MUERTO, NEW MEXICO. As Col. Alexander Doniphan (q.v.) marched south from Santa Fe (q.v.) to El Paso (q.v.) in December 1846, below the town of Valverde, he followed a route to the east of the Rio Grande (q.v.) that led for some 90 miles through a harsh and waterless desert, christened the *Jornada del Muerto* (Journey of the Dead). The army was able to reduce its time of march by this shortcut and arrived on Christmas Day at Brazito (q.v.), 30 miles north of El Paso where a battle was fought against Mexican major Antonio Ponce de León. The term *Jornada* was also applied to many other desert regions encountered by American forces.

JULIA. The schooner USS *Julia* served along the Pacific coast during the war, assisting American forces in their attack against California (q.v.) positions.

JUVERA, JULIAN (1784–1860). Julián Juvera fought in the Mexican wars for independence and in 1832 was promoted to brigadier general. He commanded a cavalry brigade in the army of Gen. Antonio López de Santa Anna (q.v.), which moved from San Luis Potosí (qv.) to Coahuila (q.v.) in February 1847 and participated in the battle of Buena Vista (q.v.).

K

KEARNY, PHILIP (1814–1862). Capt. Philip Kearny, under the command of Lt. Col. William S. Harney (q.v.), carried out a brave assault against an artillery battery near the San Antonio Gate (q.v.) following the battle of Churubusco (q.v.) and was severely wounded in the encounter.

KEARNY, STEPHEN WATTS (1794–1848). At the time of the declaration of war against Mexico, Col. Stephen Watts Kearny commanded the First Dragoons at Fort Leavenworth, Kansas (q.v.). A veteran of the War of 1812, Kearny was one of two individuals, with David E. Twiggs (q.v.), to be commissioned at the rank of brigadier general in the regular army by congressional action in May 1846. His command, designated as the Army of the West (q.v.), was strengthened by the addition of 1,000 mounted Missouri volunteers, the Mormon Battalion (q.v.), of approximately 500 men, and several additional units. In early June, Kearny set out on the Santa Fe Trail (q.v.), and advanced to Bent's Fort (q.v.) and eventually into New Mexico (q.v.), marching 850 miles over very forbidding territory. Although threatened by Gov. Manuel Armijo (q.v.), the Army of the West entered Santa Fe (q.v.) on August 18, 1846, without a fight. News of Kearny's promotion to permanent brigadier general arrived just before his triumphant entry into the New Mexican capital.

In the following months, Kearny took steps to strengthen the civil society of New Mexico, ordering the formation of a code of law, drawn up by Col. Alexander Doniphan (q.v.) and Pvt. Willard P. Hall (q.v.). At the same time, the general took steps to bring various Indian groups, including the Pueblos and Navajos (q.v.), under control through a combination of force and negotiations.

On September 25, 1846, Kearny departed from Santa Fe with a force of over 300 men, mostly dragoons (q.v.), moved south along the Rio Grande (q.v.), then turned west near Socorro. At that point, he sent all but about 100 of his men back to Santa Fe, having heard that California (q.v.) had surrendered to the United States. Guided by the famous mountain man Kit Carson (q.v.), Kearny followed the Gila River (q.v.) for some 450 miles through a harsh and forbidding region, reaching the Colorado River on November 22, 1846. Passing through the California desert, Kearny reached Warner's Ranch (q.v.) on December 2. Four days later, the small American force clashed at the battle of San Pascual (q.v.) with the Californios (q.v.) commanded by Capt. Andrés Pico (q.v.), and they suffered a number of casualties. Kearny was himself wounded. Commo. Robert Stockton (q.v.) sent a rescue force, and Kearny's very tired and bedraggled army reached San Diego (q.v.) on December 12, 1846.

Following his recovery, General Kearny came into conflict with Commodore Stockton over the latter's appointment of John C. Frémont (q.v.) as governor of California. By March 1847, the question of authority was settled as the general negotiated with Commo. W. Branford Shubrick (q.v.). Eventually these incidents led to Frémont's court martial and a bitter clash between Kearny and Sen. Thomas Hart Benton (q.v.).

KENDRICK, PETER R. Peter R. Kendrick, Roman Catholic Bishop of St. Louis, Missouri, indicated that he would supply a priest to accompany the force of Gen. Stephen W. Kearny (q.v.) in the march to Santa Fe (q.v.), but that promise was never carried out.

KENLY, JOHN REESE (1822–1891). One of the Maryland volunteers who accompanied Gen. Zachary Taylor (q.v.) in the invasion of northern Mexico, John R. Kenly recorded his experiences in an 1873 book entitled *Memoirs of a Maryland Volunteer*.

KER, CROGHAN. Capt. Croghan Ker commanded a squadron of dragoons (q.v.) in the Army of Observation (q.v.) in the lower Rio Grande Valley (q.v.). He saw action at the battles of Palo Alto (q.v.), May 8, 1846, and Resaca de la Palma (q.v.), May 9, 1846.

KILBURN, CHARLES LAWRENCE (1819–1899). Lt. Charles L. Kilburn was assigned to the artillery (q.v.) battery of Lt. Braxton Bragg (q.v.) during a crucial point in the battle of Buena Vista (q.v.). Kilburn served as a brigadier general in the Union army during the American Civil War.

KING, RICHARD. Richard King came to the Rio Grande (q.v.) as a civilian during Gen. Zachary Taylor's (q.v.) campaign in Texas and northern Mexico. King was initially a pilot and later a captain on a steamboat that transported U.S. troops on the river and remained in the area after the Treaty of Guadalupe Hidalgo (q.v.). He married a Hispanic woman from Texas and began buying old Spanish land grants in the area. Over time he built the King Ranch, the largest cattle holding in Texas, and became one of the most powerful figures in the state. King's role in postwar Texas symbolized the influence that former soldiers and others drawn by the war to the region had on its subsequent history.

KINNEY, HENRY L. A trading post on the Nueces River (q.v.) established by Henry L. Kinney in 1838 became the town of Corpus Christi, Texas (q.v.). After the invasion of northern Mexico, Gen. Zachary Taylor (q.v.) placed Kinney in charge of establishing a supply system between the river port of Camargo, Tamaulipas (q.v.), and the inland village of Cerralvo, Nuevo León (q.v.), conferring upon him the rank of major. Kinney was later promoted to colonel.

KIRBY SMITH, EPHRAIM (1807–1847). Capt. Ephraim Kirby Smith, or Kirby-Smith, graduated from West Point in 1836 and joined the Fifth Infantry Regiment. In 1846, as a company commander in the Fifth, he fought in several battles under the command of Gen. Zachary Taylor (q.v.). Shifted to the invasion force of Gen. Winfield Scott (q.v.) in early 1847, Kirby Smith fought in all of the major engagements from Veracruz (q.v.) to the Valley of Mexico (q.v.). With the illness of Bvt. Lt. Col. Charles F. Smith, Kirby Smith took command of the Light Battalion of Infantry in its attack against the fortified position at Molino del Rey (q.v.), September 8, 1847, and was killed in that action. His letters to his wife, published posthumously in 1917 as *To Mexico with Scott: Letters of Ephraim Kirby Smith to His Wife*, give an important insight into the war, especially the American campaign around Mexico City (q.v.).

KRIBBEN, CHRISTIAN. Lt. Christian Kribben assumed the position of editor of the English-language newspaper *The Anglo Saxon* on March 18, 1847, following the occupation of Chihuahua (q.v.) by the force of Col. Alexander Doniphan (q.v.).

L

LAGUNA DE ENCENILLAS. The Laguna de Encenillas was a large body of water that furnished relief for the volunteer force of Col. Alexander Doniphan (q.v.) on its march from El Paso (q.v.) to Chihuahua (q.v.). Doniphan reached that point on February 25, 1847.

LAGUNA DE TERMINOS. A strategic salt lagoon located between the states of Yucatán (q.v.) and Tabasco (q.v.), the Laguna de Terminos played an important role in U.S. naval operations during the war.

LA JOYA PASS, VERACRUZ. Approximately 10 miles west of Jalapa (q.v.), the capital of the state of Veracruz, is the formidible La Joya Pass. It became a favorite spot for Mexican guerrilla (q.v.) forces to attack U.S. convoys and came to be known in American annals as "La Hoya."

LALLY, FOLLIOT T. After Gen. Winfield Scott (q.v.) marched to Mexico City (q.v.), the route between Veracruz (q.v.) and Puebla (q.v.) was only lightly garrisoned. A reinforcement column of some 1,000 men marched from Veracruz on August 6, 1847, under the command of Maj. Folliot T. Lally. Encountering major guerrilla attacks at the Paso de Ovejas (q.v.) and Cerro Gordo (q.v.), Lally had lost almost 10 percent of his force by the time he arrived in Jalapa (q.v.). He later joined Brig. Gen. Joseph Lane (q.v.) in his march to Puebla to relieve the besieged force of Col. Thomas Childs (q.v.).

LA MESA, BATTLE OF (January 9, 1847). The broad plain between the San Gabriel (q.v.) and Los Angeles Rivers in western California was known as La Mesa. On January 9, 1847, the day after the battle of San Gabriel (q.v.) the U.S. force under Commo. Robert F. Stockton (q.v.) defeated Cap. José María Flores (q.v.) and his Californios (q.v.) in the battle of La Mesa. This opened the way for the American occupation of Los Angeles (q.v.). *See also* SAN GABRIEL, BATTLE OF.

LANDERO, JUAN JOSE (1802–1869). Brig. Gen. Juan Jóse Landero assumed command of the city of Veracruz (q.v.) with the resignation of Brig. Gen. Juan Morales (q.v.). Pressured by the bombardment of the combined U.S. naval and army forces, Landero asked for a truce on March 26, 1847. Gen. Winfield

Scott (q.v.) ordered the firing to cease, and Landero was persuaded to surrender the city on the following day. Both he and Morales were imprisoned by Mexican authorities in the Castle of Perote (q.v.) on charges of treason.

LANE, JAMES HENRY (1814–1866). Col. James H. Lane commanded the Third Indiana Volunteers in the battle of Buena Vista (q.v.), February 22–23, 1847.

LANE, JOSEPH (1801–1881). In 1846, Joseph Lane was a respected lawyer, active in politics in his home state of Indiana. With the outbreak of war with Mexico, he was appointed as a brigadier general in the Indiana volunteers. His brigade played a major role at the battle of Buena Vista (q.v.), but the Second Indiana suffered major casualties due to the misunderstanding of an order on the part of its commander, Col. William A. Bowles (q.v.). Lane's brigade (consisting of regiments from Indiana and Ohio) was shifted from Gen. Zachary Taylor's (q.v.) army to the operation against Veracruz (q.v.), which thus strengthened the army of Gen. Winfield Scott (q.v.). On September 19, 1847, Lane marched inland from Veracruz with a force of some 1,700 men to reestablish communications and relieve the besieged Col. Thomas Childs (q.v.) at Puebla (q.v.). Following the death of Maj. Samuel H. Walker (q.v.) by snipers in Huamantla (q.v.), Lane allowed his troops to sack that town in retaliation. On October 12, 1847, the column lifted the siege at Puebla and carried out a very effective series of operations in the following months against the Mexican guerrilla (q.v.) forces around that city.

LANE, WALTER P. (1817–1892). Maj. Walter P. Lane commanded a battalion of Texas cavalry that was a part of the Army of Chihuahua (q.v.). Lane's unit was severely criticized by Gen. John Wool (q.v.) for its lack of discipline.

LA PAZ, BAJA CALIFORNIA. La Paz, a small village on the remote coast of Baja California and capital of that territory, became the target of various U.S. expeditions in the course of the war. Comdr. Samuel F. DuPont (q.v.) sailed into the harbor on the USS *Cyane* (q.v.) in September 1846, gaining control of the town and capturing nine small ships. This action led to negotiations with Gov. Francisco Palacio Mirranda for the neutralization of Baja California. The port was, however, involved with further actions in the following months, and, on July 21, 1847,

Lt. Col. Henry S. Burton (q.v.) occupied La Paz with two companies of New York volunteers. On November 18–27, 1847, a Mexican force under Capt. Manuel Pineda attempted to expel the Americans but without success. Following the ratification of the Treaty of Guadalupe Hidalgo (q.v.), the American forces departed from most of Baja California but were delayed in leaving La Paz until September 1, 1848, thus making it the last Mexican territory to be evacuated. This was primarily due to the desire on the part of Colonel Burton to protect the collaborators, some 300 of whom joined in the departure.

LARKIN, THOMAS O. (1802–1858). Thomas O. Larkin, one of the early U.S. businessmen to settle in California (q.v.), was appointed consul in Monterey (q.v.). He provided important commercial and political information to Washington and at the same time warned of British intrigues relating to the region. Pres. James K. Polk (q.v.) was convinced by Larkin's reports that it would be possible to carry out the annexation of California. With the arrival of news that war had broken out between the United States and Mexico, Larkin hoped that a peaceful arrangement for the annexation of California might be negotiated with Gen. José María Castro (q.v.). Those efforts were thwarted, however, by the ambitious actions of Commo. Robert Stockton (q.v.) and the scheming of John C. Frémont (q.v.).

LA VALETTE, ELIE A. F. Capt. Elie A. F. La Valette, commander of the frigate USS *Congress* (q.v.), demanded the surrender of the Pacific port city of Guaymas (q.v.) on October 19, 1847. That demand having been rejected, La Valette carried out a bombardment on the 20th, and marines landed that same afternoon. The port remained under U.S. control throughout the war. La Valette also played an important role in the capture of Mazatlán (q.v.) on November 10, 1847. Following the Treaty of Guadalupe Hidalgo (q.v.), he transferred Mazatlán to Mexican authorities on June 13, 1848.

LA VEGA, ROMULO DIAZ DE. *See* DIAZ DE LA VEGA, ROMULO.

LAS VEGAS, NEW MEXICO. The village of Las Vegas, New Mexico, is located southeast of Santa Fe (q.v.), on the eastern slope of the Sangre de Cristo Mountains. In August 1846, as Gen. Stephen W. Kearny's (q.v.) Army of the West (q.v.) approached from Ratón Pass, New Mexico Gov. Manuel Armijo (q.v.) proposed negotiations at Las Vegas. Kearny rejected the offer, pressing ahead to that town and then on to Santa Fe.

LAS VIGAS, VERACRUZ. A small village on the National Highway (q.v.) between Jalapa (q.v.) and Perote (q.v.), Las Vigas is located in a narrow pass in the mountains. Well suited for an ambush, the town became an important center for Mexican guerrilla operations.

LAWSON, THOMAS (d. 1861). Surgeon General Thomas Lawson, a personal friend of Gen. Winfield Scott (q.v.), was critical of the way in which Gen. Zachary Taylor (q.v.) handled the assignment of surgeons during his campaign in northern Mexico. In December 1846, as General Scott visited New Orleans (q.v.), Lawson joined him to discuss health-related problems involved with the landing of the American army at Veracruz (q.v.). He joined the expedition to Mexico and remained with Scott's army until early 1848. During his absence from Washington, the duties of his office were carried out by acting surgeon general Henry Heiskell.

LEE, ROBERT E. (1807–1870). Capt. Robert E. Lee, of the West Point class of 1829, commissioned in the Corps of Engineers (q.v.), joined the army of Gen. John Wool (q.v.) during its march from San Antonio, Texas (q.v.), to the Rio Grande (q.v.) and assisted in the construction of a "flying bridge" that enabled Wool to cross into Mexico near present-day Eagle Pass. He accompanied Wool in his march to Saltillo (q.v.) but left for the Brazos (q.v.) in January 1847, where he was assigned to the personal staff of Gen. Winfield Scott (q.v.), assisting in operations against Veracruz (q.v.). During the siege of that port city, Lee distinguished himself as an untiring and effective officer, especially in the placement of artillery batteries (q.v.). His keen perceptions were a factor also in the battle of Cerro Gordo (q.v.) where he and Lt. P. G. T. Beauregard (q.v.) marked a trail that allowed General Scott to flank the strong Mexican position. The highlight of Lee's career in the war, however, came in the Valley of Mexico (q.v.). He was involved in the choice of an invasion route around Lake Chalco (q.v.) and demonstrated great bravery and stamina in leading U. S. forces across the pedregal (q.v.) in the initial conflicts south of Mexico City. Lee won the highest praise from General Scott for his outstanding service, and he was brevetted to major for Cerro Gordo, lieutenant colonel for Contreras (q.v.) and colonel for Churubusco (q.v.). He was wounded during the battle of Chapultepec (q.v.). Lee was later to serve as commanding general of the Confederate Army of Northern Virginia during the American Civil War.

LEIDESDORFF, WILLIAM B. William B. Leidesdorff was one of the early U.S. merchants to settle in the Mexican territory of California (q.v.) and served as U.S. vice consul in Monterey (q.v.). When Commo. David Sloat issued an order for the seizure of San Francisco (q.v.) on July 7, 1846, Leidesdorff translated that document into Spanish.

LEITENSDORFER, EUGENE. Eugene Leitensdorfer was one of the early American traders in the region of Santa Fe, New Mexico (q.v.), and enjoyed a special relationship with the Pueblo Indians. He assisted Gen. Stephen Kearny (q.v.) in his negotiations with Governor Manuel Armijo (q.v.) of New Mexico.

LEON, ANTONIO PONCE DE (1794–1847). Antonio León initiated his military career as a member of the Spanish Royal Army but joined the movement in 1821 for Mexican independence under Agustín Iturbide. In 1843, he was promoted to brigadier general and, with the invasion of the Valley of Mexico (q.v.) by Gen. Winfield Scott (q.v.), commanded the Oaxaca Brigade of the Mexican National Guard. General León was posted at the Molino del Rey (q.v.) and in the battle for that position, September 8, 1847, was killed.

LEONIDAS LETTER. On September 16, 1847, a letter signed "Leonidas" was published in the New Orleans *Picayune*, describing the heroic and brilliant actions of Gen. Gideon Pillow (q.v.) during the battle of Contreras (q.v.). Other such letters appeared in various publications in the United States; on his arrival in Mexico, Gen. Winfield Scott (q.v.) reacted angrily. The commander's action created ill feelings on the part of Pillow and several other high-ranking officers. The Leonidas letter was, however, only one of the factors that led to charges against General Scott and his eventual relief from command by order of Pres. James K. Polk (q.v.).

LEVANT. The sloop USS *Levant*, under Comdr. Hugh N. Page, served along the Pacific coast of California and Mexico.

LEXINGTON. The storeship USS *Lexington*, commanded by Lt. Theodorus Bailey (q.v.), transported the force of Lt. Col. Henry

S. Burton (q.v.) to Baja California (q.v.), leading to the occupation of La Paz (q.v.). The vessel continued to blockade the Pacific coastal region throughout the war.

LINARES, NUEVO LEON. The town of Linares is located in a well-watered and fertile plain, 80 miles south of Monterrey, Nuevo León (q.v.), on the eastern slope of the Sierra Madre Oriental. It was an important point during the march of the U.S. forces from Monterrey to Tampico (q.v.).

LINCOLN, ABRAHAM (1809–1865). When the resolution calling for war against Mexico was debated in the U.S. House of Representatives, Abraham Lincoln, a Whig (q.v.) congressman from Illinois, spoke against the measure, questioning whether the Mexican attack against Capt. Seth B. Thornton (q.v.) had actually taken place on "American soil." Lincoln, along with many other Whigs, continued to oppose the foreign policy of Pres. James K. Polk (q.v.). In 1860, Lincoln was elected as the first Republican president of the United States and saw the nation enter the struggle for union.

LITTLE, JESSE C. On May 21, 1846, Jesse C. Little, a leader in the Mormon Church, met with Pres. James K. Polk (q.v.) and reached an agreement in which between 500 and 1,000 Mormons would be organized into a military force to serve under Gen. Stephen W. Kearny (q.v.) in his campaign for New Mexico (q.v.) and California (q.v.). The Mormon Battalion (q.v.) marched from Santa Fe (q.v.), across Sonora (present-day southern Arizona), and to California under Lt. Col. Philip St. George Cooke (q.v.). Most of the members were discharged in California and became an important part of the population of the western region of the United States. *See also* MORMON BATTALION.

LITTLE CABINET. As Gen. Winfield Scott (q.v.) arrived at Lobos Island (q.v.) he pulled together a small group of trusted and highly trained officers, calling it his "little cabinet." Members were Col. Joseph Gilbert Totten (q.v.), Lt. Col. Ethan Allen Hitchcock (q.v.), Capt. Robert E. Lee (q.v.), and Capt. Henry Lee Scott who served as secretary for the group. This was in effect the first organized field staff, and it served Scott very well throughout the entire campaign.

LIVERMORE, ABIEL ABBOT (1811–1892). Rev. Abiel Abbot Livermore was a Unitarian minister from New Hampshire who won a prize from the American Peace Society (q.v.), February 1847, for his book *The War with Mexico Reviewed*, an attack against the policy of Pres. James K. Polk (q.v.).

LIVINGSTON, J. W. (1804–1885). Lt. J. W. Livingston commanded the USS *Congress* (q.v.) that transported Commo. Robert Stockton (q.v.) to San Pedro, California, on August 6, 1846, initiating the campaign to wrest California (q.v.) from Mexican control.

LLANO, MANUEL MARIA DE (1799–1863). Gov. Manuel María de Llano of Nuevo León was appointed by Gen. Pedro de Ampudia (q.v.) to negotiate with the U.S. commission following the battle of Monterrey (q.v.), September 24, 1846. The settlement resulted in an armistice for which Gen. Zachary Taylor (q.v.) was roundly criticized by Pres. James K. Polk (q.v.) and other members of the Democratic administration in Washington.

LOBOS, ISLA DE. The Isla de Lobos (Lobos Island) is a low-lying coral island some 65 miles southeast of Tampico (q.v.). It was used by Commo. David Conner (q.v.) in his operations in the Gulf of Mexico; later Gen. Winfield Scott (q.v.) selected it as a rendezvous point for his transports in the amphibious attack against Veracruz (q.v.). Scott arrived at Lobos on February 22, 1847, awaiting troops and supplies that had been delayed, and on March 2, he set out for Antón Lizardo (q.v.) and the landing at Veracruz.

LOCKWOOD, SAMUEL. Lt. Samuel Lockwood commanded the steamer USS *Petrita* (q.v.) in the Home Squadron (q.v.), based at Antón Lizardo (q.v.). On March 6, 1847, he guided that ship on a reconnaissance of Veracruz (q.v.) harbor. Aboard were Commo. David Conner (q.v.), Gen. Winfield Scott (q.v.), and most of the top commanders of the invasion force. In the course of the voyage, the *Petrita* came under fire from San Juan de Ulúa (q.v.) but was not hit. Later, as commander of the USS *Scorpion*, Lockwood continued activities in the Gulf of Mexico, including expeditions up the Grijalva and Usumacinta Rivers.

LOGISTICS. *See* QUARTERMASTER DEPARTMENT.

LOMBARDINI, MANUEL MARIA (1802–1853). Maj. Gen. Manuel María Lombardini commanded one of the infantry divisions in the army of Gen. Antonio López de Santa Anna (q.v.)

that met Gen. Zachary Taylor's (q.v.) force at Buena Vista (q.v.). Lombardini led the main assault against the American position; his division suffered heavy casualties and the general was wounded.

LONGSTREET, JAMES (1821–1904). A graduate of the West Point class of 1842 and commissioned in the infantry, Lt. James Longstreet served with Gen. Zachary Taylor (q.v.) in northern Mexico. He was later shifted as a member of the Eighth Infantry Regiment to participate in the invading force at Veracruz (q.v.). Longstreet was brevetted to captain for Churubusco (q.v.) and to major for Molino del Rey (q.v.), and he was then severely wounded in the assault against Chapultepec (q.v.). He was to serve as a general in the Confederate army during the American Civil War.

LOPER, ROBERT F. Capt. Robert F. Loper was an agent for the U.S. Army who supervised the building of the surfboats (q.v.) for the invasion of Veracruz (q.v.).

LOPEZ URAGA, JOSE (1810–1855). Col. José López Uraga commanded the Mexican Fourth Infantry in the battle of Palo Alto (q.v.) and participated in other encounters in northeastern Mexico. During the battle of Monterrey (q.v.), López Uraga commanded the strong position known as the Tenería (q.v.).

LORING, WILLIAM WING (1818–1886). Maj. William W. Loring of the Tennessee volunteers served under Gen. Gideon J. Pillow (q.v.), seeing important action in the battle of Contreras (q.v.), August 19, 1847. Promoted to lieutenant colonel, Loring suffered the loss of an arm during the occupation of Mexico City (q.v.) and was evacuated in November 1847. He was later to serve as a corps commander for the Confederacy.

LOS ANGELES, CALIFORNIA. Soon after news of the declaration of war between the United States and Mexico, Lt. John C. Frémont (q.v.) and Commo. John D. Sloat (q.v.) moved to occupy the California towns of Monterey (q.v.), Sonoma (q.v.), and San Francisco (q.v.). Gov. Pio Pico (q.v.) and Gen. José María Castro (q.v.) of Mexico concentrated their forces farther south at Los Angeles, a town of approximately 1,500 inhabitants. On the approach of Commo. David Stockton (q.v.), the Californios (q.v.) abandoned the city and the U.S. flag was raised on August 13, 1846. In late September, however, the Californio elements rebelled and forced Lt. Archibald H. Gillespie (q.v.) to surrender. Los Angeles remained under Mexican control until after the battle of San Gabriel (q.v.), January 8, 1847. By January 10, 1847, U.S. elements had consolidated control of Los Angeles and all of southern California.

LOVE, JOHN (d. 1881). Lt. John Love commanded a small detachment of dragoons charged with protecting the line of communication along the Santa Fe Trail (q.v.). In March 1848, Love, with an artillery battery, supported Brig. Gen. Sterling Price (q.v.) in Chihuahua (q.v.), marching 200 miles over the harsh region south of El Paso (q.v.) in only four days.

LOVELL, MANSFIELD (1822–1884). Following the battle of Chapultepec (q.v.) and the attack into Mexico City (q.v.), Gen. John A. Quitman (q.v.) sent Lt. Mansfield Lovell, along with Lt. P. G. T. Beauregard (q.v.), to arrange for the surrender of the citadel (q.v.), a key point guarding the passage to the center of Mexico City.

LOWD, ALLEN. In early May 1846, Capt. Allen Lowd commanded an artillery battery (four 18-pounders) under Maj. Jacob Brown (q.v.) at Fort Texas (q.v.). Captain Lowd was unsuccessful in his attempt to set fire to Matamoros (q.v.) with "hot shot" from his battery but was able to hold out against the Mexican siege until Gen. Zachary Taylor (q.v.) sent reinforcements after the battle of Resaca de la Palma (q.v.). *See also* FORT BROWN.

LOWELL, JAMES RUSSELL (1819–1891). James Russell Lowell joined a number of other U.S. intellectual leaders in opposing the war with Mexico. He was among the most effective, publishing harsh satirical attacks against Pres. James K. Polk (q.v.) and his administration in the *Biglow Papers* (q.v.).

M

MACKALL, WILLIAM WHANN (1818–1891). William Whann MacKall served with Gen. Zachary Taylor's (q.v.) army as a captain of artillery (q.v.) in the northern campaign. Later he was an assistant adjutant general in the First Division of Gen. Winfield Scott's (q.v.) army. He was brevetted captain for Monterrey (q.v.) and major for Contreras and Churubusco (q.v.). During the Civil War, he fought in the Confederate army.

MACKENZIE, ALEXANDER SLIDELL (1803–1848). In July 1846, Pres. James Knox Polk (q.v.) sent Alexander Slidell Mackenzie as an unofficial agent to Havana, Cuba, to conduct secret negotiations with the exiled Mexican strongman, Antonio López de Santa Anna (q.v.). Mackenzie's oral instructions from the president were to inform Santa Anna that he would be allowed by authorities to pass through the American blockade (q.v.) to return to Mexico. Mackenzie told Santa Anna that, if the former dictator subsequently regained power, the United States would be willing to negotiate a treaty with his government settling the outstanding disputes between the two countries in a manner consistent with the administration's policies. When Mackenzie put Polk's oral terms in writing and showed them to Santa Anna, Polk became furious. The president nonetheless allowed Santa Anna to return to Mexico and asked Congress for funds to support a possible settlement. Mackenzie, a commander in the navy, was the brother of John Slidell (q.v.), Polk's diplomatic representative to Mexico in 1845. Mackenzie was one of several secret agents—some official, some unofficial—whom Polk employed during the war.

MACKENZIE, SAMUEL (d. 1847). Samuel Mackenzie, who graduated from West Point in 1818, participated in the battles of Palo Alto (q.v.) and Resaca de la Palma (q.v.), the siege of Veracruz (q.v.), the battle of Cerro Gordo (q.v.), the skirmish of Amozoc (q.v.), the capture of San Antonio (q.v.), and the battles of Churubusco (q.v.) and Molino del Rey (q.v.). Although a captain of artillery (q.v.), Mackenzie led an infantry charge in the final assault on Chapultepec Castle (q.v.) in the battle for Mexico City (q.v.).

MACKINTOSH, EDWARD. As the British consul general in Mexico, Edward Mackintosh assisted the Mexicans and Americans in arranging a preliminary military armistice in August 1847. The agreement, accepted by Gen. Winfield Scott (q.v.) and Gen. Antonio López de Santa Anna (q.v.), proved only a temporary delay in the fighting. Realizing that the truce was being used by Santa Anna to reinforce his army, Scott resumed offensive operations against Mexico City.

MAGOFFIN, JAMES WILEY (1799–1868). As a prominent trader along the Santa Fe Trail (q.v.) with good contacts with officials in northern Mexico, James Wiley Magoffin answered the administration's unofficial request for him to persuade the leaders in New Mexico (q.v.) to acquiesce to U.S. military occupation. Traveling with Gen. Stephen Watts Kearny's (q.v.) army from Fort Leavenworth (q.v.) to Santa Fe (q.v.), Magoffin, acting with Philip St. George Cooke (q.v.) as Kearny's advance emissary, arrived in Santa Fe on August 12, 1846. Most observers believe Magoffin was influential in Gov. Manuel Armijo's (q.v.) decision to depart New Mexico rather than fight the approaching American army.

MAGOFFIN, SAMUEL. Brother of James Wiley Magoffin (q.v.) and husband of Susan Shelby Magoffin (q.v.), Samuel Magoffin was a Santa Fe (q.v.) trader during the years of the war with Mexico.

MAGOFFIN, SUSAN SHELBY. The wife of Samuel Magoffin (q.v.), Susan Magoffin is known by historians primarily because of a diary she kept about her impressions of life in New Mexico (q.v.) and Chihuahua (q.v.) during the period of the U.S. occupation. It was published as *Down the Santa Fe Trail and into Mexico: The Diary of Susan Shelby Magoffin, 1846–1847.*

MAGRUDER, JOHN BANKHEAD (1810–1871). An artillery (q.v.) officer, John Bankhead Magruder saw action as a battery commander at Cerro Gordo (q.v.) and in the battles for Mexico City (q.v.). He won brevets to major at Cerro Gordo and lieutenant colonel at Chapultepec (q.v.), where he was wounded in action. Magruder was a major general in the Confederate army during the Civil War.

MANIFEST DESTINY. In the 1840s, the idea that the United States had a special mission to expand the nation westward and spread its government and culture to other peoples came to be known as the concept of Manifest Destiny. It therefore was a key factor in influencing a large segment of the American people to support war with Mexico and the seizing of that nation's territory by force. Manifest Destiny was not a new idea for the nation, having been under different names a driving force in the republic from its founding. James Knox Polk (q.v.) ran for president on an expansionist platform underpinned by this creed, and as president, he was its dedicated agent. The term was supposedly coined by John Louis O'Sullivan (q.v.), editor of the *Democratic Review*, in 1842.

MANSFIELD, JOSEPH KING FENNO (1803–1862). Joseph King Fenno Mansfield was the senior engineer officer in Gen. Zachary Taylor's (q.v.) army. He was responsible for the design and construction of Fort Brown (q.v.) (located where Brownsville, Texas [q.v.], is today). As with most of the combat engineers (q.v.), Mansfield performed reconnaissance along the campaign trail and before battle. He was a captain at the border early in the war and later won brevets to major, lieutenant colonel, and colonel. Mansfield saw action at Fort Brown, Monterrey (q.v.) (where he was wounded), and Buena Vista (q.v.). In the Civil War, he rose to major general of U.S. Volunteers and was killed in action at Antietam.

MARCY, RANDOLPH BARNES (1812–1887). Infantry officer Randolph Barnes Marcy, West Point class of 1832, participated in the occupation of Texas (q.v.) in 1845–1846. During the war with Mexico, he served at Palo Alto (q.v.) and Resaca de la Palma (q.v.). In the first two years of the Civil War, he was chief of staff to his son-in-law, the commander of the Army of the Potomac, Gen. George Brinton McClellan (q.v.). By the Civil War's end, he had won two brevets to brigadier general.

MARCY, WILLIAM LEARNED (1786–1857). Formerly governor of New York, William Learned Marcy was Pres. James Knox Polk's (q.v.) secretary of war during the conflict with Mexico. Although a weak administrator, Marcy was a loyal cabinet officer for Polk. As a supporter of Polk's war policies, he was a key participant in strategic planning and, along with the president, managed the war on a day-to-day basis. Throughout the war, Marcy's department provided substantial support to the military commanders and their forces despite the government's limited resources. Although a faithful Democrat, Marcy lacked Polk's pettiness and bitter partisanship toward political opponents; his advice often steered the president toward more objective decisions, such as the selection of Winfield Scott (q.v.) as the commander of the southern campaign in Mexico. As with many politicians in the 1850s, Marcy's association with the war with Mexico probably assisted him in retaining a high government position in later years. He was secretary of state from 1853 to 1857 during the administration of Franklin Pierce (q.v.), who had served under him as a volunteer general in the war with Mexico.

MARIN, NUEVO LEON. Marín is a small Mexican town about 25 miles east of Monterrey (q.v.). The Mexican general Pedro de Ampudia (q.v.) initially planned to oppose the army of Zachary Taylor (q.v.) at Marín but later decided to fall back and defend at Monterrey. On September 15, 1846, Taylor halted his advance at Marín to allow the army to close ranks before continuing on to Monterrey. After the battle for Monterrey, Marín remained on the American resupply route that ran from the Rio Grande (q.v.) to the interior in the northern theater and became a center for Mexican guerrilla actions against the invading army.

MARIN, TOMAS (1805–1873). A Mexican naval officer, Commo. Tomás Marín prepared the defenses at the port of Alvarado (q.v.) on the Gulf coast before the second American attempt by Commo. David E. Conner (q.v.) to capture the city in October 1846.

MARINE CORPS, U.S. At the outset of the war with Mexico, the U. S. Marine Corps was composed of approximately 60 officers and 1,200 enlisted men. The size of the Corps increased after March 1847, when Congress authorized a modest addition to officer and enlisted marine billets before the opening of a second front at Veracruz (q.v.). The Marine commandant during the war was Col. Archibald Henderson, who had led the Corps since 1820 (and who would remain its chief until 1859). It was practice at the time of the war for the Corps to keep more than half of the Marines at sea. Some were aboard ships of the Home Squadron (q.v.) (operating in the Gulf of Mexico) while most deployed Marines were with the Pacific Squadron (q.v.) on the West Coast. During this period, Marines were also aboard vessels in Brazilian (two ships) and African (four ships) waters.

The Marines performed a dual role in the war with Mexico, joining the navy's bluecoats as assault troops against objectives ashore and augmenting the army in land campaigns. Marines saw combat in numerous brief, but often fierce battles in the campaign in California (q.v.), principally in the attacks the navy made against Mexican strong points along the Pacific coast. Marines also participated briefly in support of Zachary Taylor's (q.v.) operations along the Rio Grande (q.v.) in the summer of 1846. A unit of a hundred Marines joined bluecoats from the Home Squadron to reinforce army troops at Fort Polk (q.v.) near Point Isabel (q.v.), while Taylor's troops were fighting at Palo Alto (q.v.) and Resaca de la Palma (q.v.). After these battles, Marines patrolled along the mouth of the Rio Grande while Taylor secured the Matamoros (q.v.) area.

Marines played a more substantial role in the southern campaign of Gen. Winfield Scott (q.v.). A Marine company—variously listed as a detachment, company, squadron or battalion—drawn primarily from the Home Squadron but possibly also from the individual states, was assigned to Brig. Gen. William J. Worth's (q.v.) First Division for the amphibious landing at Veracruz on March 9, 1847. The unit was under the command of Capt. Alvin Edson (q.v.) and came directly under Worth's Third Artillery, commanded by Lt. Col. Francis S. Belton (q.v.). The Marines participated in the entire siege operation against Veracruz, losing one man to Mexican fire, and were withdrawn to the Home Squadron soon after the city surrendered at the end of March. Edson became ill during the operation, was evacuated to the frigate *Raritan*, and died aboard the ship in July.

In May, after Winfield Scott's army had fought at Cerro Gordo (q.v.) and moved to Jalapa (q.v.) and beyond, Pres. James Knox Polk (q.v.) ordered Colonel Henderson to send six companies of Marines from the Home Squadron to join Scott's army. Henderson did not have the Marines to send and asked the Navy (q.v.) Department to order Commo. Matthew Calbraith Perry (q.v.) to provide them from the Home Squadron. Perry protested that the loss of his Marines would threaten his hold on a number of Gulf port cities he was garrisoning at the time. Throughout 1847, Marines participated in the Home Squadron's operations against Gulf and river strong points and were frequently left to secure the towns against Mexican guerrilla attacks. Eventually the order to Perry was rescinded. Colonel Henderson had a skeleton of a Marine regiment hastily recruited. Entirely untrained, the 291 raw recruits and 23 officers were dispatched from Fort Hamilton, New York, to the war zone.

The marines sent were to be assigned to Brig. Gen. Franklin Pierce's (q.v.) brigade of volunteers (q.v.) and regulars that was to depart Veracruz for the front in the summer of 1847. The Marine "regiment" of recruits was under the command of Bvt. Lt. Col. Samuel E. Watson (q.v.). Maj. Levi Twiggs (q.v.), a veteran of the War of 1812, like Watson, was second in command. Once in Mexico, Commodore Perry added the few Marines he could spare from the Home Squadron. The unit, still too small for a regiment, was reorganized into a battalion and left Veracruz as scheduled with Pierce, who assigned Watson the mission of rear guard. On the National Highway (q.v.) on the way to Puebla (q.v.), Watson had constantly to fight off guerrilla attacks against Pierce's column. In Puebla, the Marine battalion was augmented by a battalion of the Second Pennsylvania Volunteers, and, still under Watson's command, it became the Second Brigade in Brig. Gen. John Anthony Quitman's (q.v.) Fourth Division. On arriving in the Valley of Mexico (q.v.), Quitman's division was in reserve and missed the fighting in the initial battles in the campaign for the capital. Quitman was brought forward for the final offensive against Mexico City (q.v.), however, where the Marines saw their heaviest fighting of the war in the Chapultepec (q.v.) assault and at the fight for the San Cosmé gate (q.v.). Major Twiggs was killed while leading a storming party of Marines at Chapultepec (Twiggs's commander, Sam Watson, died of illness two months later). Three marines distinguished themselves and won brevets for the attack on the San Cosmé strongpoint: Capt. George H. Terrett who, with Lt. Ulysses S. Grant of the army, led the charge on the gate, and two officers under Terrett's command, 1st Lt. John D. Simms and 2nd. Lt. Charles A. Henderson. The latter was the son of the commandant. Watson's battalion suffered 30 casualties while fighting in Scott's army. Eight Marines (Major Twiggs and seven enlisted men) were killed in action; 21 Marines died as a result of disease (Watson, Lt. Henry Walsh, and 19 enlisted men), and one enlisted Marine died from an attack while on liberty in Mexico City.

The refrain in the Marine Corps's anthem, "from the halls of Montezuma," recognizes the Marine contribution to the desperate combat that resulted in the capture of Mexico City and to the overall U. S. victory in the war with Mexico.

MARSHALL, HUMPHREY (1812–1872). As a colonel, Humphrey Marshall commanded the First Kentucky Cavalry Regiment at the battle of Buena Vista (q.v.). On the first day of the battle, Gen. Zachary Taylor (q.v.) placed Marshall in command of a task force consisting of his regiment plus one other cavalry regiment and an infantry battalion. His mission—which was partially accomplished—was to block the Mexican attack against the American left. Forces under his command during the two-day battle experienced intense combat action, at times were routed, and suffered high casualties. Marshall survived the battle and the war and later served as a brigadier general for the Confederacy in the Civil War.

MARSHALL, THOMAS (1793–1853). Thomas Marshall, a Kentuckian, was one of the six brigadier generals appointed by

Pres. James Knox Polk (q.v.) from civilian life after the declaration of war in 1846. Marshall served in both the northern and southern theaters under Gen. Zachary Taylor (q.v.) and Gen. Winfield Scott (q.v.); his volunteer division of infantry was one of the last to depart Mexico City (q.v.) at the end of the occupation in June 1848.

MASON, JAMES L. (1817–1853). Maj. James L. Mason graduated from West Point in 1836. An engineer officer in Maj. Gen. William Worth's (q.v.) division, Mason participated in the siege of Veracruz (q.v.) and performed key reconnaissance missions at Cerro Gordo (q.v.) and in the battles for Mexico City (q.v.). Mason was brevetted a lieutenant colonel before being severely wounded at the battle of Molino del Rey (q.v.).

MASON, JOHN YOUNG (1799–1859). A college classmate of Pres. James Knox Polk (q.v.) at the University of North Carolina, John Young Mason was a lawyer and jurist before becoming secretary of the navy in the last year of the John Tyler administration. He next served his friend Polk as attorney general for a year before replacing George Bancroft (q.v.) in 1846 as secretary of the navy for the duration of Polk's administration (1846–1849).

MASON, RICHARD BARNES (1797–1850). Col. Richard Barnes Mason of the First Regiment of Dragoons (q.v.) was sent by Pres. James Knox Polk (q.v.) to be the commanding officer of the Tenth Military Department (California [q.v.] and Oregon territories). Mason succeeded Brig. Gen. Stephen Watts Kearny (q.v.) as governor when Kearny returned to the East May 31, 1847. Mason was brevetted brigadier general for his contribution to the war with Mexico.

MASSACHUSETTS. Gen. Winfield Scott (q.v.) used the *Massachusetts*, an army steamer, as his flagship for the Veracruz (q.v.) operation in March 1847.

MATAMOROS, TAMAULIPAS. At the beginning of hostilities in the spring of 1846, the Mexican city of Matamoros, situated on the right bank of the Rio Grande (q.v.), became the headquarters for the Mexican Army of the North (q.v.) under Gen. Mariano Arista (q.v.). Arista fortified the city and awaited the arrival of Gen. Zachary Taylor's (q.v.) army from Corpus Christi (q.v.). Taylor established his camp in a cornfield across the river from

Matamoros and constructed a large, bastioned, earthen fort (Fort Texas [q.v.], later Fort Brown [q.v.]; presently the site of Brownsville, Texas [q.v.]). After the American victories in the battles of Palo Alto (q.v.) and Resaca de la Palma (q.v.), Arista's army fled south. Taylor occupied Matamoros and made camp just outside the city. It was the first foreign city ever to be occupied by U. S. military forces. American occupation troops, especially the volunteers (q.v.), were unruly; they mistreated the locals, committing numerous atrocities and depredations against the Mexicans in the summer of 1846. U.S. military governors of Matamoros were later able to impose a degree of discipline on their soldiers, and relations with the Mexicans improved somewhat before occupation terminated at the end of the war. In the border city of Matamoros today, there are no historical markers or other visible reminders of the two-year American occupation.

MATSON, HENRY J. Henry J. Matson, a British naval commander, was stationed off Veracruz (q.v.) at the time of the American invasion in March 1847. His observations supported Gen. Winfield Scott's (q.v.) reports regarding Mexican casualties (far less than the Mexicans claimed) and General Scott's contention that the civilians in the city were given fair warning of the American bombardment before firing commenced.

MAY, CHARLES AUGUSTUS (1817–1864). An officer with the Second Regiment of Dragoons (q.v.), Capt. Charles Augustus May served as Gen. Zachary Taylor's (q.v.) chief of cavalry. He saw extensive combat and performed key reconnaissance missions for Taylor in the northern theater. At the battle of Resaca de la Palma (q.v.), Taylor ordered May to lead a cavalry charge to take a Mexican artillery battery that was bringing effective fire on American positions. May's bold charge directly into the Mexican battery failed to capture the guns. Some news reports published in the United States—later proved false—credited May with capturing Gen. Rómulo Díaz de la Vega (q.v.) during the charge. May's charge *was* daring, however, and it disrupted the Mexican battle formation; for his actions he won a double brevet (major for Palo Alto [q.v.] and lieutenant colonel for Resaca de la Palma), awards resented by many of the officers and men who knew he did not deserve credit for the capture of Gen. Díaz de la Vega. At Buena Vista (q.v.), May again saw battle at the center, winning another brevet (this time to colonel) for his actions in that desperate fighting.

MAZATLAN, SINALOA. Parts of the coast of the state of Sinaloa were occupied by U. S. naval forces in November 1847. Mazatlán, the principal west coast port, was captured on November 11 by a 730-man landing party from the *Independence* (q.v.), the *Congress* (q.v.), the *Erie*, and the *Cyane* (q.v.) under the command of Capt. Elie A. F. La Valette (q.v.). Shortly thereafter, Col. Rafael Telles sent troops to nearby Urias; this threat to U.S.-occupied Mazatlán was thwarted by forces under Lt. George L. Selden and Lt. Stephen C. Rowan (q.v.). Thereafter, only two small skirmishes took place in the vicinity before Mazatlán was fortified, and a garrison of between 400 and 500 men was established.

McCALL, GEORGE ARCHIBALD (1802–1868). A graduate of West Point, Capt. George Archibald McCall led a battalion of regulars of the Fourth Infantry Regiment in Gen. Zachary Taylor's (q.v.) army at the battle of Resaca de la Palma (q.v.). During the Civil War, he became a major general in the Union army.

McCLELLAN, GEORGE BRINTON (1826–1885). George Brinton McClellan graduated second in his West Point class of 1846. He served as a second lieutenant of engineers (q.v.) in Gen. Winfield Scott's (q.v.) army in 1846–1847, participating in the landing at Veracruz (q.v.) and siege of the city and fort. His *The Mexican War Diary of General George B. McClellan* (published in 1917), provides some astute—if occasionally arrogant— observations of the war, especially considering the young age of its author. In the Civil War, McClellan was a major general and for a time Pres. Abraham Lincoln's (q.v.) senior commander as commanding general of the Army of the Potomac.

McCLELLAN, JOHN (1805–1854). A graduate of the West Point class of 1826, John McClellan served in the war with Mexico in the Corps of Topographical Engineers (q.v.). He participated in the siege of Veracruz (q.v.), the battles of Cerro Gordo (q.v.) and Churubusco (q.v.), and the assault on Mexico City (q.v.). For his distinguished service, he won brevets to major and lieutenant colonel. After the war, he helped survey the boundary between Mexico and the United States.

McCULLOCH, BENJAMIN (1811–1862). Benjamin McCulloch's unit, a company of Texas Rangers (q.v.) attached to Gen. Zachary Taylor's (q.v.) army, performed reconnaissance and raid missions during the campaign in northern Mexico. McCulloch's company was part of the First Texas Volunteer Regiment. Along the Rio Grande (q.v.) in the summer of 1846, Taylor sent McCulloch to scout possible roads to Linares (q.v.) as an alternate to the Camargo (q.v.) route. In the march from Camargo to Monterrey (q.v.), McCulloch's company skirmished with 200 Mexican cavalry troops near Ramos (q.v.), driving the larger force from the village. In the battle for Monterrey on September 21, 1846, McCulloch's rangers held off a daring charge by a troop of Mexican lancers west of the city. McCulloch's command later participated in the close-in fighting in the center of the city during September 22 and 23.

Before the battle of Buena Vista (q.v.), McCulloch performed a valuable mission for Gen. John Ellis Wool (q.v.) and Gen. Zachary Taylor when he took his rangers 20 miles south of Saltillo (q.v.) to gather information on the Mexican army's strength around Agua Nueva (q.v.) and Encarnación (q.v.). McCulloch boldly entered General Antonio López de Santa Anna's (q.v.) lines and made it safely back to report his intelligence to Taylor. From McCulloch's accurate reports of the Mexican army's strength, Taylor knew he faced serious battle. In the Civil War, McCulloch became a brigadier general in the Confederate army and was killed on March 7, 1862, at the battle of Pea Ridge, Arkansas.

McDOWELL, IRVIN (1818–1885). Irvin McDowell graduated from West Point in 1838 and was promoted to first lieutenant in 1842. In 1846, he became aide-de-camp to Brig. Gen. John Wool (q.v.) in the northern theater in Mexico and held that position throughout the war. At Buena Vista (q.v.), McDowell won a brevet to captain. In May of 1861, at the beginning of the Civil War, McDowell was promoted three grades (major to brigadier general) and appointed to lead Union forces in the first major battle of the war. His defeat two months later at the battle of First Manassas (Bull Run) forever marked his career, which continued until 1882.

McINTOSH, JAMES S. (d. 1847). A veteran of the War of 1812, by 1846 James S. McIntosh was one of the toughest, most hardbitten, regular officers in the army. Called "Old Tosh" by his men, Lt. Col. McIntosh initially commanded the Second Brigade in Taylor's (q.v.) army at Corpus Christi (q.v.), a command that included the Fifth and Seventh Infantry Regiments. He led the Fifth Infantry in the battle of Palo Alto (q.v.) on May

8, 1846. Aggressive by nature, McIntosh was one of only three senior officers (of 10) under Taylor who voted early on May 9 to continue the attack. In that day's fighting at Resaca de la Palma (q.v.), McIntosh fought in bloody, hand-to-hand combat and survived being bayoneted through the mouth and cheek. In the battle, McIntosh won a brevet to colonel. He later transferred to Gen. Winfield Scott's (q.v.) army in the southern theater. On June 4, 1847, he led a 700-man contingent out of Veracruz (q.v.) on a mission to guard a critical supply train bound for Scott's army at Puebla (q.v.). McIntosh fought the Fifth Infantry again at Churubusco (q.v.) on August 20. At Molino del Rey (q.v.), he commanded Col. Newman S. Clarke's (q.v.) brigade. He was wounded three times, once severely, in the suicidal assault on the Casa Mata (q.v.), an action that resulted in his old regiment, the Fifth, suffering 38 percent casualties. Molino del Rey ended the war for McIntosh. He died on September 26, 1847, from wounds received in that battle.

McKEE, WILLIAM R. (1808–1847). A West Point graduate, Col. William R. McKee commanded the Second Kentucky Regiment of Volunteers in Gen. Zachary Taylor's (q.v.) army in the northern campaign. McKee fought his regiment in the heaviest part of the battle of Buena Vista (q.v.) and was killed, along with his second in command, Lt. Col. Henry Clay, Jr. (q.v.), rallying the men of the Second Kentucky.

McLANE, LOUIS (1786–1857). As U. S. minister in London in 1845–1846, Louis McLane's reporting kept the Polk administration informed of British attitudes about the Oregon (q.v.) question and the war with Mexico. McLane was a militant regarding the war, advising Polk that a vigorous campaign producing a stream of victories would win skeptical British opinion to the American side.

McLANE, ROBERT M. (1815–1898). Pres. James Knox Polk (q.v.) sent Robert M. McLane, then an army major, as a personal courier to Maj. Gen. Zachary Taylor (q.v.) in November 1846. His mission was to inform Taylor that he should not advance his army south of Monterrey (q.v.) and that he would be required to furnish units for a forthcoming operation at Veracruz (q.v.). Taylor ignored Polk's order and proceeded south to Saltillo (q.v.). McLane was the son of Louis McLane (q.v.), U.S. minister to Great Britain. In the late 1850s, Robert McLane was again involved with Mexico when in a diplomatic role he negotiated a treaty with the Liberal faction under Benito Juárez. The McLane-O'Campo Treaty gave the United States perpetual transit rights across various routes in Mexico and even allowed Washington to use troops to keep them open. The treaty was condemned by Mexican nationalists, who portrayed Juárez and his followers as traitors to the nation. The treaty was also poorly received by the U.S. Senate, which defeated it by a vote of 27 to 18.

McNAMARA, EUGENE. Eugene McNamara was an Irish priest who, in 1845, obtained a questionable land grant from local Mexican officials for a fanciful scheme to settle 10,000 Irish Catholics in California (q.v.) The project, however unrealistic it may have been at the time, nevertheless strengthened suspicions in the Polk administration of British designs on California.

McNUTT, JOHN (1819–1881). From 1846 to 1847, John McNutt, an 1840 West Point graduate, commanded the ordnance depot at Point Isabel, Texas (q.v.). He was promoted to first lieutenant in March of 1847.

McREE, SAMUEL (1801–1849). After his graduation from West Point in 1820, Samuel McRee began his military career as an infantry officer. From the late 1830s until his death, however, he had quartermaster (q.v.) assignments. During the war, he was chief quartermaster of Gen. Winfield Scott's (q.v.) army, for which he was brevetted lieutenant colonel.

McSHERRY, RICHARD. Richard McSherry, M.D. (at times spelled M'Sherry), was an acting surgeon of the regiment of U.S. Marines (q.v.), which was attached to Gen. Winfield Scott's (q.v.) army during the war with Mexico. A collection of McSherry's letters from the war zone was published in 1850 as *El Puchero: A Mixed Dish from Mexico, Embracing General Scott's Campaign.*

MEADE, GEORGE GORDON (1815–1872). As a young lieutenant in the topographical engineers (q.v.), George Gordon Meade served in both Zachary Taylor's (q.v.) and Winfield Scott's (q.v.) armies during the war with Mexico. He was present with Taylor's army at Corpus Christi (q.v.) during the winter of 1845–1846 and along the Rio Grande (q.v.) the following summer. At the battle for Monterrey (q.v.), Meade accompanied Gen.

William Jenkins Worth's (q.v.) division in the turning movement to the west of the city and performed scouting missions before the attacks on Federation Hill (q.v.) and Independence Hill (q.v.). Transferring to Winfield Scott's army, Lieutenant Meade joined the General in Chief's staff at Veracruz (q.v.), accompanying Scott and his generals on the important reconnaissance mission aboard the *Petrita* (q.v.) March 6, 1847. At Cerro Gordo (q.v.), Meade was with Gen. Gideon Pillow's (q.v.) brigade, serving as a scout and messenger between Pillow and Scott during the battle. His memoirs, *The Life and Letters of George Gordon Meade, Major-General United States Army*, provide an excellent account of his war experiences in Mexico. As a major general 16 years later, Meade was appointed by Pres. Abraham Lincoln (q.v.) to lead the Union army against Robert E. Lee (q.v.) at Gettysburg in July 1863.

MEDICAL AND HEALTH ISSUES. Statistics showing that almost 10 percent of all U.S. soldiers who served in the war died from disease or other non-combat causes illustrate the primitive state of medical care for the troops. Over 100,000 men left the United States for the war in Mexico: of these, 1,500 died as a result of combat action, and over 10,000 died of disease. The ratio of death from disease to killed in action (seven to one) was better than that for the American Revolution but much worse than the ratio for the Civil War, which was two to one. The death rate from disease for soldiers during the war was 10 times the rate for civilians in the United States during the period. There was no known cure for the deadliest diseases of the war—yellow fever (q.v.), cholera, smallpox, typhoid, diarrhea, dysentery, and malaria—and a soldier's individual vitality and natural immunity were often his only hope for his survival. Abysmal sanitation practices among the troops (especially among the volunteers [q.v.]) added to serious health problems. Although unhealthy drinking water caused widespread illness, it was wrongly blamed for some of the most serious diseases of the war. Unknown to medical personnel at the time, the mosquito carried malaria, the deadly disease of yellow fever (called *el vómito* in Mexico), and other tropical fevers that devastated the ranks.

U.S. Army troops fell victim to disease far more frequently than their naval counterparts because of soldiers' exposure to unhealthy environments, crude living conditions, and inadequate medical care. The treatment provided by military doctors and their assistants fell far short of the requirements of the battlefield. The Army Medical Department, located in New York City and headed by Surgeon General Thomas Lawson (q.v.), was responsible for filling authorized medical billets and furnishing medical supplies to the army in the field. By and large, it did a creditable job of carrying out these functions. Two of the most serious shortcomings in army medical care were, first, that the professional knowledge of military doctors, or surgeons, as they were officially called, was poor—they often were ignorant of how to treat disease properly. Second, there were too few surgeons authorized to the units. If the regular surgeons lacked sufficient knowledge, they were nonetheless as competent as civilian doctors and had to pass examinations to obtain their appointment. The same cannot be said for doctors in volunteer units, contract surgeons, or medical attendants or assistants in all units, who often were entirely bereft of any medical training.

Medical science contributions to American society from the war during this medical dark age were few. Surgeons did prove the value of vaccinations for smallpox—the use of the measure prevented thousands of soldiers from getting the disease. The practice of using massive doses of quinine alleviated the devastating effects of malaria and other fevers. A medical innovation of the war that was not fully exploited was the use of ether as an anesthetic for surgery. Although ether was used to a limited degree, many military doctors had superstitions about its effects and chose not to employ it during operations.

If U.S. military medical care in the war was inadequate, most observers noted that it was far superior to that available in the Mexican army. American visitors to hospitals and other places where Mexican sick and wounded were held invariably reported nightmarish scenes of sick and dying men in unimaginably filthy quarters. Serious wounds more often than not resulted in death. Although some U.S. medical officers reported observing skillful, dedicated Mexican surgeons at work, these reports were rare. The deficient medical support for Mexican troops only reflected the general lack of combat and combat service support provided to the army by a government that was near bankruptcy through the war years.

MEJIA, FRANCISCO (1822–1901). Brig. Gen. Mejía was the 24-year-old, untested commander of Mexican forces at Matamoros (q.v.) on the Rio Grande (q.v.) in March 1846. In early April, Mejía sent his second in command to meet Gen. Zachary Taylor's (q.v.) emissary to discuss the Mexican and American intentions. After being relieved of command by Gen. Pedro de Ampudia (q.v.), Mejía led subordinate units against Taylor's forces in the first battles near Matamoros in May 1846. Later in the year, he commanded at Monterrey (q.v.) in the early hours of the battle for the city. After again being superseded as commanding general, Mejía led troops as a subordinate commander during the battle. He later commanded troops at the Angostura (q.v.) pass (battle of Buena Vista [q.v.]) in February 1847.

MEJIA, TOMAS (1820–1867). Tomás Mejía fought at Monterrey (q.v.) and Buena Vista (q.v.). As a member of Emperor Maximilian's inner circle in the 1860s, his power was feared by the regime's enemies. Mejía was executed with Maximilian on the Hill of the Bells by Benito Juárez's forces on June 19, 1867.

MENDOZA, NICOLAS. Col. Nicolás Mendoza commanded an infantry brigade under Gen. Pedro de Ampudia (q.v.) at the battle of Monterrey (q.v.). Later promoted to general, he and his men were forced to retreat at the battle of Contreras (q.v.) in August of 1847.

MERRILL, MOSES E. (1804–1847). On his graduation from West Point in 1826, Moses E. Merrill began his career as an infantry officer. During the war with Mexico, he saw action at Palo Alto (q.v.), Resaca de la Palma (q.v.), Monterrey (q.v.), Veracruz (q.v.), San Antonio (q.v.), and Churubusco (q.v.) before being mortally wounded while leading an assault at Molino del Rey (q.v.). He attained the rank of captain.

MERRITT, EZEKIEL. In June 1846, encouraged by the presence of a band of adventurers and explorers under Bvt. Capt. John C. Frémont (q.v.) of the U.S. Army Corps of Topographical Engineers (q.v.), Ezekiel Merritt led a group of fellow American settlers in a revolt against the Mexican authorities in California (q.v.). Merritt's party captured the town of Sonoma (q.v.) and the former Mexican *comandante general* in California, Gen. Mariano Guadalupe Vallejo (q.v.). The insurgents' short-lived successes led them, with Frémont's tacit support, to proclaim California a separate and independent nation, which they called the California or Bear Flag (q.v.) Republic.

MERVINE, WILLIAM (1791–1868). Capt. William Mervine, with a party from his ship, the USS *Cyane* (q.v.), participated in the seizure of Monterey (q.v.), California (q.v.), on July 7, 1846. In a ceremony in Monterey's plaza, Mervine hoisted the American flag over the customs house and read a proclamation to the citizens declaring Upper California to be part of the United States. Later the resident Mexicans (called Californios [q.v.]), led by Capt. José María Flores (q.v.), revolted against American occupation and reestablished control. In October of 1846, Mervine, commanding the USS *Savannah*, led a force of sailors and marines (q.v.) from his ship, along with some American civilians, in a futile attempt to retake Los Angeles (q.v.) from the Mexicans.

MEXICALZINGO, DISTRITO FEDERAL. Mexicalzingo was a small village five miles south of Mexico City (q.v.). In August of 1847, as the American army approached the capital, reconnaissance by engineer captains Robert E. Lee (q.v.) and James L. Mason (q.v.) revealed the village to be heavily defended. Their reports and other factors influenced Gen. Winfield Scott (q.v.) to choose another route in his advance on the Mexican capital.

MEXICAN WAR. This term originated with historians and other writers in the United States to refer to the U.S. war with Mexico. It is never used in Mexico, where the war is normally called in Spanish, *la invasion Norteamericana*, or the North American invasion (followed by the dates 1846–1848, to distinguish it from other U.S. invasions of Mexican territory).

MEXICO CITY, DISTRITO FEDERAL. Mexico City, the capital of Mexico at the time of the war, as it is today, played a critical role in the political and military life of the nation in the 1840s. In 1847, it was a beautiful city of 200,000 residents, retaining its splendor from the colonial era when it was the seat of Spanish government in Madrid's northern colony of New Spain. At the time of the war, governments were changed by coups d'état there, armies gathered in the city and marched out to meet the invading American forces, and, in both the broad valley that held the capital and in Mexico City itself, the most critical, desperately fought, and costly battles of the war were fought in late summer of 1847. After those battles were won, Gen. Winfield Scott (q.v.) knew that to control the capital would be to control the vital, strategic center of the nation. Scott therefore did not attempt to send occupation forces throughout the entire country; although many provincial centers remained occupied, many never saw American troops. Scott's army occupied Mexico City until a peace was negotiated, signed, and finally approved by both governments. After the general's departure in February 1848, the American army, on orders from the administration, soon withdrew from the capital (June 1848), returning control to Mexican authorities after an American military occupation of nine months.

MICHELTORENA, JOSE MANUEL (1802–1853). In 1843, the caudillo Antonio López de Santa Anna (q.v.) sent Brig. Gen. José Manuel Micheltorena to be governor of California (q.v.) with the mission of reasserting central government control in that rebellious territory. Micheltorena alienated the Californios (q.v.), and they rebelled again, driving him from office in February 1845. Two years later Micheltorena served as Santa Anna's chief of staff at the battle of Buena Vista (q.v.).

MIER, NUEVO LEON. A small town located near the Rio Grande (q.v.), Mier lay along Gen. Zachary Taylor's (q.v.) route from Camargo (q.v.) to Monterrey (q.v.). American forces occupied the town on July 31, 1846; Mier subsequently served as a training camp for Taylor's army during his campaign in northern Mexico (1846–1847).

MILES, DIXON S. (1804–1862). A regular captain, then major, with the Seventh Infantry, Dixon S. Miles served first with Zachary Taylor's (q.v.) army (William Jenkins Worth's [q.v.] brigade) and later in Winfield Scott's (q.v.) campaign. Miles won a brevet to lieutenant colonel for action in the battle of Monterrey (q.v.). Miles commanded the city of Veracruz (q.v.) from August 11 to December 23, 1847. He died of wounds received at Harper's Ferry, Virginia, during the Civil War.

MILITARY ACADEMY, U.S. Founded during Thomas Jefferson's administration in March 1802, the U. S. Military Academy at West Point, New York, provided the regular army with a nucleus of well-trained, professional junior officers to fight in the war with Mexico. Initially, the academy's primary mission was to prepare military engineers (q.v.), and most graduates entered active service as second lieutenants in the Corps of Engineers. Some of them remained on engineer duty, while others transferred into the various branches, such as artillery (q.v.) or infantry. Later, however, the academy commissioned officers directly into the various branches of the army, with only the top graduates being offered the more coveted commissions as engineers.

The war with Mexico was the first war in which the army in the field was officered primarily by West Pointers. Academy graduates served in command and staff positions throughout the force, leading both regular and volunteer troops. The leadership provided to the army from West Point graduates during the war with Mexico drew high praise from many observers and senior officers. Gen. Winfield Scott, although not a West Pointer, repeatedly praised the performance of academy officers during the war, in his memoirs, and in testimony before Congress. On the latter occasion, Scott argued that, without West Pointers, the war might have lasted four or five years with more defeats than victories during the first years. The General in Chief felt that the presence of West Point officers made it possible in two campaigns to conquer a vast country in two years without the loss of a single battle.

MINON, JOSE VICENTE (1802–1878). As a brigadier general, José Vicente Miñón commanded a cavalry brigade under Gen. Antonio López de Santa Anna (q.v.) at the battle of Buena Vista (q.v.). Miñón screened far in advance of Santa Anna's army during its march north from San Luis Potosí (q.v.). At Encarnación (q.v.), a unit of lancers from Miñón's force captured a mounted company of Arkansas volunteers (q.v.) under Maj. Solon Borland (q.v.). At Buena Vista, Miñón's cavalry attempted to disrupt the American rear and capture Saltillo (q.v.), missions that failed because of American counterattacks.

MISSISSIPPI. The USS Mississippi, a first-class steam frigate, was assigned to the Home Squadron (q.v.) in the Gulf of Mexico at the beginning of the war. Secretary of the Navy George Bancroft (q.v.) assigned command of the Mississippi to Commo. Matthew Calbraith Perry (q.v.) in August of 1846; the ship was Perry's flagship when he assumed command of the Home Squadron in March 1847.

MISSISSIPPI RIFLES. The First Regiment of Mississippi Rifles was a regiment of volunteers (q.v.) commanded by Col. Jefferson Davis (q.v.). Its second in command was Lt. Col. Alexander K. McClung. The regiment was unique in that its soldiers were equipped with rifles instead of the muskets most units used in the war. See also BUENA VISTA, BATTLE OF; DAVIS, JEFFER-

SON; MONTERREY, BATTLE OF; VOLUNTEERS; WEAPONRY.

MISSOURI COMPROMISE. This U.S. congressional agreement in 1820 established a line (36′ 30″ north latitude), extending west from the southern boundary of Missouri, above which from that time slavery would be "forever prohibited." The Missouri Compromise was thus a central part of most debates about annexing Texas (q.v.) during the 1830s and 1840s. The debate intensified during the period of conflict with Mexico; in the 1845–1848 period, northern antislavery Whigs (q.v.) and Democrats feared that much of the land gained from Mexico would fall below the line of 1820 and be added to the Union as slave territory.

MITCHELL, ALEXANDER M. (1813–1861). Col. Alexander M. Mitchell, a West Point graduate of the class of 1835, was a colonel in the First Ohio Volunteers during the war with Mexico. He was severely wounded at the battle of Monterrey (q.v.). Subsequently, he served as military governor of Monterrey (q.v.) from April 1847 until his unit was disbanded in June of that year.

MITCHELL, DAVID D. (1806–1861). David D. Mitchell was a lieutenant colonel under Col. Sterling Price (q.v.) in the Second Regiment of Missouri Volunteers. During the Chihuahua (q.v.) campaign, Mitchell joined Col. Alexander W. Doniphan (q.v.) in the First Regiment of Missouri Mounted Volunteers and participated in the battle of Sacramento (q.v.) and the occupation of Chihuahua City (q.v.).

MIXCOAC. Mixcoac was a village five miles southwest of the center of Mexico City (q.v.). In early September 1847, Mixcoac was the staging base for Brig. Gen. Gideon Pillow's (q.v.) division before the final attack on the city.

MODERADOS. After independence and until the late 1850s and the War of the Reform, the *Moderados*, a faction of the reformist movement, struggled to create liberal democracy in 19th-century Mexico. As with the *Puros* (q.v.), who also fought for a government by the people, the *Moderados* sought a government based on Anglo-Saxon democracy modeled on the U.S. Constitution. Whereas the *Puros* were primarily from the popular classes of mestizo society, the *Moderados*, while including some mestizos, also encompassed wealthy landowners and members of the professional classes who were imbued with the ideas of Jefferson and Rousseau. The *Moderados* tended to be, as the name implies, more moderate in their approach to politics; they were less anti-church than the *Puros*, less opposed to the military, and less stringently nationalistic. After the U. S. invasion in 1846, the *Moderados*, like most Mexicans incensed by this violation of their sovereignty, were nevertheless realistic about the grim chances for ultimate victory and therefore open to negotiating a peace. After Gen. Winfield Scott's (q.v.) victorious campaign in the Valley of Mexico (q.v.), the *Moderados* gained control of the government and negotiated the Treaty of Guadalupe Hidalgo (q.v.), ending the war and losing vast territories to the United States. *See also PUROS.*

MOLINO DEL REY, BATTLE OF (September 8, 1847). A lull in Gen. Winfield Scott's (q.v.) campaign in the Valley of Mexico (q.v.) occurred after the battles of Contreras and Churubusco (q.v.) (August 20, 1847). A tentative armistice was signed on August 24, negotiated by the diplomat Nicholas Philip Trist (q.v.) in talks with senior Mexican officers. Scott, aggravated by reports that Gen. Antonio López de Santa Anna (q.v.) was breaking the truce by building up his forces, carrying out reconnaissance and allowing attacks on American supply trains around Mexico City (q.v.), told Trist to inform the Mexican army that the truce would end on September 6. Information reached Scott that Santa Anna was collecting church bells in the city and having them cast into cannon in a nearby foundry. The alleged foundry was in a group of buildings called Molino del Rey (q.v.), located 1,000 yards to the west of Chapultepec Castle (q.v.) and about two miles west of the city's walls. The buildings were thickly constructed stone structures. Several hundred yards to the west of Molino del Rey was a large stone building known as the Casa Mata (q.v.), which Scott's engineers (q.v.) reported was a powder magazine. Defenses at the Molino del Rey complex of buildings were manned by forces under the commands of Brig. Gen. Antonio León (the Oaxaca Brigade) and Brig. Gen. Joaquín Rangel (q.v.). The Casa Mata defenses were manned by Brig. Gen. Francisco Pérez (q.v.) and Brig. Gen. Simeon Ramírez (q.v.).

Scott, having decided to make this complex his first objective after fighting resumed, assigned the task to Maj. Gen. William Worth's (q.v.) division. Scott's plan called for Maj. Gen. David Twiggs's (q.v.) division and one of Brig. Gen. Gideon Pillow's (q.v.) brigades to make a feint against the southern gates of the city two miles to the east; Worth led the main attack at Molino del Rey. Scott reinforced Worth with artillery (q.v.) batteries led by Capt. Simon H. Drum (q.v.) and Capt. Benjamin Huger (q.v.), a cavalry squadron under Maj. Edwin Vose Sumner (q.v.), and an additional infantry brigade commanded by Col. George Cadwalader (q.v.). Among Worth's organic units for the attack were a brigade under Lt. Col. John Garland (q.v.); a battalion under Lt. Col. Charles Ferguson Smith (q.v.), commanded for the battle by Capt. Ephraim Kirby Smith (q.v.); Col. Newman S. Clarke's (q.v.) brigade, commanded by Col. James S. McIntosh (q.v.); an artillery unit under Col. James Duncan (q.v.); and a special unit of assault troops under Maj. George S. Wright (q.v.). Worth had over 3,000 men for the predawn attack on September 8, 1847.

The battle went badly for William Worth. The most critical mission fell to Major Wright, who commanded a storming party made up of 500 carefully selected men. After a brief artillery bombardment to soften the defenses, Worth ordered Wright to assault the objective. The storming party quickly masked the supporting artillery, and Wright assaulted in the face of withering fire from the Mexicans, which included an unexpected counterattack by a unit from Chapultepec to the east. Wright's force was devastated. It lost 11 of its 14 officers and over a third of its soldiers in the assault. The Mexican positions, from the foundry complex to the Casa Mata, were vastly more fortified and difficult to dislodge than reports had indicated, and the results of the battle made Molino del Rey one of the bloodiest of the war. Because the American artillery batteries were mostly positioned directly and closely behind the infantry units, their fires were masked too soon by the units that assaulted in straight lines from their original positions; the guns could not do proper damage to the Mexican positions before the assaulting troops went to the bayonet. The Mexican forces fought tenaciously, and repeated infantry assaults were required, all costly for Worth's force. Artillery eventually played a key role, especially in reducing the Casa Mata after infantry assaults had failed and the troops withdrew to allow the guns room to work. After a violent two-hour, close-in fight on the right of the line in front of the Molino buildings—one that ended only with a series of desperate bayonet charges by Worth's men—the Americans finally drove the enemy from the complex. The irony of the Molino del Rey battle—perhaps the most costly in lives per minute of all battles during the war—

was that it was unnecessary. The report of guns being cast there proved false. There was no foundry; the location was therefore not a threat, and Scott could have bypassed it and moved directly on Chapultepec, his next objective, or to the city itself. Molino del Rey resulted in approximately 2,000 Mexican casualties. Worth's force lost 787 men, about 25 percent of those committed. Of these, 116 were killed in action, including some of Worth's best officers, among these the young infantry captain, Ephraim Kirby Smith, and Col. James McIntosh, who died from wounds received in the battle. Lt. Col. Ethan Allen Hitchcock (q.v.), who participated in the battle, later wrote that it was a pyrrhic victory, more of which Scott's small army could not afford.

MONCLOVA, COAHUILA. Monclova, located northwest of Monterrey (q.v.), was the intermediate staging area for Brig. Gen. John Ellis Wool's (q.v.) force as it marched from San Antonio (q.v.), Texas (q.v.) to Chihuahua (q.v.). After a change of orders, Wool marched from Monclova to Parras (q.v.); from there he joined Taylor's army at Saltillo (q.v.).

MONROE DOCTRINE. Pres. James Knox Polk's (q.v.) policies during the war with Mexico, as well as his moral support for the idea of Manifest Destiny (q.v.), were in his view consistent with the Monroe Doctrine. This 1823 doctrine of Pres. James Monroe warned European powers to keep "hands off" the Western Hemisphere; Polk's carefully structured yet aggressive policies were designed for similar purposes. Great Britain had long made claim to the Oregon Territory, and there was a clear sense in the nation in the 1840s that it had set its sights as well on California (q.v.). Polk developed policies—often couched within the framework of the Monroe Doctrine—designed to thwart any British attempt to secure California from Mexico.

MONTERDE, J. M. Gen. J. M. Monterde of Mexico fought as part of Gen. Antonio López de Santa Anna's (q.v.) army in the defense of Mexico City (q.v.). He was captured at the battle of Chapultepec (q.v.) in September of 1847.

MONTEREY, CALIFORNIA. In the early 1840s, Monterey was a small, lightly garrisoned port in Upper California on Mexico's west coast. After the start of hostilities, American sailors and marines under Commo. John Drake Sloat (q.v.), commander of the Pacific Squadron (q.v.), captured the village and its customs house on July 7, 1846. Monterey became the operating base of the Pacific Squadron for the remainder of the war.

MONTERREY, ARMISTICE OF. After the Mexicans lost the battle for Monterrey (q.v.), a six-man commission negotiated an armistice on September 25, 1846. For the Mexicans, the members of the commission were Gen. Tomás Requeña (q.v.), Gen. José María Ortega (q.v.), and the Nuevo León governor, Manuel María del Llano (q.v.). The American representatives were Gen. William J. Worth (q.v.), Gen. and former Texas Gov. James Pinckney Henderson (q.v.), and Col. Jefferson Davis (q.v.).

The armistice terms were as follows: (1) the Mexican army would give up the citadel fortress and leave Monterrey within the week, (2) the cavalry would retain its horses, officers would keep their sidearms, and the Mexican army would retain one field battery of six guns; and (3) the line between the two opposing forces would run from the Rinconada Pass (q.v.) to Linares (q.v.) and Parras (q.v.). On receiving news of the armistice, Pres. James Knox Polk (q.v.) roundly condemned Gen. Zachary Taylor's (q.v.) decision to release the Mexicans and to stop his offensive temporarily. Polk immediately issued orders to cancel the agreement. On receiving orders from Secretary of War William Marcy (q.v.) to end the armistice, Taylor sent notice to Gen. Antonio López de Santa Anna (q.v.) on November 10, 1846, that he would resume hostilities on the 13th.

MONTERREY, BATTLE OF (August 20–24, 1846). After occupying Matamoros (q.v.) in May 1846, Gen. Zachary Taylor (q.v.) spent the summer preparing for an offensive in northern Mexico. His strategic objective was the city of Monterrey (q.v.), located about 200 miles from the Rio Grande (q.v.). When scouting parties reported that the direct route between Matamoros and Monterrey lacked water, Taylor decided on an axis of advance that would take his army up the Rio Grande and then west on a route that would follow or parallel the San Juan valley. After spending over a month in the disease-ridden town of Camargo (q.v.) on the right bank of the San Juan River, Taylor marched his army out in mid-August, passing through Cerralvo (q.v.) and Marín (q.v.) before arriving at the northern edge of Monterrey on September 19.

The defenses of the city were formidable. Houses and forts were of stone or strong adobe construction. To the south and west, the city was protected by sharply rising hills and the Santa Catarina River. The eastern and northern approaches

were fairly open; there the Mexicans had dug ditches and fortified buildings, one of which, the citadel (or Black Fort [q.v.], as
the Americans called it), mounted with 12 guns and defended
by 400 troops, was an extremely difficult defensive challenge
for Taylor's troops. To the east of Monterrey's center, two fortified structures, Fort Diablo (Devil's Fort) and La Tenería (the
Tannery) guarded the city. On the western side of Monterrey
lay two fortified hills. Federation Hill (q.v.), south of the Santa
Catarina River, held an artillery (q.v.) position and a stone fort
called El Soldado (q.v.). On the other, taller hill (Independence
Hill [q.v.]), on the north side of the river, stood another gun
battery and a structure called the Obispado, or Bishop's Palace
(q.v.), a ruin of a stone edifice that the Mexicans protected with
troops and heavy guns. To the west of the city ran the strategically important road to Saltillo (q.v.), the artery for resupply
and reinforcement for the Mexican army in Monterrey. The
commander of Mexican forces in the city, Gen. Pedro de Ampudia (q.v.), had approximately 7,300 troops and 42 guns
under his command.

After Maj. Joseph K. Mansfield (q.v.), Taylor's chief engineer,
assessed these fortifications and reported his results to Taylor
on the evening of September 19, Taylor, assisted by his aide,
Capt. William W. S. Bliss (q.v.), drafted his plan for taking the
city. It was to be a two-directional attack. One attack would go
against the northeastern end of the city and would be launched
from the direction of Taylor's headquarters at Walnut Springs
(a grove of trees to the north of the city that the Mexicans called
El Bosque de Santo Domingo [q.v.]). The other would be a
flanking movement to the west of the city. Taylor chose Brig.
Gen. William Jenkins Worth (q.v.) to make the attack to the
west with a 2,000-man force. Worth's mission was to execute a
turning movement by circling around the city where he could
cut the Saltillo road and take the commanding hills on that side
of Monterrey.

Worth began his march at 1400 hours on September 20, with
Col. John Coffee Hays's (q.v.) regiment of Texans leading the
way. After a four-hour march covering six miles, Worth was
sighted and fired on by a large unit of cavalry. He withdrew
without a fight, however, and bivouacked his force in the open
for the cold, drizzling night. To the east on September 20, Taylor had marched his troops out in front of Monterrey to demonstrate and divert the Mexicans' attention from Worth's
movements. Little contact was made in that sector.

On September 21, Worth started out at 0600. At 0700, when

his advanced element of Texas Rangers (q.v.) reached a point about 300 yards from the Saltillo road, it was charged by 200 Mexican lancers under Lt. Col. Juan N. Nájera (q.v.), an advance guard of a 1,500-man cavalry brigade under Gen. Manuel Romero (q.v.). With the support of two batteries (James Duncan's [q.v.] and William Mackall's [q.v.]) firing over the heads of the dismounted Texans, the Americans drove the lancers back. It was a short but violent fight that resulted in 100 Mexican casualties, including the daring and gallant Nájera, who was killed leading his men in the charge. Worth continued the turning movement. At the Saltillo road, he chose Capt. Charles Ferguson Smith (q.v.) to lead a storming party to assault Federation Hill. It consisted of three light infantry companies (actually artillerymen fighting as infantry; they were called "red-legged infantry") and six companies of Texas Rangers—about 300 men total. Smith moved west to find a suitably shallow point to wade his men across the Santa Catarina. After crossing under fire from the Mexican positions on the heights, Smith's force made its way to the base of the 400-foot high, steeply sloping hill. At that point, Worth grew impatient and sent Col. Persifor Smith's (q.v.) Second Brigade to join Capt. Charles Ferguson Smith in the attack. Together they assaulted the objective, taking the artillery position on the western end of the hill and El Soldado Fort, a defensive structure on the eastern end. Worth had Federation Hill.

On the eastern side of the city on September 21, Taylor ordered probing attacks by Gen. David E. Twiggs's (q.v.) division (commanded by Col. John Garland [q.v.] because Twiggs was indisposed after taking a laxative) and Gen. William O. Butler's (q.v.) division. Taylor's idea was to make a demonstration or diversion, not to assault the fortifications. Garland apparently took Taylor's vague order otherwise and moved forward in a full attack. His lead elements immediately drew fire from the Tannery and the Citadel, crippling his right flank. On the advice of Maj. Mansfield, who was on the battlefield and knew the Mexican defenses, Garland soon withdrew the bulk of his forces, although some of his men remained engaged. Aware that Garland had been repulsed, Taylor rushed John Anthony Quitman's (q.v.) brigade and additional units into the field to reinforce the attack. A series of frantic infantry assaults on the fortified positions of La Tenería and Fort Diablo followed, with Taylor's (q.v.) forces suffering heavily from the intense Mexican fire from these positions and from the strong point at the Purísima Bridge (q.v.). Taylor himself, dismounted and leading small units of infantry, was in the thickest of the fight as he attempted to rally his men and save the attack. Units in the most intense combat were the First, Third, and Fourth Infantry Regiments (regulars); the Maryland and District of Columbia battalion of volunteers (q.v.) under Lt. Col. William H. Watson (q.v.); a brigade commanded by volunteer Brig. Gen. Thomas L. Hamer (q.v.) of Ohio which included the First Ohio Regiment of Volunteers under Col. Alexander M. Mitchell (q.v.); the First Tennessee Volunteer Regiment under Col. William B. Campbell (q.v.), and the Mississippi Rifles, a regiment under Col. Jefferson Davis (q.v.). The artillery batteries engaged were under Capt. Randolph Ridgely (q.v.) and Capt. Braxton Bragg (q.v.). After some of the bloodiest fighting at Monterrey, the Tannery position was at last taken by Capt. Electus Backus (q.v.) of the First Infantry with help from Davis's Mississippians, but across the line resistance could not be broken. Taylor finally gave the order to withdraw to Walnut Springs, leaving one unit to hold the Tannery.

September 21 at Monterrey was probably the worst day for Zachary Taylor in his 40 years of service. The cost of this desperate series of engagements, fights that he had not planned for or desired, was dear. Taylor had 394 men killed or wounded. Among the wounded were Gen. William Butler and Col. Alexander Mitchell; among the dead were Lt. Col. William H. Watson and Maj. Philip Norbourne Barbour (q.v.), two of Taylor's most respected officers.

On September 22, Worth pursued his attack at 0300 hours, seizing Independence Hill and the Obispado on its eastern tip, while Taylor rested his forces. On September 23, Taylor renewed his attacks on the fortified positions in the eastern sector and discovered that Fort Diablo and the strong point at Purísima Bridge had been abandoned. His troops, some led by Taylor himself, continued the attack west through the city toward Monterrey's main plaza. Worth, from his position at the Obispado and without orders from Taylor, did the same thing, working his way block by block in often hand-to-hand street fighting toward the plaza. Worth ordered his men to use pickaxes and cut holes in the buildings through which the troops could pass, thereby avoiding the raking fire in the streets from Mexican muskets and artillery. During his move to the plaza, Worth loosed a 10-inch mortar on the cathedral after hearing that General Ampudia had moved his headquarters and ammunition stores there that morning. At nightfall the attack halted, but Worth continued to lob an occasional round toward the plaza. Early on September 24, Ampudia sent word to Taylor that he wanted a ceasefire and was ready to surrender the city under terms allowing his men to leave with all armaments and military property. Taylor refused the offer but appointed a commission to negotiate terms with Ampudia's representatives. The resulting agreement allowed the Mexican army to depart as Taylor's occupied Monterrey. Strategically, it was an important victory for the United States. It demonstrated that the U.S. Army could move 200 miles into the interior of Mexico and capture an important regional city. But it was costly from a military viewpoint. The "Three Glorious Days," as Gen. Winfield Scott later called them, nearly made Taylor's army combat ineffective, at least for a time. After the battle, the Texas volunteers departed since their enlistment had expired. In addition, Taylor suffered 531 casualties, mostly from his disastrous attacks on September 21. Of these, 120 men were killed in action, losses that would take Taylor some time to rebuild. For the concluding agreement at Monterrey. *See also* MONTERREY ARMISTICE.

MONTERREY, NUEVO LEON. At the time of the war, Monterrey, in the state of Nuevo León about 200 miles from the Rio Grande (q.v.), was the largest city in the northern region of the country. It had from 10,000 to 15,000 civilian inhabitants and a strong military garrison. The city lay in a beautiful setting in a valley on the north bank of the Santa Catarina River; it was surrounded dramatically on three sides by ranges of the Sierra Madre Oriental. The Mexican military at first planned to abandon the city and make a defense against the American advance at Saltillo (q.v.). They changed plans, however, and reinforced Monterrey before the arrival of Gen. Zachary Taylor's (q.v.) army in September 1846. Today Monterrey is the third largest city in Mexico and a major industrial center. *See also* MONTERREY, BATTLE OF.

MONTGOMERY, JOHN B. The Home Squadron's (q.v.) sloop *Portsmouth*, commanded by Captain John B. Montgomery, arrived June 1, 1846, in San Francisco Bay. From its anchor near the villages of Yerba Buena (q.v.) and San Francisco (q.v.), Montgomery awaited news of U.S. relations with Mexico and Commo. John Drake Sloat's (q.v.) instructions. The night of July 8, he received Sloat's orders to take the San Francisco Bay area. After landing unopposed the next morning and raising the U. S. flag at the customs house in San Francisco, Montgomery left a modest garrison under Marine Lt. Henry B. Watson to protect the area. In March 1847, Montgomery oversaw the peaceful surrender of San José del Cabo (q.v.) and San Lucas, Baja California; in these instances, he did not leave a garrison behind. Montgomery next accepted the peaceful surrender of La Paz (q.v.), the capital of Baja California. *See also* SAN FRAN-CISCO; YERBA BUENA.

MONTGOMERY, THOMAS J. (1822–1854). An infantry officer and West Point graduate of 1845, Lt. Thomas J. Montgomery participated in battles at Palo Alto (q.v.), Resaca de la Palma (q.v.), Monterrey (q.v.), Veracruz (q.v.), San Antonio (q.v.), Churubusco (q.v.), Molino del Rey (q.v.), and the assault on Mexico City (q.v.). After the war and before his death, he attained the rank of captain.

MONTGOMERY, WILLIAM READING (1801–1871). Captain William Reading Montgomery, an 1825 West Point graduate, was with the Eighth Regiment of Infantry in both the northern and southern campaigns. He fought at Palo Alto (q.v.) and Resaca de la Palma (q.v.) on the Rio Grande (q.v.). In Gen. Winfield Scott's (q.v.) army, he fought at Cerro Gordo (q.v.), San Antonio (q.v.), Churubusco (q.v.), Molino del Rey (q.v.), Chapultepec (q.v.) and in the battles for Mexico City (q.v.). Montgomery was wounded at Resaca de la Palma and Molino del Rey. He received brevets to major for Palo Alto and Resaca de la Palma and to lieutenant colonel for Molino del Rey. In the Civil War, he was a brigadier general of U. S. Volunteers.

MONTOYA, PABLO (d. 1847). Pablo Montoya was one of the major conspirators behind the uprising in Taos (q.v.), New Mexico (q.v.). This event resulted in the savage murder of Gov. Charles Bent (q.v.) and other Americans in Taos, in the village of Mora, and at other locations throughout the surrounding region. Montoya was captured after troops under Col. Sterling Price (q.v.) put down the uprising in a short, bloody campaign. He was quickly tried and hung by American authorities.

MOORE, BENJAMIN D. (d. 1846). Benjamin D. Moore commanded a company of dragoons (q.v.) with Brig. Gen. Stephen Kearny's (q.v.) Army of the West (q.v.). In California (q.v.), at the battle of San Pascual (q.v.), Moore died while leading his dragoons into a headlong attack against a much larger force of Mexican (Californio) cavalry.

MORA Y VILLAMIL, IGNACIO (1791–1870). Brig. Gen. Ignacio Mora y Villamil was chief of Mexican engineers under Gen. Antonio López de Santa Anna (q.v.) and one of the strongman's senior lieutenants. He fought at Buena Vista (q.v.) and was later the commander at San Luis Potosí (q.v.). Mora was one of the diplomatic emissaries in negotiations between Santa Anna and Gen. Winfield Scott (q.v.) during and after the battles for Mexico City (q.v.). On February 22, 1848, Mora, with Gen. Benito Quijano (q.v.) and the American generals William Worth (q.v.) and Persifor Smith (q.v.), signed the accord establishing the end of hostilities between the two armies.

MORALES, FRANCISCO. Morales was governor of the state of Nuevo León at the time of the American occupation of its capital, Monterrey (q.v.), in September of 1846.

MORALES, JUAN (1802–1847). Brig. Gen. Juan Morales commanded at Veracruz (q.v.) in March of 1847 when American troops landed at nearby Collado Beach (q.v.). On the night of March 25, during the bombardment and siege of Veracruz by the joint American force, Morales claimed illness, turned over command to Brig. Gen. Juan José Landero (q.v.), and fled the city by sea. For these actions Gen. Antonio López de Santa Anna (q.v.) had Morales imprisoned at the notorious San Carlos de Perote fortress (q.v.), where he was freed when U.S. forces occupied Perote and its famed prison in late April.

MORGAN, GEORGE WASHINGTON (1820–1893). As a colonel, George Washington Morgan commanded the Second Regiment of Ohio Volunteers, which saw action under Gen. Zachary Taylor (q.v.) in the northern campaign. Later he was given command of the newly formed Fifteenth Regiment of Infantry, part of Gen. Gideon Pillow's (q.v.) division in the battles for Mexico City (q.v.). It was composed of men from Ohio, Michigan, Wisconsin, and Iowa. Morgan was brevetted brigadier general for action at Contreras (q.v.) and Churubusco (q.v.). In the Civil War, he was brigadier general of U. S. Volunteers.

MORMON BATTALION. The Mormons, persecuted in Illinois, sought assistance from the Polk administration to emigrate to California (q.v.). Pres. James Knox Polk (q.v.), after conferring with a church elder, Jesse C. Little (q.v.), who represented Mormon leader Brigham Young, agreed to allow the army to recruit a Mormon battalion. This unit, called the Battalion of Iowa

Mormon Volunteers, was formed at Council Bluffs, Iowa Territory, in June 1846 and was commanded by a regular officer, Capt. (brevetted lieutenant colonel) James Allen (q.v.). Allen died during the march west from Fort Leavenworth (q.v.), and the battalion was led for the remainder of the journey to New Mexico by Lieutenant, then Capt. Andrew Jackson Smith (q.v.). At Santa Fe (q.v.), another regular officer, Captain Philip St. George Cooke (q.v.), assumed command of the battalion and the lieutenant colonelcy it carried and led the battalion on a grueling march across mostly desert terrain to California. There the Mormon Battalion, attrited by harsh conditions from 500 to 350 men, joined Stephen W. Kearny's (q.v.) Army of the West (q.v.) after the military action of the California campaign had ended. The majority of the battalion's troops were mustered out after one year of active service. Many of the Mormon soldiers stayed in the region to become citizens of the territory that soon became the state of California.

MORRIS, LEWIS N. (1800–1846). Capt. Lewis N. Morris of the Third Infantry Regiment was brevetted major for action at the battles of Palo Alto (q.v.) and Resaca de la Palma (q.v.). He was killed September 21, 1846, at the battle of Monterrey (q.v.).

MOSQUITO FLEET OR FLOTILLA. This was the name given to the small squadron of light-draft steamers and gunboats Commo. Matthew Calbraith Perry (q.v.) used to give fire support to the amphibious assault at Veracruz (q.v.) in March 1847. The squadron, commanded by Comdr. Josiah Tattnall (q.v.), consisted of the steamers *Spitfire* and *Vixen* and the gunboats *Bonita* (q.v.), *Reefer*, *Petrel*, *Falcon*, and *Tampico*. During the siege of Veracruz and its fort, San Juan de Ulúa (q.v.), the squadron moved in close to the city to join the land batteries in the bombardment on March 22, 1847. On both March 22 and 23, Commander Tattnall brought the squadron dangerously close to Veracruz, within grapeshot of Mexican batteries, to bring effective fire on the city. Commodore Perry, believing that the commander had exceeded his orders, attempted to have him withdraw the squadron on March 23. Tattnall ignored Perry's order and continued to fire for a time until the commodore sent another officer by boat to deliver his order in person. Tattnall's daring action raised morale of American soldiers and sailors alike and brought praise from officers on neutral ships of war observing offshore. *See also* TATTNALL, JOSIAH.

MULEJE. Mulejé, a village on the gulf side of the Baja California (q.v.) peninsula, was one of the centers of opposition to the American occupation of Baja California. At Mulejé, in October 1847, a band of loyalists successfully resisted a landing attempt by a party from the U.S. sloop of war *Dale* (q.v.).

MUNROE, JOHN (d. 1861). John Munroe, a West Pointer of the class of 1814, was a major in the Second Regiment of Artillery in Gen. Zachary Taylor's (q.v.) army. Taylor placed Munroe in command of the supply base at Point Isabel (q.v.) near the mouth of the Rio Grande (q.v.) when the army arrived in March 1846. Munroe fought in the battle for Monterrey (q.v.) and at Buena Vista (q.v.), where he was charged with the critical defense of the hacienda headquarters buildings. He held off a determined attack by Mexican cavalry under Brig. Gen. Julián Juvera (q.v.). For his actions in combat, Munroe received brevets of lieutenant colonel for Monterrey and colonel for Buena Vista. He served as Taylor's chief of artillery (q.v.) from July 1846 until November 1847.

MURDER. The killing of non-combatants or soldiers not engaged in battle by persons on both sides of the conflict was widespread. Extensive documentation indicates that innocents were randomly assassinated in Mexico throughout the period of the American invasion and occupation. Some of this was perpetuated by Mexican citizens infuriated by the U.S. invasion of their country. Many episodes resulted from undisciplined American soldiers, especially volunteers (q.v.), carrying out unconscionable acts against innocent natives. Some accounts blame the Texas volunteers for many of the unwarranted killings and murders; the Texans had particular grievances rooted in their long conflict with Mexico in the 1830s and early 1840s. Certain of the Arkansas volunteer units have also been cited by historians examining the record as responsible for atrocities against Mexicans. Some U.S. commanders, Winfield Scott (q.v.) and John Ellis Wool (q.v.) among them, maintained firm discipline and largely prevented widespread acts of terror by their soldiers. Zachary Taylor (q.v.), on the other hand, did not keep a tight rein on his subordinate units; the often despicable behavior of his volunteers and their unwarranted attacks on civilians may have reflected the general's leadership style. Taylor consistently condemned such acts, however. There were instances in which U.S. military authorities tried American soldiers for murdering civilians and, if they were found guilty, executed them on the spot. In some cases, commanders simply discharged the guilty soldiers from the service and sent them back to the United States.

MURPHY, TOMAS (1810–1869). As the Mexican minister to Great Britain from 1844 to 1845, Tomás Murphy attempted to persuade the British authorities to support Mexico in its claims for Texas (q.v.) and California (q.v.). By 1845, Murphy became convinced that Lord Aberdeen (q.v.) would not risk war with the United States by supporting these claims.

N

NAJERA, JUAN N. (d. 1846). In the battle of Monterrey (q.v.), Lt. Col. Juan N. Nájera commanded the Jalisco cavalry regiment. The regiment was part of the advance guard of a 2,000-man cavalry and infantry force that defended the Saltillo (q.v.) road to the west of Monterrey. On September 21, the second day of the battle, Nájera led a hellbent-for-leather charge with his cavalrymen against the leading unit of Gen. William J. Worth's (q.v.) division—a company of Texas Rangers (q.v.) under Capt. Ben McCulloch (q.v.). This opening of the Monterrey battle was short, bloody, and, for the Mexicans, costly, as they suffered heavy casualties, including the gallant Nájera, who died within minutes of leading his bold charge against the Texans.

NARROWS, THE. See ANGOSTURA.

NATIONAL BRIDGE. See PUENTE NACIONAL, VERACRUZ.

NATIONAL HIGHWAY. The National Highway or Road, known in 19th-century Mexico as the *Camino Nacional*, was the historic route over which Hernán Cortés marched from Veracruz (q.v.) to conquer the center of Aztec power at Tenochtitlán in the Valley of Mexico (q.v.). Gen. Winfield Scott (q.v.) chose this road for his army's march from Veracruz to Mexico City (q.v.). It ran northwest from Veracruz through Corral Falso, Cerro Gordo (q.v.), Jalapa (q.v.), La Joya (q.v.), and Las Vigas (q.v.). At Las Vigas, it turned southwest, continuing through Perote (q.v.) and Amozoc (q.v.) to Puebla (q.v.). From Puebla, the road completed its course to Mexico City in a northwesterly fashion, passing to the north and in the shadow of the 18,000-foot peak of Popocatépetl before descending into the Valley of Mexico and the nation's capital.

NAVAJO INDIANS. Navajos in the New Mexico (q.v.) region had been hostile to white settlers in the period leading up to the war with Mexico. When Brig. Gen. Stephen Watts Kearny (q.v.) arrived with his army from Fort Leavenworth (q.v.) in 1846, he charged one of his commanders, Col. Alexander Doniphan (q.v.), of the First Missouri Mounted Volunteers, with the task of solving the Navajo problem. In October and November 1846 Doniphan and his senior officers departed Santa Fe (q.v.) to seek out the Navajo leaders, including their chief, Narbona. Doniphan was able to arrange a peace treaty calling for an end to hostilities with 500 Navajos.

NAVY, MEXICAN. In the mid-1840s, the Mexican government had few resources to support its armed forces adequately in the war with the United States. The limited support it did have went to its armies, although supplying land forces was often a haphazard affair immediately before battle. The Mexican navy got scant support. Historical records are unclear about the exact number of naval vessels belonging to the Mexican government at the time of the war. Naval records in the *Archivo General de la Nación* (general archives) in Mexico City listed 16 ships in government service for 1845. These included 11 schooners, three brigs, and only two steamships. These naval ships were designed to patrol the rivers and the coasts and were clearly not prepared to challenge the U.S. Navy in blue water. The active service of all of the ships listed here ended prematurely and somewhat disastrously during the war years. Two schooners were burned at Guaymas (q.v.) in October 1846, and three were captured by the U.S. Navy (q.v.) at Tampico (q.v.) in November of that year. The other six schooners listed were scuttled in the Alvarado River by the Mexicans in April 1847. All three brigs were scuttled in the Alvarado at the same time as the schooners. The two steamers, built in Great Britain, were repossessed by British interests in May 1846 for failure of the Mexican government to meet contractual agreements.

NAVY, U. S., AND NAVAL OPERATIONS. At the start of the war, the majority of the U.S. Navy's ships of war were deployed either with the Home Squadron (q.v.) in the Gulf of Mexico or with the Pacific Squadron (q.v.) along the Pacific coast. War legislation passed by Congress in 1846 called for a manpower increase in the navy from 7,500 to 10,000 men. During the war, the navy had difficulty recruiting sailors because of competition from the merchant marine, which paid higher wages at the time—and the navy's strength never exceeded 8,100 men.

In 1846, the navy had sufficient large ships for a conflict with Mexico, a nation that had no effective blue-water navy. For its primary mission to blockade (q.v.) the Gulf and Pacific coasts and seize ports with its bluecoats and marines, however, the U.S. Navy needed more small, shallow-draft boats. Although part of this requirement was met by capturing Mexican vessels, most of it came from new construction and especially from direct purchase on the economy of small steamers, schooners, gunboats, brigs, and storeships.

Although sailors and marines fought on land on numerous occasions in California (q.v.) and, to a lesser extent, in the Gulf theater, the sea services did not suffer the high number of casualties of the army. The navy's greatest troop losses came from diseases such as scurvy, ague, and yellow fever (q.v.).

The U.S. Navy's greatest contributions to Gen. Zachary Taylor's (q.v.) and Gen. Winfield Scott's (q.v.) campaigns in northeastern and southeastern Mexico were in logistics support, coastal blockades, the occasional landing of troops to assist the army ashore, and the furnishing of naval gunfire both from sea and ashore during the assault at Veracruz (q.v.).

The most prominent naval officers in the war's Gulf campaigns were Commo. David E. Conner (q.v.) and Commo. Matthew Calbraith Perry (q.v.), the Home (Gulf) Squadron's commanders in the 1845–1848 period. Both officers were commended by General Scott, as well as their superiors in Washington, for their cooperation with the army in joint operations during the war. Because of his key role during the invasion of Veracruz and in operations against river ports along the coast, Comdr. Josiah Tattnall (q.v.) also stood out among the naval officers in the Gulf of Mexico. The navy provided similar support in the California campaign. On the West Coast, it played a large role with bluecoats and marines in a few small but closely fought land engagements and a significant political role in the establishment of U.S. rule in the California Territory. The Pacific Squadron's most important leaders during the war were three of its commanders: John Drake Sloat (q.v.), Robert Field Stockton (q.v.) and William Branford Shubrick (q.v.). Shubrick especially stood out because of his well-planned campaign that neutralized the whole California coast north of Acapulco (q.v.) from the summer of 1847 to the spring of 1848. Pres. James

Knox Polk's (q.v.) secretaries of the navy, George Bancroft (q.v.) and John Young Mason (q.v.), also served the administration in important capacities, working tirelessly during the war to build up their service and participating as advisors to the president on numerous occasions as he planned the war's strategy (q.v.). *See also* BANCROFT, GEORGE; CONNER, DAVID E.; HOME SQUADRON; MARINE CORPS, U. S.; MASON, JOHN YOUNG; *OHIO*; PACIFIC SQUADRON; PERRY, MATTHEW CALBRAITH; SHUBRICK, WILLIAM BRANFORD; SLOAT, JOHN DRAKE; STOCKTON, ROBERT FIELD; AND TATTNALL, JOSIAH.

NEW MEXICO. Like California (q.v.) and Texas (q.v.), New Mexico was a territory on the far northern fringe of Spain's New World empire. Until 1821, it was thinly populated and largely closed by Spain to American trade and immigration. After Mexico won its independence in 1821, few restrictions were placed on Americans coming into New Mexico. A flourishing trade developed between St. Louis, Missouri; Santa Fe (q.v.), New Mexico (q.v.); and Chihuahua, Chihuahua (q.v.). A large part of this commerce consisted of both Mexican hides and gold being exchanged for finished goods. The route, which followed a southwesterly course from Fort Leavenworth (q.v.), was known as the Santa Fe Trail (q.v.). Some Americans, mostly traders, settled in the New Mexico region in the 1820s and 1830s, and by the mid-1840s Santa Fe trade was rapidly growing. In 1831, William and Charles Bent (q.v.) established a successful trading post (Bent's Fort [q.v.]) on the Arkansas River at present-day Las Animas, Colorado; the Bents re-supplied the caravans on the Santa Fe Trail and traded goods with Americans and Mexicans alike. New Mexico was ruled from Santa Fe in the 1840s by Manuel Armijo (q.v.), who as governor served as both head of the civil government and *commandante general* (the military chief of the territory). He had scant supervision from Mexico City (q.v.), as the central government lacked the interest and resources to enforce federal laws in the territory. Armijo's rule was corrupt and self-aggrandizing, and the results were a disaffected population. Although there was some resistance when General Stephen Watts Kearny's (q.v.) Army of the West (q.v.) arrived from Fort Leavenworth to occupy New Mexico in the late summer of 1846, the population in general benignly accepted American rule. *See also* ARMIJO, MANUEL; BENT'S FORT; KEARNY, WILLIAM WATTS; TAOS REBELLION.

NEW ORLEANS, LOUISIANA. As the primary U. S. port and commercial center on the Gulf of Mexico, New Orleans supplied both Mexico and Texas (q.v.) during the Texas revolution for independence. Mexico continued to rely on supplies from New Orleans until the implementation of the American blockade (q.v.) in the Gulf at the start of the war. Once the war began, New Orleans became the principal port of embarkation for troops going to Mexico, and it remained the primary port from which U.S. forces were supplied.

NEWSPAPERS. The popular press provided the American public with a steady stream of reports from Mexico during the war period. The conflict was the first U.S. war covered by newspaper correspondents. On the home front, the major newspapers were identified with political parties and thus were pro- or anti-war depending on whether they were Democratic or Whig (q.v.). Two Washington, D.C., newspapers, the *Union* and the *National Intelligencer*, were examples of this partisanship. The *Union* was Democratic and strongly supportive of Pres. James Knox Polk's (q.v.) war policies; the *Intelligencer* was a Whig paper and very anti-war in its policies.

Newspapers fought in the so-called "penny press" wars of the time, competing vigorously to gain advantage in their coverage of the battles in Mexico. Major newspapers from cities such as New Orleans (q.v.) and New York sent their own reporters to Mexico with the American field armies, while many volunteer soldiers sent first-hand accounts back for their hometown papers. Two New Orleans papers, the *Delta* and the *Picayune*, typified the penny press competition. The *Picayune*'s co-owner, George Wilkins Kendall, went to Mexico as his own frontline war correspondent. He joined Gen. Zachary Taylor's (q.v.) entourage in Texas (q.v.) as a journalist on Taylor's staff and went on operations with Capt. Ben McCulloch's (q.v.) Texas Ranger (q.v.) company. Later Kendall served as a volunteer aide to Brig. Gen. William Jenkins Worth (q.v.). These contacts gave Kendall inside information on the army's operations that he used in dispatches he sent back to New Orleans. The *Picayune* probably had the best coverage of the war because of Kendall's ingenuity and resourcefulness as a reporter. After the war, Kendall wrote and published extensively about the war and his experiences.

Because of slow communication, often accounts from the battlefields would be published in major port cities in the United States before the news reached the U.S. government.

The stories were telegraphed to Washington before the official reports of the same events reached the capital, which made it difficult for the government to put its spin on events of the war. Stories were frequently provided to reporter-friends of the major military and civilian figures of the war (such as Kendall) to ensure their own views of events were published in order to promote personal advancement or partisan politics.

In the war zone, newspapers—both official and unofficial—were established to entertain the troops and keep them informed of news from home; they were also sent to the United States and became additional sources for news of the war. Newspapers were established in most of the major cities occupied by American forces. Examples of the larger papers include the *Anglo Saxon* in Chihuahua; the *American Star* (q.v.) in Jalapa; the *Free American*, *American Eagle* (q.v.), and *Genius of Liberty* in Veracruz (q.v.); the Matamoros *American Flag* (q.v.) and *Reveille*, and the *North American*, *American Star* and *Echo del Comercio* (q.v.) in Mexico City (q.v.). The *American Star* in Mexico City was edited by Harvard graduate John H. Warland, a sergeant in the Ninth Infantry (the "New England" regiment) and became the official voice of Gen. Winfield Scott's (q.v.) army. Small "army camp" newspapers, such as the four-page *Picket Guard* in Saltillo (q.v.), often edited by soldiers, also sprang up for brief periods. Unofficial papers, such as the *Free American* in Veracruz, were sometimes suppressed by the army, although generally censorship of an army composed of so many undisciplined volunteers (q.v.) and camp followers was unsuccessful.

NINO PERDIDO GATE. The Niño Perdido Gate was one of the police and customs stations (called *garitas* in Mexico) controlling access to Mexico City (q.v.) over causeways running into the city from all directions. The Niño Perdido Gate approached the capital from the south.

NINOS HEROES. Mexican folklore holds that six military academy cadets gave their lives in the defense of Chapultepec Castle (q.v.) during the American assault on the building in the battle for Mexico City (q.v.). The *niños héroes* (heroic children) are immortalized today by an enormous statue at the base of the castle.

NORIEGA, LUIS. Gen. Luis Noriega commanded Mexican cavalry at the battle of Palo Alto (q.v.) in May 1846. Later in the war, he was captured by American forces in the fight for Chapultepec Castle (q.v.) (September 1847).

NORTHEASTERN MEXICO INDEPENDENCE MOVEMENT. The northeastern Mexico independence movement sprang from strong federalist dissatisfaction in that region with several centralist governments in power after 1834. The northeastern federalists established, through a unilateral and essentially meaningless proclamation, the Republic of the Rio Grande in 1839. This republic existed a short time in name only, but the federalist efforts to create a separate nation in northeastern Mexico continued through the 1840s and later in the century. In 1846, Gen. Antonio Canales (q.v.) of Camargo (q.v.) and other Mexican strongmen in the northeast attempted to gain American support for a rebellion against the central Mexican government. Gen. Zachary Taylor (q.v.) was first approached to support the movement when his army was at Corpus Christi (q.v.); later the separatists again sought his assistance at Matamoros (q.v.). Taylor relayed all requests to Washington; the administration refused direct support but sent word that cooperation with American policies and military forces by all groups would be welcomed. The federalist idea to establish an independent republic in northern Mexico that would ally with Washington and accept the annexation of Texas (q.v.) to the United States was never realized.

NORTHERS. Northers were fierce storms that blew in on the Gulf coast of Mexico from Canada. They usually did not include rain, but their violent winds played havoc with American ships at sea and troops on shore throughout the war years. Several northers (known as *nortes* in Mexico) in March 1847 severely affected the U.S. landing and siege at Veracruz (q.v.).

NUECES RIVER. In the 1820s and 1830s, Mexico considered the Nueces River to be the boundary between its states of Tamaulipas and Tejas (Texas) (q.v.). After Texas declared its independence in 1836—an act Mexico never officially recognized—the Lone Star Republic began to claim the Rio Grande (q.v.) as the southwest boundary, indicating that the Nueces was within its territory. Mexico never acknowledged the Rio Grande as the border but over time came to accept, tacitly at least, the Nueces (100 miles farther north). The region between the Nueces and the Rio Grande Rivers was still largely unoccupied territory in the 1840s. When Gen. Zachary Taylor's (q.v.) army moved across this region (19th-century maps called it the "Wild Horse Desert") and occupied the left bank of the Rio Grande in the spring of 1846—an action to back up the claim of the newly annexed state of Texas—Mexico considered it an invasion of its territory.

O

OBISPADO. *See* BISHOP'S PALACE.

O'BRIEN, JOHN PAUL JONES (1818–1850). As a captain at Buena Vista (q.v.), John Paul Jones O'Brien commanded an artillery (q.v.) section that played an important role in holding the American left flank. In some of the most desperate fighting of that battle, O'Brien's three-gun section was left bereft of infantry protection; O'Brien was wounded and forced to abandon his guns to the enemy assault. For his gallantry in action, he was brevetted major.

OCCUPATION OF CONQUERED REGIONS. The invading American forces occupied portions of Mexican territory that lay in the path of the armies, as well as limited areas outside of these zones. The principal cities along the campaign routes were occupied, therefore, as were selected cities within 100 to 200 miles of these routes. Gen. Winfield Scott (q.v.)—the General in Chief of the army, commander of the final campaign against Mexico City (q.v.), and strategic architect of the war— never planned to occupy the entire country. Scott realized the vastness of the territory and the limited size of his army. Examples of the pattern of limited occupation could be seen in both the northern and southern campaigns. In the northern theater, Matamoros (q.v.), Monterrey (q.v.), and Saltillo (q.v.) were occupied; outlying cities such as Monclova (q.v.), Parras (q.v.), and Victoria (q.v.) were also occupied, as were smaller towns, such as Camargo (q.v.) and Cerralvo (q.v.), which were used as intermediate supply bases for the army. In the southern campaign, besides Tampico (q.v.), Veracruz (q.v.), Jalapa (q.v.), Puebla (q.v.), and Mexico City, outlying cities such as Cuernavaca and Toluca (q.v.) were occupied by American troops. Occupations in the larger cities generally lasted from the time of conquest (e.g., in Matamoros after May 1846, and in Veracruz after March 1847), until the final withdrawal of the armies in the summer of 1848. In the smaller cities such as Victoria and Parras, occupations were relatively brief.

Occupation government was under military governors appointed by the senior generals (Gen. John Ellis Wool [q.v.] governed Saltillo, Gen. William Jenkins Worth [q.v.] governed Veracruz and Puebla, and Gen. John Anthony Quitman [q.v.] governed Mexico City). Local officials were normally allowed to continue performing their duties with American oversight. One of the largest problems of the occupation officials was to control the outrages perpetuated by both sides—assault, murder (q.v.), rape, theft, plunder of private property, and the like, especially acts committed against Mexican civilians by American volunteer troops. Gen. Zachary Taylor (q.v.) believed he did not have the right to punish soldiers for crimes against civilians; his position was that they would have to be tried by civil courts, which did not exist in Mexico. Taylor normally discharged flagrant violators and sent them back to the United States. Generals Wool and Scott, however, established military commissions to try soldiers for these crimes. All of the general officers, including Taylor, issued orders from time to time imploring the troops to respect the rights of Mexicans. Pres. James Knox Polk (q.v.) insisted that the Mexicans be forced to contribute money to support the occupation armies, believing that this harassment would cause them to put pressure on their government for peace. Both Taylor and Scott thought that this practice would further alienate the civilian populace and exacerbate the problem of obtaining supplies on the economy, and they largely did not carry out the policy. Scott did levy taxes in Mexico City, however, and Polk's order to collect tax at the ports for goods leaving and entering Mexico was implemented in American-controlled areas.

OHIO. The ship-of-the-line USS Ohio saw service in both the Home (q.v.) and Pacific (q.v.) Squadrons during the war. At 2,757 tons, the Ohio was the heaviest ship in the navy at the time and carried the largest crew (820 men) and most firepower. Its armament included 12 eight-inch shell guns, twenty-eight 42 pounders and forty-four 32 pounders. On March 23, 1847, Commo. Matthew Calbraith Perry (q.v.) brought in the Ohio to use its heavy guns against the fortress of San Juan de Ulúa (q.v.) in the attack on Veracruz (q.v.). Besides their firepower, the large ships of the line were valuable because their large crews could be used for shore duty to reinforce army troops. This role was critical during the campaign in California (q.v.), where the Pacific Squadron furnished bluecoats to secure ports and other key locations, usually but not always in conjunction with army forces.

OPPOSITION IN THE UNITED STATES TO THE WAR WITH MEXICO. With the possible exceptions of the Philippine and Vietnam Wars, the war with Mexico was the United States' most controversial. There were no public opinion polls in the mid-19th century to judge exactly how the American people viewed a particular issue. Although historians have frequently written that "most people" felt one way or the other about the war with Mexico, it is not possible to determine today how most of the American public felt about the war at the time. It is sufficient to say that a segment of the population, a large but extremely vocal minority, strongly opposed the war, a large sector vigorously supported it, and large numbers remained indifferent. Considerable opposition was purely political, that is, Whigs (q.v.) opposing a Democratic president or Democratic opponents of the president speaking out against Pres. James Knox Polk's (q.v.) policies. Much opposition was moral or religious, especially from the Congregationalists, Unitarians, and Quakers, who viewed the war as pure aggression against a weak nation. Many prominent literary figures of the time opposed the war, voicing their opposition in essays, poems, and prose that were widely read by the public. The antislavery movement in the northeast was one of the loudest voices against the war. The abolitionists (q.v.) and those opposed to the extension of slavery into new territories were convinced that Polk's war policies were aimed at extending slave territory into land seized from Mexico. In response to this, the Wilmot Proviso, an amendment to an appropriations bill, was introduced in Congress by Rep. David Wilmot (q.v.) of Pennsylvania to ensure that slavery would not be extended into any territory the United States gained from Mexico. Although it did not pass and drew little attention at the time, the subsequent emotional debates over the Wilmot Proviso reflected the controversy and divisiveness of the war itself.

Members of each of the aforementioned groups expressed their opposition by joining peace organizations, such as the American Peace Society (q.v.). Some prominent southerners opposed the war on conservative, constitutional grounds, arguing that the Constitution did not allow inclusion of new states from territories seized by force of arms; they feared also that new territories would intensify the debate over slavery, possibly destroying the delicate balance in the Senate between slave and free states. Some northern business groups opposed the war, fearing that it might bring Britain in on the side of Mexico, affecting access to British credit or resulting in British boycotts or blockades damaging to their interests. Although opponents of the war existed in all sections of the country, New England was the region of greatest opposition. Regional leaders in New England felt that national expansion as a result of the war could only weaken their economic and political power.

To put opposition to the war in proper context, it should be noted that there *was* great support for the war among various elements of the population in all parts of the country; this was most prevalent in the days and weeks following Gen. Zachary Taylor's (q.v.) first victories along the Rio Grande (q.v.) when war fever was fresh across the land. There was a season of excitement about the war as men rushed to volunteer from practically all of the states, especially from the northwest (Indiana, Illinois) and southwest (Mississippi, Louisiana, and Texas [(q.v.]). Polk had enthusiastic support from many prominent politicians and ordinary people who truly believed that it was America's destiny and mission to carry its values to foreign lands. And many enthusiasts saw opportunity for advancement, both personal and for society as a whole, in new territories that the war might bring into the nation. As the war dragged on in 1847, with reports of high casualties from battle and disease filtering back to town and city and with Mexico refusing to fight or negotiate a peace, support lessened, and voices of opposition in press and Congress rose to new heights. But Polk had sufficient support when he needed it. He brilliantly played on the people's sense of patriotism and on the idea that they would not fail to support their fellow citizens who had already been placed in harm's way. Important appropriation bills for the military, therefore, although passionately debated by the politicians, invariably passed through Congress at critical times in the war, and at its end, Congress ratified a treaty that ended the war on terms that accomplished Polk's original goals (and more) by bringing into the nation vast new territories. *See also* MISSOURI COMPROMISE; NEWSPAPERS; WHIGS; WILMOT PROVISO.

OREGON. The imperative for a settlement with Great Britain of the Oregon boundary complicated Pres. James Knox Polk's (q.v.) foreign policy during the crisis with Mexico in 1845–1846. The press, politicians, and members of the administration expressed concern over the possibility of simultaneous conflicts with Mexico and Great Britain. While Polk was aware of the dangers of pushing Britain too far on the Oregon question, the president, counseled to take a hard line by former president Andrew Jackson, did not waver in his determination to settle the boundary at the 49th parallel, an arrangement the American public had come to expect. Polk's aggressive policy toward Mexico in the spring of 1846 resulted in armed conflict and a declaration of war on May 12. Perhaps impressed with Polk's belligerent policy, Britain agreed to terms on Oregon one month later, and the danger for the administration of a conflict on two fronts passed.

ORIZABA, VERACRUZ. Orizaba was one of the principal towns along the southern route between Veracruz (q.v.) and Mexico City (q.v.). Gen. Antonio López de Santa Anna (q.v.) fled there after his defeat by Gen. Winfield Scott (q.v.) at Cerro Gordo (q.v.). In the 1840s, the main road to Mexico City was the National Highway (q.v.), which was the northern route that went through Jalapa (q.v.), Cerro Gordo (q.v.), and Perote (q.v.). Today the main road goes through Córdoba and Orizaba.

ORTEGA, JOSE MARIA (1793–1871). Gen. José María Ortega, after participating in the defense of Monterrey (q.v.), served as a member of the commission that negotiated the surrender of the city to General Zachary Taylor's (q.v.) forces in September 1846. At Buena Vista (q.v.), he fought under Gen. Antonio López de Santa Anna (q.v.) as commander of the Third Infantry Division.

O'SULLIVAN, JOHN LOUIS (1813–1895). John Louis O'Sullivan, publisher of the *Democratic Review* in the 1830s and 1840s, was an ardent expansionist. In 1845, he coined the term "Manifest Destiny" (q.v.), the battle cry of those in the United States who believed that America had a natural right to expand its borders across the North American continent.

OWENS, SAMUEL C. Maj. Samuel C. Owens was an irregular officer in charge of a logistics "battalion" of civilian traders and teamsters accompanying Col. Alexander Doniphan's (q.v.) brigade of Missouri volunteers. At the battle of Sacramento (q.v.) in Chihuahua (q.v.), he recklessly and inexplicably charged alone, forward of the attack formation, and was killed by enemy fire. Owens was the only U.S. fatality in the battle.

P

PACHECO, FRANCISCO. Maj. Gen. Francisco Pacheco fought as a division commander for General Antonio López de Santa Anna (q.v.) at Buena Vista (q.v.). On February 23, 1847, his division attacked over the ridge line against the American left flank and suffered heavy casualties from the V formation of the Third Indiana Regiment and Jefferson Davis's (q.v.) Mississippi Rifles.

PACHECO, JOSE RAMON (1805–1865). After the battles of Contreras and Churubusco (q.v.), and as the final assault was about to be launched on Mexico City (q.v.) by Gen. Winfield Scott's (q.v.) army, Foreign Minister José Ramón Pacheco of Mexico sent to the U.S. diplomat Nicholas Trist (q.v.) a proposal for a year-long truce. The United States was agreeable to the idea of a temporary cease-fire, and on August 23, 1847, the Mexicans and Americans sat across a table from each other near Tacubaya (q.v.) and negotiated an armistice. Because of violations of the armistice agreement (Scott's troops were harassed when entering Mexico City for supplies, and reports indicated Gen. Antonio López de Santa Anna [q.v.] was using the cease-fire to build up his army), it quickly broke down, and Scott ordered the American offensive against the city to resume. See also MOLINO DEL REY, BATTLE OF.

PACIFIC SQUADRON. The Pacific Squadron of the U.S. Navy (q.v.) operated along the West Coast during the war with Mexico. Its mission was to protect the evolving, and, in the mid-1840s, increasingly expansionist, U. S. interests in the region. Commo. John D. Sloat (q.v.) took command of the Pacific Squadron on March 24, 1845, and served until relieved by Commo. Robert F. Stockton (q.v.) on July 29, 1846. Commo. W. Branford Shubrick (q.v.) assumed command from Stockton on January 22, 1847; Shubrick was temporarily replaced by Commo. James Biddle (q.v.) on March 2, 1847; Biddle returned the Pacific Squadron to Shubrick on July 19, 1847. On May 6, 1848, Shubrick relinquished command of the Pacific Squadron to Commo. Thomas ap Catesby Jones (q.v.).

The ships of the Pacific Squadron were the *Columbus* (ship of the line), the *Congress* (q.v.) (first-class frigate), the *Cyane* (q.v.) (second-class sloop of war), the *Dale* (q.v.) (third-class sloop of war), the *Erie* (storeship), the *Independence* (q.v.) (razee), the *Julia* (q.v.) (schooner), the *Levant* (q.v.) (second-class sloop of war), the *Lexington* (q.v.) (storeship), the *Libertad* (schooner), the *Malek Adhel* (brig), the *Portsmouth* (first-class sloop of war), the *Preble* (third-class sloop of war), the *Savannah* (first-class frigate), the *Shark* (schooner), the *Southampton* (storeship), the *Warren* (second-class sloop of war), and the *Whiton* (bark, a square-rigged sailing vessel).

PADIERNA. Padierna, an Indian village located a few miles southwest of Mexico City (q.v.), was the site of a major battle on August 20, 1847, during the final American drive on the capital. American accounts refer to the engagement as the battle of Contreras (q.v.), after the village to the south of the actual battlefield. Mexican histories use the more accurate name Padierna for the battle of August 20. *See also* CONTRERAS AND CHURUBUSCO, BATTLES OF.

PAGE, FRANCIS N. (d. 1860). Lt. Francis N. Page, West Point graduate of 1841, participated in the defense of Fort Brown (q.v.), for which he was brevetted first lieutenant. He fought at the battles of Contreras and Churubusco (q.v.) before being wounded at the storming of Chapultepec Castle (q.v.). Although wounded, Page entered Mexico City (q.v.) with Gen. Winfield Scott's (q.v.) army. He was brevetted major for gallantry at Contreras and Churubusco.

PAINE, ROBERT TREAT (d. 1910). A Whig politician from North Carolina, Col. Robert Treat Paine was commander of the only North Carolina unit in the war, the First Regiment of North Carolina Volunteers. Paine, whose appointment was controversial in North Carolina because he had had no previous military experience, served under Gen. John Ellis Wool (q.v.) in the northern theater after Buena Vista (q.v.). A strict disciplinarian—rare for a volunteer officer—Paine was unpopular with many of his officers and soldiers. At one point, in August 1847, Paine used force to put down a rebellion among his troops, shooting two of his men, killing one. General Wool, also a stern leader and disciplinarian, stood behind Paine and approved Paine's discharge of two of his junior officers for inappropriate conduct and insubordination. Pres. James Knox Polk (q.v.), as often was his practice, did not stand behind Wool, his general in the field. He overturned Paine's and Wool's actions and restored the lieutenants' commissions on a technicality. Paine was brought before a court of inquiry for the soldier's death and absolved. After the war, he returned to North Carolina, was elected to the U.S. Congress in the mid-1850s, and served as a commissioner for Mexican claims resulting from the war.

PALO ALTO. Located on a plain at a point approximately 10 miles from the Rio Grande (q.v.), Palo Alto is alternately described by historians and depicted on old maps as a pond or road junction; it was the site of the first major battle of the war. *See also* PALO ALTO, BATTLE OF.

PALO ALTO, BATTLE OF (May 8, 1846). After the ambush of Capt. Seth Thornton's (q.v.) force on April 24, 1846, Gen. Zachary Taylor (q.v.) informed Washington that hostilities had commenced. Taylor continued to construct his Army of Occupation's (q.v.) fortification, then called Fort Texas (q.v.), across the Rio Grande (q.v.) from Matamoros (q.v.). Needing supplies and fearing the Mexicans would attack his mostly undefended base at Point Isabel (q.v.), the general departed Fort Texas on May 1 with 2,000 troops. His purpose was to reinforce the defenses at the Point Isabel base (called Fort Polk [q.v.]) and gather supplies to bring back to Fort Texas. Arriving on May 2, his men immediately began building defenses around Fort Polk. Taylor, hearing a bombardment back at Matamoros, sent Capt. Samuel H. Walker (q.v.) with some of his Texas Rangers (q.v.) to Fort Texas to see how it was holding out. When Walker returned on the 5th, he reported that Fort Texas was under fire but holding up well. Taylor waited two more days before starting his return trip, taking with him approximately 300 wagons, hundreds of mules and oxen, and two huge, 18-pounder howitzers, each pulled by five yoke of oxen.

Taylor expected opposition from Mexican forces that reports indicated had crossed the Rio Grande. He issued an order to his men that the departure would be at 1500 hours and assured them that they had his "every confidence." Taylor also stressed to his infantry, as was his practice, that in the event of combat "their main dependence must be in the bayonet." The army marched seven miles before bivouacking along the road. At dawn the next morning, May 8, the army struck out for Fort Texas, moving 11 miles across the flat, sandy plain of the Rio Grande valley.

At a site called Palo Alto, Taylor's scouts came on the Mexican army. It was led by Gen. Mariano Arista (q.v.), who in April had replaced Gen. Pedro de Ampudia (q.v.) as the commanding general of Mexican troops in the north. The previous day Arista had recalled Ampudia (who after being replaced by

Arista in April took over a subordinate unit) from his invest-
ment of Fort Texas to be his second in command. With 4,000
men, Arista's force outnumbered Taylor's by about two to one;
he had only 12 artillery (q.v.) pieces, however, to the Americans' 20. Arista, aware of Taylor's approach, had positioned his
army across the Matamoros road with his infantry on line, supported by artillery to the rear and cavalry troops protecting
each flank. Arista's cavalry was commanded by Gen. Anastasio
Torrejón (q.v.) (left flank) and Gen. Luis Noriega (q.v.) (right
flank). His infantry was under Colonel José López Uraga (q.v.),
Gen. José María García (q.v.), and General Rómulo Díaz de la
Vega (q.v.).

After two of Taylor's engineer officers, Lt. Jacob Blake (q.v.)
and Lt. Lloyd Tilghman, quickly reconnoitered the Mexican
positions, Taylor halted his army and had his men refill their
canteens in a nearby pond. He then deployed his troops to give
battle. Arista strangely allowed this deployment to occur uncontested. Taylor had Col. (later general) David Twiggs (q.v.)
commanding his right. Under Twiggs were Col. James S. McIntosh's (q.v.) Fifth Infantry, the Third and Fourth Infantries
under Lt. Col. John Garland (q.v.), artillery batteries under
Capt. Samuel Ringgold (q.v.) and Lt. Randolph Ridgely (q.v.),
and dragoons (q.v.) under Capt. Charles A. May (q.v.). Taylor's
left was under Lt. Col. William G. Belknap (q.v.), who commanded the Eighth Infantry. Belknap had a battalion of "red-
legged infantry" under Lt. Col. Thomas Childs (q.v.) and artillery under Capt. James Duncan (q.v.).

The fight that followed was the first standing battle for the
U.S. Army against a regular force since the battle of New Orleans in 1815. Palo Alto was essentially an artillery duel. Arista
opened fire from a range of one-half mile. The Mexican fire was
not effective, the solid shot (Arista did not have high explosive
ammunition) often falling short and rolling into the American
positions. The troops would see it coming and dodge aside. On
the other hand, Taylor's artillerymen were better trained, and
their ammunition more diverse and effective. After the opening
exchanges, Arista sent Torrejón's cavalry to the left to flank Taylor's right and reach the vulnerable American supply train to
the rear. Twiggs redeployed both infantry and artillery to stop
Torrejón's charge. The batteries, under Ringgold and Ridgely,
maneuvered forward and opened with their six-pounders
(called "flying artillery" since they were rapidly deployed on
the battlefield with teams of horses). The accuracy of the American fire caused Torrejón's cavalry to withdraw.

When these forces pulled back, Taylor adjusted his line toward the enemy's position. Artillery and infantry were rotated forward in a counter-clockwise move, allowing the artillery to rake the Mexican lines. Taylor sent Captain May's dragoons to his right flank to attempt to penetrate the Mexican left and capture their guns. Arista's troops held their ground, and the strong resistance turned May back. General Arista then rotated his units clockwise to again square with Taylor's line. He next attempted to envelop Taylor's left in order to reach the supply trains from that flank. To carry this out, General Noriega led a cavalry charge in that direction, but Taylor's artillery, fought by Duncan on his left, quickly turned back Noriega.

During the fight, which was mostly an artillery duel but included considerable musket fire, an artillery charge started a fire on the dry plain. Smoke obscured the vision of both armies and combat ceased; after an hour the fight resumed briefly before Arista made a decision at dusk to withdraw from the field. The devastating accuracy of the American artillery had forced the decision. Arista's troops had been demoralized by the murderous blasts; in three hours the general had suffered over 200 casualties, about 100 of these killed in action. Taylor's units had lost about 50, five of these killed, including Captain Ringgold, developer of the flying artillery concept, who died of wounds a few days after the battle.

The battle was far from decisive. Taylor had retained the battlefield, however, and his losses were light. Significantly, he had protected his supply trains, critical for his army once it was reunited with the troops at Fort Texas. He did not have to go to the bayonet, as he had presumed before the battle. The accuracy and mobility of his artillery made him more appreciative of that arm's utility; the old general would continue to talk about the bayonet, but he would increasingly use his artillery. Palo Alto was significant for another reason. It was a battle fought only with regulars on the American side (which also applied to the battle the next day at Resaca de la Palma [q.v.]). This gave the regular regiments considerable pride in their accomplishments; they knew the volunteer units would soon be in the theater of war, and they wanted the chance to prove their mettle before the volunteers (q.v.) arrived.

Arista's army was still intact, although his men were dispirited. He pulled his army a short distance south of the battlefield and camped for the night. Taylor left him alone. The next morning Arista withdrew five miles farther south toward the river.

There he prepared for more battle, which Taylor soon gave him. For the follow-on to the battle of Palo Alto, *see* RESACA DE LA PALMA, BATTLE OF.

PAREDES Y ARRILLAGA, MARIANO (1797–1849). In the early 1840s, Gen. Mariano Paredes y Arrillaga, commander of an army at San Luis Potosí (q.v.), was the main rival to Gen. Antonio López de Santa Anna (q.v.) for national power. An opportunist and monarchist, he was uncompromising in his opposition to any peaceful settlement of the Texas (q.v.) problem with the United States. In December 1845, Paredes made a *pronunciamento* (a proclamation backed up with force) against the José Joaquín de Herrera (q.v.) government in Mexico City (q.v.) and, with the backing of his army, rode into Mexico City and seized the presidency. He followed a warlike policy from the start of his short-lived regime, instructing all commanders sent to the Rio Grande (q.v.) to take the initiative against Gen. Zachary Taylor's (q.v.) army by going on the offensive at the first opportunity. Paredes's actions for the four months after January 1846 made war much more likely, notwithstanding other factors in Mexico or the military deployments of the U.S. troops. Paredes held the presidency until forced out by Santa Anna loyalists in July 1846. He went into exile, making an abortive attempt at regaining power when he returned to Mexico in 1847.

PARRAS, SAN FERNANDO DE, COAHUILA. During the war, Parras was a town of about 5,000 residents in the center of a rich agricultural and wine-producing zone in the state of Coahuila (q.v.). Gen. John Ellis Wool's (q.v.) force of 3,000 men arrived at Parras on December 5, 1846, on its way from San Antonio (q.v.) to Chihuahua (q.v.). After 12 days there, Gen. Zachary Taylor (q.v.) ordered Wool to cancel his planned invasion of Chihuahua and to join the main body at Saltillo (q.v.).

PARROTT, WILLIAM. One of Pres. James Knox Polk's (q.v.) initial actions regarding Mexico was to send Dr. William Parrott as an unofficial agent to Mexico City (q.v.) to report on the mood of the people and their government regarding peacefully settling difficulties then extant between the two nations. Although Parrott's reputation was somewhat cloudy, he was chosen because he had lived for years in Mexico, was fluent in Spanish, and supposedly had a sense of Mexican political life. He reported to Washington that Mexico was eager to negotiate with the United States and would welcome the re-establishment of diplomatic relations. Parrott returned to Washington in November after several months as Polk's confidential agent in the Mexican capital. He was immediately sent back to Mexico to accompany John Slidell (q.v.), Polk's choice as minister plenipotentiary to the Mexican government.

PASO DE BARTOLO. See SAN GABRIEL, BATTLE OF.

PASO DE OVEJAS. The Paso de Ovejas was a pass in the foothills of the mountains along the route of Gen. Winfield Scott's (q.v.) campaign from Veracruz (q.v.) to Mexico City (q.v.). After Scott's army fought the battle of Cerro Gordo (q.v.) and moved into the Valley of Mexico (q.v.), Paso de Ovejas, 20 miles southeast of Cerro Gordo, became a center of Mexican guerrilla (q.v.) attacks against American resupply columns from Veracruz.

PATTERSON, ROBERT (1792–1881). Irish-born Robert Patterson came to the United States when his father was exiled for participating in the Irish Rebellion. Patterson was a soldier in the War of 1812, rising to the rank of colonel in the Pennsylvania militia at 21 years of age and then to captain in the U. S. infantry. After the war, he left the army, made a fortune in private business, and rose to major general in the Pennsylvania militia.

When Patterson returned to the army as a volunteer general in 1846, Pres. James Knox Polk (q.v.) briefly considered him for overall command in Mexico although he had not been on active duty for 32 years. Polk tended to favor Patterson because he was a good Democrat and political ally, but he realized that he could not groom him for the presidency because his foreign birth made him ineligible. Polk, although generally ignorant of military affairs, also realized that Patterson lacked the necessary military experience and did not have the confidence of the army. Fifty-three years old at the start of the war with Mexico in 1846, Patterson was the second-ranking officer in the war as a senior major general after Gen. Winfield Scott (q.v.).

Despite his seniority, Patterson commanded a volunteer division under Gen. Zachary Taylor (q.v.) in the northern theater in 1846. He later marched with his division to occupy Tampico (q.v.) and join Scott's army for the Veracruz (q.v.) operation in March 1847. Arriving at Cerro Gordo (q.v.) before Scott's arrival, Patterson overruled Gen. David Twiggs's (q.v.) order for an immediate attack before the main body of troops under Scott had closed on the site, a decision that most historians of the war believe saved many American lives and preserved chances for the eventual victory. In May, after the battle of Cerro Gordo, Patterson led seven regiments of discharged volunteer soldiers back to the United States. In December 1847, he returned to the theater and served Scott in the occupation forces after the fall of Mexico City (q.v.). Patterson again returned to civil life after the war.

In the interval between the Mexican and Civil Wars, he acquired sugar and cotton plantations in the South, played a major role in the development of the sugar industry in Louisiana, and owned about 30 cotton mills in Pennsylvania. In addition, he was a promoter of the Pennsylvania Railroad. At the beginning of the Civil War, he was reinstated as major general for the Union and commanded in the Shenandoah Valley campaign during the battle of First Manassas (Bull Run), where his reticence and indecisiveness would draw sharp criticism. Patterson had a reputation as a good subordinate commander who was indecisive when operating independently. After the war, he published *A Narrative of the Campaign in the Valley of the Shenandoah in 1861*.

PAYNE, MATTHEW M. (d. 1862). During the war, Lt. Col. Matthew M. Payne commanded the Fourth Artillery Regiment. He was brevetted colonel for Palo Alto (q.v.) and Resaca de la Palma (q.v.). During Resaca de la Palma, he was seriously wounded. Payne served as one of the members of the court in the court-martial of Lt. Col. John Charles Frémont (q.v.) that convened at Fort Monroe, Virginia, in November 1847.

PEACE TERMS. *See* GUADALUPE HIDALGO, TREATY OF.

PECK, JOHN JAMES (1821–1878). Commissioned a brevet second lieutenant upon graduating eighth in the West Point class of 1843, John James Peck joined the artillery (q.v.). Transferred to Gen. Zachary Taylor's (q.v.) army in Texas (q.v.) in 1845, Peck fought in all of the battles of Taylor's campaigns in Texas (q.v.) and northern Mexico with the exception of Buena Vista. He later moved on to the army of Gen. Winfield Scott (q.v.) and fought in the entire southern campaign from Veracruz (q.v.) to Mexico City (q.v.). Peck received brevets to captain for gallantry and meritorious conduct at the battles of Contreras and Churubusco (q.v.) and to major for Molino del Rey (q.v.). After the war, he fought in the Indian campaigns in the West before resigning from the army in 1853. In civilian life, he became active in politics and business. During the Civil War, Peck reentered active service for the Union as a brigadier general of volunteers (q.v.) and earned a major generalcy during the Peninsular Campaign in 1862. Thereafter, Peck saw action as brigade, division, or district commander throughout the war. After the Civil War, he resumed civilian life, participating actively in Democratic politics and serving as president of the New York State Life Insurance Company from 1867 until his death in 1878.

Peck's total combat service in the six years of the two wars in which he served was equal to or superior to that of any of his West Point contemporaries from that era. He left a valuable participant record of the war with Mexico in his letters home during the conflict. This collection of detailed, descriptive, and beautifully written letters was published in 1970 as part of the book *The Sign of the Eagle: A View of Mexico—1830 to 1855.*

PECK, WILLIAM G. William G. Peck graduated number one in the West Point Class of 1844. He entered the topographical engineers (q.v.) and participated in Lt. John Charles Frémont's (q.v.) third expedition through the Rocky Mountains in 1845. During the war with Mexico, he returned to the West, serving in Gen. Stephen Watts Kearny's (q.v.) army.

PEDREGAL. The pedregal was an extensive field of hardened lava several miles to the south and west of Mexico City (q.v.). The American army had to cross the pedregal to position units for the battle of Contreras and the final advance on Mexico City. The lava field, about three miles across and two miles from north to south, still exists today in the vicinity of Mexico's National University.

PENA Y BARRAGAN, MATIAS DE LA (1789–1850). A Mexican brigadier general and political conspirator, Matias de la Peña y Barragán sided with Gen. Antonio López de Santa Anna (q.v.) after the battle of Buena Vista (q.v.) and wrote to the caudillo requesting his return to the capital. Peña fought in the battles for Mexico City (q.v.) against Gen. Winfield Scott's (q.v.) forces, several times rallying his troops to counterattack the American positions.

PENA Y PENA, MANUEL DE LA (1789–1850). In 1845, Manuel de la Peña y Peña was the Mexican foreign minister during discussions with the Polk administration over the Texas (q.v.)

question and other border issues. At that time, Peña, a *Moderado* (q.v.), was strongly in favor of negotiating with Polk's representative, John Slidell (q.v.), and argued that Mexico's failure to do so would bring war and irreparable harm to the nation for generations to come. Although his position was supported by the president at the time, José Joaquín de Herrera (q.v.), the government came under increasing pressure from ultranationalist sectors who refused to compromise. The Slidell mission, therefore, was turned back by the Herrera government. At the end of the war, the aging Peña y Peña, still a moderate opposed to the extremist factions who preferred guerrilla (q.v.) warfare to negotiations, served as acting president at the time of the peace talks that eventually produced the Treaty of Guadalupe Hidalgo (q.v.).

PENSACOLA, FLORIDA. Pensacola was the principal naval base for the Home Squadron (q.v.) operating in the Gulf of Mexico. The fleet made regular voyages back to Pensacola from Antón Lizardo (q.v.), its temporary base in Gulf waters, for resupply, even occasionally making the entire 900-mile round trip solely for water replenishment.

PEREZ, FRANCISCO (1847). Brig. Gen. Francisco Pérez was a brigade commander under Gen. Antonio López de Santa Anna (q.v.) and fought in some of the heaviest combat of the war. He commanded a brigade in the army that marched from San Luis Potosí (q.v.) to Agua Nueva (q.v.) in January-February 1847 and led the final charge on the last day at Buena Vista (q.v.). Surviving Buena Vista, he later fought in the battles for Mexico City (q.v.); most accounts agree that Pérez fought bravely in defending the bridge at Churubusco (q.v.) and in the defense of Chapultepec (q.v.), where he was killed in action when American troops stormed the castle.

PERFECTO DE COS, MARTIN. *See* COS, MARTIN PERFECTO DE.

PEROTE, VERACRUZ. Perote is a town on a high valley plain west of Jalapa (q.v.). On April 22, 1847, the advance guard of Gen. William Jenkins Worth's (q.v.) division reached the city, and the invading force occupied the town and the notorious fort on its periphery—San Carlos de Perote. San Carlos was a castle-like fortress, forbidding in its dust-grey appearance, where Texans from the Mier (q.v.) Expedition had been incarcerated in the early 1840s. Worth discovered and released some of the Mexican officers from Veracruz (q.v.) who had been imprisoned as punishment for surrendering the port city. Perote and its fort remained occupied by the United States for the rest of the war, serving as a way station for supply and anti-guerrilla units as well as a holding base for sick or wounded soldiers. The fort of San Carlos still serves as a Mexican prison today.

PERRY, MATTHEW CALBRAITH (1794–1858). Called "Old Bruin" by his men, Matthew Calbraith Perry, the famed naval officer (a fame largely gained later in the Orient), was chosen by Secretary of the Navy George Bancroft (q.v.) in the fall of 1845 to succeed Commo. David E. Conner (q.v.) as commander of the Home Squadron (q.v.) in the Gulf of Mexico. Since Conner's tour of duty had not ended, Perry did not immediately report on station. In August 1846, Bancroft gave Perry command of the ship of the line *Mississippi* (q.v.) and ordered him to the Gulf as Conner's second in command, awaiting further orders to assume command upon Conner's departure. In January 1847, Perry returned to Norfolk for repairs to the *Mississippi*. While there he visited officials in Washington, including the new secretary of the navy, John Young Mason (q.v.). Perry apparently convinced the administration that it was time for him to replace Conner, and orders were issued on March 3. Perry returned to Veracruz (q.v.) with these orders in hand on March 21, in the midst of Gen. Winfield Scott's (q.v.) siege of the city and fort. Unfortunately for Conner, much of the credit for the joint army-navy cooperation and the critical naval gunfire support in the huge operation went to Perry. This was unfair to Conner, who had worked tirelessly with the administration and with Scott during the previous year to prepare every detail of that historic and successful undertaking. After the surrender of Veracruz, Perry commanded the squadron for the remainder of the war. He led expeditions to capture the Gulf and river ports of Alvarado (q.v.) and Tuxpan (q.v.)—as well as the ports on the Yucatán (q.v.) peninsula still flying the Mexican tri-color—and continued to enforce the blockade (q.v.) of the Gulf coast that Conner had established almost two years earlier.

PETRITA. The *Petrita* was a small steamer captured from the Mexicans by the U.S. Navy and placed into service with the Home Squadron (q.v.). On March 6, 1847, Commo. David E. Conner (q.v.) arranged for Gen. Winfield Scott (q.v.) to accompany him on the *Petrita* for a reconnaissance of Collado Beach (q.v.), Veracruz (q.v.), and the fort of San Juan de Ulúa (q.v.). The General in Chief took with him his major subordinates (Gen. William Jenkins Worth [q.v.], Gen. David Twiggs [q.v.], and Gen. Robert Patterson [q.v.]) and members of his "little cabinet" (q.v.) and other engineer officers—among them Captains Robert E. Lee (q.v.) and Joseph E. Johnston (q.v.), and Lieutenants Pierre Gustave T. Beauregard (q.v.) and George Meade (q.v.). During the reconnaissance, Mexican batteries on shore fired all around the little ship (which did not return fire), endangering the key commanders as well as the rising stars of the U.S. Army before the *Petrita*'s captain turned beyond range of enemy fire.

PHELPS, JOHN WOLCOTT (1813–1885). John Wolcott Phelps, West Point class of 1836, was assigned to the Fourth Artillery in the war with Mexico and participated in the battle of Monterrey (q.v.) and the siege of Veracruz (q.v.). Later he fought at Cerro Gordo (q.v.), Contreras and Churubusco (q.v.), and Molino del Rey (q.v.). He was brevetted captain for gallantry at Contreras and Churubusco. During the Civil War, Phelps became a brigadier general of U.S. volunteers.

PICKETT, GEORGE EDWARD (1825–1875). George Edward Pickett, last in the West Point class of 1846, participated in the siege of Veracruz (q.v.), the battle of Cerro Gordo (q.v.), the capture of San Antonio (q.v.), the battles of Contreras and Churubusco (q.v.), the battle of Molino del Rey (q.v.), the storming of Chapultepec Castle (q.v.), and the assault on Mexico City (q.v.). He was brevetted first lieutenant for Contreras and Churubusco and captain for Chapultepec. Pickett resigned his federal commission in June 1861 to serve in the Confederate army, where, as a general, he led the tragic charge during the last day of the battle of Gettysburg that historians would forever record in his name.

PICO, ANDRES (1810–1876). Capt. Andrés Pico was a brother of the former insurgent governor of California (q.v.), Pio Pico (q.v.). Andrés Pico led the Californios (q.v.) against Gen. Stephen Watts Kearny's (q.v.) force at San Pascual (q.v.), practically annihilating the Americans until a relief force finally arrived to drive away the besieging troops. Inheriting responsibility for command of all of the Californios when José María Flores (q.v.) fled to Sonora (q.v.), Andrés Pico—after Los

Angeles (q.v.) had fallen to the Americans and his defeated forces were in retreat—signed the so-called Convention of Cahuenga (q.v.) with Bvt. Capt. John Charles Frémont (q.v.), gaining for the native population all of the rights and privileges that Commo. Robert Stockton (q.v.) had previously denied them.

PICO, JESUS. During his march south in California (q.v.), Bvt. Capt. John Frémont (q.v.) captured Jesus Pico, the Californio (q.v.) commander at San Luis Obispo. Pico, who had violated his parole from a previous apprehension by again taking up arms, was court-martialed and sentenced to death. Frémont, realizing Pico's potential as an ally, spared the Californio the gallows. In gratitude, Pico served Frémont as a negotiator, attempting to convince the Californios still resisting Frémont's advance to surrender. In talks with Andrés Pico (q.v.) south of Santa Barbara, Jesus Pico arranged a surrender of the Californios that led to the disputed Convention of Cahuenga (q.v.). See also PICO, ANDRES, and FREMONT, JOHN C.

PICO, PIO (b. 1801). Pío Pico served as the governor of the breakaway Mexican province of California (q.v.) in 1846. He was the last civil governor of California before American forces under John Charles Frémont (q.v.), Robert Field Stockton (q.v.) and Stephen Watts Kearny (q.v.) defeated the Californios (q.v.) and the region became part of the United States.

PIERCE, FRANKLIN (1804–1869). A graduate of Bowdoin College and lawyer in his native New Hampshire, Franklin Pierce at the outbreak of war had already served four years in the House of Representatives and five in the U.S. Senate. As a Democrat in Pres. James Knox Polk's (q.v.) confidence, Pierce had turned down an offer to join the administration as attorney general. When war came, he enlisted as a private in a New Hampshire unit and soon won appointment as a colonel. In March 1847, Polk used one of his congressional authorizations to make his fellow Democrat a brigadier general. In command of a brigade, Pierce led a train of troop and supply reinforcements from Veracruz (q.v.) in June 1847. After several delays caused by Mexican resistance and sickness among his men, Pierce arrived in Puebla (q.v.) on August 6, 1847. In the Valley of Mexico (q.v.) offensive, Pierce's brigade fought as part of Gideon Pillow's (q.v.) division. Pierce saw some action, but because of injury from a horse accident he missed the battles of

Contreras and Churubusco (q.v.), and at Chapultepec (q.v.) he was out of action due to illness. Gen. Winfield Scott (q.v.) apparently respected the New Englander's abilities and used him on delegations in truce negotiations with Mexican officials. After the war, Pierce returned to New England and continued to be active in the Democratic Party. Four years later, he won his party's nomination for president. It was a great irony that his opponent, whom he defeated in the general election in the fall of 1852, was the Whig (q.v.) candidate Winfield Scott. Pierce was the 14th president of the United States, 1853–1857.

PILLOW, GIDEON JOHNSON (1806–1878). Before the war with Mexico, Gideon Johnson Pillow was a law partner of President James Knox Polk (q.v.) in Columbia, Tennessee. He earned Polk's undying loyalty when he was instrumental in securing the Democratic nomination for his friend and business colleague in 1844; he later owed his appointment as brigadier general of volunteers (q.v.) to his relationship with the president. Although through his political connections he had earlier been named a brigadier general in the Tennessee militia, Pillow had never seen combat or even active military service before 1846 and was widely considered by officers and men alike to be incompetent as a division commander in the war. Pillow participated for a short time in the northern theater under Gen. Zachary Taylor (q.v.) and saw most of his war duty in the Veracruz (q.v.)–to–Mexico City (q.v.) campaign under Gen. Winfield Scott (q.v.). His lack of leadership ability was particularly evident at the battle of Cerro Gordo (q.v.), where Scott's forces carried the day despite Pillow's failure to execute his mission to take the Mexican right.

As a major general, Pillow later led his volunteer division during the battles around Mexico City, and he attempted after the surrender to take credit for the gallantry and generalship of Scott and others. His alleged misappropriation of government property (two captured howitzers were discovered in his wagon baggage), fabricated battle reports, and surreptitious communications with the press led to a court-martial and a court of inquiry based on charges by Scott at the close of hostilities. Although not completely exonerated by these military courts, Pillow escaped punishment or even official reprimand for his actions. He continued to enjoy the president's warm friendship and support, celebrating the end of the court of inquiry by dining with Polk at the White House. After the war, Pillow returned to private life and his interests in law and politics, assisting Franklin Pierce (q.v.) in obtaining the Democratic nomination for president in 1852. Gideon Pillow surfaced again in the profession of arms in the Civil War. He played a brief and undistinguished role for the Confederacy as a general of volunteers early in that conflict—an experience which refurbished his reputation as an incompetent and buffoon.

PLAN DEL RIO. Plan del Rio was a small village located northwest of Veracruz (q.v.) on the National Highway (q.v.). It was situated on the Rio del Plan. Here Gen. David Twiggs (q.v.). halted the American army to prepare for the attack on Gen. Antonio López de Santa Anna's (q.v.) forces at Cerro Gordo (q.v.). *See also* CERRO GORDO, BATTLE OF.

PLYMPTON, JOSEPH (d. 1860). Lt. Col. Joseph Plympton commanded the Seventh Infantry Regiment. He positioned his regiment on the Jalapa (q.v.) road to block a Mexican retreat in the battle of Cerro Gordo (q.v.) in April 1847. For this action Plympton won a brevet to colonel.

POINT ISABEL, TEXAS. Situated 10 miles north of the juncture of the Rio Grande (q.v.) and the Gulf of Mexico on the Laguna Madre, the small village of Point Isabel was a key base of operations and a resupply link from New Orleans (q.v.) and Pensacola (q.v.) for the U.S. Army. Although separated from the Gulf by Padre Island, Point Isabel was more suited to the needs of Gen. Zachary Taylor's (q.v.) army than was the Rio Grande, the entrance to which was too shallow to make it navigable for most ships. Access to Point Isabel was through the narrow straights of Brazos Santiago Pass (q.v.), located about five miles southeast of Point Isabel. Since this passage was also shallow, it was often necessary to use barges to transport men and equipment across the lagoon to the port. The military installation that surrounded the supply depot at Point Isabel was called Fort Polk (q.v.).

POLK DOCTRINE. Pres. James Knox Polk's (q.v.) foreign policy was essentially a reaffirmation of the Monroe Doctrine (q.v.). Polk did not want outside powers to gain a foothold in North America or in territories where America's interests could be threatened. In September of 1845, six months after Polk took office, his administration instructed the U.S. diplomatic representative in the Hawaiian Islands that it was the firm policy of the U.S. government to protect the independence of the islands.

This came at a time when rumors indicated that Great Britain had intentions of annexing them. In October 1845, the administration informed the American consul in Monterey (q.v.), California (q.v.), then Mexican territory, that the U.S. government would oppose the colonization of any part of the North American continent by a foreign monarchy. In his first message to Congress in December of that year, Polk stated that "it should be distinctly announced to the world that it is our settled policy that no future European colony or dominion shall, with our consent, be planted or established on any part of the North American continent." The president, in instructions to his secretary of state, James Buchanan, made it clear that his doctrine applied to Britain's or any other nation's designs on California or "any other part of the Mexican territory."

POLK, JAMES KNOX (1795–1849). Born in Mecklenburg County, North Carolina, to a strict Presbyterian family, raised and educated in Tennessee, James Knox Polk returned to his native state in 1816 to attend the university in Chapel Hill. After graduation, he went back to Tennessee, read law, and served as a state legislator. In 1825, he won a seat in the U.S. House of Representatives where he served seven terms. Although accused of possessing a humorless, cold reserve, Polk had a solid reputation in Congress for industry, integrity, and absolute loyalty to the Democratic Party. His hard work earned him the speakership of the House in 1835. After four years as Speaker, Polk returned to Tennessee in 1839 and ran successfully for governor. Defeated in the gubernatorial campaigns of 1841 and 1843, Polk's political career seemed at an end before his surprise nomination as the Democratic standard-bearer in the 1844 presidential election. Polk, who had been an ardent supporter of Andrew Jackson, won Old Hickory's endorsement and ran on a platform calling for low tariffs, banking reform, and Texas (q.v.) annexation. Victorious in the fall of 1844 over the Whig (q.v.) candidate, Henry Clay (q.v.), Polk became the 11th president in 1845 amid a national spirit of Manifest Destiny (q.v.). As chief executive, Polk followed an alternatively aggressive and cautious foreign policy that led to war with Mexico and diplomatic settlement of the nation's northwestern boundary dispute with Great Britain.

Polk's conduct of the war with Mexico revealed a president largely innocent of military matters but one nevertheless determined, as he had been throughout his political career, to become enmeshed in the details of governance. Polk's lack of knowledge of the military, combined with a determination to be involved in the campaigns, caused problems in the management of the war and the public's support of it. He often issued vague orders to his commanders in the field and then failed to support them wholeheartedly when the results of his directives proved unpopular. He was highly suspicious and contemptuous of his two most senior commanders in the war, Gen. Zachary Taylor (q.v.) and Gen. Winfield Scott (q.v.), constantly second-guessing their decisions and rarely giving them due credit for victories on the battlefield. After Taylor's victory against superior numbers at Monterrey (q.v.), Polk condemned Taylor's truce arrangement with the Mexicans. He did this despite not having provided guidance for the army commander in the event major cities were conquered and American forces were battered and placed at risk, as Taylor's were after the hard-fought battle for Monterrey. The president criticized Scott for cutting his army off from its supply line to the coast after it reached Puebla (q.v.) in the summer of 1847, ignoring the tactical imperatives on the ground that caused Scott to make that decision. Polk often complained that Taylor's and Scott's actions were motivated by political ambition (which had some validity, since both generals were Whigs with eyes on the White House), while at the same time his own policies were invariably framed in partisan politics. His futile attempt to persuade Congress to appoint his erstwhile friend, Democratic Missouri senator (and military amateur) Thomas Hart Benton (q.v.), as the commanding general of the army in Mexico demonstrated the president's ignorance of military command requirements.

Throughout the conflict with Mexico, Polk closely followed detailed reports of tactical, diplomatic, administrative, and logistical events of the war, discussing these for hours in long sessions with his cabinet and close advisors. He delegated little and was involved in practically all decisions regarding conduct of the war. Polk was generous with his criticisms of subordinates whose performance did not meet his standards and generally critical of any individual or group who opposed his policies. He was at the same time niggardly with praise for the many civilian and military officials whose efforts brought the war to a successful close. Polk was especially critical of the press during the war, accusing reporters of anti-war propaganda that in his view encouraged the enemy and protracted the war. Although on occasion wavering in his commitment to pursue an aggressive war policy (in late summer of 1846, when the public begin to tire of a war seemingly at a stalemate, the president talked about going on the defensive and following a policy of "inactive occupation"), in the end Polk stayed a policy course that forced a treaty on Mexico which was accepted by a largely expansionist American public in 1848.

Polk clearly had resolve; he was a strong president in the tradition of his predecessors George Washington and Andrew Jackson and his successor wartime president, Lincoln. Unlike the historical judgments of these national leaders, however, those rendered Polk, while often admitting his general competence as president, omitted references to greatness. But Polk played an indispensable role at a critical time in the nation's history, one that other chief executives—perhaps even Lincoln, who condemned the war with Mexico on moral grounds—could not have filled. Some historians have argued that James K. Polk was the ideal man for the age of American expansionism: while Manifest Destiny was not of his creation, he was its ideal agent. Historians credit Polk's performance as a commander in chief with bringing the war to a conclusion that over time proved highly beneficial to the United States, while they nonetheless criticize him for overzealousness in supervision, for creation of discord in relations with his principal commanders, and for political pettiness during a time of national emergency. Polk was succeeded in the presidency by Zachary Taylor (whom he loathed and belittled) and died on June 15, 1849, at 54 years of age, three months after leaving the White House. During the four years of his presidency, Polk kept a meticulous diary that has served for 150 years as a superb source for historians of the period. It was published in four volumes in 1910 as *The Diary of James K. Polk during His Presidency, 1845 to 1849*.

POLK, WILLIAM H. (1815–1862). William H. Polk was a brother of Pres. James Knox Polk (q.v.). As an army major, on May 22, 1848, William Polk commanded troops who accompanied the U.S. diplomatic delegation from Mexico City (q.v.) to Querétaro (q.v.) to deliver ratification documents pertaining to the Treaty of Guadalupe Hidalgo (q.v.). The official exchange of these documents occurred on May 30, an act that formally brought the war to an end.

POLKO REBELLION. The Mexican Congress, pressed for money to finance the war, enacted laws on January 11 and February 4, 1847, that initially gave the government the authority to pledge or sell church property and ultimately authorized the seizure of an initial five million pesos worth of church property. Despite a strong public outcry against these laws, anticlerical and pro-war vice president Valentín Gómez Farías (q.v.)—who was in fact running the country while President Antonio López de Santa Anna (q.v.) led the army—invoked them.

The ensuing revolt, known as the *Polko* Rebellion and begun on February 27, 1847, stopped Gómez Farías after about one and one-half million pesos had been collected. The revolt was named for the *Polkos*, an elite military group formed in Mexico City (q.v.) in the fall of 1846 and made up of the following four regiments: Independencia and Bravo, composed primarily of artisans; Hidalgo, composed primarily of clerks; and Victoria, composed largely of merchants, professionals, and wealthy individuals. The name *Polkos* has been attributed either to the militia regiments' having adopted a polka for their hymn or to their proclivity for festive dancing. The results of the rebellion were that desperately needed troops were delayed in reaching Veracruz (q.v.) and its surrounding area, Gómez Farías was ousted from the vice presidency, and Santa Anna annulled the two offensive laws. Moses Y. Beach (q.v.), the American editor of the *New York Sun*, apparently played a role in the crisis. Beach had been sent to Mexico City by Secretary of State James Buchanan (q.v.) to investigate the chances for a peace settlement and had encouraged the military units and clergy to resist the government's attempt to confiscate church property. *See also* BEACH, MOSES Y.

POPE, JOHN (1822–1892). After his graduation from West Point in 1842, John Pope became a topographical engineer. During the war with Mexico, Pope served at Monterrey (q.v.) and Buena Vista (q.v.), where he was brevetted first lieutenant and captain, respectively. In the Civil War, he played a prominent role for the Union as major general in the U.S. Army.

PORTER, DAVID DIXON (1813–1891). Born in Pennsylvania, David Dixon Porter was the son of Capt. David Porter, who—as a senior U.S. naval officer—commanded the Mexican Navy in 1826. Young David Porter accepted a commission as a midshipman in the Mexican naval forces during his father's tenure as commander. After being captured and released by the Spanish navy in 1828, Porter joined the U.S. Navy as a midshipman. During the war with Mexico, he served as a lieutenant aboard the steamer *Spitfire*, commanded by Comdr. Josiah Tattnall (q.v.). Porter participated in the attack on Veracruz (q.v.) and the second Tabasco (q.v.) campaign, where he was commended by Commo. Matthew Calbraith Perry (q.v.) for successfully leading a force of 70 men to storm the main fort of Tabasco city. After the war, Porter remained in the navy (with the exception of the 1849–1855 period) and rose steadily in rank and positions of responsibility. During the Civil War, he commanded large naval units on the Mississippi and along the Gulf and Atlantic coasts. Remaining in the navy after that conflict, Porter eventually became its senior officer with the death of Admiral Farragut in 1870.

PORTER, FITZ-JOHN (1822–1901). A West Point graduate of 1845, Fitz-John Porter participated in the siege of Veracruz (q.v.); the battles of Cerro Gordo (q.v.), Contreras (q.v.), and Molino del Rey (q.v.); the storming of Chapultepec (q.v.); and the assault on Mexico City (q.v.), where he was wounded at the Belén Gate (q.v.). He received a brevet to captain for Molino del Rey and one to major for Chapultepec. During the Civil War, he became major general of U.S. volunteers and brevet brigadier general and colonel of regulars. After refusing to lead what he considered to be a suicidal assault during Second Manassas, his commanding officer, Gen. John Pope (q.v.), charged him with disobedience. Porter was court-martialed and cashiered out of the army in January 1863. After the war, congressmen who believed Porter had been unfairly treated by Pope introduced a bill to exonerate him. An act of Congress in 1886 restored Porter to his regular army rank of colonel (retired).

PORTER, JOHN B. (d. 1869). After entering the army in 1833, John B. Porter served as a medical officer in the Florida, or Seminole, War and in the war with Mexico. At Veracruz (q.v.), where he commandeered a Franciscan convent on the seacoast to serve as a general hospital, he distinguished himself in 1847 during an outbreak of yellow fever (q.v.).

PORTER, THEODORIC H. After Col. Trueman Cross (q.v.) disappeared along the banks of the Rio Grande (q.v.) in April 1846, Lt. Theodoric H. Porter was sent with a 10-man force to search for him. In a subsequent ambush, Porter was killed by Mexican troops. Since Porter was a respected and promising young officer and the son of the navy's distinguished Commo. David Porter (q.v.), his death at the hands of the Mexicans

stirred strong emotion among the American soldiers of Gen.
Zachary Taylor's (q.v.) army.

PRENTISS, JAMES H. (1809–1848). Twelfth in the West Point class
of 1830, James H. Prentiss served initially in the First Artillery.
In Gen. Zachary Taylor's (q.v.) army during the war with Mexico, Prentiss was assistant adjutant general to Brig. Gen. John
Ellis Wool (q.v.) during the march through Chihuahua (q.v.)
before returning to his old unit, the First Regiment of Artillery,
to take command of a heavy gun battery.

PRICE, STERLING (1809–1867). Sterling Price, a Virginian who
moved to Missouri as a young man, served in the Missouri legislature before his election to the U. S. Congress, where he
served four years. He resigned to fight in the war with Mexico
as a colonel commanding the Second Regiment of Missouri
Mounted Volunteers in Gen. Stephen W. Kearny's (q.v.) Army
of the West (q.v.). When Kearny departed Santa Fe (q.v.) for
California (q.v.) in September 1846, he left Price in command
of U.S. forces in the territory of New Mexico (q.v.). Price led a
500-man contingent composed of five companies of his regiment, augmented by other available troops, to quell the violent
Taos Rebellion (q.v.) in February 1847.

In March 1848, after a year of occupation duty in New Mex-
ico, Price, unaware that a peace treaty had been signed,
marched a column south from El Paso (q.v.) and reoccupied
Chihuahua City (q.v.) for the United States. After meeting no
resistance there and without orders from higher authorities,
Price moved 60 miles south and on March 16, 1848, engaged a
Mexican force defending Santa Cruz de Rosales (q.v.). The almost day-long battle resulted in over 20 dead or wounded
American soldiers and a greater number of Mexican casualties.
The surrender of the Mexican force at Santa Cruz marked the
end of hostilities in the northern theater and the last major
fighting of the war.

After the war with Mexico, Price became governor of Missouri and a major general and commander of the state militia
in the 1850s. He fought for the Confederacy throughout the
Civil War, rising to major general, CSA. After the Civil War,
he returned to Mexico and attempted unsuccessfully to form a
colony of confederate exiles; from Mexico he returned to St.
Louis, where he died September 29, 1867. See also SANTA
CRUZ DE ROSALES; CHIHUAHUA; TAOS REBELLION.

PRINCE, HENRY. First Lt. Henry Prince, an 1835 graduate of West Point, served with the Fourth Infantry Regiment in the war with Mexico. He fought at the National Bridge (q.v.) on the road from Veracruz (q.v.) to Jalapa (q.v.); at the capture of San Antonio (q.v.) in the Valley of Mexico (q.v.); and at the battles of Contreras and Churubusco (q.v.), and Molino del Rey (q.v.). He was seriously wounded at Molino del Rey. For his bravery, he was brevetted captain for Contreras and Churubusco and major for Molino del Rey.

PUEBLA, PUEBLA. Puebla was an important Mexican city of 80,000 inhabitants in 1847. Situated at 7,000 feet altitude, the city was located less than 100 miles southeast of Mexico City (q.v.). After the battle at Cerro Gordo (q.v.), Gen. Antonio López de Santa Anna (q.v.) moved his reconstituted army to Puebla on May 11, 1847, to await Gen. Winfield Scott's arrival. When Scott's leading division under Gen. William Jenkins Worth (q.v.) appeared on the outskirts of Puebla several days later, Santa Anna, lacking the support of the populace, had second thoughts about contesting the Americans there and decided to abandon the city. Puebla officials, encouraged by the clergy, surrendered the city to Worth on May 15. The remainder of the army, along with Scott himself, arrived in Puebla within two weeks. Scott received reinforcements in early June, bringing his effective fighting strength to 8,000 men (2,200 others were on the sick list). Scott stayed at Puebla for two and a half months, gathering and training his army for the coming battle for the capital. Additional units arriving in the summer brought the army's numbers in Puebla to 10,700. On August 7, the army marched out of Puebla for the campaign in the Valley of Mexico (q.v.); a small force under Col. Thomas Childs (q.v.) remained as a garrison.

While Scott was carrying out his campaign against Mexico City in September, Brig. Gen. Joaquín Rea (q.v.) began a siege of Puebla that lasted over a month. Rea was reinforced by General Santa Anna after the latter retreated when the capital fell to the Americans in September. Santa Anna left the siege lines on September 30 to intercept an American relief column under Gen. Joseph Lane (q.v.). Santa Anna was unable to halt Lane's advance after Lane defeated his forces at Huamantla (q.v.) on October 9. On the 12th, Lane's troops arrived at Puebla and broke the siege; Puebla thereafter remained occupied by elements of Scott's army until they withdrew from Mexico in mid-1848. Although never again subjected to a siege, the region around Puebla remained a center of Mexican guerrilla (q.v.) activity against Scott's forces as they moved to and from Mexico City in the months after October 1847.

PUEBLO OF TAOS, NEW MEXICO. *See* TAOS REBELLION.

PUENTE NACIONAL, VERACRUZ. The Puente Nacional, or national bridge, was a picturesque stone bridge across the Río Antigua on the National Highway (q.v.) from Veracruz (q.v.) to Jalapa (q.v.). It was in the path of Gen. Winfield Scott's (q.v.) army in its march to Mexico City (q.v.). The heavy stone structure and its surrounding hills witnessed guerrilla (q.v.) warfare activity and numerous small battles throughout the southern campaign.

PURISIMA BRIDGE. The Purísima Bridge, a fortified position on a bridge over the Ojo de Agua canal in the eastern section of Monterrey (q.v.), was a point of strong Mexican resistance during Gen. Zachary Taylor's (q.v.) assault on the city. *See also* MONTERREY, BATTLE OF.

PUROS. Champions of social revolution in Mexico in the mid-19th century, the *Puros* were part of the broader federalist movement arising after independence from Spain. They fought for a liberal democracy patterned on the United States and sought the abolishment of clerical and military *fueros* (privileges), the confiscation of church property, and the abandonment of the caste system existing in 19th-century Mexico as a legacy of the Spanish colonial system. The *Puros* consisted largely of the mestizo class, those of mixed Spanish and Indian blood. They vigorously opposed Texas (q.v.) annexation to the United States, preferring to go to war than accept losing that province. Although most parties resisted the American invasion after the war began, the *Puros* were especially vigorous in opposing any peace agreement with the invading army that would give up its northern provinces to the "Colossus of the North." Even after Mexico City (q.v.) had been captured by Gen. Winfield Scott's (q.v.) army in September 1847, the *Puros* took the extremist position of wanting to continue the conflict through guerrilla warfare in the outlying areas. After the war, the *Puros* blamed the Conservatives for Mexico's defeat and the loss of national territory. The reform movement (*La Reforma*) under Benito Juárez grew out of the *Puro* political faction in the decade after 1848. *See also* MODERADOS.

Q

QUARTERMASTER DEPARTMENT. In 1845, the Quartermaster Department—led since 1818 by quartermaster general, Maj. Gen. Thomas Sidney Jesup (q.v.)—was ill prepared for war. Congress had cut military manpower after the Seminole War as well as funds needed to maintain readiness. Wagons were scarce, wagon parts were not interchangeable, and experienced teamsters were hard to find; animals to pull wagons were in short supply; sufficient drivers were unavailable. Both ocean-going ships and shallow-draft boats for transport of troops and supplies were lacking. Clothing and equipment—the responsibility of the Quartermaster Department since the abolishment of both the Clothing Bureau in 1841 and the Office of the Commissary General of Purchases in 1842—were barely sufficient for a peacetime army manning frontier posts.

At the beginning of the war with Mexico, the Quartermaster Department had a staff of 31 of its 37 authorized officers. Throughout the war, the department had no quartermaster units. This meant that quartermaster officers only supervised logistics planning and execution—actual work (as with the engineers [q.v.]) had to be accomplished by line troops. What the department lacked in quantity, however, it made up for in quality, experience, and resourcefulness. Lt. Col. Thomas F. Hunt (q.v.) and Col. Trueman Cross (q.v.) had entered active service shortly after Jesup was made quartermaster general; they and Col. Henry Stanton had frequently developed their decision-making and leadership skills as acting quartermaster general when Jesup had to be away from Washington. Although Congress authorized regimental quartermasters to be appointed within volunteer units in the summer of 1846, the Quartermaster Department did not begin to increase in size until 10 months after the outbreak of war.

Before the conflict—from June 1845 when the War Department (q.v.) ordered Gen. Zachary Taylor (q.v.) to move from Fort Jesup (q.v.) to Texas (q.v.) and May 1846 when the war started—Jesup made an inspection tour of the army, leaving Colonel Stanton in charge. Key posts were filled by respected officers: Lieutenant Colonel Hunt went to New Orleans; Maj. Osborn Cross (q.v.) (son of Col. Trueman Cross) was assigned to Fort Jesup, Capt. George W. Crossman was sent to Taylor's headquarters, and Col. Trueman Cross was sent to the southwest in charge of Hunt and six other quartermaster officers assigned to Texas.

James K. Polk (c. 1849). Daguerreotype. Courtesy Amon Carter Museum, Fort Worth, Texas.

D. ANTONIO LOPEZ DE SANTA ANNA,

General de Division,

varias veces Presidente de la Republica Mejicana

Zachary Taylor and His Staff at Walnut Springs (1847). William Garl Brown, Jr.; oil on canvas. NPG. 71.57. National Portrait Gallery, Smithsonian Institution. Taylor third from left; William W. S. Bliss, fourth from left; Braxton Bragg, standing, sixth from left.

Zachary Taylor (1848). Sarony and Major lithography company, NPG. 85.163. National Portrait Gallery, Smithsonian Institution.

Pedro de Ampudia (c. 1847). The Benson Collection, University of Texas, Austin.

Mariano Arista. The Benson Collection, University of Texas, Austin.

William Jenkins Worth (1844). Lithograph by Charles Fenderich. Edward D. Weber Lithography Company, 1844. NPG 66.99. National Portrait Gallery, Smithsonian Institution.

John Ellis Wool (c. 1862). Photograph by Charles DeForest Fredricks, NPG. 80.329. National Portrait Gallery, Smithsonian Institution.

John Macrae Washington (c. 1847). Daguerreotype. Courtesy Amon Carter Museum, Fort Worth, Texas.

Jefferson Davis. (1849). George Lethbridge Saunders, watercolor on ivory. NPG. 79.228. National Portrait Gallery, Smithsonian Institution.

Stephen Watts Kearny (c. 1847). Carruth & Carruth, Printers, Oakland, California. U.S. Naval Historical Center Photograph.

Alexander W. Doniphan (c. 1850). Portrait from William Elsey Connelley, *Doniphan's Expedition and the Conquest of New Mexico and California* (Kansas City: Bryant & Douglas, 1907).

David E. Conner. U.S. Naval Historical Center Photograph.

Matthew Calbraith Perry (c. 1855). Unidentified photographer. Daguerreotype. NPG 77.206. National Portrait Gallery, Smithsonian Institution.

Franklin Pierce (c. 1848). Benjamin W. Thayer Lithography company. NPG. 77.275. National Portrait Gallery, Smithsonian Institution.

Robert E. Lee (c. 1861). Charles G. Crehen, after photograph by Mathew Brady. NPG 84.83. National Portrait Gallery, Smithsonian Institution.

Thomas J. Jackson (c. 1863). Dominique C. Fabronius, after unidentified artist. Louis Prang Lithography company. NPG. 76.45. National Portrait Gallery, Smithsonian Institution.

Ulysses S. Grant (c. 1848). From U. S. Grant, *Personal Memories of U.S. Grant,* Vol. I (New York: Webster, 1885).

View of Chapultepec and Molino del Rey. Lithograph by N. Currier. Prints and Photographs Division, Library of Congress.

At the outset of the war, the Quartermaster Department was stretched to supply Taylor's army. The 300-plus wagon train in Taylor's army during its march to the Rio Grande (q.v.) was composed largely of scavenged wagons and animals. As the war progressed, however, the situation was alleviated to a great extent as additional wartime funds were allocated by Congress and as the department settled into the rhythm of supplying a war different than those that the United States had fought before. The number of quartermaster officers increased; wagons were built, wagon trains were staffed, and animals were procured; ships were built or acquired to facilitate the flow of men and supplies; packaging was waterproofed and slimmed down in size to better meet the hardships of long supply lines; goods were manufactured; the supply process was improved for the duration of the war by allowing the department to make purchases on the open market instead of by the slow and less flexible process of bidding; and market prices settled back down somewhat from their surge due to the military's sudden need for transport and equipment at the war's outset.

The department's job was complicated by numerous factors. Most important among them were that (1) the volunteer force increased at a fast and uneven rate, which made it difficult to know what supplies, equipment and transport would be needed; (2) in the northern Mexico campaign in 1846, Taylor, unlike Winfield Scott in the southern campaign the following year, was slow to requisition wagons and steamboats; (3) the War Department was unaccustomed to procuring the type of shallow-draft steamboats needed, and it was difficult to get these weakly powered boats to their destinations; (4) the army, accustomed to cumbersome comforts, bulky rations, and the convenience of wagons, was reluctant to travel light, a necessity in the mobile warfare demanded in the Mexican campaigns; (5) topographical surveys had not been made of the Rio Grande or many harbors and bays, which made it difficult to provide for water transport; (6) the Quartermaster Department had the responsibility of supplying multiple, geographically separated armies over the long, insecure supply lines of the armies of Generals Zachary Taylor, John E. Wool (q.v.), Stephen Watts Kearny (q.v.), and Winfield Scott; and (7) sorely needed funds were always slow to be authorized and slow to arrive in the coffers of the Quartermaster Department.

The heightened wartime responsibility of the Quartermaster Department did not end with the close of hostilities. The logistics process had to be reversed as the nation returned to peace—troops had to be returned to the United States, animals had to be disposed of, ships had to be sold, and surplus property in Mexico had to be auctioned or returned to the United States.

The great captains of the war—Taylor, Scott, and many of their fellow senior officers—frequently criticized the lack of timely logistics support during the war in their letters and reports. But the tasks were great, and the Quartermaster Department performed admirable service under circumstances unique in America's military history.

QUERETARO, QUERETARO. After Gen. Antonio López de Santa Anna (q.v.) abandoned Mexico City (q.v.) in September 1847, half of his forces went with him to carry out the siege of Puebla (q.v.), and half were sent 150 miles north to Querétaro under the command of ex-president and general José Joaquín de Herrera (q.v.). The following month, Querétaro became the temporary capital of Mexico as the United States continued its occupation of Mexico City. After both nations ratified the Treaty of Guadalupe Hidalgo (q.v.), a U.S. force under the command of Pres. James Knox Polk's (q.v.) brother, Maj. William H. Polk (q.v.), traveled to Querétaro in late May 1848 to exchange ratification documents with the Mexican government.

QUIJANO, BENITO (1800–1865). During the lull after the battles of Contreras and Churubusco (q.v.), Brig. Gen. Benito Quijano served as a commissioner for Gen. Antonio López de Santa Anna (q.v.) in negotiations to arrange a cease-fire. The agreement proved temporary, and fighting soon resumed. In February, after the Treaty of Guadalupe Hidalgo (q.v.) had been signed, Quijano again sat for the Mexicans in negotiations that arranged a final armistice between his country and the United States.

QUITMAN, JOHN ANTHONY (1798–1858). The son of a Lutheran pastor in New York who wanted his son to also enter the ministry, John Anthony Quitman was well educated by private tutors. Instead of following in his father's footsteps, however, he taught English at a Pennsylvania college before studying law and being admitted to the bar in Ohio. He later moved to Natchez, Mississippi, where he became a prominent politician. He served in the Mississippi legislature and was briefly acting governor of Mississippi. Quitman raised a company of volunteers (q.v.) called the Fencibles and took them to Texas in 1836, although they missed seeing action in the Texas revolution.

In the war with Mexico, Quitman was one of the six brigadier generals of volunteers appointed from civilian life as a result of congressional authorizations in May 1846. Quitman and his volunteer troops joined Taylor's army and participated in the battle of Monterrey (q.v.) before moving south in December 1846 to join Gen. Winfield Scott's (q.v.) gathering army. Quitman took part in the siege of Veracruz (q.v.) and commanded a brigade through the battle of Cerro Gordo (q.v.) and a division after his promotion to major general in the late spring of 1847. He led his division in the battles for Mexico City (q.v.) in August and September 1847. Quitman's division spearheaded the attack on Chapultepec (q.v.) on September 13. Later that day, leading a composite force gathered from the Chapultepec assault, he was the first to reach the defenses guarding the center of the city. In fierce combat to take the Belén Gate (q.v.) and repulse counterattacks from the citadel (q.v.), Quitman's force suffered high casualties, among those most of his staff and artillery officers. At daybreak on September 14, 1847, the battle for Mexico City ended when Quitman led his division into the central plaza after Gen. Antonio López de Santa Anna's (q.v.) army withdrew. For two months, Quitman served as the first military governor of Mexico City before returning to the United States. Although criticized by some as vain and obsessed with personal glory, Quitman was considered by most observers to be one of the more professional and effective of the volunteer generals in the war.

After the war with Mexico, he became governor of Mississippi. While in office, Quitman was charged with violating U.S. neutrality laws with regard to a filibustering expedition to liberate Cuba. Although he was never convicted of the charge, he resigned the governorship. Quitman was elected to two terms in the U.S. Congress before dying while in office on July 17, 1858.

R

RAILROADS. During the war with Mexico, a regiment of Pennsylvania militia traveled by train to New Orleans (q.v.) en route to Gen. Winfield Scott's (q.v.) army. This event marked the first time that U.S. troops were transported by rail to their wartime destination. Most of the strategic movement of troops from the

United States to Mexico was by river and sea transportation. In Mexico, railroad tracks had been laid in the vicinity of Veracruz but locomotives were not put in use in that country until after the war.

RAMIREZ, SIMEON. Brig. Gen. Simeon Ramírez commanded one of the four infantry brigades under Gen. Pedro de Ampudia (q.v.). Although Ramírez was not an engineer, Ampudia charged him with constructing defensive works in northern Mexico. Furthering Gen. Antonio López de Santa Anna's (q.v.) briefly held policy of destroying fortifications in the path of Gen. Zachary Taylor's (q.v.) army, it was at Ramírez's urging that the Tenería redoubt in Monterrey (q.v.) was leveled—only to have to be hurriedly rebuilt for the Mexican defense of the city.

Ramírez commanded a brigade in the battle of Molino del Rey (q.v.) in September 1847. By repositioning his artillery (q.v.), he induced U.S. engineers to believe that the mill had been abandoned. This lured American forces into intense Mexican fire that devastated Maj. George S. Wright's (q.v.) assault troops. Despite heavy losses, U.S. forces pressed the attack, sending Ramírez and the bulk of the Mexican forces into flight.

RAMOS, NUEVO LEON. The village of Ramos lay along Gen. Zachary Taylor's (q.v.) route as he marched on Monterrey (q.v.) in September 1846. Taylor's lead elements, a party of Texas Rangers (q.v.) under Capt. Ben McCulloch (q.v.), briefly engaged a Mexican cavalry force attempting to block the Americans' advance near Ramos as the army moved through the village on the way to Monterrey. The Camargo (q.v.)-Cerralvo (q.v.)-Ramos-Marín (q.v.)-Monterrey-Saltillo (q.v.) route remained the main supply line for Taylor's army during its occupation of northern Mexico for the rest of the war. Throughout this time, the vicinity of Ramos was a center of Mexican guerrilla (q.v.) activity against American forces. In February 1847, as both sides positioned themselves for the battle of Buena Vista (q.v.), Gen. José Urrea (q.v.) led his forces in isolating the guards of a 110-wagon supply train near Ramos and massacred the nearly 50 teamsters who manned the train (this was known as the "Ramos Massacre"). Although Taylor thereafter increased counterinsurgency operations around Ramos, guerrilla action in the area after the massacre continued to be a threat to American forces until the occupation ended in 1848. Today the 19th-century town of Ramos is known as Dr. Gonzalez.

RAMSAY, GEORGE D. (1802–1882). West Pointer George D. Ramsay was a captain in the Ordnance Department during the war with Mexico. As such, he participated in the battle of Monterrey (q.v.), for which he was brevetted major. From June 1847 to May 1848, Ramsay served as chief of ordnance of Gen. Zachary Taylor's (q.v.) army. During the Civil War, as brigadier general, he was chief of ordnance of the U.S. Army.

RAMSEY, ALBERT C. (d. 1869). Col. Albert C. Ramsey commanded the 11th Regiment of Infantry, consisting of volunteer soldiers from Pennsylvania, Delaware, and Maryland. This regiment, created by the Ten Regiment Bill (q.v.) of January 1847, joined Gen. Franklin Pierce's (q.v.) brigade in Gen. Winfield Scott's (q.v.) army.

RANCHEROS. During the period of the war with Mexico and shortly thereafter, the term *ranchero* denoted a member of a group of guerrillas (q.v.) who operated in northern Mexico. They were cowhands and drovers accustomed to hard riding and exposure to harsh conditions. Normally lightly armed, they had among their weapons *lazos*, or lassos, used for snaring cattle on the ranches and unsuspecting American soldiers ambushed by the *rancheros* when they were operating as guerrillas.

RANGEL, JOAQUIN. Brig. Gen. Joaquín Rangel and his brigade left Mexico City (q.v.) on March 28, 1847, to join the force defending Veracruz (q.v.). Since the city surrendered while Rangel was en route, his mission became one of attacking Gen. Winfield Scott's (q.v.) rear positions. Subsequently, Rangel's brigade joined Gen. Antonio López de Santa Anna's (q.v.) army in the defense of Mexico City. Rangel's orders were to reinforce units under the command of Gen. Gabriel Valencia (q.v.) that were deployed south of the capital in the vicinity of Contreras (q.v.). Since Rangel arrived too late to assist Valencia, Santa Anna directed him to guard the southwestern flank of Mexico City; he was defeated there at Molino del Rey (q.v.) on September 8, 1847. After initially halting the American attack at Chapultepec (q.v.), Rangel withdrew to the San Cosmé Gate (q.v.) at the entrance to the inner city, where he was seriously wounded in one of the Americans' final attacks.

RANSOM, TRUEMAN B. (1802–1847). Col. Trueman B. Ransom commanded the Ninth Volunteer Infantry Regiment from New

England. He participated in the battle of Contreras (q.v.) in August 1847, commanding Gen. Franklin Pierce's (q.v.) brigade when Pierce was injured. Ransom died leading one of the final charges at Chapultepec Castle (q.v.) on September 13, 1847.

REA, JOAQUIN (*ca.* 1790–1850). On September 13, 1847, Mexican guerrilla leader General Joaquín Rea led a siege against Bvt. Col. Thomas Childs (q.v.), whose forces controlled three key defensive positions in Puebla (q.v.)—the citadel of San José, Fort Loretto, and the Church of Guadalupe. General Rea was joined by Gen. Antonio López de Santa Anna (q.v.) on September 21. Santa Anna remained part of Rea's siege operation in Puebla until hearing that U.S. reinforcements were under way from Veracruz (q.v.) under Gen. Joseph Lane (q.v.). On October 1, while Childs continued to hold out against Rea's forces, Santa Anna moved from Puebla in a failed effort to ambush American reinforcements. Lane and his men continued on to Puebla, arriving there on October 12 to break Rea's month-long siege. General Rea and his band fled southwest to Atlisco (q.v.), with Lane's forces in pursuit. Rea was pushed southward and his band scattered.

REEVE, ISAAC V. D. (d. 1890). During the war with Mexico, Capt. Isaac V. D. Reeve, of the Eighth Infantry Regiment, served with Gen. Zachary Taylor's (q.v.) army at Palo Alto (q.v.) and Resaca de la Palma (q.v.). Transferred to the army of Gen. Winfield Scott (q.v.), he took part in the siege of Veracruz (q.v.), the battle of Cerro Gordo (q.v.), and the capture of San Antonio (q.v.). Reeve was brevetted major for the battles of Contreras and Churubusco (q.v.) and lieutenant colonel for Molino del Rey (q.v.). Captain Reeve also fought at the storming of Chapultepec (q.v.) and the assault on Mexico City (q.v.).

REID, JOHN W. Capt. John Reid served under Col. Alexander Doniphan's (q.v.) First Missouri Mounted Volunteers in General Stephen W. Kearny's (q.v.) Army of the West (q.v.). Most notably, he participated in a 20-day trek through Navajo (q.v.) territory to meet with Navajo chief Narbona, participated in the December 1846 skirmish at Brazito on the Rio Grande (q.v.), and fought in the battle of Sacramento (q.v.) (in Chihuahua [q.v.]) in February 1847.

REJON, MANUEL CRESCENCIO (1799–1849). When Gen. Antonio López de Santa Anna (q.v.) returned from exile in Cuba in mid-August of 1846, it was Manuel Crescencio Rejón who authored Santa Anna's manifesto in which the returning general came down squarely against domination of Mexico either by a monarchy or by the church and for restoring the constitution of 1824. At Santa Anna's urging, Rejón was made minister of foreign affairs under acting president José Mariano Salas (q.v.). On August 31, 1846, Rejón sent a communication to Pres. James Knox Polk (q.v.) containing Mexico's refusal to participate in peace negotiations. After the signing of the Treaty of Guadalupe Hidalgo (q.v.), Rejón led opposition to the agreement.

RENO, JESSE LEE (1823–1862). An ordnance officer, Jesse Lee Reno, West Point class of 1846, served in Gen. Winfield Scott's (q.v.) army from the siege of Veracruz (q.v.) to the environs of Mexico City (q.v.) where he was wounded at the battle of Chapultepec (q.v.). Twice brevetted in the war (first lieutenant for Cerro Gordo and captain for Chapultepec), Reno stayed on active duty until he was killed at the battle of South Mountain in Maryland during the Civil War. In that conflict he rose to the rank of major general in the U.S. Volunteers.

REQUENA, TOMAS (1804–1850). Gen. Tomás Requeña, considered one of the more professional of the Mexican military officers, at one point was second in command of the Mexican Army of the North (q.v.) under General Francisco Mejía (q.v.). After the Mexican defeat at Monterrey (q.v.), Requeña, serving under General Pedro de Ampudia (q.v.), acted as one of the members of the commission which negotiated an armistice.

RESACA DE GUERRERO, BATTLE OF. See RESACA DE LA PALMA, BATTLE OF.

RESACA DE LA PALMA, BATTLE OF (May 9, 1846). After the engagement at Palo Alto (q.v.) on May 8, 1846, the battered forces of Gen. Mariano Arista (q.v.) withdrew a short distance and bivouacked near the battlefield. Arista had suffered over 200 casualties, 100 of which were killed in action. Many of the dead and wounded had been left on the field. The badly wounded suffered greatly during the night of May 8; troop morale sagged (the surgeon in charge of medicine chests had disappeared during the fight). At 0600 hours the following morning, Arista withdrew five miles south toward the Rio Grande (q.v.) and deployed his forces in defensive positions along a wide ravine. The depression was an old river channel long abandoned by the Rio Grande; in Spanish it was called a *resaca*, and the particular dry riverbed Arista chose was referred to by the Mexicans as "Guerrero" and by the Americans as "Palma." At that position, Arista waited with over 3,000 men for battle with Gen. Zachary Taylor's (q.v.) army.

Early on the 9th, Taylor's scouts discovered that Arista had withdrawn to the south. The general held a meeting with his senior officers to plot his next move. Seven of ten voted to hold in place and wait for reinforcements then on the way to the Rio Grande. After listening to their arguments, Taylor went with the minority and gave the order to move south for battle. At noon, he sent Capt. George A. McCall (q.v.) with a light battalion from the Fourth Infantry to conduct a reconnaissance in force of Arista's retreating army. The main body followed at 1400 hours. After five miles, McCall sent a report back at 1430 that he had made contact with Arista's outposts. By 1500, Taylor had received the report and had gone forward to scout for himself. He returned to his command post and gave orders for an attack. This time, unlike the previous day at Palo Alto, Taylor secured his large supply train with a regiment of dismounted artillerymen and two large howitzers. Arista's selected field of battle favored his defense. He knew that employment of the American artillery (q.v.) would be limited because of the terrain. A thick, nearly impenetrable chaparral covered the dry plain, making maneuver of artillery and infantry (and even observation) difficult.

Taylor decided on a frontal assault. Again he cautioned his soldiers with his watchword: they must be prepared to go to the bayonet. He knew small infantry actions would have to carry the fight since Arista's troops were hidden in the chaparral and Mexican artillery covered the Matamoros (q.v.) road, the only rapid route through his forces. Minus the men he left with the trains, Taylor had about 1,700 troops for the fight. He placed his infantry regiments on either side of the Matamoros road, his artillery on the road, and launched the attack at 1600. He sent a battery under Lt. Randolph Ridgely (q.v.) forward of the infantry to fire on the Mexican positions in order to draw their fire and to open up an avenue of approach for his regiments. In the meantime, Mexican cavalry attacked over their left flank, through the chaparral, and into Taylor's right and Ridgely's battery on the road. The Americans did not see the charge until it was on them; Ridgely fired a volley at nearly point-blank range, and the lancers fell back. Since the Mexican artillery fire still dominated the road, Taylor decided on a bold cavalry charge to take the guns. Capt. Charles A. May's (q.v.) cavalry troop was chosen. May charged at full gallop straight toward the guns, four horses abreast. Momentum carried May past the gun positions, and by the time he reined the horses, they had come under intense fire from infantry in the brush. Saddles emptied. May retreated, again at full gallop, with the Mexican artillery undisturbed.

A ferocious firefight ensued after the charge. Taylor's men continued forward in desperate attacks against the Mexican defenders obscured in the chaparral. It was close, hand-to-hand combat between small infantry units. Disorder prevailed. Officers became separated from their men, men from their companies. The heavy brush made the fighting even more cruel. Taylor's prophecy of the bayonet proved true. Taylor, as was his custom in battle, moved up to the zone of fire, sat his horse, Old Whitey, and gave orders to his units. Becoming impatient with the continuing damage from the artillery position May had failed to silence, he turned to Lt. Col. William Belknap (q.v.) of the Eighth Infantry, pointed toward the Mexican battery on the road, and told him to "take those guns, and by God keep them." Belknap assaulted with the Eighth supported by part of the Fifth Infantry and took the guns. Taylor's infantry was now pressing the attack. General Arista, who had been in his tent during most of the action working on correspondence, realized too late the seriousness of battle. At the last minute, he called for the cavalry, most of which had been in the rear, and personally led a futile counterattack against Taylor's charging regiments.

Quickly repulsed, Arista retreated, followed by his disintegrating army. The Mexican troops fled toward the river three miles away. It was a chaotic retreat—unit cohesion completely broke down as each man tried to save himself. Taylor sent Capt. Croghan Ker's (q.v.) dragoons (q.v.), Capt. James Duncan's (q.v.) battery, and companies from the Third Infantry to press the attack on the retreating troops. As with Palo Alto the day before, Arista left his wounded on the field of battle. As his men passed Fort Texas (q.v.), the American guns there opened on the Mexicans with flanking fire, causing more casualties among the fleeing troops. At the river, soldiers took small boats or swam the swiftly moving Rio Grande. Many drowned in the attempt. Ker, with the other forces Taylor had sent forward, stopped at the riverbank and did not pursue. The disaster was about as total as could have been envisioned for the Mexican army. Arista's force suffered over 250 killed and over 500 wounded and missing in the battle. One of his key subordinates, Gen. Rómulo Díaz de la Vega (q.v.), was captured during the battle (an act Captain May of Taylor's dragoon's would erroneously receive credit for, along with much publicity in newspapers on the home front).

Taylor had more damage at Resaca de la Palma (39 killed, 82 wounded) than at Palo Alto the previous day, but his victory was complete. This time, he had driven the Mexican army across the Rio Grande. The victory at Resaca de la Palma opened the way for Taylor's crossing of the river and capture of Matamoros. It would be the first foreign city to be occupied by the United States military.

REYES, IGNACIO. After the fall of Mexico City, Gen. Ignacio Reyes succeeded Gen. Antonio López de Santa Anna (q.v.) as commander in chief of the Mexican army in October 1847.

REYES, MARIANO (1815–1882). Lt. Col. Mariano Reyes was a highly regarded Mexican military engineer who fought at Palo Alto (q.v.), Resaca de la Palma (q.v.), and Monterrey (q.v.). At Monterrey, he was in charge of preparing defenses before Gen. Zachary Taylor's (q.v.) army arrived in September 1846.

REYNOLDS, JOHN FULTON (1820–1863). John Fulton Reynolds graduated from West Point in 1841 and was promoted to first lieutenant in 1846. In the war with Mexico, Reynolds served as an artillery lieutenant in Capt. Thomas Sherman's battery of the U.S. Third Regiment of Artillery. He helped successfully defend Fort Brown (q.v.) and fought both at Monterrey (q.v.) and Buena Vista (q.v.); in the latter battle his mission on the second day was to position his guns to defend the Hacienda Buena Vista against a Mexican lancer (cavalry) attack. Reynolds won brevets to captain at Monterrey and to major at Buena Vista. After the war, his star rose steadily in the army; he accompanied Gen. Albert Sidney Johnston's (q.v.) Mormon Expedition and became commandant of cadets at West Point. In the Civil War, as a major general of U.S. Volunteers, Reynolds was killed by a sniper on the first day at Gettysburg, July 1, 1863.

REYNOLDS, JOHN G. Capt. John G. Reynolds, U.S. Marine Corps (q.v.), a veteran of the Seminole Wars, commanded Company D in the Marine battalion under Lt. Col. Sam Watson (q.v.) during the battle for Mexico City (q.v.). In the assault against Chapultepec Castle (q.v.) on September 13, 1847, Reynolds led a party of 40 pioneers in the storming of the fortress. For this action he was brevetted major.

REYNOSA, TAMAULIPAS. In June of 1846, after occupying Matamoros (q.v.), Gen. Zachary Taylor (q.v.), in response to a request from Mexican officials, sent a contingent consisting of elements of the First Infantry under Col. Henry Wilson (q.v.), a section of Braxton Bragg's (q.v.) battery of artillery (q.v.) under Lt. George H. Thomas (q.v.), and a company of Texas Rangers (q.v.) to protect Reynosa, located 60 miles to the northwest. This force secured the city and the road between it and the American base at Matamoros (q.v.) in preparation for the advance of Taylor's army toward Monterrey (q.v.). Reynosa later became a critical location since it lay along the main resupply route of Taylor's army from Matamoros to northern Mexico. Mexican guerrillas (q.v.), or *rancheros* (q.v.), frequently attacked convoys proceeding through the Reynosa area.

RICHEY, JOHN ALEXANDER (d. 1847). Lt. John Alexander Richey, a native of Ohio, graduated from West Point in 1845 and fought at Palo Alto (q.v.), Resaca de la Palma (q.v.), and Monterrey (q.v.). In January 1847, he was entrusted with a copy of an important communiqué from Gen. Winfield Scott (q.v.) to Gen. Zachary Taylor (q.v.). The letter directed Taylor to send part of his regulars to Scott's army, which was preparing for the opening of a second front at Veracruz (q.v.). Richey, traveling by horse between Monterrey and Victoria (q.v.), went into the village of Villa Gran alone on January 13, 1847, to obtain provisions for his small escort force. Scott's letter was on his person. While in the village, a Mexican patrol lassoed and murdered the lieutenant, discovering the letter in the process. The letter revealing American strategy (q.v.) soon reached General Antonio López de Santa Anna (q.v.), who reacted by ordering his army to march north to attack the weakened U.S. forces at Saltillo (q.v.). Santa Anna's move north from San Luis Potosí (q.v.) toward Saltillo resulted in the battle of Buena Vista (q.v.) in February 1847.

RIDGELY, RANDOLPH (1814–1846). Lt. Randolph Ridgely, a West Point graduate, expert horseman, and highly regarded artilleryman, took over Samuel Ringgold's (q.v.) battery of "flying artillery" (q.v.) after Ringgold fell at the battle of Palo Alto (q.v.) on May 8, 1846. The following day, Ridgely drew fire to expose enemy positions and played a key role in routing the Mexican forces at the battle of Resaca de la Palma (q.v.). Ridgely also participated in the siege of Monterrey (q.v.) in September 1846. Although well known for his equestrian skills, he died in an ironic riding accident in Monterrey on October 27, 1846. Ridgely had been promoted to the rank of captain at the time of his death.

RILEY, BENNET (1787–1853). A career army officer, Bennet Riley entered military service in January 1813, during the War of 1812. After that war, he fought Indians in the Black Hawk and Seminole Wars. During the war with Mexico, he commanded the Second Infantry Regiment and subsequently became a brigade commander in Gen. David E. Twiggs's (q.v.) Second Division of Gen. Winfield Scott's (q.v.) army in southern Mexico. After commanding his brigade in the battle of Cerro Gordo (q.v.), Riley won a brevet to brigadier general and participated in the battles for Mexico City (q.v.), where his brigade played a central role in the battle of Contreras (q.v.). At that battle, Riley's engineers discovered a route to the rear of the Mexican position that allowed an envelopment and rout of the Mexican forces. He was breveted major general for his actions at Contreras. After the war, Riley served in Louisiana and Missouri before commanding the 10th Military Department in California (q.v.). He became ex-officio provisional governor of California before his death on June 9, 1853. Fort Riley, Kansas, was named in his memory.

RILEY, JOHN. John Riley was an Irishman who had been a noncommissioned officer in the British army until he deserted while stationed in Canada. He came to the United States and enlisted in the army in 1845 as a private, joining the Fifth Infantry Regiment. His unit became part of Gen. Zachary Taylor's (q.v.) army along the Rio Grande (q.v.) in 1846, just before the outbreak of hostilities between the United States and Mexico. At the American camp across from Matamoros (q.v.), Riley deserted the American army by swimming across the Rio Grande the last part of April 1846 (at least 200 others did the same thing while the army was on the Rio Grande). In Mexico, Riley assisted Mexican officers in recruiting an artillery (q.v.) unit of American deserters (q.v.) and others (mostly foreigners living in Mexico) that became part of the *Batallón de San Patricio*, or San Patricio Battalion (q.v.), a unit commanded by Lt. Col. Francisco Rosendo Moreno (q.v.). Riley served as an officer in the unit and fought with the Mexican army for the entire war. After he was captured by U.S. forces at the end of the conflict, he was tried by military court-martial and sentenced to be hung for desertion in wartime. Gen. Winfield Scott (q.v.) commuted Riley's sentence because he had deserted before the official beginning of the war. As alternative punishment, he was lashed, branded on the cheek with a D, and imprisoned. After his release upon withdrawal of the American occupation army, Riley rejoined the Mexican army and served as a major (and, according to some reports, commander) in a reorganized San Patricio unit. Shortly afterward, in July 1848, Riley was accused of involvement in an attempted coup d'état initiated by the former president and perennial strongman, General Mariano Paredes y Arrillaga (q.v.). He was jailed by Mexican authorities, and the San Patricios were disbanded for the last time. A Mexican judge released Riley from prison in September 1848, whereupon he was reinstated in the Mexican army. He served as a major for two more years before being discharged in 1850. John Riley's whereabouts after 1850 are uncertain, but circumstantial evidence suggests that he returned to his native Ireland. Riley is sometimes listed as Reilly or O'Reilly. *See also* SAN PATRICIO BATTALION.

RINCON, MANUEL E. (1784–1849). Maj. Gen. Manuel Rincón was charged by Gen. Antonio López de Santa Anna (q.v.) with the ill-fated mission of holding the Convent of San Mateo (q.v.) at Churubusco (q.v.) on August 20, 1847. In October 1847, when Santa Anna was relieved as the commander of the Mexican army by Pres. Manuel de la Peña y Peña (q.v.), his command was turned over to Rincón. After the cessation of hostilities in November 1847, Rincón was appointed a commissioner for the Mexican delegation in the peace negotiations with the United States.

RINCONADA PASS, NUEVA LEON. Rinconada Pass lay southwest of Monterrey (q.v.) in the Sierra Madre Mountains, between Monterrey and Saltillo (q.v.). During the armistice that followed the battle of Monterrey, the line between the United States and Mexican forces was drawn through the Rinconada Pass, Linares (q.v.), and Parras (q.v.). After the armistice, Gen. Zachary Taylor's (q.v.) army marched to Saltillo through this pass.

RINGGOLD, SAMUEL (1800–1846). Capt. Samuel Ringgold's battery of the Third Regiment of Artillery was with the lead elements in Gen. Zachary Taylor's (q.v.) march to the Rio Grande (q.v.), departing Corpus Christi (q.v.) on March 8, 1846. Ringgold, a West Pointer who graduated in 1818, pioneered the "flying artillery" that made an invaluable contribution in the victories at Palo Alto (q.v.) and Buena Vista (q.v.).

At Palo Alto, on May 8, 1846, in Taylor's first victory of the war with Mexico, Ringgold's battery was deployed forward to a frontline position along with the infantry. His actions in the battle were critical to the American victory. Ringgold, then a brevet major, along with his thoroughbred horse, David Branch, fell in the engagement. The horse died on the battlefield; Ringgold died May 11th at Point Isabel (q.v.) where he was buried (he was later reburied with honors in Baltimore, Maryland). Ringgold was a highly regarded officer whose prewar innovations in the employment of artillery (q.v.) greatly contributed to the ultimate success of the U.S. military in the war.

RIO GRANDE. As early as the Louisiana Purchase in 1803, the United States claimed that the Rio Grande was the southern boundary of Louisiana. When the United States annexed Texas (q.v.) in March 1845 and reasserted this Rio Grande boundary, the Mexicans regarded it as an act of aggression. Consequently, the Rio Grande became the contested frontier between Mexico and the United States. In April of 1846, Mexican forces under Gen. Francisco Mejía (q.v.) at Matamoros (q.v.) clashed with Gen. Zachary Taylor's (q.v.) forces along the river. This engagement, which precipitated the American declaration of war, occurred on the left (north) bank of the Rio Grande above Matamoros on April 25 when a patrol under Capt. Seth Thornton (q.v.) was ambushed by Mexican forces; the first major battles of the war followed in May within a few miles of the Rio Grande. These engagements were at Palo Alto (q.v.) on May 8 and at Resaca de la Palma (q.v.) the following day. Besides the key role it played in the boundary dispute between the United States and Mexico, the Rio Grande remained important during the war from a strategic viewpoint. Troops and supplies for Zachary Taylor's army in northern Mexico poured through the Brazos Santiago (q.v.) near the mouth of the river throughout the war. Steamships plied the river, bringing war material to Matamoros, Fort Brown (q.v.), and the staging base at Camargo (q.v.). The war brought men to the Rio Grande Valley who would ultimately settle there—such as the steamboat pilot and later captain Richard King (q.v.). King, as did many others, married a local woman and began to acquire land from the Mexicans. He built the great King Ranch below Corpus Christi (q.v.) and developed vast pasture lands from the inhospitable terrain over which Taylor's army had passed in the spring of 1846. So the river, although shallow and narrow in physical scope, was large in significance during the period of the war. It was—in that era, as it is today—politically, militarily, socially, and economically critical to the region and to U.S.-Mexican relations.

ROBERTS, BENJAMIN STONE (1810–1875). Benjamin Stone Roberts graduated from the U.S. Military Academy in the class of 1835 and saw duty on the Iowa and Kansas frontiers before resigning his commission to become chief engineer of a railroad. After traveling abroad, Roberts returned to the United States to practice law in Iowa and serve in the Iowa militia as a lieutenant colonel. When the war with Mexico broke out, he became a first lieutenant in the U. S. Regiment of Mounted Rifles. He served in Gen. Winfield Scott's (q.v.) army, participating in the heaviest fighting at Cerro Gordo (q.v.) in April 1847. Roberts later fought at Contreras (q.v.) and led a storming party at Chapultepec (q.v.) the following September. On orders given by Maj. Gen. John A. Quitman (q.v.), he raised the U.S. flag over the National Palace on the Grand Plaza of Mexico City (q.v.) on September 14, 1847. For his actions, Roberts won brevets to major and lieutenant colonel. After the war, he remained in the army and served in the Civil War as a brigadier general of U.S. Volunteers. He retired from the service in 1870 and resumed law practice in Washington, D.C., until his death.

ROBLES, MANUEL M. In March 1846, Lt. Col. Manuel Robles— along with Gen. Ignacio Mora y Villamil (q.v.), the Mexican army's senior engineer and commander of Veracruz—drew up plans to repair the Castle of San Juan de Ulúa (q.v.) and fortifications within Veracruz itself. Because of a lack of funds, however, not all of these plans were implemented. At Cerro Gordo (q.v.), Robles urged Gen. Antonio López de Santa Anna (q.v.) to move his defensive line for the following reasons: (1) retreat, if necessary, would be difficult from the positions Santa Anna had chosen; (2) the positions would be difficult to reinforce; (3) owing to rough terrain and thick vegetation, the enemy could maneuver too closely to the Mexican positions before fire could be brought on them; (4) cavalry would be useless because of the terrain; and (5) the battle line was too lengthy and not mutually supportive. Santa Anna decided to ignore Robles's advice, and the Mexican army's defeat at Cerro Gordo followed on April 18, 1847.

ROMERO, MANUEL (1800–1851). Gen. Manuel Romero commanded a cavalry brigade in northern Mexico. During the American offensive against Monterrey (q.v.) in September 1846, Romero's mission was to block the advance of Gen. William Jenkins Worth's (q.v.) brigade as it attempted to flank the city to the west. A cavalry troop under Romero, commanded by Lt. Col. Juan Nájera (q.v.), charged Worth's advance guard on September 21; it was a short, fierce engagement that precipitated the wider battle for Monterrey that followed during the day.

ROMERO, TOMAS. See TAOS REBELLION.

ROSENDO MORENO, FRANCISCO. Francisco Rosendo Moreno commanded the San Patricio Battalion (q.v.), known in Spanish as the *Batallón de San Patricio* or the *Legión de Extranjeros* (foreign legion). Popularly thought of in the United States as a unit composed of North American deserters (q.v.) of Irish descent, sources indicate that the majority were probably neither Irish nor deserters. Many were foreigners, however, and clearly a minority were Irish who had deserted from the U.S. Army along the Rio Grande (q.v.) in the spring of 1846. The battalion and Rosendo Moreno were captured at Churubusco (q.v.) on August 20, 1847. See also RILEY, JOHN; SAN PATRICIO BATTALION.

ROWAN, STEPHEN C. Lt. Stephen C. Rowan led the landing party from the sloop of war *Cyane* (q.v.) to raise the American flag at San Diego (q.v.), California (q.v.), on July 29, 1846. He led another landing party from the *Cyane* on September 2, 1846—this time to take the town of San Blas, Baja California (q.v.). In November 1847, Rowan led one of two forces sent out to intercept Mexican forces that threatened Mazatlán (q.v.). Losses in the skirmish were one American and four Mexicans killed; 20 Americans and an unknown number of Mexicans were wounded.

S

SABINE RIVER. The United States acquired Florida through the Adams-Onís Treaty with Spain that was signed in February

1819 and implemented in 1821. This treaty also established the Sabine River as the boundary between the United States and Spanish territory. After Mexican independence, the river was generally recognized as the boundary between the United States and the Mexican province of Texas (q.v.). It was to the east of the Sabine River, between the Sabine and the Red River, that Lt. Col. Zachary Taylor (q.v.) built Fort Jesup (q.v.) in 1822 as a border fort to protect settlers against Indian raids. In the early 1830s, before Texas became a separate republic, Texans began to claim the Rio Grande (q.v.) as their boundary with Mexico. After the battle of San Jacinto in 1836, the Mexican general on the field of battle in Texas signed a treaty granting Texas her independence, although the central government in Mexico City (q.v.) never approved the agreement. Mexico thus still considered Texas part of its territory. Thereafter, the Texans reiterated their claim that the Rio Grande was their boundary with Mexico, while Mexico recognized the Nueces River (q.v.) as the boundary between her states of Tamaulipas and Texas. After numerous failed attempts to reconquer Texas in the late 1830s and early 1840s, Mexico would have apparently lived with this confusing situation and tolerated Texas's independent stance had it not been annexed to the United States in 1845. When Zachary Taylor's army (Taylor had returned to Fort Jesup in 1844) crossed the Sabine River in that year for the purpose of protecting the newly annexed state of Texas, nationalist elements in Mexico exploded. The border issue, defined by the dispute over the Rio Grande, the Nueces, and the Sabine Rivers, emerged anew to play a central role in the war between Mexico and the United States.

SACRAMENTO, BATTLE OF (February 28, 1847). The battle of Sacramento was as unconventional as the colorful but highly respected man who led it and the undisciplined but seasoned men who fought it. In early 1847, Col. Alexander Doniphan (q.v.) was ordered to take his First Missouri Mounted Infantry south from New Mexico (q.v.) through El Paso (q.v.) del Norte to join Gen. John Ellis Wool's (q.v.) forces in Chihuahua (q.v.). Doniphan discovered on departure from New Mexico that Wool had been diverted from the Chihuahua objective. The Missourian faced a difficult choice: to move forward into enemy territory without the expected support of Wool's troops or to return to Santa Fe (q.v.). Hoping that his men would choose to move southward, the democratically inclined Doniphan let his 1,000-man contingent vote on their course of action; they chose to continue to march. The Doniphan army was accompanied by over 300 civilian wagons of teamsters and traders who had joined them along the way and who made up a rag-tag auxiliary force. Where the road intersected the Sacramento River, approximately 3,000 Mexicans under the commands of Gov. Angel Trías Alvarez (q.v.), Gen. José A. Heredia (q.v.), and Gen. José María García Conde (q.v.) blocked their path from a series of redoubts and breastworks that formed a solid defensive position.

Confident that the Americans had no choice but to continue along the route toward their positions rather than face the suicidal terrain off the road, the Mexicans anticipated an easy victory. But Doniphan did the unexpected. Using his cavalry in the lead, he plunged the bulk of his force, with its almost 400 military and civilian wagons, to the right, down into a steep ravine (the Arroyo Seco [q.v.]) and up the 40- to 50-foot sharp gradient on the other side. It was a frantic maneuver wherein frenzied, desperate men used every available method, humane and inhumane, to force panicked animals to perform the seeming impossible. Realizing what Doniphan's men had done and discovering that his artillery (q.v.) fire was out of range, the Mexican commander ordered a cavalry attack. The charge was repulsed by accurate fire from Doniphan's artillery. The tall, red-haired, Missourian then maneuvered his men behind the Mexican forces. The ensuing combat devolved into grisly hand-to-hand fighting. When the fight stilled, 300 Mexicans lay dead and an equal number suffered wounds (most of the dead were probably killed from artillery fire)—a sharp contrast to the surprisingly light American casualties (one killed, eight wounded). As the remaining Mexican forces scattered, Doniphan's troops moved on to take Chihuahua the following day, March 1, 1847.

SACRAMENTO, CALIFORNIA. *See* SUTTER, JOHN AUGUSTUS.

ST. JOSEPH'S ISLAND. In July 1845, Gen. Zachary Taylor (q.v.) and his advance element, the Third Infantry, sailed aboard the steamer *Alabama* from New Orleans (q.v.), Louisiana, to St. Joseph's Island, one of the barrier islands offshore from Corpus Christi (q.v.). It was separated from the mainland by Aransas Bay and was situated between Matagorda Island to its north and Padre Island to its south. They arrived, along with their escort, the Home Squadron's (q.v.) sloop *St. Mary's*, on July

25th and set up an interim camp on St. Joseph's Island before continuing 25 miles in small boats to their Corpus Christi destination. On August 2, they were joined by the main body of Taylor's army.

SALAS, JOSE MARIANO (1797–1867). Brig. Gen. José Mariano Salas, as commander of the Hidalgo Battalion in Mexico City (q.v.) in 1846, was a participant in the power struggles for control of the government in the chaotic months after the American invasion. He became Mexico's acting president on August 6, 1846, and served as head of the government for four months until, on December 6, the Congress elevated Gen. Antonio López de Santa Anna (q.v.) once again to the presidency. In August 1847, Salas commanded cavalry in the battles around the capital before he was captured at the battle of Contreras (q.v.) on August 20.

SALTILLO, COAHUILA. Saltillo, the capital of the state of Coahuila (q.v.), is located approximately 80 miles southwest of Monterrey. In the war, the city was never an objective of the Polk administration after Monterrey fell to Zachary Taylor's (q.v.) army in September 1846. Secretary of War William Marcy (q.v.) ordered Taylor to halt his advance southward and to establish a defensive line in the vicinity of Monterrey. Taylor ignored these orders and decided on his own to march south and occupy Saltillo, which he peacefully accomplished the following November after it had been abandoned by Mexican forces the previous month. Once in Saltillo, Taylor left Gen. William Jenkins Worth (q.v.) in command and returned temporarily to Monterrey. In January 1847, Gen. Winfield Scott (q.v.) ordered Worth to move his division of regulars and join his army in preparation for opening a second front at Veracruz (q.v.). The loss of Worth's division and other units drawn away by Scott considerably weakened Taylor's position at Saltillo. In early 1847, Gen. Antonio López de Santa Anna (q.v.), after intercepting a message indicating American strength at Saltillo would be reduced, moved north from San Luis Potosí (q.v.) with a 20,000-man army to attack Taylor's diminished defenses. Santa Anna's march north resulted in the legendary battle of Buena Vista (q.v.), several miles south of Saltillo, in February 1847. After the battle, U.S. troops continued to occupy Saltillo for the remainder of the war, although major troop movements south across the desert to San Luis Potosí never occurred.

SAN AGUSTIN, DISTRITO FEDERAL. South of Mexico City (q.v.) and below the pedregal (q.v.) lava beds, on the road between the capital and Acapulco (q.v.), lay the town of San Agustín. During the war, its importance came from Gen. Winfield Scott's (q.v.) use of the town as his headquarters during the battles for Mexico City.

SAN ANGEL, DISTRITO FEDERAL. The town of San Angel was situated southwest of Mexico City (q.v.) and north of the pedregal (q.v.) lava beds. Gen. Antonio López de Santa Anna (q.v.) made his base at San Angel during the battle of Contreras (q.v.) in August of 1847. After the fall of Mexico City, Gen. Robert Patterson's (q.v.) division was headquartered at San Angel.

SAN ANTONIO, DISTRITO FEDERAL. The village of San Antonio, on the highway leading into Mexico City (q.v.) from the south, was a critical defensive site for the Mexican government because it restricted American options for approaching the capital. Gen. Winfield Scott (q.v.) discovered the town's importance when reconnaissance revealed that San Antonio could not easily be flanked; to its west lay the extremely rugged pedregal (q.v.) lava fields and to its east was an impassable marshy area. North of the heavily defended town ran a causeway that led into Mexico City. Realizing the difficulty and the potentially high cost of taking the Mexican defenses at San Antonio by frontal assault, Scott ordered his forces to halt before the town, to threaten the position with patrols, and to await the Mexican response. He then used the delay to look at methods to advance on the capital without taking San Antonio. Scott's engineers found a possible but difficult route around the Mexican defenses immediately west of San Antonio in the lava beds and another farther west that would completely flank the pedregal. While Scott was deploying his forces on August 20, 1847, during and after the battle of Contreras (q.v.), Gen. Antonio López de Santa Anna (q.v.) decided to withdraw from San Antonio north to Churubusco (q.v.). The Mexican forces were thus attacked by Scott's army as they fled north along the causeway from San Antonio and after they arrived at Churubusco. The costly fight Scott feared at San Antonio was therefore avoided, occurring instead at Churubusco, a location more favorable for maneuver during an American assault.

SAN ANTONIO GATE. The San Antonio Gate, known in Spanish as the *Garita de San Antonio*, was a police and customs station at the southeastern corner of Mexico City (q.v.) on the road that led south to Churubusco (q.v.). This gate controlled access to Mexico City over the San Antonio causeway, the road that ran from the village of San Antonio (q.v.) north to Churubusco. Gen. David Twiggs (q.v.) created a diversion at the San Antonio Gate to lure Mexican troops away from Chapultepec (q.v.) when that position was stormed by U. S. forces on September 13, 1847.

SAN ANTONIO, TEXAS. San Antonio (in the 19th century some-times known as San Antonio de Bexar or simply Bexar) was one of the few occupied settlements in the Mexican territory of Texas (q.v.) at the time of Mexican independence in 1821. It was the site of the Alamo (q.v.), the old Spanish mission where Gen. Antonio López de Santa Anna's (q.v.) troops massacred Texas defenders in 1836. During the war, San Antonio served as a way station and rendezvous point for U.S. Army forces as they traveled overland to the Rio Grande (q.v.). In June 1846, the Polk administration ordered widely dispersed units to gather at San Antonio to await the arrival of Gen. John E. Wool (q.v.). General Wool arrived there in mid-August en route to Gen. Zachary Taylor's (q.v.) theater of operations and spent the next month organizing the gathering forces into the Centre Division (q.v.). Wool departed San Antonio for Chihuahua City (q.v.) the last week in September with his 2,000-man composite army of regulars and volunteers (q.v.).

SAN CARLOS DE PEROTE. *See* PEROTE, VERACRUZ.

SAN COSME GATE. The San Cosmé Gate, known in Spanish as the *Garita de San Cosmé,* was a fortified stone police and cus-toms station at the northwest edge of Mexico City (q.v.) that controlled access to the capital from the west. It was through this gate that Gen. William J. Worth (q.v.) and his men, aided by other units, finally fought their way into the capital. The intense fighting at the San Cosmé Gate resulted in the serious wounding of the Mexican general Joaquín Rangel (q.v.).

SANDERS, JOHN (1810–1858). After graduating second in the West Point class of 1834, John Sanders entered the engineers (q.v.). When the war with Mexico broke out, he served in Gen. Zachary Taylor's (q.v.) army at the battle of Monterrey (q.v.)—for which he won a brevet to major. Sanders later served under Gen. Winfield Scott (q.v.) during the siege of Veracruz (q.v.).

SAN DIEGO, CALIFORNIA. In 1846, San Diego was a small Mexican village consisting of a few adobe houses several miles northeast of the present California (q.v.) city. From the time Bvt. Capt. John C. Frémont's (q.v.) troops peacefully took San Diego with assistance from a landing party under Lt. Stephen C. Rowan (q.v.) from the sloop *Cyane* (q.v.) in late July 1846, the town saw periodic activity in the war with Mexico. From San Diego on August 8, 1846, Frémont and his troops marched northward for the first advance on Los Angeles (q.v.). The lightly defended San Diego garrison under Ezekial Merritt (q.v.) was abandoned for a few days in October of 1846 when it was threatened by a detachment under Francisco Rico. The Americans regained possession of the town after Merritt's band was reinforced by 52 men under the command of Lt. George Minor. The Americans maintained a precarious hold on the site until Commo. Robert F. Stockton (q.v.) made it his base of operations. Stockton arrived offshore on Friday, October 30, 1846, on the frigate *Congress* (q.v.), which went aground while trying to enter the harbor. After a brief trip to San Pedro, Stockton returned to San Diego on November 15, and this time his ship was able to cross the sandbar and enter the harbor to protect the city.

It was into San Diego that Brig. Gen. Stephen Watts Kearny (q.v.) and his battle-weary men trudged on December 12, 1846, after the long march from Fort Leavenworth (q.v.) and near disastrous battle with the Californios (q.v.) at San Pascual (q.v.); and it was from San Diego that Stockton and Kearny's combined force departed on the campaign to reconquer Los Angeles on December 29, 1846.

SAN FRANCISCO, CALIFORNIA. San Francisco and Yerba Buena were small villages strategically located on a protected bay on the Pacific coast, north of Monterey (q.v.), California (q.v.). During the war with Mexico the villages were combined and officially given the name of San Francisco. On July 9, 1846, under orders from Commo. John Sloat (q.v.) of the Pacific Squadron (q.v.), Comdr. John B. Montgomery, of the sloop *Portsmouth*, accepted the surrender of San Francisco. During the surrender ceremony, Montgomery spoke to the local citizens, assuring them that American rule would not be oppressive, nor would it disrupt their normal daily routines. Montgomery also read a proclamation from Commodore Sloat. After the peaceful surrender, Montgomery proceeded to inspect the Presidio and the artillery (q.v.) battery at San Joaquín, to select a new battery position on Telegraph Hill, and to call on the native population to form a militia to protect the town. Thereafter, San Francisco remained under U. S. control as one of the navy's strong points in California during the war.

SAN GABRIEL, BATTLE OF (January 8, 1847). The battle of San Gabriel took place at the Bartolo Ford on the San Gabriel River, approximately 12 miles south of Los Angeles (q.v.). It pitted a force of 450 Californios (q.v.) under Capt. José María Flores (q.v.) against the approximately 500 sailors, marines, and army troops under Commo. Robert F. Stockton (q.v.). Second in command of the American force was army Brig. Gen. Stephen Watts Kearny (q.v.). Discovering that the Americans planned to cross at the Bartolo Ford, Flores arrived there first on the night of January 7 and prepared positions on elevated ground on the north bank of the San Gabriel. When Stockton's force arrived at the Bartolo Ford during the early afternoon of January 8, Kearny ordered the artillery (q.v.) to cover the American crossing of the knee-deep river. Stockton countermanded the order and had the force cross without fire support. Infantry, artillery, and mounted troops crossed first, followed by the main body, which Stockton had formed into a square with cattle and supply wagons in the center. As soon as the artillery was in place, Stockton personally directed its fire against Flores's forces. Despite the Mexican attempts to halt the crossing with cavalry charges and artillery fire (the latter being highly ineffective), American artillery and rifle fire soon forced them to withdraw. Within 90 minutes of the first contact at the ford, Stockton's force had overwhelmed the enemy and taken the ridge to the north of the river. The Mexicans retreated, and Stockton continued to his next objective, Los Angeles. The Mexicans named this confrontation the battle of Paso de Bartolo; the Americans called it the battle of San Gabriel.

SAN GERONIMO, DISTRITO FEDERAL. San Gerónimo was located to the west of the road between Contreras (q.v.) and Mexico City (q.v.). Col. Bennet Riley's (q.v.) brigade occupied the abandoned town of San Gerónimo before participating in the battle of Contreras in August 1847.

SAN JOSE DEL CABO, BAJA CALIFORNIA. The village of San José del Cabo was located at the southern tip of Baja California (q.v.). When a contingent from the American sloop of war *Portsmouth* landed on March 29, 1847, to demand the town's surrender, the ultimatum was rejected. The following day, however, the town's officials surrendered to a 140-man landing force that immediately hoisted the U. S. flag. Commo. William Branford Shubrick (q.v.) arrived at San José on October 29, 1847, to begin a campaign in the Gulf of California, the body of water that separated Baja California from mainland Mexico. The town subsequently changed hands several times. On November 19, Mexicans unsuccessfully attempted to retake the town. In January 1848, a fresh attempt was successful, although the Mexicans were soon driven out by another American landing.

SAN JUAN BAUTISTA. *See* TABASCO, TABASCO.

SAN JUAN DE ULUA, CASTLE OF. A prime consideration of Gen. Winfield Scott (q.v.) in planning the amphibious landing at Veracruz (q.v.) was the imposing fortress guarding the city, San Juan de Ulúa. The fort, a formidable obstacle for Scott's forces, was an immense structure situated on the Gallega Reef, 1,000 yards offshore of the port city. Constructed with massive walls and firing positions, the old colonial-era fort could hold over 1,000 defenders and 128 heavy guns. Scott had naval ships go in close to bombard the fortress on March 9, the day of the landings. The next day, March 10, 1847, Scott's naval commander, Commo. David E. Conner (q.v.), ordered Comdr. Josiah Tattnall (q.v.) to take his sidewheel steamer *Spitfire* and a small flotilla and go in close to shore to create a diversion by again bombarding the fort. As expected, these bombardments inflicted little damage. San Juan de Ulúa was again bombarded by Tattnall's flotilla on March 23. During the entire siege operation, the fortress intermittently placed effective fire on the American forces deployed along the south of the siege line around the city. Fortunately for Scott's forces, no serious attack on the fortress was necessary because the Mexicans surrendered it along with the city of Veracruz on March 27, 1847. *See also* VERACRUZ.

SAN LUIS POTOSI, SAN LUIS POTOSI. It was from San Luis Potosí, northwest of Mexico City (q.v.), that General Mariano Paredes y Arrillaga (q.v.), commander of the Army of the North (q.v.), launched a drive on the capital to take over the presidency from José Joaquín de Herrera (q.v.) in early January 1846. On October 8 of that year, Gen. Antonio López de Santa Anna (q.v.) established his base at San Luis Potosí. There he gathered an army from soldiers scattered in garrison duty throughout central Mexico and from the recruitment of fresh troops. Santa Anna's intent was to take the new army and drive Gen. Zachary Taylor's (q.v.) forces from northern Mexico. Despite financial problems, apathy of the people, and political preoccupations, Santa Anna—having been declared ad interim president of Mexico by the Liberal-led Mexican Congress in December 1846—was able to gather 20,000 men for his army. Santa Anna marched north from San Luis Potosí across the high desert toward Saltillo (q.v.) on January 27, 1847, a move that culminated in the battle of Buena Vista (q.v.) the following month. After the battle, the defeated army retraced the long trek back to San Luis Potosí; Santa Anna arrived on March 9 and his demoralized and worn-out soldiers straggled in during the ensuing weeks. After falsely claiming victory, Santa Anna left Gen. Gabriel Valencia (q.v.) in San Luis Potosí with approximately 4,000 men and returned to Mexico City.

SAN MATEO CONVENT. One of the three actions of the battle of Churubusco was the attack on the Franciscan Convent of San Mateo by Gen. David Twiggs's division. The convent was defended by Gen. Manuel Rincón's (q.v.) troops. See also CONTRERAS AND CHURUBUSCO, BATTLES OF.

SAN PASCUAL, BATTLE OF (December 6, 1846). The battle of San Pascual was a near-disastrous engagement for Brig. Gen. Stephen W. Kearny's (q.v.) forces. In early December of 1846, Kearny's approximately 150 exhausted men arrived in California (q.v.) after their long march from New Mexico (q.v.). Approaching San Diego (q.v.) on the 6th, they encountered a group of Californios (q.v.) at the village of San Pascual under the command of Capt. Andrés Pico (q.v.). Although lacking good intelligence on the enemy force, Kearny decided to attack. He sent Capt. Benjamin D. Moore (q.v.) out front to lead the charge with his sabre-armed dragoons (q.v.). Moore galloped into the Mexican position and immediately engaged in an unequal fight with better-armed and rested Californian lancers. After a brief but violent fight that inflicted heavy casualties on the Americans, Kearny was saved when marine captain Archibald H. Gillespie (q.v.) reinforced him with infantry and artillery (q.v.). Pico withdrew his troops, taking with him a captured American artillery piece.

It had been a costly fight for Kearny's force. Unique for the war with Mexico, Kearny lost more men killed (18) than wounded (13). Captain Moore and several other junior officers were killed; Gillespie was wounded, as was Kearny who temporarily turned command over to Capt. Henry Turner, also wounded in the fight. On December 7, Kearny's band continued its weary march toward San Diego. At Rancho San Bernardo, the bone-tired Americans clashed again with Pico's troops, who had remained in the area to harass Kearny's column. Turner and Kearny held their deteriorating position, waiting reinforcements from Commo. Robert F. Stockton (q.v.). When the 180-man relief force under Lt. Andrew V. F. Gray (q.v.) arrived on December 10, Kearny's diminished column proceeded on to San Diego.

SAN PATRICIO BATTALION. The first unit that eventually became the nucleus of the San Patricio Battalion was formed by Irish-born John Riley (q.v.) after he deserted the American army on the Rio Grande (q.v.) in 1846. Riley named the unit, designed its shamrock flag, and made every effort to have the 150-man force appear more Irish than it actually was. Although it consisted of a number of Irish Catholic soldiers, they did not constitute a majority. The San Patricio Battalion also contained non-Irish U.S. Army deserters (q.v.) and non-Mexicans who had been residing in Mexico before and during the war.

At its inception, the San Patricio unit was an artillery (q.v.) company; it later evolved into two companies. In July 1847, Gen. Antonio López de Santa Anna (q.v.) redesignated the San Patricios as an infantry unit and the two companies merged into the newly created *Legión de Extranjeros* or foreign legion. John Riley became one of the two company commanders under the commander, Col. Francisco Rosenda Moreno (q.v.).

The San Patricios fought in four major battles of the war. In the northern campaign, they fought as artillerymen at Monterrey (q.v.) and Buena Vista (q.v.) (at the latter, one-third of San Patricios were either killed or wounded). In the southern campaign, they fought as infantrymen at Cerro Gordo (q.v.) and at the defense of the San Mateo Convent (q.v.) in the battle of Churubusco (q.v.). Reports indicate they fought bravely and ferociously; and knowing their punishment would be severe indeed, they avoided capture by American forces at all costs. At Churubusco, 60 percent of the San Patricios were either killed or wounded and the remainder captured. Among the captured was John Riley. Of the captured, 70 were accused of desertion in wartime, tried by court-martial, and sentenced as the last battle for Mexico City (q.v.) was in progress. All but 2 of the 70 were sentenced to be hanged as traitors. Gen. Winfield Scott (q.v.) confirmed the death sentence of 50 San Patricios, pardoned 5, and reduced the sentence of 15—including that of their leader, John Riley. Throughout the battles in which the San Patricios participated, the highly devout Catholic women of Mexico came to their aid and comfort because of their reputation (which was at least in part deserved) for being good Catholic soldiers. *See also* RILEY, JOHN.

SANTA ANNA, ANTONIO LOPEZ DE (1794–1876). Gen. Antonio López de Santa Anna so dominated Mexican political and military life from the late 1820s to 1855 that historians have frequently referred to that period in Mexican history as the "Age of Santa Anna." Born in Jalapa (q.v.) in the state of Veracruz in 1794, Santa Anna joined the Spanish Army at 16 and rose rapidly within the military of Spain and, after 1821, when Mexico won her independence, the Mexican Republican Army. An opportunist whose one consistent trait seemed to be a thirst for power, Santa Anna shifted his political allegiance between conservative and liberal factions throughout his career. Generally considered a mediocre military tactician, Santa Anna was nonetheless brave and flamboyant, characteristics that assisted in raising armies and motivating troops before combat—but in the end doing little to win key battles. Elected to the presidency in 1833 at the age of 39, Santa Anna led the army to put down the Texas (q.v.) revolt two years later. In March of 1836, his troops besieged the Texans at the Alamo (q.v.) mission in San Antonio (q.v.), eventually slaughtering all of its defenders. A few days later Santa Anna's army defeated the Texans again at Goliad, massacring several hundred prisoners after they had surrendered. Six weeks later at San Jacinto the Texans took revenge, turning on the advancing Mexicans in a surprise attack, killing hundreds and capturing Santa Anna. A subordinate general to Santa Anna then signed a treaty granting Texas its independence.

After his capture, Santa Anna was sent to Washington where he was interviewed by Pres. Andrew Jackson, released, and sent back to Mexico in disgrace. In 1838, he regained his reputation by losing a leg in the defense of Veracruz (q.v.) against an attempted invasion by France. Santa Anna rode his new acclaim back into the president's chair in the early 1840s. At the time of the war with the United States in 1846, however, he had been overthrown and sent into exile in Cuba. While in Cuba he convinced the Polk administration that he could arrange for a peaceful settlement of the Texas issue if he were allowed to return to Mexico. Pres. James Knox Polk (q.v.) ordered the U.S. Navy (q.v.) to allow Santa Anna to pass through the Gulf coast blockade (q.v.). After returning, Santa Anna soon convinced Mexican leaders that he was the person to lead the army against the American invasion. He raised an army in San Luis Potosí (q.v.) and marched it north to confront Gen. Zachary Taylor's (q.v.) army south of Saltillo (q.v.). Meeting Taylor's force at Buena Vista (q.v.), Santa Anna fought a bloody two-day battle in February 1847; on the third day, he surprised Taylor (whose troops had suffered high casualties in the fighting) by withdrawing his force and giving the Americans the field of battle. Santa Anna later raised another army to oppose Gen. Winfield Scott's (q.v.) invasion at Veracruz. Meeting Scott's army at Cerro Gordo (q.v.) near his Jalapa home, Santa Anna was thoroughly defeated by the Americans. Withdrawing to Mexico City (q.v.), Santa Anna made elaborate plans to defend the capital. In August and September 1847, Scott's army repeatedly defeated Santa Anna's forces in a series of hard-fought battles for the capital city. The fighting ended with a Mexican surrender to Scott's army. After the Mexican capitulation, Santa Anna escaped and again went into exile, leaving his country 40 percent smaller in territory because of the disastrous war with the United States. He was recalled from exile once again to resume the presidency (and presumably save the country) in 1853, serving in regal splendor as a supreme dictator and selling additional territory to the United States in the 1854 Gadsden Purchase. He served until his last overthrow in 1855. After a final exile, Santa Anna returned to his native soil and died an impoverished old man in Mexico City in 1876.

SANTA CRUZ DE ROSALES, CHIHUAHUA. In early 1848, after a year of occupation duty in New Mexico (q.v.), Sterling Price (q.v.), unaware that a peace treaty had been signed, marched a column south from El Paso (q.v.) and took the city of Chihuahua (q.v.). After meeting no resistance there and without orders from higher authorities, Price moved 60 miles south on March 16, 1848, pursuing a Mexican force that established a defense at Santa Cruz de Rosales. Despite information from the Mexican commander that a peace treaty had been signed in Mexico City (q.v.) ending the war, Price decided to attack. The almost day-long battle resulted in 23 dead or wounded American soldiers. Historians have noted that the surrender of the Mexican force at Santa Cruz marked the end of hostilities in the

SCOTT, HENRY LEE • 247

war with Mexico; in reality, however, this distinction belongs to the engagement at Todos Santos (q.v.). *See also* TODOS SANTOS, BAJA CALIFORNIA.

SANTA FE, NEW MEXICO. In the early 19th century, Santa Fe developed as a trading center for the exchange of goods between Mexicans coming north from Chihuahua (q.v.) and Anglo-Saxon traders traveling across the Great Plains from the United States. After Mexican independence, trade grew rapidly, and by 1825, the route along the Arkansas River from St. Louis to Santa Fe came to be known as the Santa Fe Trail (q.v.). The town was a collection of mud or adobe buildings, including the Palace of the Governors, which was a long, one-story building on the north side of the plaza with a long portico held up by tree trunks. Santa Fe became one of the first bustling, freewheeling, gambling, and drinking frontier towns. It was also a place of interaction between Mexicans and Americans for 20 relatively peaceful years before the war between Mexico and the United States in 1846.

As the Army of the West (q.v.) advanced on Santa Fe in the late summer of 1846, Gov. Manuel Armijo (q.v.) fled, thereby allowing Brig. Gen. Stephen Watts Kearny (q.v.) and his troops to peacefully occupy the town of 3,000 on August 18, 1846. From Santa Fe, American troops deployed to Taos (q.v.) and other parts of New Mexico (q.v.) to pacify the region and establish U.S. rule. From Santa Fe, U.S. forces also launched expeditions to conquer California (q.v.) and to participate in the campaign against Mexican armies in northern Mexico.

SANTA FE TRAIL. The Santa Fe Trail was the route along the Arkansas River from St. Louis, Missouri, to Santa Fe (q.v.), New Mexico (q.v.). First used by traders in the early years of the 19th century, it was the route followed by Gen. Stephen Watts Kearny's (q.v.) Army of the West (q.v.) in its march from Fort Leavenworth (q.v.) to Santa Fe in the summer of 1846.

SCAMMON, ELIAKIM PARKER (1816–1894). Eliakim Parker Scammon, West Point graduate of the class of 1837, served with Gen. Winfield Scott (q.v.) at the siege of Veracruz (q.v.). He was later dismissed from the army for disobedience of orders. Scammon's reputation was restored in the Civil War, where he rose to colonel and brigadier general of U.S. volunteers.

SCOTT, HENRY LEE (1815–1886). Henry Lee Scott graduated from West Point in 1833 at 18 years of age and was commissioned in the infantry. As a captain, Scott served as aide-de-camp to Maj. General Winfield Scott (q.v.) from 1842 to 1848 and also held the job of General Scott's chief of staff from January 1847 to February 1848. Henry Scott, who was not related to General Scott, was a principal member of the general's "little cabinet" (q.v.) during the war. He was brevetted major for the battles of Contreras and Churubusco (q.v.) and lieutenant colonel for Chapultepec (q.v.). After the war, he served as General in Chief Scott's senior aide-de-camp from 1850 to 1861. Scott took a year's leave of absence in 1861 and wrote the reference work *Military Dictionary*. He retired from active service in 1862.

SCOTT, WINFIELD (1786–1866). Born in Virginia to a minor landed family, Winfield Scott matriculated in 1805 at the College of William and Mary. After a brief period in Williamsburg, he departed to study law privately and was admitted to practice in 1806. In the wake of the *Chesapeake-Leopard* affair, Scott enlisted for his first military duty, serving as a corporal in a Virginia cavalry troop in 1807. In the summer of 1808, Scott began his career as an officer, obtaining a commission from President Jefferson as a captain of artillery (q.v.). In 1810, the army court-martialed Captain Scott for insubordinate remarks he repeatedly made about the general in chief, Gen. James Wilkinson, and he was suspended from duty for 10 months. The incident (Scott had repeatedly called Wilkinson a traitor) would be indicative of numerous others during Scott's career when his temper would dictate his actions. His stubbornness and independence of character, revealed in intemperate remarks or letters, caused discord in his relations with associates and several times resulted in disapproval or even reprimand from superiors.

After returning to active service, Scott won fame and rank in the War of 1812, becoming a national hero after the battles at Chippewa and Lundy's Lane. Promoted to brigadier general at age 27 in March 1814, he was breveted major general in July of that year. Over the next 25 years, Scott participated in the latter stages of the Black Hawk War in 1832, fought in the Seminole War in 1837, and the next year commanded troops along the Canadian border. Scott later won acclaim for effectively implementing Andrew Jackson's controversial order to remove the Cherokees from several southern states. A broadly talented soldier-statesman, Scott competently served the government during the 1840s in several diplomatic roles and authored the army's first manual on tactics (q.v.) and drill. In 1841, he became general in chief of the army and a permanent major general—positions he held until his retirement in November 1861. At the outbreak of war with Mexico, Pres. James Knox Polk (q.v.) appointed Scott commanding general of the field army in May 1846. Polk soon withdrew the appointment because of the general in chief's impolitic comments in letters to the secretary of war that made the president suspicious of Scott's loyalty to the administration. Scott had further irritated the impatient Polk as he tarried in Washington rather than departing immediately for the war theater. Scott had argued that time was needed to properly recruit, organize, and train the newly activated units before precipitously deploying them to the war zone. After failing in an attempt to get Congress to appoint Sen. Thomas Hart Benton as the army field commander (thus bypassing both Scott and Maj. Gen. Zachary Taylor [q.v.], the latter then in northern Mexico), Polk again turned to Scott as the commander of a new front to open on Mexico's southeastern Gulf coast.

Before his appointment, Scott had written a strategic plan for opening the new front. "Vera Cruz and Its Castle" was a concept for a massive invasion at Veracruz (q.v.) on the Gulf coast and a subsequent campaign that would take the American army to the Mexican capital. It became the campaign plan that eventually won the war. Before departing for the theater of operations, Scott meticulously organized and equipped an army to land on the Mexican coast. He obtained reports on the conditions in the region from the navy, requisitioned sea transports from both army and naval sources, and ordered a contract for assault or surfboats (q.v.) to be built to specifications that the general in chief approved—the first ever made for this purpose for the U.S. military. Scott designated rendezvous points north of Veracruz and at the Rio Grande (q.v.) and in late 1846 went to the Brazos Santiago (q.v.) at the opening to the Rio Grande to "gather an army" for the invasion.

During the buildup and staging process, Scott worked closely with the navy to prepare for the joint amphibious landing at Veracruz in March 1847. The invasion, under Scott's direct command and conducted with his characteristic precision, was the largest amphibious operation of the United States before the North African campaign in 1942. After a siege forced the fortified city of Veracruz to capitulate, Scott moved his army toward Mexico City (q.v.). Along the route Hernán Cortés had taken 300 years earlier, Scott fought a series of successful battles that culminated in the capture of Mexico City on September 14, 1847. His six-month-long offensive against Mexico, conducted in the interior of a hostile nation against superior numbers with an army cut off from its supply line to the coast, has been hailed as one of history's great military campaigns. The Duke of Wellington, who had closely followed the war from across the Atlantic, commented of Scott's feat that the campaign was "unsurpassed in military annals" and that Scott was "the greatest living soldier." During the occupation of Mexico City in late 1847 and early 1848, Scott brought charges against some of his senior commanders for writing reports he considered false and insubordinate. Among those he arrested were Maj. Gen. William Jenkins Worth (q.v.) and Maj. Gen. Gideon Pillow (q.v.), the latter a political ally and former law partner of President Polk. These controversies, along with reports that reached Washington of an earlier scheme to pay the Mexican general, Antonio López de Santa Anna (q.v.), for quitting the war, resulted in Scott's relief in January 1848 and in the administration's call for a court of inquiry to investigate his performance of duty in Mexico. Scott was eventually cleared by the court. After turning down an offer by a group of prominent political figures in Mexico City to be dictator of that nation, Scott returned to the United States in April 1848. Although he was ignored upon his return by an ungrateful Polk, he was hailed by the public and Congress. Congress voted the general in chief a medal to show the nation's gratitude.

Scott continued his military career after the war with Mexico. He remained general in chief of the army and won the Whig (q.v.) nomination for president in 1852. Defeated in the fall election by one of his former volunteer generals in Mexico, the Democrat Franklin Pierce (q.v.), Scott received from Pierce and the Congress a promotion three years later to brevet lieutenant general. Although a temporary rank—which he carried until his retirement—Scott thus became the nation's second three-star general after Washington. Still head of the army on the eve of the Civil War, the aging and deteriorating Virginia-born Scott remained loyal to the Union and prepared another strategic plan, this one to defeat the rebellious Confederate states. Referred to by some as "The Anaconda Plan," it called for a deliberate buildup of the army, a total blockade of the South, and an invasion of the Mississippi Valley to divide the South in half before defeating it by sending an army through its heartland. The plan, although derided by the press and impatient northern politicians in 1861, ultimately proved to be the strategy (q.v.) successfully pursued by the Lincoln administration. Winfield Scott retired from active service in November 1861. He wrote his memoirs and spent his retirement years in poor health, but he lived to see the Union restored in 1865 before passing away at West Point in May 1866 at the age of 79.

SEMMES, RAPHAEL (1809–1877). Navy Lt. Raphael Semmes commanded the brig *Somers* that wrecked off the Gulf coast on December 8, 1846, while participating in the U.S. blockade (q.v.) of Mexico. Half of the men on board—32 sailors—perished in the catastrophe. Although Semmes faced a court of inquiry as a result of the incident, he was absolved of all blame. He then became a flag lieutenant to Commo. David E. Conner (q.v.), serving in the siege of Veracruz (q.v.) and the Tuxpan (q.v.) expedition. Subsequently, he was assigned to Gen. Winfield Scott's (q.v.) army at Jalapa (q.v.) and given a mission by the navy to secure from Mexican authorities the release of a midshipman, R. Clay Rogers. Rogers had been captured during an aborted raid against Mexican positions along the coast. Although he was in full uniform, Rogers was held as a spy. Semmes was thus the only naval officer to accompany the land forces during Scott's campaign for Mexico City. Scott never officially recognized Semmes assignment to his army and refused to accept his credentials since the navy had not officially communicated the assignment to the general in chief. During the Civil War, Semmes gained fame as the commander of the Confederate raider *Alabama*. Semmes's *Service Afloat and Ashore during the Mexican War*, published in 1851, is a useful contribution to primary source material on the war.

SHACKLEFORD, MUSCOE L. (1813–1847). Upon his graduation from West Point in 1836, Muscoe L. Shackleford served as a lieutenant in the Second Artillery. He fought at Monterrey (q.v.), Veracruz (q.v.), Cerro Gordo (q.v.), Amozoc (q.v.), San Antonio (q.v.), and Churubusco (q.v.) before being killed leading his company in an assault on the enemy's works at Molino del Rey (q.v.).

SHANNON, WILSON (1802–1877). Pres. John Tyler appointed the former governor of Ohio, Wilson Shannon, as ambassador to Mexico in the late summer of 1844. Soon after his arrival, Gen. Antonio López de Santa Anna (q.v.) released 120 prisoners from the Mier (q.v.) Expedition, apparently to win favor with the new envoy. Any illusions Shannon held about establishing good relations, however, were shattered as the Mexican government grew increasingly hostile over the Tyler administration's efforts to annex Texas (q.v.). Although by autumn Shannon became extremely discouraged in his mission, he remained in his post until the end of 1844 before returning to the United States.

SHERMAN, WILLIAM TECUMSEH (1820–1891). Lt. William Tecumseh Sherman graduated sixth in his West Point class of 1840 and spent his initial years in service in Florida, South Carolina, and Georgia. During the conflict with Mexico, Sherman sailed with F Company of the Third Artillery on the *Lexington* (q.v.) to protect its cargo of ordnance supplies as it traveled from New York around Cape Horn to California (q.v.). He arrived in Monterey Bay on January 26, 1847. His assignment in California meant that he missed seeing combat action during the war. On the verge of resigning his commission, he decided to remain on active duty when Gen. Persifor Smith (q.v.), a veteran of considerable action during the war and commander of the division of the Pacific after the war ended, made the young Sherman his aide-de-camp and acting assistant adjutant general. Sherman did resign his commission in September 1853, briefly becoming a banker, then a lawyer, and finally the superintendent of what is now Louisiana State University.

In 1861, when the army was increased in size, Sherman reentered military service. He later rose to major general in the Civil War and subsequently replaced Gen. Ulysses S. Grant (q.v.) as general of the army.

SHIELDS, JAMES (1806–1879). Born in Ireland, James Shields emigrated to the United States in 1826. He settled in Illinois, fought in the Black Hawk War, practiced law, served in the state legislature, and served on the Illinois Supreme Court. Shields was one of the five volunteer brigadier generals whom Pres. James Knox Polk (q.v.) appointed at the beginning of the war with Mexico. After serving briefly under Gen. Zachary Taylor (q.v.), Shields participated in the siege of Veracruz (q.v.) in March 1847. At Cerro Gordo (q.v.) in April, he led 300 largely untrained volunteers (q.v.) in a desperate assault against a Mexican position manned by 2,000 cavalry supported by an artillery (q.v.) battery. In the attack Shields fell gravely wounded, miraculously surviving a gunshot wound in the head with the assistance of a Mexican surgeon. He later distinguished himself at the battles of Contreras and Churubusco (q.v.) in August

1847 before again being wounded at the battle of Chapultepec (q.v.) in September of that year.

After the war, Shields renewed his political career in his home state, which he represented for almost six years in the U.S. Senate. Defeated for reelection, he moved to the Minnesota Territory. He served in the U.S. Senate for an abbreviated term after Minnesota achieved statehood. Once more failing to be reelected, he moved to California (q.v.) where he remained until the start of the Civil War, whereupon he served as a general in the Union army. At war's end, after a brief period in California, he settled in Missouri. From Missouri, he again returned to the U.S. Senate to fill an unexpired term but refused to run thereafter because of illness.

SHUBRICK, WILLIAM BRANFORD (1790–1874). A South Carolinian by birth, William Branford Shubrick spent a year at Harvard before entering the U.S. Navy in 1806. Because of a close, lifelong friendship with fellow shipmate James Fenimore Cooper, Cooper dedicated his books *The Pilot* and *The Red Rover* to Shubrick. At the start of the war with Mexico, he had been a career officer for nearly 40 years. As a commodore, Shubrick sailed from New York on the razee *Independence* (q.v.) on August 22, 1846, with orders to succeed John Drake Sloat (q.v.) as commander of the Pacific Squadron (q.v.). His orders conflicted with those of James Biddle (q.v.), a commodore then serving in the Far East. Shubrick arrived on the West Coast before Biddle and commanded the squadron briefly from January 22, 1847, until Biddle's assumption of command on March 2. Biddle turned the command back over to Shubrick on July 19 of that year and Shubrick remained as the squadron's commander until May 6, 1848, when he relinquished command to Commo. Thomas ap Catesby Jones (q.v.). During his tenure, Shubrick frequently worked with U.S. Army forces in joint operations along the Pacific coast.

SITGREAVES, LORENZO (1810–1888). Joining the topographical engineers (q.v.) upon his graduation from West Point in 1832, Lorenzo Sitgreaves served as a first lieutenant during the war with Mexico. He marched with Gen. John Ellis Wool's (q.v.) Centre Division and fought at the battle of Buena Vista (q.v.), where he was brevetted captain for gallantry in action. In the Civil War, Sitgreaves remained loyal to the Union and rose to lieutenant colonel.

SLACK, WILLIAM B. (d. 1874). During the war with Mexico, marine Lt. William B. Slack participated in the occupation of the port of Tuxpan (q.v.), served with the Third Artillery at the siege of Veracruz (q.v.) and took part in the captures of Tabasco (q.v.) and Tamulté. In the brief period when the United States held the port of Tabasco, Slack was its military commandant. He was brevetted captain for his service in the war.

SLAVERY. See WILMOT, DAVID.

SLIDELL, JOHN (1793–1871). Pres. James Knox Polk (q.v.) chose John Slidell—diplomat, Louisiana politician, and brother-in-law of Commo. Matthew Calbraith Perry (q.v.)—to serve as U.S. minister to Mexico with the mission of negotiating the Texas-Mexico boundary and purchasing New Mexico (q.v.) and California (q.v.). Slidell arrived at the port of Veracruz (q.v.) on November 30, 1845, and in Mexico City (q.v.) on December 6, much earlier than Pres. José Joaquín de Herrera (q.v.) had expected. Herrera was not hostile to the Slidell mission, being inclined to avoid war by negotiating the two nations' differences. Although for political reasons Herrera did not receive Slidell after the diplomat arrived in the capital, the fact that his government allowed Slidell that far brought intense pressure on the president from ultranationalists within the army. These forces, led by Gen. Mariano Paredes y Arrillaga (q.v.), overthrew Herrera on December 31. The new government was intensely anti-American and determined not to negotiate with the United States. Slidell therefore left the country, sailing from Veracruz on March 30. These events effectively ended the Polk administration's efforts to avoid war through diplomacy in 1845. After the fall of Veracruz during the second year of the war, Slidell was again considered by President Polk as an emissary to the Mexican government before Polk decided instead to send Nicholas P. Trist (q.v.), chief clerk of the State Department.

SLOAT, JOHN DRAKE (1781–1867). A seasoned naval leader who had served in the War of 1812, Commo. John Drake Sloat assumed command of the Pacific Squadron (q.v.) at Callao, Peru, on March 24, 1845. He arrived in the port of Mazatlán (q.v.), on the west coast of mainland Mexico, on November 18, 1845. His orders were to avoid hostilities with Mexico unless and until there was a declaration of war. Upon learning of the Thornton (q.v.) incident (April 25, 1846) and the battles of Palo Alto (q.v.) (May 8, 1846) and Resaca de la Palma (q.v.) (May 9, 1846), Sloat was faced with the dilemma of following his instructions to the letter or commencing hostilities. He chose to delay, a controversial decision for which he was later criticized. His detachment of seamen and marines peaceably took Monterey (q.v.) and proclaimed annexation of California (q.v.) on July 7, 1846. On July 29, 1846, he turned over command of the Pacific Squadron to Robert F. Stockton (q.v.) and continued on active duty until retiring from the service in September 1855. *See also* THORNTON, SETH B.

SMITH, ANDREW JACKSON. During the march from Fort Leavenworth (q.v.) to New Mexico (q.v.), Lt. Andrew Jackson Smith, a West Point graduate of 1838 serving with the First Regiment of Dragoons, temporarily assumed command of the Mormon Battalion (q.v.) after the death of the battalion's first commanding officer, Lt. Col. James Allen (q.v.). Smith was posted to garrison duty in California (q.v.) during the rest of the war. During the Civil War, he rose to major general of U.S. volunteers.

SMITH, CHARLES FERGUSON (1807–1862). A West Point graduate of the class of 1825, Charles Ferguson Smith served in artillery (q.v.) units before returning to the academy for 13 years to teach infantry tactics (q.v.) and serve as commandant of cadets. Afterward, he had assignments in New York and Pennsylvania before joining Gen. Zachary Taylor's (q.v.) army as a regular army captain at the time of the war with Mexico.

On the march from Corpus Christi (q.v.) to the Rio Grande (q.v.), Captain Smith's command was the first to cross the Arroyo Colorado (q.v.) after Mexican officers had warned Taylor that to cross the stream would mean battle. Smith's four-company unit, part of Gen. William Jenkins Worth's (q.v.) brigade, forded the 80-foot-wide stream located 30 miles north of Matamoros (q.v.) on March 20, 1846. Although expecting battle at the Arroyo Colorado that would have started the war, the American troops crossed unopposed. Smith participated in the battles of Palo Alto (q.v.) and Resaca de la Palma (q.v.) in May 1846. In the campaign for Monterrey (q.v.), Smith commanded a line of skirmishers on September 21, 1846, when General Worth's force was charged by a strong force of lancers under Lt. Col. Juan Nájera (q.v.). Smith and a unit of Texas Rangers (q.v.) under Capt. Sam Walker (q.v.) held off the charge and killed or wounded more than 100 of the Mexican cavalry, including their commander. In the same battle, Smith's troops forded the Santa Catarina River and attacked Mexican forces on Federation Hill (q.v.). Smith's unit, after being joined by Col. Persifor Smith's (q.v.) brigade, successfully carried the hill, a terrain feature critical to command of the city.

Transferred to Gen. Winfield Scott's (q.v.) forces in the south, Smith's light infantry battalion—composed of two artillery and two infantry companies—helped block the Mexican retreat from San Antonio (q.v.) in the battle for Mexico City (q.v.). On September 8, 1847, a temporary illness caused Smith to relinquish command of his battalion before it stormed the Mexican position in the costly battle of Molino del Rey (q.v.). After the capital fell to Scott's army, Smith commanded a 500-man force that worked with the Mexican police to maintain order in the capital and enforce the martial law that Scott had declared. Although still a regular captain at the end of hostilities, for the various actions he participated in during the war, Smith won brevets to major, lieutenant colonel, and colonel. In the Civil War, Charles Ferguson Smith rose to major general of volunteers in the Union army; he died in Tennessee in April of 1862 as a result of an accident.

SMITH, EPHRAIM KIRBY. See KIRBY SMITH, EPHRAIM.

SMITH, GUSTAVUS WOODSON (1822–1896). From his graduation from West Point in 1842 until he retired from the army in 1854, Gustavus Woodson Smith served in the engineers (q.v.). During the war with Mexico, as a regular second lieutenant and later brevet first lieutenant and captain, he alternately served as second-ranking company officer and commander of a company of sappers, miners, and pontoniers. His company helped open the Matamoros (q.v.)–Victoria (q.v.)–Tampico (q.v.) road and participated in Gen. Winfield Scott's (q.v.) campaign in the southern theater. Smith helped strengthen defenses at Puebla (q.v.) and cleared the road around Lake Chalco (q.v.); thereafter, he fought at the battles of Contreras and Churubusco (q.v.). Smith's unit prepared positions for artillery (q.v.) batteries before the attack on Chapultepec (q.v.). Smith was twice breveted—to first lieutenant for Cerro Gordo (q.v.) and to captain for Contreras. After the war, he held a number of civilian engineering positions in the 1850s before joining the Confederate forces in the Civil War. In that conflict, Smith held the rank of major general before resigning after he was passed over for promotion to lieutenant general. Before the war's end, however, he went to Georgia and accepted a position as a major general in the Georgia state militia. After the Civil War, Smith wrote or edited several military histories, including one on his experiences with the combat engineers in the war with Mexico. This account, useful for historians of the war as one of the few participant accounts of the engineers, was first published in 1896. It was republished in 1964 in *The Military Engineer* as "Company A Engineers in Mexico, 1846–1847."

SMITH, HENRY (d. 1847). After a brief stint in the artillery (q.v.), Henry Smith, a West Point graduate of 1815, served alternately as a quartermaster and infantry officer until he resigned from active service in 1836. In March 1847, Smith was reappointed to the army in the rank of major in the Quartermaster Corps (q.v.). He was immediately ordered to Veracruz (q.v.), landing at the port city soon after the amphibious operation had been successfully executed by Gen. Winfield Scott's army. Smith became ill soon after arriving in Veracruz and died there on July 24, 1847.

SMITH, JOHN LIND (d. 1858). Maj. John Lind Smith was the senior staff engineer officer of the regular engineers on Gen. Winfield Scott's (q.v.) personal staff. He was in charge of construction of batteries, bridges, and other structures and positions—and, perhaps of more importance for an army on the offensive, he supervised the engineers under him as they carried out their reconnaissance missions. After his officers went out to scout routes and gather intelligence, Scott frequently asked Smith to summarize the information gained by the other engineers (among these Smith's second in command, Capt. Robert E. Lee [q.v.], the second ranking engineer; and lieutenants Zealous B. Tower [q.v.], John G. Foster [q.v.], George B. McClellan [q.v.], Pierre G. T. Beauregard [q.v.], and others) and present it during preoperation briefings of the commanders and staff. Smith was breveted to lieutenant colonel for Cerro Gordo (q.v.) and colonel for Contreras and Churubusco (q.v.).

SMITH, JUSTIN HARVEY (1857–1930). Justin Harvey Smith, graduate and valedictorian of the Dartmouth class of 1877, continued his education at Union Theological Seminary. He entered the workforce on both the business and editorial sides of Charles Scribner's Sons and Ginn & Company before retiring from publishing in 1898 to accept a teaching position in the Dartmouth history department. Smith resigned from Dartmouth to concentrate on writing his two-volume epic, *The War with Mexico*, which was published in 1919. It won the Pulitzer Prize in 1920 and the first Loubat Prize in 1923. While serving on the Historical Manuscripts Commission of the American Historical Association, he edited "Letters of General Antonio López de Santa Anna (q.v.) Relating to the War between the United States and Mexico, 1846–1848," which appeared in the *Annual Report of the American Historical Association* for 1917. Justin Harvey Smith remains the foremost scholar of the war with Mexico.

SMITH, MARTIN LUTHER (1819–1866). Second Lt. Martin Luther Smith entered the topographical engineers (q.v.) after his graduation from West Point in 1842. During the war with Mexico, he won a brevet to first lieutenant for his reconnaissance work and map making in the Valley of Mexico (q.v.). Smith served as an engineer in the Confederate army during the Civil War.

SMITH, PERSIFOR FRAZER (1798–1858). Persifor Frazer Smith was a graduate of Princeton and as a young man practiced law in New Orleans. As a volunteer officer, Smith had experience in the Florida Indian campaigns. At the start of the war with Mexico, as a brigadier general, he commanded two regiments of Louisiana volunteers along the Rio Grande (q.v.). He next took command of the second brigade in the Second Division of regulars in Gen. Zachary Taylor's (q.v.) army where he carried the rank of brevet brigadier general. In the campaign against Monterrey (q.v.) in September 1846, Smith, under the direct command of Brig. Gen. William Jenkins Worth (q.v.), led his brigade in the critical fight for Federation Hill (q.v.). After he was reassigned to Gen. Winfield Scott's (q.v.) army at Veracruz (q.v.), Smith commanded a brigade under Gen. David Twiggs (q.v.) consisting of two companies of Mounted Riflemen (without horses), the First Artillery, and the Third Infantry.

Because of illness, Smith missed the fighting at Cerro Gordo (q.v.) in April 1847. He participated in the battles of Contreras and Churubusco (q.v.) in August and in the storming of Chapultepec (q.v.) the following month. Smith's tactical leadership at Contreras was considered critical; David Twiggs, his division commander, credited Smith with the victory there. When Mexico City (q.v.) fell in September 1847, Gen. John A. Quitman (q.v.) and Smith marched on foot before their battle-weary troops to the palace on the plaza where the U.S. flag was raised, whereupon General Scott arrived on horseback in full dress uniform to the troops' cheers. Smith, following Quitman, was the second military governor of Mexico City. He participated in the armistice negotiations and, once a treaty was reached, helped plan and execute the evacuation of U.S. troops.

SONOMA, CALIFORNIA. On June 10, 1846, Ezekiel Merritt (q.v.) led a group of 12 U.S. citizens in an attack against a small unit of Californios (q.v.) near Sonoma. A few days later, Merritt led another force to seize the Californio general, Mariano Guadalupe Vallejo (q.v.), the founder of Sonoma and commander of the northern Californio forces. It was at Sonoma on July 4, 1846, that the Bear Flaggers precipitately declared California's (q.v.) independence. Here, the following day, John Charles Frémont (q.v.) became the leader of the newly organized California Battalion, made up of U.S. citizens belonging to Frémont's quasi-military unit and Americans already present in California.

SOTO, JUAN. Juan Soto served as Mexican governor of the state of Veracruz. As Gen. Winfield Scott's (q.v.) army approached the port of Veracruz, Soto zealously but unsuccessfully attempted to collect taxes for sufficient provisions from a financially strapped citizenry and to enlist a cadre of regular troops to defend the city and state.

After the fall of Veracruz, he was directed to marshall money, supplies, and troops to join Gen. Valentín Canalizo (q.v.) in fortifying Corral Falso and Cerro Gordo (q.v.), southeast of Jalapa (q.v.) on the National Highway (q.v.). Later he was also asked to do the same to fortify Orizaba (q.v.). Soto's efforts toward these ends were frustrated, however, because the state of Veracruz had exhausted virtually all of its available resources under the American blockade (q.v.).

STEVENS, ISAAC INGALLS (1818–1862). After graduating first in his West Point class of 1839, Isaac I. Stevens joined the engineers (q.v.) in Mexico. He participated in the siege of Veracruz (q.v.), the battle of Cerro Gordo (q.v.), the reconnaissance of El Peñon (q.v.), and the battles in the Valley of Mexico (q.v.). Stevens, who was badly wounded at the San Cosmé Gate (q.v.), won two brevets—to captain for the battles of Contreras and Churubusco (q.v.) and to major for Chapultepec (q.v.). In civilian life after the war, Stevens was governor of the Washington Territory and *ex officio* superintendent of Indian affairs. In 1861, he returned to active military service as a colonel with the New

York Volunteers before becoming a brigadier general and major general in the U.S. Volunteers. Stevens was killed while leading a charge at the battle of Chantilly in Virginia on September 1, 1862.

STOCKTON, ROBERT FIELD (1795–1866). Born in Princeton, New Jersey, Robert F. Stockton attended the College of New Jersey (now Princeton) before being commissioned as a U.S. naval officer in 1811. Before the war with Mexico, he had enjoyed a distinguished career in the navy and the merchant marine, serving in the War of 1812 and the Algerine War of 1800–1815. On July 29, 1846, Commo. Robert F. Stockton took command of the Pacific Squadron (q.v.)—a naval force that would become unique for its land campaigns in the conquest for California (q.v.). Stockton, having become good friends with Capt. John Charles Frémont (q.v.), unofficially incorporated Frémont's battalion of Bear Flaggers into his command as the "California Battalion." When Stockton's unopposed forces occupied Los Angeles (q.v.) in August 1846, he claimed California for the United States, declared martial law, and installed himself as provisional governor. The discontented Californios revolted, however, and retook Los Angeles at the end of September 1846. After Stockton and Brig. Gen. Stephen Watts Kearny (q.v.) defeated the Californians at the battles of San Gabriel (q.v.) and La Mesa (q.v.) on January 8 and 9, 1847, respectively, they marched with their troops 12 miles to retake Los Angeles the following day. On January 13, the Convention of Cahuenga (q.v.) was signed by Frémont and Gen. Andrés Pico (q.v.). Although the treaty contained generous terms that Stockton had previously refused, he named Frémont the military governor of California over Kearny, who had been appointed to that position by Pres. James Knox Polk (q.v.). This controversial situation was resolved on January 22, 1847, when Stockton relinquished command to Commo. William Branford Shubrick (q.v.), who recognized Kearny's authority. Stockton resigned from the navy in 1850 and served in the U.S. Senate as a Democrat from New Jersey from March 1851 until January 1853.

STONE, CHARLES P. (1824–1887). Ordnance officer Charles P. Stone, seventh in the West Point class of 1845, fought in Mexico at Veracruz (q.v.), Amozoc (q.v.), Contreras (q.v.), Molino del Rey (q.v.), Chapultepec (q.v.), and Mexico City (q.v.). He was twice brevetted—to first lieutenant for Molino del Rey and to captain for Chapultepec. He resigned his commission in 1856 and, after a brief stint in banking, returned to Mexico to work for the Mexican government as head of a scientific commission that surveyed public lands in Sonora and Baja California. He later became acting U. S. consul in Guaymas (q.v.). Returning to the U.S. Army during the Civil War, he served as inspector general with the rank of colonel. He subsequently was brigadier general of U.S. Volunteers.

STRATEGY. Until U.S. General in Chief Winfield Scott (q.v.) made his lasting imprint on the United States–Mexican War, the war strategies of both countries during the war were developed by men who lacked either the vision to determine long-range national goals or the ability to implement successful strategies to achieve them.

Mexico's broad goal during the war years was to protect its territory and its people from complete subjugation to the American invaders. Since the country was in a state of political chaos during the 1840s, however, internal rivalries prevented its leaders from implementing a clear-cut strategy in pursuit of this end. Conservative and Liberal parties battled for power, fierce loyalty to regional caudillos overrode alliances with political groups, and the central government changed too frequently for a consistent strategy to be maintained by federal officials. In addition, rivalry existed between the power structure in the capital and generals in the field, resulting in generals ignoring politicians' directives or politicians failing to support armies raised outside the capital by their generals. Even the one cause that could unite the country—opposition to the hated Yankee invader—was not supported universally in Mexico. In 1848, after the fall of Mexico City (q.v.), a group of Conservatives offered Gen. Winfield Scott the dictatorship of the nation.

The United States' ultimate goal of having a nation that spread from coast to coast evolved slowly. Although Pres. James Knox Polk (q.v.) discussed the desirability of California (q.v.) becoming part of the nation, he initially limited his objectives to focus on bringing Texas (q.v.) into the Union. His strategy was to send Gen. Zachary Taylor's (q.v.) army to protect Texas and the Rio Grande (q.v.) border. When Mexico refused to capitulate after the first victories along the Rio Grande in May 1846, Polk realized that stronger measures were necessary. He ordered Taylor to move his army southward into northern Mexico and to capture the new strategic center of gravity, Monterrey (q.v.). Once Taylor had seized Monterrey and scattered army and naval forces the administration had sent to California had won a few small battles, Mexico still refused to treat with the U.S. government. Polk, seeing the failure of his strategy, went on the strategic defensive by ordering Taylor to establish a defensive line from Monterrey to the Gulf coast.

During the late summer of 1847, Polk and his "kitchen cabinet," which consisted of Secretary of War William Marcy (q.v.), Secretary of the Navy George Bancroft (q.v.) (and after September 9, when Bancroft resigned, John Mason), the president's confidant, Sen. Thomas Hart Benton (q.v.) of Missouri, and others, began to talk of a long-range strategic plan for the war. Their focus was now on Mexico City as the new strategic center of gravity. While these talks were in progress, Winfield Scott, the administration's senior uniformed officer but not part of Polk's inner circle, presented to the president a written plan he titled "Veracruz and Its Castle, Thence Upon the Capital." In it, Scott specifically called for raising a new army that would open a front (in reality, a new theater of war) on the Gulf coast of Mexico. The army and navy would conduct a joint amphibious assault at Veracruz, besiege the city and its fortress, and execute an overland campaign to conquer Mexico City. Strategic centers along the way and in the Valley of Mexico (q.v.) would be occupied. Scott presented his plan to Polk in late October 1846, and the president approved it. Appointed by Polk as the commander of the new army, Scott executed the plan to perfection, and Mexico City was in American hands by September 1847. Since the war, historians have generally praised Scott as a true strategic thinker, one of the few in U.S. military history. Scott's reputation as a strategist was enhanced in 1861 at the beginning of the Civil War. The general prepared the Anaconda Plan, a strategy to build an army methodically, embargo the South, and eventually invade the region and split it into two parts. Although the plan at first drew ridicule in the press and from a restless northern public, over time it became President Lincoln's (q.v.) strategy to defeat the South. It has been recognized since as a successfully planned and executed strategy. *See also* POLK, JAMES KNOX; SCOTT, WINFIELD.

SUMNER, EDWIN VOSE (1797–1863). Edwin Vose Sumner, a respected career army officer from Massachusetts, served in the Black Hawk War before the war with Mexico. At the outbreak of the war with Mexico in 1846, Major Sumner was on the frontier. He took two companies of dragoons (q.v.) to join Gen. Stephen Watts Kearny's (q.v.) Army of the West (q.v.) and was with Kearny when Santa Fe (q.v.) was peaceably occupied. Sumner then joined Gen. Winfield Scott's (q.v.) army, serving in the Second Regiment of Dragoons under Col. William S. Harney (q.v.). Scott, lacking confidence in Harney, unsuccessfully tried to transfer him to Gen. Zachary Taylor's (q.v.) army and to substitute Sumner in his stead; this caused strained relations between Sumner and his superior officer.

In the envelopment of Veracruz (q.v.), Sumner led an advance guard of two companies in Gen. David Twiggs's (q.v.) Second Division. Wounded in the fierce fighting at Cerro Gordo (q.v.), he went on to distinguish himself at the battles of Molino del Rey (q.v.) and San Cosmé Gate (q.v.) in September 1847. For his actions he was awarded the rank of brevet colonel. After the war, Sumner served as military commandant of the Department of New Mexico. In the Civil War, he rose to major general of U.S. Volunteers.

SURFBOATS. Gen. Winfield Scott (q.v.) wanted small assault boats to put his troops ashore during the amphibious landing at Veracruz (q.v.). Since they were not in existence at the time, he gave his requirements to his logistician, army Quartermaster Gen. Thomas S. Jesup (q.v.). The surfboats Scott requested were the first specially constructed for an American amphibious assault. Scott's specifications called for flat-bottomed, double-ended, broad-beamed rowboats that were to be constructed in three different lengths, which thus allowed the boats to be nested in transport. Forty-seven sets, or 141 boats, were ordered; the price was $795 each, and delivery time was to be one month. Each surfboat would carry approximately 40 men (one platoon) plus a crew of eight sailors, with a naval officer in command. The boats were designed by Lt. George M. Totten (q.v.) and built under a contract negotiated with a Philadelphia builder by Jesup's agent, Capt. Robert F. Loper (q.v.). *See also* SCOTT, WINFIELD.

SUTTER, JOHN AUGUSTUS (1803–1880). Sutter's Fort, first known as New Helvetia, was established in California (q.v.) at the juncture of the Sacramento and the American Rivers by the German-born, Swiss-raised, Mexican-naturalized entrepreneur, Capt. John Augustus Sutter, whose German name was Johann August Suter. He was accorded the title of captain because of his service in the Swiss army, in which he purportedly reached that rank. As his personal popularity and the success of his empire in the hinterlands mushroomed, he came to enjoy the moniker "General."

Using Indian labor, Sutter erected a fortified post to protect the 50,000 acres he had purchased or acquired through grants from the Californians. Sutter's enterprises included farming, ranching, mining, fishing, trading, and shipping. He hired Indian mercenaries to defend his interests. He welcomed Americans as they migrated into the area, and Sutter's Fort soon became a popular gathering place for newcomers. It was to Sutter's Fort that Bvt. Capt. John C. Frémont (q.v.) came with a small band of 63 men on December 9, 1845. Although Frémont seized the fort on July 11, 1846, it was later returned to Sutter.

After the war with Mexico, Sutter served as a delegate to the California constitutional convention and unsuccessfully ran for governor. The gold rush of 1849, which focused on an area 40 miles from Sutter's Fort, marked the beginning of Sutter's slide into bankruptcy as his workers left him in search of fortune. Sutter eventually lost most of the land he had been granted. He spent the last 10 years of his life in Pennsylvania with the exception of summers in Washington. Sutter's Fort became the present-day city of Sacramento, California.

SUTTER'S FORT, CALIFORNIA. *See* SUTTER, JOHN AUGUSTUS.

SWIFT, ALEXANDER J. (1810–1847). Alexander J. Swift, whose father was in the first West Point graduating class, also attended the academy, graduating first in the class of 1830. Swift entered the engineers (q.v.) and in 1840 was chosen by the chief of engineers for professional study in Europe. He attended the French school for engineer officers at Metz, France. Upon his return to the United States, Swift was given command of the first company of engineers authorized by Congress (before, engineer officers were assigned individually to combat units). The new company, referred to as Company A, Corps of Engineers, or the Company of Sappers, Miners and Pontoniers, consisted of 100 enlisted men and three officers. The other officers assigned to the company were Lt. Gustavus W. Smith (q.v.) and Lt. George B. McClellan (q.v.). Swift deployed from New York with the company in September of 1846 and landed at Brazos Santiago (q.v.) on October 12. While in Camargo (q.v.), near the Rio Grande (q.v.), Swift contracted one of the diseases that so devastated the ranks of the army in that pestilence-ridden town and had to stay behind in a hospital in Matamoros (q.v.)

when the company joined the campaign. Although still suffering from serious illness, Swift rejoined his company for the amphibious landing at Veracruz (q.v.) in March of 1847. His condition required his relief from command immediately after the landing. Captain Swift was evacuated to New Orleans (q.v.) where he died on April 24, 1847.

SWORDS, THOMAS (1807–1886). A West Point graduate of 1829, Thomas Swords served in the Quartermaster Corps (q.v.) during the war with Mexico. His first assignment in the war was that of chief quartermaster in the Army of the West (q.v.) under Gen. Stephen Watts Kearny (q.v.). In that capacity he participated in the battle of San Pascual (q.v.), California (q.v.). Swords then served in the quartermaster general's office in Washington before transferring to Veracruz (q.v.) in 1848. For his Veracruz duty, he was brevetted lieutenant colonel for meritorious conduct in a war zone. During the Civil War, he served as chief quartermaster to various army departments with the rank of regular colonel. In 1865, Swords received brevets to brigadier general and major general for his entire Civil War service.

T

TABASCO, TABASCO. Tabasco, a shallow river port, was located 72 miles up the Tabasco River from the Gulf of Mexico. Also known as San Juan Bautista, Tabasco was briefly occupied by the U.S. Navy Home Squadron's (q.v.) second in command, Commo. Matthew Calbraith Perry (q.v.), on October 25, 1846. Fearing for his men's safety, Perry recalled them to their ships later that day. On the 26th, Mexican gunfire prompted return fire by Perry's squadron. Perry then agreed to a cease-fire at the request of community leaders in Tabasco but was forced to resume bombardment after Mexican forces again fired on his ships. Because he did not have the manpower to hold the port against Mexican resistance, he abandoned it for the safety of Frontera (q.v.) at the mouth of the Tabasco River. Until July of 1847, when Perry retook the town, Tabasco was the only significant Gulf coast port held by the Mexicans. A month after retaking Tabasco, however, Perry again decided to abandon it—this time in deference to yellow fever (q.v.) as well as to guerilla (q.v.) assaults by the Mexicans. Today, the town is known as Villahermosa, and the river upon which it is located is known as the Grijalva River (q.v.).

TACTICS AND TRAINING. Battle drill and training for combat for both Mexicans and Americans were in the Napoleonic tradition. Although tactical maneuvering to flank the enemy was used on the battlefield, armies commonly fought by marching head-on into each other over open ground. Battles were waged with companies or regiments on line with soldiers in close formation, two or three ranks deep. Adversaries marched into each other in a cadence directed by their commander. During the war years, U.S. Army regulations called for three rates of march in battle: common time (90 steps per minute), quick time (110 steps per minute), and double quick time (165 steps per minute). Double quick time was a full run, and this order was given for charging a position. If the defender was well entrenched, the attacker marched deliberately, building up a rate of fire on the march in the hope that defenses would crumble and the defenders flee. If this happened, then the rate of march for the attackers would steadily increase as they pursued fleeing forces.

Training, therefore, focused on drilling soldiers to maintain close order, to march forward at a pace determined by their officers, and to mass their musket fire on vulnerable enemy positions. Basic drill was essentially marching and the manual of arms for the musket (and, for a minority of units, the rifle). The general in chief of the army, Maj. Gen. Winfield Scott (q.v.), had for 40 years been a stern advocate of a strict training regimen, one guided by published army drill and training regulations and carried out by spending long days on the drill field. Early in his career, Scott had chaired a commission that wrote the first standard edition of U.S. drill regulations; in the mid-1830s, Scott wrote *Infantry Tactics*, the new standard for drill manuals of the day. Although not a West Pointer, Scott greatly admired the professionalism of the U.S. Military Academy (q.v.) and the young officers it produced. He took full advantage of the leadership provided by these officers, and he always gave them high praise and credit for the army's successes in the war. The rigorous training standards Scott introduced after taking command of the army in 1841 produced, after five years, a tough, professional fighting force. Years after the war, Ulysses S. Grant (q.v.) wrote that the regular U.S. Army in the spring of 1846 was the best, man for man, to ever take the field of battle.

TACUBAYA, DISTRITO FEDERAL. The town of Tacubaya lies south of Chapultepec (q.v.) in the center of present-day Mexico City. As the final assault was about to be launched on Mexico City (q.v.) by Gen. Winfield Scott's (q.v.) army, Foreign Minister José Ramón Pacheco (q.v.) of Mexico sent, via Nicholas P. Trist (q.v.), a letter to Secretary of State James Buchanan (q.v.) saying that he would meet with Trist and proposing a year-long truce. The United States agreed to a temporary cease-fire, and on August 23, 1847, the Mexicans and North Americans met near Tacubaya to negotiate an armistice. Their agreement, however, quickly broke down. The next month, in September 1847, Tacubaya served as the headquarters of Gen. Winfield Scott and Gen. William Jenkins Worth (q.v.) before the battle of Molino del Rey (q.v.).

TALCOTT, GEORGE. In 1842, Lt. Col. George Talcott functioned as the senior ordnance officer in the army when Col. George Bomford became unable to carry out his duties fully. During the war with Mexico, Talcott served on Secretary of War Marcy's (q.v.) executive staff as chief of the Ordnance Bureau. When Bomford died in 1848, Talcott received the colonelcy that came with the position.

TALCOTT, GEORGE H. (1811–1854). Eleventh in the West Point Class of 1831, George H. Talcott served alternately as an artillery and ordnance officer. After participating in the Seminole War, Talcott was assigned to Mexico where, as a major, he commanded artillery in the Voltigeur Regiment (q.v.) at Cerro Gordo (q.v.), Contreras and Churubusco (q.v.), and Molino del Rey (q.v.). In the latter battle in September 1847, Talcott was seriously wounded, causing him to be put on sick leave until July 1848. He was brevetted lieutenant colonel for gallant and meritorious conduct at Molino del Rey.

TAMPICO, TAMAULIPAS. Tampico, situated a few miles up the Pánuco River from the Gulf of Mexico, was 210 miles north of Veracruz (q.v.). At the beginning of the war, it was second only to Veracruz in its importance to Mexico as a port. Along with most of the Gulf coast, Tampico was blockaded after May 1846 by the Home Squadron (q.v.) under Commo. David E. Conner (q.v.). During the summer, the Polk administration briefly considered Tampico as the launching site for an invasion of central Mexico but gave up the idea after discovering that no good routes existed from there to Mexico City (q.v.). Gen. Antonio

López de Santa Anna (q.v.) made the decision to abandon Tampico after receiving word that it was an objective of American forces. This allowed Commodore Conner's forces to occupy the town in mid-November 1846, without a fight. Thereafter, Tampico served as a gathering point for U.S. forces that were en route to join Gen. Winfield Scott's (q.v.) army during the buildup for the invasion of Veracruz.

TAOS, NEW MEXICO. In 1847, Taos, with 3,000 inhabitants, was the third largest town in New Mexico (q.v.). Located 80 miles north of Santa Fe (q.v.), Taos was an early trading post and the home of Indians and whites who were of both Hispanic and Anglo origin. Christopher "Kit" Carson (q.v.) made his home in Taos beginning in 1825. After the American occupation of New Mexico in 1846, Taos became a center of native resistance to the occupation by U.S. troops. *See also* TAOS REBELLION.

TAOS PUEBLO, NEW MEXICO. *See* TAOS REBELLION.

TAOS REBELLION. When forces under the command of Gen. Stephen Watts Kearny (q.v.) met little resistance in occupying Santa Fe (q.v.) in August 1846, it appeared to American authorities that imposition of U.S. rule throughout New Mexico (q.v.) would be peaceful. This hope was soon shattered when a plot brewed against the Americans at year's end. The first leaders of the conspiracy were arrested by authorities in Santa Fe. The rebellion spread, however, to outlying villages in the north. Leaders of the movement were Pablo Montoya (q.v.) and Tomás Romero. The newly appointed American governor, Charles Bent (q.v.), while maintaining his official post at Santa Fe, kept a home in the trading town of Taos (q.v.), 80 miles to the north. Returning there to visit his family on January 17, 1847, Bent encountered angry Indians outside the town. Confronting the governor, they relayed to him their complaints about "gringo" rule in the territory. Bent, thinking he had pacified the mob with his words, continued to his home in Taos. During the night of January 18, a wild gang of discontents descended on the Taos jail, killing two officials. The next morning, the excited mob showed up at Bent's home, demanding entry and threatening his life. Rather than depart out the rear of his dwelling where he could have escaped by horse, Bent decided to remain and attempt to reason with the rebels. He was thereupon attacked, scalped alive, and brutally slain by the frenzied mob. The savages spared Bent's wife and his sister-in-law, Josefa Jaramillo Carson, a houseguest and the young wife of the scout Christopher "Kit" Carson. The rebellion extended to other towns; a mob killed seven Americans at nearby Arroyo Hondo (q.v.), and eight were slaughtered at Mora.

When the report of the Taos massacre reached Santa Fe, Col. Sterling Price (q.v.), then in command at the territorial capital, departed with approximately 400 men to put down the rebellion. Price met resistance from native forces at Canada and Embudo Pass, defeating the New Mexicans in pitched battles at both sites. After marching over rough mountain terrain through snow two feet deep, Price's force reached Taos on February 2, 1847. The rebels made their defense against the Americans in the Pueblo of Taos, an Indian village north of the Taos plaza where they had fortified the church. Price, aware of the savagery of the recent uprising, was determined to give no quarter. During February 3 and 4, he pounded the pueblo with artillery (q.v.); on the 4th, his forces attacked the village, burning part of it and killing an estimated 150 New Mexicans in a furious assault. Price's attack on Taos brought the New Mexican rebellion to a close. Of the conspirators, Romero and Montoya were taken alive. Romero was subsequently murdered by an American while in jail awaiting trial; Montoya was tried, sentenced, and hung in the Taos plaza, along with several other members of the rebellion. After the Taos uprising, American rule in New Mexico continued largely unchallenged by the native population. Today Taos is a center for artists that draws thousands of tourists each year. Among the attractions are the Taos Pueblo (where the ruins of the church are proudly preserved by the Indians) and the former home of Governor Bent.

TATTNALL, JOSIAH (1795–1871). A career officer, Josiah Tattnall served in the U.S. Navy (q.v.) from 1812 to 1861. Before the war with Mexico—in February 1837, when Gen. Antonio López de Santa Anna (q.v.) had been released by U.S. authorities after his visit to Washington and interview with Pres. Andrew Jackson at the White House—the fallen dictator was furnished U.S. naval transport back to Mexico with Lt. Comdr. Tattnall in command. Tattnall accompanied Santa Anna ashore in Veracruz (q.v.) and briefly visited with him at his nearby estate.

During the war with Mexico, Comdr. Tattnall participated in the peaceful surrender of Tampico (q.v.), a shallow Gulf of Mexico port on the Pánuco River, in November 1846. In the ensuing days, he led two expeditions upriver to capture and destroy Mexican armaments. When the Veracruz landing occurred at Collado Beach (q.v.) on March 9, 1847, Tattnall, from his ship, the *Spitfire*, commanded the "Mosquito Fleet" (q.v.) of small steamers and gunboats in support of the assault troops. The day after the initial landings, Tattnall led a brief but effective diversionary attack on the Castle of San Juan de Ulúa (q.v.). He led yet another—and dramatically daring—bombardment of the castle on March 23 that evoked cheering from both U.S. troops ashore and American and foreign seamen on ships in the harbor. Tattnall's at-risk position caused the newly arrived commanding officer of the Home Squadron (q.v.), Commo. Matthew Calbraith Perry (q.v.), to withdraw the young officer's flotilla. Still in command of the *Spitfire* in April (with Commodore Perry aboard), Tattnall was wounded when the squadron took Tuxpan (q.v.). At the beginning of the Civil War in 1861, Tattnall resigned his commission in the U.S. Navy to enter first the Georgia navy and then the Confederate States navy.

TAYLOR, FRANCIS (1805–1858). Capt. Francis Taylor, an artillery (q.v.) officer in Gen. David Twiggs's (q.v.) division, marched with the division from Veracruz (q.v.) in April 1847 and was present at the battle of Cerro Gordo (q.v.) later that month. On August 16, 1847, in the Valley of Mexico (q.v.), supporting fire from Capt. Francis Taylor's field battery (Company K) of the First Regiment of Artillery was critical in halting a Mexican attack led by Gen. Juan Alvarez (q.v.) against Twiggs's division at the village of Ayotla (q.v.), north of Lake Chalco (q.v.). A few days later, Captain Taylor and his men fought valiantly but had to withdraw at the battle of Churubusco (q.v.). A month later, Taylor commanded his unit in the fiercely fought battle of Chapultepec (q.v.). He was brevetted major for Cerro Gordo and lieutenant colonel for Churubusco.

TAYLOR, JOSEPH. Joseph Taylor was a brother of Gen. Zachary Taylor (q.v.). During the war with Mexico, he served as a lieutenant colonel in the army's Subsistence Department. During 1847, Taylor served along the Rio Grande (q.v.) until ill health required his transfer back to the United States.

TAYLOR, RICHARD (1826–1879). Richard "Dick" Taylor was the son of Gen. Zachary Taylor (q.v.). In the late spring of 1846, the 20-year-old Taylor visited his father along the Rio Grande (q.v.) at the time of the first engagements of the war. During and after the conflict, he managed his father's plantations in Mississippi and Louisiana. As a general officer in the Confederate army, Richard Taylor fought in numerous battles throughout the Civil War.

TAYLOR, ZACHARY (1784–1850). Born in Virginia, Zachary Taylor moved with his family to Kentucky, where he was raised on a frontier plantation near Louisville. In 1808, with little formal education behind him, Taylor entered the army as a first lieutenant in the Seventh Infantry Regiment. He fought in the War of 1812, earning promotion to brevet major and later major for combat actions. In the drawdown after the war, the army reduced Taylor to the rank of captain in June 1815. He resigned from the army and returned to Kentucky to take up farming. Through family contacts with Pres. James Madison, Taylor was reinstated as a major in 1816. Taylor's connection to Texas (q.v.) and the borderlands began in 1821 when, as a lieutenant colonel, he moved four companies of the Seventh Infantry across the Red River to a location near Natchitoches in Louisiana to construct a frontier fort. The mission of the fort—which was named Cantonment Jesup after Taylor's friend, Army quartermaster general Thomas Sidney Jesup (q.v.)—was to defend against Indian attacks and possible Mexican incursions in the territory recently acquired by treaty from Spain. After promotion to colonel, Taylor commanded troops in the Black Hawk War, where he fought in the last stages of the battle of Bad Axe, and in Florida, where in 1837 he won a brevet promotion to brigadier general after demonstrating bravery and tactical leadership in an impressive victory against the Seminoles at Lake Okeechobee. From his long service in the Indian campaigns along the frontier, Taylor earned the nickname "Old Rough and Ready" from his troops because of his willingness to share their hardships in the field.

When relations with Mexico deteriorated in 1844 over the issue of Texas annexation, the army sent Taylor back to Louisiana to command the First Military District at the fort he had constructed 23 years earlier. At Fort Jesup (q.v.) during 1844–1845, he drilled his Army of Observation (q.v.), steadily increasing its size as reinforcements came in from along the frontier. In June 1845, as Texas annexation drew near, Taylor moved his army of 4,000 troops to Corpus Christi (q.v.), about 100 miles east of the Rio Grande (q.v.). After remaining in camp under miserable conditions at Corpus Christi during the winter of 1845–1846, Taylor moved his force—now named the

Army of Occupation (q.v.) of Texas—to the left bank of the Rio Grande in March.

Mexico, considering Taylor's move a violation of her sovereignty, challenged the American incursion, and the war began. Zachary Taylor, often criticized by historians for lacking not only strategic vision but also an ability to plan a theater campaign competently and employ an army on the battlefield, proved yet again in the first battles of the war his fearlessness and leadership in combat. In the May 1846 border battles of Palo Alto (q.v.) and Resaca de la Palma (q.v.), Taylor calmly led his regiments to decisive victories against Mexican forces superior in numbers. In late May, Pres. James Knox Polk (q.v.) brevetted Taylor a major general for his victories; in June, he received the permanent rank. Taylor next occupied Matamoros (q.v.) across from the earthen fortification (Fort Brown [q.v.]) which he had built on the Rio Grande. This act was the first time American troops had occupied a foreign city. After staging in Matamoros and up the river in Camargo (q.v.) in the summer of 1846, Taylor moved his army across the plains and valleys of northern Mexico to Monterrey (q.v.). In a series of costly assaults against the heavily fortified city, Taylor's army forced the Mexicans to withdraw under an armistice on September 24 of that year. President Polk later criticized Taylor for not pushing the Mexican forces at Monterrey to complete defeat. This "armchair" criticism embittered Taylor, who as a field leader had shared the risks of disease and desperate combat of his troops in the May–September 1846 period. Polk's criticism, and the president's jealousy over Taylor's growing national acclaim resulting from his victories on the battlefield, created a lasting estrangement between the two.

After Polk rescinded the Monterrey armistice, Taylor, ignoring orders from the administration to hold at Monterrey and open a road to Tampico (q.v.), moved forces 50 miles south and occupied the city of Saltillo (q.v.) on November 16, 1846. From November to February, Taylor moved back and forth from Saltillo to Monterrey and from Monterrey to Victoria (q.v.), attempting to both establish realistic lines of defense and support the administration's plan to open a second front along the Gulf coast. During this period, he had to give up most of his regular units for the second front campaign. In February 1847, a Mexican army under Gen. Antonio López de Santa Anna (q.v.) moved north from San Luis Potosí (q.v.), threatening Taylor's advance guard below Saltillo. Taylor reinforced his units at the Angostura Pass south of Saltillo and waited in defensive positions as Santa Anna's army of approximately 15,000–20,000 troops approached. On February 22, after Taylor refused a demand to surrender his 4,600-man force composed mostly of volunteers (q.v.), Santa Anna attacked, and the battle the Americans called Buena Vista (q.v.) ensued. After fierce engagements on the 22 and 23, Taylor's bloodied army held the field; to the Americans' surprise, dawn of the 24th revealed that Santa Anna had decided to retreat. After reports reached the United States that American forces retained the battlefield against overwhelming numbers of enemy forces at Buena Vista, Taylor's popularity soared throughout the nation. The victor of Buena Vista returned to the United States in the fall of 1847 amid demands that he run for the presidency the following year. Nominated as the Whig (q.v.) candidate for president in 1848, Taylor, without campaigning, won the election over Democrat Lewis Cass (q.v.). Taylor's administration was marked by the growing controversy over the introduction of slavery into the territories newly gained from the war that made him a national figure; it was an introduction that the southern-born president and slaveowner ironically opposed. Taylor's term ended with his sudden death in July 1850, after he participated in the ceremonies for the laying of a cornerstone of the Washington Monument.

Although Taylor's long career as an army officer brought him national fame and a heroic image, he has not been universally praised by military historians. Though most praise him for his gallantry in battle and for his superb ability to motivate soldiers to fight under difficult conditions, they are frequently critical of his generalship, faulting him for a lack of strategic foresight and for his lifelong disinterest in making detailed operational plans. Historians concede, however, that Zachary Taylor was a beloved figure, popular among his men—a view surviving participant accounts of the war clearly support.

TECOLUTO, VERACRUZ. In May 1846, the Polk administration began a naval blockade (q.v.) of the major ports along Mexico's Gulf coast. The following July, the Mexican government designated smaller ports, among them Tecoluto, as ports of entry. Consequently, the American blockade was extended to include this small port town.

TEHUANTEPEC, ISTHMUS OF. Rights of passage across this narrow stretch of land separating the Gulf of Mexico and the Pacific Ocean in southern Mexico were prominent in the original objectives of the Polk administration at the beginning of the war. The orders sent with the diplomat Nicolas Trist (q.v.) in the spring of 1847 called for rights for an American passage across the isthmus. By the time of the Treaty of Guadalupe Hidalgo (q.v.) in 1848, Great Britain had already obtained rights across the isthmus from Mexico; there was, therefore, no mention of these rights in the Mexican-American treaty ending the war.

TELEGRAPH HILL. The prominent terrain feature, Telegraph Hill, was situated southeast of Jalapa (q.v.) near the small village of Cerro Gordo (q.v.). From Telegraph Hill (on Mexican maps it is listed as El Telégrafo) and the adjacent hill, Atalaya (q.v.), Gen. Antonio López de Santa Anna (q.v.) concentrated defensive forces to halt Gen. Winfield Scott's (q.v.) army as it advanced from Veracruz (q.v.). See also CERRO GORDO, BATTLE OF.

TENERIA, LA. See MONTERREY, BATTLE OF; RAMIREZ, SIMEON.

TEN REGIMENT BILL. Secretary of War William Marcy (q.v.) submitted a report to Congress on December 5, 1846, stating that the regular army at that time was 7,000 men below authorized strength. Marcy's report forwarded the Polk administration's recommendation that 10 regiments (9 of infantry, 1 of dragoons [q.v.]) be added to the active force to support the army in Mexico. Most members of the House of Representatives were still sensitive to charges of being unpatriotic if they failed to support an army at risk in the field, and the House quickly approved the troop request. The legislation was known as the 10 Regiment Bill. The Senate, not directly responsible to the electorate, balked, however. Polk had at the same time requested that Congress create a lieutenant generalcy. He planned to appoint to the new rank his friend and fellow Democrat, Sen. Thomas Hart Benton (q.v.), and to send him to the theater of war as the commanding general. The Whigs (q.v.) and John C. Calhoun (q.v.) Democrats, infuriated by the idea of such a political and unprofessional appointment, threatened to block the troop legislation. While a compromise was soon reached on the 10 Regiment Bill, which the Senate passed February 10, 1847, the senators turned down Polk's request for the special three-star general's billet. The significance of the troop legislation was that the new units, made up of raw recruits but officered mostly with regulars, allowed Polk to implement his strategic policy of prosecuting the war in Mexico until a peace satisfactory to his administration could be won.

TENNERY, THOMAS DOUTHIT (1819–1891). Thomas Douthit Tennery was a private soldier, though an uncommon one, in Col. Edward D. Baker's (q.v.) Fourth Illinois Volunteer Regiment, one of several volunteer regiments from that state to fight in the war with Mexico. As a private, Tennery was unusual because of his good educational background and his superb ability to express himself in writing—a quality rarely found among enlisted soldiers of the day. In recent years, historians and others have come to know Tennery through his diary, *The Mexican War Diary of Thomas D. Tennery*, published by the University of Oklahoma Press in 1970. A study of his diary gives the reader the rare opportunity to view Mexico, the war, and the everyday experiences of the volunteer soldiers in the ranks through the eyes of one of those soldiers. Tennery's prose is vivid, poignant, and at times breathtaking when describing the deaths of his fellow soldiers. Although not the only such published account available, Tennery's is perhaps the most valuable.

TERRES, ANDRES. During the battle for Mexico City (q.v.), the Mexican general Andrés Terrés commanded the Morelia Battalion at the Belén Gate (q.v.) when Gen. Antonio López de Santa Anna (q.v.) took refuge there after the fall of Chapultepec (q.v.). The Belén Gate was critical to the defense of the capital because it lay across the major avenues of approach from the south and west. When it fell and Terrés withdrew his exhausted troops to the *ciudadela* (citadel) garrison, formerly a tobacco factory within the city's walls, the fate of the capital was determined. In his memoirs, Santa Anna attributed the fall of the city to Terrés's decision to withdraw, criticism unwarranted since Terrés had fought well. General Terrés was considered a professional officer, respected by Mexicans and Americans alike.

TEXAS, FORT. *See* FORT BROWN.

TEXAS RANGERS. This wild and unruly group of Texas (q.v.) volunteers (q.v.) was motivated by a long-standing hatred of Mexicans and exhilarated at the opportunity to treat them with the same brutality as the Mexicans had earlier treated the Texans. The Texas Rangers' obsession with taking revenge for

Mexican atrocities at the battles at the Alamo (q.v.), Goliad, and other places during their long struggle for independence caused these undisciplined soldiers to be a constant irritant to generals Zachary Taylor (q.v.) and Winfield Scott (q.v.) during the war. The group's commander was Colonel John Coffee Hays (q.v.); among notable Texas Rangers were Ben McCulloch (q.v.), who lived to fight in the Confederate army, and Samuel H. Walker (q.v.), who was killed at Huamantla (q.v.).

Known for their outlandish appearance, explosive Texas yells, and Colt revolvers, the Texas Rangers joined Taylor's army on the Rio Grande (q.v.) in the northern campaign. They served primarily as scouts, operating independently in advance of the main body of troops. They performed raids against specific targets, often concentrating on Mexican guerrilla (q.v.) units, and frequently carried out intelligence missions to provide information on Mexican troop movements for the American forces. After participating in the desperate battle for Monterrey (q.v.), most of the Rangers returned to Texas after their initial six-month enlistments terminated in the autumn of 1846. A Texas Ranger company under Captain McCulloch joined General Taylor's army in early 1847 and performed critical reconnaissance missions before the battle of Buena Vista (q.v.). A newly formed Texas Volunteer Regiment joined General Scott's army after the invasion of Veracruz (q.v.), and the Rangers belonging to that unit fought throughout the southern campaign. Scott, like Taylor earlier in the war, found the Rangers disruptive of good discipline and gross violators of the rights of the native civilian population. Scott frequently threatened the Rangers with court-martial and banishment from the theater. In the end, however, Scott recognized the value of the Texans' bravery and superb fighting skills, tolerated their abuses (as had Taylor), and permitted them to remain with his army. At war's end the Texas Rangers returned as heroes to their native state. They remain celebrated as such today.

TEXAS, REPUBLIC OF. Texas, a far north territory of Spain's New World empire—and, after 1821, the remote Mexican state of *Tejas*—remained a sparsely populated land until Anglo settlers under Moses and Stephen Austin began arriving from the United States in the 1820s. They came invited, first by Spain, then by the Mexican Republic, with the understanding under the latter that they would be good citizens of Mexico. They received grants of land and, in turn, were obligated to live under

Spanish law (no trial by jury) and become Roman Catholics. Mostly southerners, many brought slaves to work the newly cleared cotton lands. As their numbers grew, they became restless under Mexican government. Disdaining the carelessness and incompetence of their Hispanic rulers, the Texans made several attempts at rebelling against Mexican authority. In 1826, in Nagodoches, the Texans' leader, Haden Edwards, declared Texas the independent republic of Fredonia. These rebellions were quickly put down by the Mexican army. In the mid to late 1820s, Mexico City began to realize that the 25,000 Anglos in Texas were a potential threat to Mexican sovereignty. Most remained Protestants, and their culture—as well as that of their slaves—was alien to the Mexicans' Spanish and Indian heritage. In 1829, Mexico outlawed slavery in Texas (it was already illegal elsewhere in the country). The following year, the Mexican government forbade further immigration into Texas from the United States, attached Texas to the state of Coahuila (q.v.), and restricted the Texans' trade to official Mexican ports of entry. These new laws and changes were virtually impossible for Mexico to enforce, and they created hostility and resentment among the largely Anglo populace.

By the mid-1830s, the Texans became convinced that they should separate from Mexico and were willing to fight for independence. As armed rebellion grew, the Mexican government sent the army to quell the unrest. In 1835, one force sent north by the Mexican dictator Antonio López de Santa Anna (q.v.) was defeated by the Texans at San Antonio (q.v.) and driven back into Mexico. Santa Anna himself led the next army to put down the Texas rebellion. As he was moving toward Texas with an army of several thousand, the Texans held a convention at Washington-on-the-Brazos, 200 miles east of San Antonio, and established an independent republic. Arriving at San Antonio in February 1836, Santa Anna caught a small force of Texans defending an old Spanish mission called the Alamo (q.v.). Inside the mission were 150 Texans led by Col. William Barrett Travis, who refused to surrender. After a two-week siege, Santa Anna attacked, slaughtering the entire garrison, which included David Crockett (q.v.) and James Bowie. Two months later, after fleeing east from San Antonio in the wake of Santa Anna's advance, the Texans, now led by Sam Houston (q.v.), turned and surprised the resting Mexican army at Lynchburg Ferry. In the ensuing battle of San Jacinto, the Texans thoroughly defeated the Mexican army and captured Santa Anna.

The victory won Texas its de facto independence, although Mexico refused to recognize it officially.

For the next nine years, Texas remained an independent nation called the Lone Star Republic. There was occasional conflict between Texas and Mexico, but trade continued and coexistence was relatively peaceful. During this period—1836 to 1845—Texas claimed that its border with Mexico was the Rio Grande (q.v.). Mexico alternately claimed the border to be either the Nueces River (q.v.), 100 miles to the north of the Rio Grande, or the Sabine River (q.v.), much further east. During this time, Mexico City tolerated Texas's claims, preferring not to make a major issue of the boundary lines. In 1845, when Texas was finally annexed to the United States and Washington decided to send troops to the Rio Grande to protect Texas sovereignty from Mexican incursions, Mexican national pride demanded that it defend what it had long considered its territory. When Gen. Zachary Taylor's (q.v.) army moved from Corpus Christi (q.v.) to the Rio Grande in the spring of 1846, therefore, the crisis was precipitated. Though historians consider other issues as underlying causes of the conflict between the United States and Mexico, the occupation of the left bank of the Rio Grande by the American army must be considered a direct, immediate cause of the war.

TEXCOCO LAKE. Lake Texcoco was one of the three lakes in the immediate vicinity of Mexico City, the other two being Lake Xochimilco (q.v.) and Lake Chalco (q.v.). Lake Texcoco was located north and northeast of Mexico City and protected the capital from invasion from that direction.

THOM, GEORGE (1819–1891). A West Point graduate of 1839, George Thom was a second lieutenant in the topographical engineers (q.v.) during the war with Mexico. He participated in several combat actions while serving as aide-de-camp to Brig. Gen. (of volunteers) Franklin Pierce (q.v.). He served in the Union army during the Civil War and was brevetted lieutenant colonel, colonel, and brigadier general at the end of the conflict for his service throughout the war years. Remaining in the army after the Civil War, Thom served as a regular colonel in numerous engineer positions for the next 18 years.

THOMAS, CHARLES (d. 1878). Commissioned in the army in 1813, Maj. Charles Thomas, was assigned to St. Joseph's Island (q.v.) during the war with Mexico. His mission was to accompany ships from Brazos Santiago and to establish a new supply depot at Point Isabel (q.v.). While at Point Isabel, he was temporarily appointed chief quartermaster with Gen. Zachary Taylor's (q.v.) Army of Occupation (q.v.). Thomas, who won a brevet to lieutenant colonel for his contributions to the war with Mexico, later became quartermaster in Gen. John Ellis Wool's (q.v.) division. He served in the Union army during the Civil War and was brevetted both to brigadier and major general for his military service.

THOMAS, GEORGE HENRY (1816–1870). A Virginian, West Point graduate of 1840, and career army officer, George Henry Thomas first gained combat experience in the Second Seminole War. In the war with Mexico, he was a member of the Third Regiment of Artillery in Gen. Zachary Taylor's (q.v.) army. After taking Matamoros (q.v.), Taylor assigned Lieutenant Thomas to the forces marching on the town of Reynosa (q.v.) when Mexican officials there requested the protection of the American army; this action opened the way for Taylor's move westward along the Rio Grande (q.v.). Thomas later saw action under Taylor at Monterrey (q.v.) and fought his gun section in the heaviest fighting in the battle of Buena Vista (q.v.). For these actions he won brevets to captain (Monterrey) and major (Buena Vista). In the Civil War, Thomas rose to major general in the Union army and gained the sobriquet "Rock of Chickamauga" for his actions in Tennessee.

THOMAS, LORENZO (1804–1875). Lorenzo Thomas graduated 17th in the West Point class of 1823 and entered the army as second lieutenant of infantry. After serving in the Seminole War, Thomas, as a major, was chief of staff to Gen. William Orlando Butler (q.v.) in the war with Mexico. For his gallantry at Monterrey (q.v.), he was brevetted lieutenant colonel. After the war, one of his assignments was chief of staff to Gen. Winfield Scott (q.v.). During the Civil War, he rose to brigadier general and served as adjutant general of the army. Thomas was credited with organizing the colored troops from March 1863 to August 1865. At the close of the war, he received a brevet to major general for meritorious service during the conflict. Thomas retired in 1869 with more than 45 years of active service.

THORNTON, EDWARD (1817–1906). A British diplomat with a long and distinguished career, Sir Edward Thornton was assigned as attaché to Mexico in February of 1845 (after the war, in 1853, he became secretary of legation in Mexico). Nicholas P. Trist (q.v.), sent by Pres. James Knox Polk (q.v.) to Mexico to negotiate a settlement between the two nations, received word via Thornton on June 10, 1847, that Gen. Antonio López de Santa Anna (q.v.) was willing to enter peace talks. Thornton also communicated to Trist the British belief that part of the $3,000,000 Trist was authorized by the U.S. government for a peace settlement would expedite peace negotiations if it found its way into appropriate hands. At a meeting attended by Trist, Gen. Winfield Scott (q.v.), and some of Scott's generals, it was decided that $10,000 would be advanced immediately, with $1,000,000 to follow when the treaty was signed. It is believed, but uncertain, that Thornton and British consul Edward Mackintosh (q.v.) delivered the $10,000; to whom the money went is not known, and the bribery scheme (q.v.) was unsuccessful.

In November 1847, Thornton unofficially notified the Mexicans on Trist's behalf of the American diplomat's recall by the Polk administration and urged them to act quickly in negotiating peace. Thornton, along with General Scott, Foreign Minister Manuel de la Peña y Peña (q.v.), and others, successfully urged Trist to ignore his recall and continue his efforts to secure a treaty. *See also* BRIBERY SCHEME; TRIST, NICHOLAS P.

THORNTON, SETH B. (d. 1847). When Gen. Zachary Taylor (q.v.) received reports of Mexican troops crossing the Rio Grande (q.v.) on April 24, 1846, he ordered a mounted patrol of 63 dragoons (q.v.) under Capt. Seth B. Thornton to investigate. The next day Thornton rode into an ambush set by Gen. Anastasio Torrejón (q.v.), who had crossed the river 14 miles upstream from Matamoros (q.v.) with 1,600 cavalry and infantry the previous day. The ambush, which occurred at Rancho de Carricitos (q.v.), resulted in 11 Americans killed, 6 wounded, and the rest captured—including Thornton and his second in command, Capt. William J. Hardee (q.v.). After Taylor reported the action to Washington, the Polk administration used the news of a Mexican force crossing the Rio Grande and attacking American troops as justification for calling for a congressional recognition of a state of war. In May, after the April 25th ambush, Thornton and his command were exchanged for Mexican prisoners taken in the battle of Resaca de la Palma (q.v.). Fifteen months later, in August 1847, Thornton was killed early in the battles for Mexico City (q.v.) by an artillery (q.v.) round fired from a Mexican battery at San Antonio (q.v.).

TIBBATTS, JOHN W. (d. 1852). While a member of the U.S. House of Representatives from Kentucky, Democrat John W. Tibbatts unsuccessfully fought in February 1846 for a boundary settlement with Mexico along the Sierra Madre Mountains. In Congress, Tibbatts supported the Polk administration's war policy. During the war, he was appointed colonel and commanded the 16th Infantry Regiment, a unit formed of men from Kentucky, Indiana, and Illinois. The 16th, which served in the northern theater under Zachary Taylor (q.v.), was one of the 10 regular regiments authorized by Congress in January 1847.

TODOS SANTOS, BAJA CALIFORNIA. On November 1, 1847, Commo. William Branford Shubrick (q.v.), commander of the Pacific Squadron (q.v.), sent a party under Lt. Mongomery Lewis to investigate reports that Mexican forces were camped at the Pacific coast town of Todos Santos, situated near the tip of Baja California (q.v.). By the time Lewis's force arrived, the Mexicans had left.

At Todos Santos, on March 30, 1848, the last shots of the war were fired when forces under Lt. Col. Henry S. Burton (q.v.) of the First Regiment of New York Volunteers routed the Mexicans under Baja California governor Mauricio Castro (q.v.). Castro was captured shortly thereafter at nearby Santiago.

TOLUCA, ESTADO DE MEXICO. It was in Toluca, located 65 miles west of Mexico City (q.v.), that interim president Manuel de la Peña y Peña (q.v.) briefly established his seat of government in November 1847, after the fall of the capital and the resignation of Gen. Antonio López de Santa Anna (q.v.). When the peace treaty was ratified, the garrison at Toluca was one of the first abandoned by U.S. troops.

TOMPKINS, DANIEL D. (1800–1863). Tenth in his West Point class of 1820 and a veteran of the Florida (or Seminole) Wars, Daniel D. Tompkins served as a quartermaster captain and major during the war with Mexico. As such, he was assigned to Philadelphia, Cincinnati, and New Orleans (q.v.). For his contribution to the war effort, he was breveted lieutenant colonel. During the Civil War, Tompkins served as a colonel of quartermaster in New York City from 1861 until his death on active duty in 1863.

TORNEL Y MENDIVIL, JOSE MARIA (1789–1853). Diplomat, minister of war, general, and cunning *politico*, José María Tornel y Mendívil held a deep hatred for the United States. In 1830, as Mexican minister to the United States, he complained to the Andrew Jackson administration of the government's failure to enforce Mexico's laws prohibiting further migration of Americans to Texas (q.v.). While in Washington, he also worked unsuccessfully to secure recognition of a firm boundary along the Sabine River (q.v.). As minister of war in July 1843, Tornel sent a directive to Gen. Adrian Woll (q.v.), two years before the U.S. annexation of Texas, instructing Woll to withdraw to the Rio Grande (q.v.). This action indicated that Mexico considered the Rio Grande to be its boundary, an impression that Tornel probably did not intend. That same month, he ordered the governors of four northern departments, including California (q.v.), to expel Americans on their soil and refuse entry to all others. In 1846, Tornel was clearly a warhawk. He asked the Mexican Congress to declare war and influenced Pres. Mariano Paredes y Arrillaga (q.v.) to announce by executive order a defensive war against the United States. Also in April 1846, Tornel restored Gen. Mariano Arista (q.v.) to head of the Division of the North and ordered him to attack Zachary Taylor's invading forces.

Tornel avidly opposed peace negotiations with the United States and exhorted the clergy to preach violence against the American invaders in September 1847. Later that month, after the U.S. flag was raised in the plaza of the capital, a mob that included both released convicts (who could not be controlled by Mexican authorities) and the Mexican populace, on orders from Tornel, attacked U.S. troops with paving stones and all available weapons. The mob was forcibly quelled by U.S. troops.

TORREJON, ANASTASIO. Gen. Mariano Arista (q.v.) ordered Gen. Anastasio Torrejón to cross the Rio Grande (q.v.) upstream from Matamoros (q.v.) at La Palangana in April of 1846. Torrejón and his 1,600 cavalry and infantry troops overwhelmed a small U.S. contingent commanded by Capt. Seth B. Thornton (q.v.). This engagement marked the beginning of the war. Subsequently, Torrejón led his cavalrymen in the northern campaign at the battle of Palo Alto (q.v.) on May 8, 1846, at Resaca de la Palma (q.v.) the next day, and at the battle of Monterrey (q.v.) the following September. He later commanded cavalry at the battle of Buena Vista (q.v.) in February 1847. Torrejón also participated in the campaign in the Valley of Mexico (q.v.), fighting at Contreras (q.v.) in August and at the San

Cosmé Gate (q.v.) in September 1847. Torrejón was one of the senior Mexican officers who saw extensive combat action and survived the war. Despite the fact that he normally commanded a cavalry force of 1,000–1,500 regulars, he never won any great victories, nor did he influence battles at critical junctures. One of the most respected historians of the war, Justin H. Smith, has observed that Torrejón's greatest talent, perhaps, was his "instinct of self-preservation," since he always lived to fight another day.

TOTTEN, GEORGE M. (1809–1884). Lt. George M. Totten, U.S. Navy (q.v.), designed the surfboats (q.v.) (sometimes called flatboats) requested by Gen. Winfield Scott (q.v.) during the preparation for the invasion of Veracruz (q.v.). Totten later commanded the *Water Witch*, a third-class steamer that joined Commo. Matthew Calbraith Perry's (q.v.) Home Squadron (q.v.) at Veracruz (q.v.) in the autumn of 1847. *See also* SURF-BOATS.

TOTTEN, JOSEPH GILBERT (1788–1864). Col. Joseph Gilbert Totten, an 1805 graduate of West Point, served on the executive staff of the U.S. War Department (q.v.) as chief engineer. During the war with Mexico, Gen. Winfield Scott (q.v.) took Totten with him in the southern campaign and made him a member of what Scott termed his "little cabinet" (q.v.). Totten played a key role in planning the Veracruz (q.v.) operation of March 1847. When the Veracruz shelling stopped, Totten, along with Gen. William Jenkins Worth (q.v.) and Gen. Gideon Pillow (q.v.), was appointed by Scott to negotiate the city's surrender with three commissioners appointed by Mexican general Juan José Landero (q.v.). Totten was brevetted brigadier general at Veracruz; after the surrender, he served as Scott's official courier to carry the news of the port's fall back to the Polk administration. During the Civil War, Totten served as chief engineer of the U.S. Army. On April 21, 1864, the U.S. Congress authorized Totten a brevet promotion to major general. He died the following day.

TOWER, ZEALOUS BATES (1819–1900). After his graduation as first in his class of 1841 at West Point, Zealous Bates Tower entered the engineers (q.v.). Before the war with Mexico, he participated in the construction of fortifications at the entrance to Virginia's Hampton Roads harbor. During the war, he served in Gen. Winfield Scott's (q.v.) army. At Cerro Gordo (q.v.) in April of 1847, Tower—along with Capt. Robert E. Lee (q.v.), Lt. Pierre G. T. Beauregard (q.v.), and other engineer officers—went out in advance of the main body on reconnaissance missions to determine possible routes of attack. For this action Tower won a brevet to first lieutenant. As did most engineers on Scott's staff, Tower served the army in the same capacity before the battles of Contreras and Churubusco (q.v.), and the battle of Chapultepec (q.v.). For his service at Contreras and Churubusco, he was brevetted captain; for Chapultepec, he was brevetted major. Although wounded at Chapultepec, Tower survived the war and continued his military career. He became a major general during the Civil War and retired from active service in 1883.

TOWSON, NATHAN (d. 1854). As a member of the executive staff of the War Department (q.v.), Brig. Gen. Nathan Towson served as paymaster general of the army. He was appointed by Pres. James Knox Polk (q.v.) to be president of the court of inquiry to investigate the charges and countercharges surrounding Col. James Duncan (q.v.), Gen. Winfield Scott (q.v.), Gen. Gideon Pillow (q.v.), and Gen. William Jenkins Worth (q.v.).

TRIAS ALVAREZ, ANGEL (1809–1867). In August 1846, Angel Trías Alvarez became governor of the northern Mexican state of Chihuahua. The state's capital, Chihuahua (q.v.) City, located 350 miles northwest of Monterrey (q.v.), became a strategic objective of Washington because of its commercial prominence as a trading link to the United States. Trías, despite lack of support from Mexico City (q.v.) (in late 1846, Gen. Antonio López de Santa Anna [q.v.] began drawing off forces from Chihuahua and elsewhere in preparation for the Saltillo [q.v.] campaign), rallied the citizenry of Chihuahua and worked with the military commander, Gen. José Antonio Heredia (q.v.), to build up defenses in anticipation of an American advance on the area. Gen. José María García Conde (q.v.) took military command of Chihuahua in February 1847, while Trías remained governor. Conde established a strong defensive position above Chihuahua City north of the Sacramento River to block the American advance. Despite Trías's and Conde's efforts, the U.S. volunteer force under Col. Alexander Doniphan (q.v.) defeated the Mexicans at the battle of Sacramento (q.v.) on February 28 and Chihuahua fell to the Americans.

Trías remained governor of Chihuahua after the battle. One year later, he faced another offensive against the region by forces under Brig. Gen. Sterling Price (q.v.). Price, without permission from higher authority and unaware that a peace treaty had been signed with the Mexican government, invaded Chihuahua from El Paso (q.v.) in March 1848. At Chihuahua City, representatives of Governor Trías, who had fled the city with his forces on the Americans' arrival, informed Price that the treaty had been signed. Price doubted the report and continued to press southward. At Santa Cruz de Rosales (q.v.), he was met by Trías, who again informed Price that the war was over. Still refusing to believe the news, Price attacked the town of Santa Cruz on March 16. After a day's battle, which resulted in over 20 American soldiers killed or wounded along with many Mexican casualties, Trías surrendered to Price. *See also* PRICE, STERLING.

TRIPLER, CHARLES S. (1806–1866). Charles S. Tripler entered the regular army as a surgeon in 1830. He saw service on the frontier and in the Seminole Wars, apprenticed under surgeon Walter V. Wheaton at West Point, and was chief surgeon for Gen. David Twiggs's (q.v.) division in the war with Mexico. During the Civil War, he served as medical director of the Army of the Potomac until he became medical director for the Northern Department.

TRIST, NICHOLAS PHILIP (1800–1874). On April 10, 1847, Pres. James Knox Polk (q.v.) appointed Trist, the chief clerk of the State Department, as his executive agent to negotiate a peace with Mexico. Although Polk would have preferred sending Secretary of State James Buchanan (q.v.) on the mission, he did not want to have the secretary away from Washington for an extended period during a time of crisis and decided on Trist instead. The office of chief clerk was a fairly important one in that era since it was essentially, in today's context, the undersecretary of state's position. After a second front had successfully been opened at Veracruz (q.v.), Trist accompanied Gen. Winfield Scott (q.v.). Trist's instructions were to arrange a peace as soon as the army's progress convinced the Mexicans to come to the negotiation table. At first, his relations with Scott were contentious; Scott feared the civilian official would interfere with his military operations. The two began to pass acrimonious notes back and forth between intermediaries. By the end of May 1847, however, the diplomat and the general had become fast friends, partly because Scott made amends by sending the temporarily indisposed Trist a jar of guava marmalade from his private stores.

Trist, who carried with him to Mexico a draft treaty written by the State Department, was a determined man, bent on accomplishing a mission he knew would be difficult to complete with the proud Mexicans. In July, Scott and Trist, along with some of Scott's general officers, agreed to attempt to bribe the Mexican strongman, Gen. Antonio López de Santa Anna (q.v.), into accepting U.S. peace terms, an effort that quickly failed. After the fall of the capital in September 1847, Polk grew restless with Trist's lack of progress. Under pressure at home for terms even more favorable than those originally planned, and fearing that Trist's presence with the army would convey to the Mexicans an undue American eagerness to end the war, the president sent an order to recall his envoy. The order arrived in Mexico City (q.v.) in the middle of November. Trist, who had made an opening with Mexican moderates that he felt had a chance for success, decided to disregard Polk's order and remain on the job. The diplomat was concerned that failure to treat with the moderates would reinforce the position of the radical *Puros* (q.v.) and result in a prolonged guerrilla (q.v.) campaign against American forces. He sent Polk a 65-page letter justifying his actions (which caused Polk to write in his diary that Trist was an "impudent and unqualified scoundrel") and continued to negotiate. On February 2, 1848, near Mexico City, Trist signed the Treaty of Guadalupe Hidalgo (q.v.), a document that ended the war, brought vast territories into the United States, and forever changed the nation's relations with its neighbor to the south. Trist returned to the United States and to an ungrateful president. Not only was he without a job, the administration refused to even pay his official expenses in Mexico—a situation that a subsequent Congress would correct to Trist's satisfaction. *See also* GUADALUPE HIDALGO, TREATY OF; THORNTON, EDWARD.

TROUSDALE, WILLIAM (1790–1872). Col. William Trousdale commanded the 14th Infantry Regiment, which participated in the southern campaign under Gen. Winfield Scott (q.v.). The 14th Infantry was one of the regiments authorized by the 10 Regiment Bill (q.v.) in February 1847 and was made up of men from Illinois, Tennessee, and Louisiana. Trousdale saw action as its commander in the battles of Churubusco (q.v.) and Chapultepec (q.v.). For his leadership during the assault on Chapultepec Castle, Trousdale won a brevet to brigadier general.

TURNBULL, WILLIAM (1800–1857). William Turnbull graduated ninth in the West Point class of 1819 and entered the army as an artillery (q.v.) officer. In the 1830s, he joined the topographical engineers (q.v.). In the war in Mexico, Major Turnbull was chief topographical engineer on the staff of Gen. Winfield Scott (q.v.). Turnbull participated in Scott's campaign from Veracruz (q.v.) to Mexico City (q.v.). For gallantry in action he received brevets to lieutenant colonel for Contreras and Churubusco (q.v.) and colonel for Chapultepec (q.v.). After the war, Turnbull remained on active duty until his death in 1857.

TUXPAN, VERACRUZ. Tuxpan was a shallow river port 140 miles north of Veracruz (q.v.) a few miles up a river of the same name. Along with the port of Alvarado (q.v.), which was captured by the Home Squadron (q.v.) in early April, Tuxpan was one of the last ports on the Gulf coast to still fly the Mexican red, white, and green tricolor after the fall of Veracruz in March 1847. Situated on the left bank of the river, Tuxpan was defended by eight guns located at several strong points (La Peña, La Palmasola, Hospital Hill) between the Gulf and the town. These positions and the town itself were garrisoned by about 400 troops under the command of Gen. Martín Perfecto de Cos (q.v.). After the surrender of Veracruz and the capture of Alvarado, Commo. Matthew Calbraith Perry (q.v.) began planning an attack on Tuxpan. Forming a 1,500-man force and a flotilla of some 15 ships, Perry entered the river on April 17. Bombarding the Mexican gun positions as he proceeded upstream, Perry then dropped off landing parties to assault each fort. At La Peña, the *Spitfire*, under Comdr. Josiah Tattnall (q.v.) and with Commodore Perry aboard, received heavy musket fire, wounding Tattnall and three of his officers. General Cos abandoned Tuxpan without a fight, however, and Perry proceeded to occupy it. After securing all military articles of value for his squadron and destroying the remainder, Perry's occupation force evacuated Tuxpan on April 22, 1847.

TWIGGS, DAVID EMANUEL (1790–1862). When Gen. Zachary Taylor (q.v.) moved the main body of his army by sea to Corpus Christi (q.v.) in the summer of 1845, he sent Col. David Emanuel Twiggs (q.v.) overland with his Second Dragoons. At Corpus Christi during the winter of 1845–1846, Twiggs was the second-ranking regular officer after Taylor. When Taylor moved his army south to the Rio Grande (q.v.) in the spring of 1846, Twiggs's unit led the army's order of march. After the battles of Palo Alto (q.v.) and Resaca de la Palma (q.v.) in May 1846, Twiggs—who had been in the army over 35 years and had seen previous action in the War of 1812 and the First Seminole War—was promoted to brigadier general on the same congressional orders that made Taylor a major general. After taking Matamoros (q.v.), Taylor designated Twiggs military governor of the city. At Monterrey (q.v.), Twiggs temporarily relinquished command due to illness. There his division saw action in the attacks on the north and east of the city and suffered high casualties.

Twiggs later transferred to the southern theater and was one of Gen. Winfield Scott's (q.v.) three division commanders (along with William Jenkins Worth [q.v.] and Robert Patterson [q.v.]) during the Veracruz (q.v.) landings. After the surrender of the port city, Scott chose Twiggs to lead the march from Veracruz to Jalapa (q.v.). On arriving ahead of the rest of the army at Cerro Gordo (q.v.), Twiggs made a hasty decision to attack Gen. Antonio López de Santa Anna's (q.v.) position with his division. This attack did not occur, however, because of the arrival of General Patterson, who overturned Twiggs's decision to wait for Scott and the remainder of the American forces. During the two-day battle, Twiggs led his division against strong resistance on the Mexican left flank, suffering severe casualties but eventually taking Santa Anna's main position on the high ground east of Cerro Gordo village. Twiggs subsequently participated in the battles in the Valley of Mexico (q.v.): Contreras (q.v.) (known to the Mexicans as Padierna), Molino del Rey (q.v.), and Chapultepec (q.v.). After the occupation of Mexico City (q.v.), Scott sent Twiggs back to Veracruz in December 1847 to be the commander of that department. After the war with Mexico, Twiggs remained in the army, and at the start of the Civil War, he commanded the Department of Texas. In 1861, he surrendered federal weapons and property to Confederate forces to accept a major generalcy in the Confederate army.

Like Zachary Taylor, Twiggs was not known as a brilliant officer. Winfield Scott respected Twiggs's loyalty, his long service and combat experience, his toughness and durability under hard field conditions, and the admiration many of his men held for the "Bengal Tiger," as they often called him. But Scott recognized Twiggs's shortcomings, judging him lacking in battlefield acumen and clearly unqualified to command an independent army. Few officers during that era, however, including Zachary Taylor, had ever commanded more that a few hundred troops at one time; they were experienced in small unit tactics (q.v.), often fighting Indians, nothing more. So Scott's criticism of Twiggs, although probably accurate, did not make the old soldier unique for his time.

TWIGGS, LEVI (d. 1847). Maj. Levi Twiggs, U.S. Marine Corps (q.v.), was second in command of the marine battalion (commanded by Lt. Col. Samuel E. Watson [q.v.]) that joined Gen. Winfield Scott's (q.v.) army in Puebla (q.v.). In the assault on Chapultepec Castle (q.v.), Twiggs was killed leading a composite 120-man unit of marines and volunteer army soldiers from Gen. John Anthony Quitman's (q.v.) division. Major Twiggs was the only marine officer in the battalion killed in action during the campaign.

U

UGARTE, MAURICIO (1803–1853). As Col. Stephen Watts Kearny's (q.v.) Army of the West (q.v.) advanced toward Santa Fe (q.v.), New Mexico's (q.v.) governor Manuel Armijo (q.v.) appealed to Mauricio Ugarte, *comandante general* of Chihuahua (q.v.), for reinforcements that were not forthcoming. After Santa Fe had been occupied by Kearny's forces, rumors arose that Ugarte was marching northward with troops to regain the New Mexican capital. Although he had, in fact, left Chihuahua with that intent, he aborted his mission in El Paso (q.v.) because of rumors which had reached him of a much inflated estimate of U.S. troops in Santa Fe.

URAGA, JOSE LOPEZ. As a colonel, José López Uraga commanded a brigade under Gen. Pedro de Ampudia (q.v.) in the defense of Monterrey (q.v.). Uraga had a key mission to man the defenses of the citadel, the fortification known by Taylor's troops as the "Black Fort" (q.v.). Uraga also commanded units under Gen. Mariano Arista (q.v.) in the battles of Palo Alto (q.v.) and Resaca de la Palma (q.v.) and under Gen. Antonio López de Santa Anna (q.v.) in the battle of Cerro Gordo (q.v.).

URREA, JOSE (1797–1849). In March 1836, shortly after the battle of the Alamo (q.v.) at San Antonio (q.v.), Texas (q.v.), over 300 American rebels surrendered to Gen. José Urrea near the town of Goliad. After Urrea sent a message to his superior, Gen. Antonio López de Santa Anna (q.v.), urging clemency for the prisoners, he turned them over to a subordinate, Lt. Col. Nicolás de la Portilla. Santa Anna, in reply to Urrea's communication, ordered Portilla to execute the prisoners, and Portilla carried out Santa Anna's order. The incident came to be known as the Goliad Massacre.

During the war with the United States, Urrea and his several thousand regular troops and *rancheros* (q.v.) participated in Gen. Antonio López de Santa Anna's campaign in northeastern Mexico. Urrea was based in Tula. Units under his command operated along the route between Camargo (q.v.) and Monterrey (q.v.), ambushing American convoys that resupplied Gen. Zachary Taylor's (q.v.) army.

February 1847 was a period of heightened Mexican guerrilla activity. That month, Urrea led a particularly brutal attack on a 110-wagon supply train near Ramos (q.v.) in which nearly 50 teamsters were killed; the attack became known as the Ramos Massacre. In another action, he and Gen. Antonio Canales (q.v.) mounted an offensive against Lt. Col. William Irvin's (q.v.) three companies of the Second Ohio Volunteers at Marín (q.v.), which was located on the road between Cerralvo (q.v.) and Monterrey (q.v.); the Americans were able to defend themselves and the town successfully. On the eve of the battle of Buena Vista (q.v.), which took place on February 22 and 23, Urrea was assigned the task of raiding to the east of the Sierra Madre Oriental, disrupting the American lines of communication, and threatening Monterrey. When he and his cavalry and *rancheros* struck Camargo (q.v.) on February 18, Col. Samuel Ryan Curtis (q.v.)—a West Pointer who commanded a regiment of Ohio volunteers (q.v.) and who was assigned as governor and commandant of Camargo—not only held off Urrea's forces but led his men in pursuit to Ramos, thereby opening Taylor's line of communications. As a result of these and other encounters, Curtis requested 50,000 volunteers from Washington in March 1847.

The following November, General Santa Anna reassigned Urrea from Tula because of Urrea's inability to maintain good relations with the local authorities and rally the local citizenry against the American invaders. *Also see* GUERRILLAS; *RANCHEROS*.

V

VALENCIA, GABRIEL (1799–1848). Maj. Gen. Gabriel Valencia, an early ally of Gen. Antonio López de Santa Anna (q.v.) who later became one of his most bitter enemies, moved his Army of the North (q.v.) from San Luis Potosí (q.v.) to Mexico City (q.v.) to reinforce the defenses of the capital in July 1847. The following August 18, during the deployment of units to the southwest of the capital, Valencia disobeyed Santa Anna's order to withdraw his troops north of San Ángel. Valencia decided to remain in a defensive position on a ridge near the Padierna (q.v.) ranch several miles north of the village of Contreras (q.v.). At dawn on August 20, American forces enveloped Valencia's position and completely routed the Mexicans, enraging Santa Anna, who threatened to shoot Valencia on sight. *See also* CONTRERAS AND CHURUBUSCO, BATTLES OF.

VALLEJO, MARIANO GUADALUPE (1808–1890). In the 1830s, Mariano Guadalupe Vallejo, along with J. B. Alvarado and José María Castro (q.v.), led the provincial revolt against Mexican authority in California (q.v.). Founder of Sonoma, Vallejo was a large landowner in northern California and at one point commander (*comandante general*) of the Californio forces in that area. Despite his prominence and particularly his pro-American stance, Vallejo was captured in June 1846 in a raid by American settlers led by Ezekiel Merritt (q.v.). Mariano Vallejo's brother, a pioneer winegrower in the Sonoma region, was also captured in the raid.

VALLEY OF MEXICO. The Valley of Mexico is an approximately 5,000-square-mile elliptical valley located in south-central Mexico. Since the time of the Aztecs, the valley has been the center of power for the Mexican people. It remains that today, since Mexico City (q.v.), the nation's capital, was built over the ruins of the old Aztec seat of power, Tenochtitlán. At the time of the war with Mexico, Gen. Winfield Scott (q.v.) faced numerous strong points within the valley before he could close with and capture Mexico City. From the day his lead troops under Gen. David Twiggs (q.v.) descended into the valley on August 10, 1847, until Mexico City fell, Scott's army had to endure over a month of tough fighting. The month of combat is often referred to as the campaign in the Valley of Mexico, a campaign that ended the war when Mexico City capitulated on September 14, 1847.

VANDERLINDEN, PEDRO. Dr. Pedro Vanderlinden was Gen. Antonio López de Santa Anna's (q.v.) chief medical officer. Before the battle of Buena Vista (q.v.), Santa Anna used him as a courier to take a letter to Gen. Zachary Taylor (q.v.) in which Santa Anna told Taylor that the American troops were surrounded by over 20,000 Mexicans and that he should surrender. Taylor's reply, probably written by his aide, the erudite Capt. William Bliss (q.v.), was "I beg leave to say that I decline acceding to your request."

VAZQUEZ, CIRIACO (1794–1847). One of Gen. Antonio López de Santa Anna's (q.v.) brigade commanders at the battle of Cerro Gordo (q.v.), Brig. Gen. Ciriaco Vázquez was placed in command of defenses on the strategic Telegraph Hill (q.v.). Considered a brave, strong leader, Vázquez was mortally wounded during the American assault on this position on April 18, 1847.

VERACRUZ, VERACRUZ. Veracruz, the principal port of Mexico at the time of the war (as it is today), was blockaded (q.v.) by the U.S. Navy (q.v.) under Commo. David E. Conner (q.v.) after May 1846. The fortified city was surrounded by a wall along which strong points were built. A straight, mile-long segment of the wall paralleled the coast, with Fort Santiago (q.v.) at the southeastern tip of the wall and Fort Concepción (q.v.) at the northwestern tip. The wall then extended inland in a semicircle. Opposite Veracruz, in the Gulf of Mexico, the separate San Juan de Ulúa (q.v.) fortress on the Gallega Reef dominated the entrance to the city.
   Gen. Winfield Scott (q.v.) chose Veracruz as the site for launching the second front in the war. Besides the critical need to have the port for subsequent resupply of his army as it marched inland, Veracruz controlled the entrance to the National Highway (q.v.), the major route that left from the port and ran through the mountains to Mexico City (q.v.). After a long buildup and months of cooperative planning with the navy, Scott chose March 9, 1847, as the date for the amphibious landing. On that date, with the navy furnishing transport (to supplement the army's) and fire support, Scott safely landed over 10,000 troops in a period of hours at Collado Beach (q.v.) a few miles south of Veracruz. It was the largest amphibious operation of U.S. forces before North Africa in 1942.
   Rather than conduct a costly frontal assault against the well-fortified city and fort (which some of his senior officers urged him to do to move quickly out of the coastal yellow fever [q.v.] zone into the mountains), Scott decided to besiege the city. He

invested Veracruz on three sides with his infantry and subjected it to an intense artillery (q.v.) bombardment beginning on March 22. Scott's troops were reinforced on the 24th with fire from heavy naval guns that had been emplaced on shore. On March 27, the commander of Veracruz raised a white flag, surrendering not only the city but also the fort of San Juan de Ulúa. On the 29th, the Mexican troops marched out, and Scott's army began an occupation that lasted until the last American troops were withdrawn on August 1, 1848, several months after the ratification of the Treaty of Guadalupe Hidalgo (q.v.) that ended hostilities between Mexico and the United States.

VICTORIA, TAMAULIPAS. Gen. Zachary Taylor (q.v.) made the town of Victoria one of the strong points of his occupation army after the battle of Monterrey (q.v.). Taylor sent Gen. John Anthony Quitman (q.v.) to occupy the isolated town, capital of the state of Tamaulipas, in December 1846. Taylor later quartered there himself and continued the buildup of forces in Victoria until the number in that location grew to nearly 5,000 troops. While in Victoria, Taylor received word from Gen. Winfield Scott (q.v.) to divert approximately 9,000 men from his army in the northern theater to reinforce Scott's army as it prepared for the Veracruz (q.v.) expedition.

VIGA GATE. The Viga Gate, a police and customs house located along a canal by that name, was one of the strong points protecting Mexico City (q.v.). As Gen. Winfield Scott's (q.v.) troops neared the capital, they discovered that the Viga Gate was one of five gates, or *garitas*, as the Mexicans called them (the others were San Cosmé [q.v.], Belén [q.v.], Niño Perdido [q.v.], and San Antonio [q.v.]), protecting Mexico City against attacks over likely avenues of approach from the west, south, and east.

VIGAS. *See* LAS VIGAS.

VIGIL Y ALARID, JUAN BAUTISTA. As Col. Stephen Watts Kearny's (q.v.) Army of the West (q.v.) advanced toward Santa Fe (q.v.), New Mexico (q.v.), Gov. Manuel Armijo (q.v.) appealed to Mauricio Ugarte (q.v.), *comandante general* of Chihuahua (q.v.), for reinforcements. When these were not sent and Armijo was unable to rally the support of the citizenry, he fled southward, leaving Juan Bautista Vigil y Alarid to serve as acting governor. By default, it was Vigil who greeted Kearny and agreed to the annexation of New Mexico by the United States.

VILLA DE GUADALUPE. *See* GUADALUPE HIDALGO, TREATY OF.

VOLTIGEUR REGIMENT. One of the 10 regular regiments created by Congress in February 1847, the Voltigeurs were designed as a highly mobile light infantry regiment that specialized in skirmishing. It contained an equal number of foot and cavalry soldiers. Theoretically, mules were to transport artillery (q.v.) pieces, and, when necessary, foot soldiers would hitch rides on the horses of the cavalry. In practice, however, the Voltigeurs fought as regular infantry, distinguishable from other regiments only by their gray uniforms. In the battles in the Valley of Mexico (q.v.), they fought as part of Brig. Gen. George Cadwalader's (q.v.) brigade in Gen. Gideon Pillow's (q.v.) division. Commanded initially by Col. Timothy Patrick Andrews (q.v.), the Voltigeur Regiment was led by engineer Lt. Col. Joseph E. Johnston (q.v.) during the fierce fighting as the Americans stormed Chapultepec Castle (q.v.). The regiment also fought at Churubusco (q.v.) and Molino del Rey (q.v.).

VOLUNTEERS. Upon declaration of war in May 1846, the regular U.S. Army numbered fewer than 10,000 men. The war bill, passed by Congress and signed by Pres. James Knox Polk (q.v.) on May 13, authorized the government to raise 50,000 volunteers to enlarge the active force. These new units, authorized in late spring of 1846, were state volunteer units, in contrast to the army units that were formed by the 10 Regiment Bill (q.v.). Initially, the administration decided to call up 20,000 of the authorized number from the southern and western (present-day midwestern) states, enrolling 25,000 additional volunteers in the Northeast but delaying their call to active service. The volunteers were obligated to serve for 12 months. New regiments were organized and officers appointed at the state level; general officers, however, were to be appointed by the federal government. Volunteer soldiers went to regular units or to the newly formed volunteer regiments. The size of the volunteer regiments ranged from 700 to 1,200 men each. When the bulk of the first group of volunteers completed their obligatory year of service in May 1847, 90 percent of them chose to depart the war zone to return to the United States. Intermittently, the administration made numerous other calls for volunteers throughout the war, specifying, unlike in the initial call, that they serve for the duration of the conflict.

Relations between the regulars and volunteers during the

war were often strained and at times outright combative, the regulars generally looking down on the volunteers as unkempt and undisciplined soldiers. One of the most serious problems with the volunteer soldiers was their lack of decent sanitation, which caused a higher rate of disease among their ranks than among those of the regular troops. There were frequent problems with the volunteers' treatment of Mexican nationals, especially in Gen. Zachary Taylor's (q.v.) army in the northern campaign during the first months of the conflict. Some historians have attributed the unruly conduct of the volunteers partly to Taylor's casual leadership style, which failed to impose strict discipline on his subordinates. While problems with volunteers persisted throughout the war, they appeared less pronounced in the commands of Gen. Winfield Scott (q.v.) and Gen. John Ellis Wool (q.v.), both known as strict disciplinarians. Although many instances arose of volunteers fleeing in the face of the enemy during battle (at the battle of Buena Vista [q.v.] there were approximately 1,500 deserters [q.v.]), several reports were made of volunteers performing bravely in combat. Their performance, as is universally true with inexperienced soldiers, varied widely depending on their unit leadership. Col. Jefferson Davis (q.v.), a West Pointer and a stern disciplinarian, trained his regiment of Mississippi volunteers to a high level of proficiency. Most critics give Davis's Mississippi Rifles (q.v.) high marks for their bravery and competence at Monterrey (q.v.) and Buena Vista. The Mississippi Rifles were by most accounts the only volunteer unit at Buena Vista that did not at least one time turn away and retreat in the face of Mexican charges during the battle. Volunteers participated in all battles of the war with the exception of the first two, Palo Alto (q.v.) and Resaca de la Palma (q.v.), which took place before volunteers were called. Buena Vista was fought by an army under Zachary Taylor that consisted of over 80 percent volunteer soldiers (only the artillery [q.v.] batteries were regular units in the battle). Despite the number of desertions, the volunteers' performance at Buena Vista still drew high praise from General Taylor. Volunteers later fought throughout the southern campaign of General Scott.

W

WAINWRIGHT, ROBERT A. (1814–1866). Robert A. Wainwright graduated from West Point in 1835 and was commissioned in the infantry. During his initial years of service, he served both in infantry and artillery (q.v.) billets before becoming an ordnance officer in 1838. During the war with Mexico, in 1847 and 1848, 1st Lt. Robert Wainwright commanded the Saltillo (q.v.) Ordnance Depot. In the Civil War, he served the Union in various ordnance positions and received a brevet to colonel in 1865 for faithful service to the Ordnance Department. Wainwright died as a lieutenant colonel on active duty in 1866.

WALKER, ROBERT JOHN (1801–1869). During the last days of the John Tyler administration, Senator Robert John Walker lobbied in Congress for the annexation of Texas (q.v.). When efforts for annexation were at the point of being stalled, Walker proposed a compromise giving the incoming president, James Knox Polk (q.v.), the prerogative of deciding whether to require Texas's agreement to a House resolution on annexation or to initiate new negotiations with Texas on the issue. President Tyler, after conferring with the president-elect, made the decision himself and forwarded the House resolution. President Polk made Walker his secretary of the treasury. Walker, a war hawk, became the Polk administration's most ardent expansionist. He opposed the September 1847 peace treaty with Mexico on the grounds that it did not demand sufficient territory.

WALKER, SAMUEL HAMILTON (d. 1847). Before locating in Texas (q.v.) in 1836, Samuel Hamilton Walker fought in the Indian wars in Georgia and Florida. In 1839, on a trip to New York to buy arms for the Republic of Texas, he met the famed gunsmith Samuel Colt. After examining a revolver that Colt had developed, Walker recommended several modifications that Colt adopted and later named the *Walker Colt*. On his return to Texas, Walker fought against Mexican General Adrián Woll's (q.v.) invasion of Texas. He participated in the Mier (q.v.) Expedition, was captured, and thereafter was released by the Mexicans.

In the early days of the war with Mexico, Captain Walker's company of Texas Rangers (q.v.) was the first volunteer unit in Gen. Zachary Taylor's (q.v.) army when it was fighting along the Rio Grande (q.v.) in the spring and summer of 1846. Since Walker knew the terrain in the river valley, Taylor used him for scouting missions before and after the battles of Palo Alto (q.v.) and Resaca de la Palma (q.v.). Walker performed a dangerous mission for Taylor when he returned from Point Isabel (q.v.) in early May, passing through Mexican lines to get intelligence on conditions in Fort Brown (q.v.). In the Monterrey (q.v.) campaign, Walker's unit engaged in a short but violent battle with a force of Mexican lancers on September 21, 1846. After Monterrey fell to the Americans, he mustered out of his Texas volunteer regiment as a lieutenant colonel.

Walker next became a regular army captain in a newly organized unit, the Regiment of U.S. Mounted Rifles. After joining Gen. Winfield Scott's (q.v.) army in the southern theater, Walker's unit—part of Col. John C. ("Jack") Hays's mounted regiment of Texas Rangers—continued to lead reconnaissance and raid missions in advance of the main body of troops. In June 1847, Walker was sent to Las Vigas (q.v.) (on the road between Jalapa [q.v.] and Perote [q.v.]) to clear guerrillas (q.v.) from the town. Walker surprised the guerrilla force and laid waste to the town on June 20, allowing the resupply convoys from Veracruz (q.v.) to proceed on the National Highway (q.v.). Walker, a highly popular officer among his men, was killed in a similar raid on October 9, 1847, when his unit charged in advance of the main force at Huamantla (q.v.).

WALNUT SPRINGS. *See* EL BOSQUE DE SANTO DOMINGO.

WAR DEPARTMENT, U.S. In 1846, the War Department was led by William Marcy (q.v.), a former Democratic governor of New York and political ally of Pres. James Knox Polk (q.v.). The department consisted of Marcy, the bureau chiefs on his executive staff and their officers, as well as the army in the field. On Marcy's executive staff were Bvt. Brig. Gen. Roger Jones (q.v.), adjutant general; Lt. Col. George H. Talcott (q.v.), chief of the ordnance bureau; Maj. Gen. Thomas S. Jesup (q.v.), quartermaster general; Brig. Gen. Nathan Towson (q.v.), paymaster general; Dr. Thomas Lawson (q.v.), surgeon general; Bvt. Brig. Gen. George Gibson (q.v.), commissary general of subsistence; Col. Joseph G. Totten (q.v.), chief engineer; and Col. John J. Abert (q.v.), chief topographical engineer. Each of these specialty bureaus or branches had officers assigned to army staffs in the field. At the beginning of the war, there were, for example, approximately 40 regular or combat engineers (q.v.) assigned to the army, several dozen topographical engineers, and 31 quartermaster officers, all assigned to the staffs of army commands. Each of the other specialty bureaus had a limited number of officers authorized in each army unit.

The bureau chiefs often stayed in their jobs for decades (Jesup was named quartermaster general in 1818, Jones began

serving as adjutant general in 1825, Towson had served continuously as paymaster general since 1822, and Gibson was appointed commissary general of subsistence in 1818) and saw
many secretaries of war come and go. They were powerful men
in their own right and were reluctant to take direction from
Marcy, who had a reputation as a weak administrator. President Polk, an intensely active executive who wanted to be involved in all details of the management of war with Mexico,
frequently bypassed the secretary to deal directly with the bureau chiefs. Before 1844, the chiefs sent their budget requests
directly to the secretary of the treasury who in turn would sub-
mit them to Congress. Polk insisted that Secretary Marcy consolidate all bureau requests for his review and adjustments
before they were forwarded to the treasury.

Polk became intimately involved in personnel matters of the
War Department; if he wanted an officer promoted he would
not hesitate to call Adjutant General Jones to the White House
to discuss the matter. Polk would also interfere with operational aspects of the war, making decisions about the movement of supplies and troops in the theaters of war in Mexico
and involving himself in various details of the campaigns. In
many aspects, Polk served as his own war secretary during the
conflict with Mexico and at times as his own general in chief.

The army was led by the commanding general (often called,
in the mid-19th century, the general in chief). At the outset of
the war with Mexico, this position was filled by Maj. Gen. Winfield Scott (q.v.) who, as the ranking officer in the army, had
been in the billet since 1841. The army consisted of eight regiments of infantry, two regiments of dragoons (q.v.) (horse soldiers), four regiments of artillery (q.v.), and, after May 1846,
one company of engineers. The actual strength of the army at
the start of the war was under 10,000 men, although the total
number authorized by law was 780 commissioned officers and
16,218 enlisted men. Much of the force was spread out over
frontier posts in the West, and its experience had been limited
to Indian campaigns. The most seasoned officers, such as Scott
and Brig. Gen. Zachary Taylor (q.v.), had no experience leading
units larger than a regiment (800–1,000 men). Many of the company and field grade officers in the 1840s were West Point graduates and were dedicated, well-respected leaders who knew
how to train and fight soldiers in combat. Trained on the model
of the European armies of the day, the regular U.S. army in
1846 was considered a professional fighting force. In the first
battles of the war along the Rio Grande (q.v.), Zachary Taylor

had only regular units in his army, and their victories at Palo Alto (q.v.) and Resaca de la Palma (q.v.) attested to the regular army's professionalism at the time. As the army increased by thousands of regulars and volunteers (q.v.) from 1846 to 1848, the effectiveness of units varied, depending on the quality of leadership. *See also* ARTILLERY; ENGINEERS; MARCY, WILLIAM; MEDICAL AND HEALTH ISSUES; POLK, JAMES KNOX; QUARTERMASTER DEPARTMENT; SCOTT, WINFIELD; TAYLOR, ZACHARY; TEN REGIMENT BILL; VOLUNTEERS.

WARD, JAMES N. (1823–1858). A West Point graduate of 1845, James N. Ward was a second lieutenant of infantry in the Third Regiment of Infantry in the war with Mexico. Ward participated in the Veracruz (q.v.) operation and was wounded during the assault on the heights at Cerro Gordo (q.v.). For gallantry in action at Cerro Gordo, he received a brevet to first lieutenant. After being wounded, he became ill and was evacuated from the theater. Ward died on active duty as a regular captain with the Third Infantry in 1858.

WARNER, WILLIAM H. (1812–1849). After a brief period with the First Artillery, William H. Warner, West Point graduate of 1836, became a topographical engineer (q.v.). He accompanied Gen. Stephen Watts Kearny (q.v.) to California (q.v.) and was severely wounded in the battle of San Pascual (q.v.) in December 1846. For his performance at San Pascual, Warner received a brevet to captain. After the war, he participated in the exploration and survey of railroad (q.v.) routes through the Sierra Nevada mountains, where he was killed in a fight with Indians in September 1849.

WARNER'S RANCH, CALIFORNIA. After marching from Fort Leavenworth (q.v.) to Santa Fe (q.v.), Gen. Stephen Watts Kearny (q.v.) and his Army of the West (q.v.) continued westward to California (q.v.). Kearny, with the famed frontiersman Christopher ("Kit") Carson (q.v.) guiding his force, arrived at the frontier settlement of Warner's Ranch on December 2, 1846. The site was a trading post located about 1,000 miles west of Santa Fe and 50 miles northeast of San Diego (q.v.). Like Sutter's Fort (q.v.), it served as a way station for settlers coming from the east and south. While there, Kearny confirmed earlier reports of the California revolt. After a two-day stay, Kearny departed for San Diego and en route fought Andrés Pico's (q.v.) Californios (q.v.) at the small village of San Pascual (q.v.). The Californios called the area around Warner's Ranch "Agua Caliente."

WARREN, WILLIAM BARTON. William Barton Warren, an Illinois lawyer, was a battalion commander in Col. John J. Hardin's (q.v.) First Regiment of Illinois Volunteers under Gen. John E. Wool (q.v.). In November 1846, Wool placed Warren's battalion in charge of Monclova (q.v.) and the supply base there. Later, Warren commanded the garrison at Saltillo (q.v.) while Gen. Zachary Taylor's (q.v.) army prepared for and fought the battle of Buena Vista (q.v.) a few miles to the south at Angostura (q.v.) Pass. Before and during that battle, Taylor, concerned about the safety of Warren's small command and fearful that Mexican forces would go around his defenses at the pass and take Saltillo, returned to the city to check on Warren's status. Warren successfully accomplished his mission of protecting Saltillo during the battle. At the end of the war, he mustered out of the service as a lieutenant colonel.

WASHINGTON, JOHN MACRAE (1797–1853). A West Point graduate in 1817, Capt. John Macrae Washington and his light artillery (q.v.) battery (called "flying artillery," since the six-pounder guns in these batteries were rapidly moved on the battlefield by horse) joined Gen. John E. Wool's (q.v.) force in San Antonio (q.v.) in September 1846 before Wool deployed to Mexico. Washington and his battery—specifically Company B, Fourth Regiment of Artillery—distinguished themselves on the right flank of the army at Angostura (q.v.) Pass in the battle of Buena Vista (q.v.) on February 22 and 23, 1847. Washington won a brevet to lieutenant colonel at Buena Vista and later served as governor of Saltillo (q.v.). After the war, as he was en route to duty on the West Coast in 1853, Washington, along with 181 officers and men, was washed overboard and drowned when the steamer *San Francisco* encountered a fierce storm at the mouth of the Delaware River.

WATSON, SAMUEL E. In the war with Mexico, U.S. Marine Corps brevet lieutenant colonel Samuel E. Watson, who had been on active service since the War of 1812, commanded a regiment of marines hastily organized by the corps in June 1847. Because the unit was undermanned for a regiment, it was redesignated a battalion when it arrived at Veracruz. Watson's battalion was assigned to Brig. Gen. Franklin Pierce's (q.v.) brigade, which departed Veracruz for the front in July 1847. In Puebla, a battalion of volunteers was joined with Watson's command, and it was redesignated again, this time as a brigade. Assigned to Brig. Gen. John Quitman's (q.v.) division, Watson led the unit through the campaign in the Valley of Mexico (q.v.), including the assault on Chapultepec Castle (q.v.) Watson fell ill after Chapultepec and was evacuated to Veracruz where he died November 16, 1847. *See also* MARINE CORPS, U.S.

WATSON, WILLIAM H. (d. 1846). Lt. Col. William H. Watson commanded the Baltimore-Washington Battalion of volunteers (q.v.) in Gen. Zachary Taylor's (q.v.) army in the march on Monterrey (q.v.). The Baltimore Battalion, as it was commonly called, was brigaded with a regiment of regular army troops in Brig. Gen. David Twiggs's (q.v.) division of regulars. In the attack on the city of Monterrey on September 21, 1846, the division was temporarily commanded by Lt. Col. John Garland (q.v.). When it came under withering fire from Mexican fortified positions in the eastern part of the city, both Garland and Watson lost control and became separated from their men. The division took a heavy toll, suffering more casualties in the first hours of the attack on September 21 than the rest of the army suffered during three days of fighting to take the city. In addition to the many soldiers lost that morning, several senior officers were wounded or killed, including Colonel Watson.

WEAPONRY. The origin of the weapons used by the United States and Mexico during the war was largely European. Mexico relied not only on European-designed weaponry but also on European suppliers for arms for its troops during the war. Mexico did manufacture some of its arms for the war, but most were purchased abroad, whereas the United States manufactured its own. The Mexican army, unlike the American, used lances to arm some of its cavalry units, a European military tradition carried to Mexico by Spain. Another difference in Mexican weapons and equipment was the Mexican guerrilla's use of the lasso to snare unsuspecting American soldiers, especially stragglers on lonely mountain trails.

The weapons technology mentioned here was present in Mexico in the 1840s, but the nation's resources and supply system were generally not sufficient to supply arms to its field armies at the same level and in the same quality as those supplied to the U.S. Army at the time. So, though the following comments apply as well to Mexico, the reader is reminded that ordnance available in Mexico was generally inferior to that available to American forces.

The basic soldier's weapon for both sides in the United States-Mexican War was the smoothbore, flintlock musket. A musket was defined as a smoothbore shoulder arm that was muzzleloaded and at least 53 inches or longer. Although the rifle had appeared generations before the war (the Kentucky or Pennsylvania rifles were used on the frontier), the U.S. Army still used the musket in the 1840s, as did the Mexican army. The two reasons for this were that the musket cost less than a rifle to manufacture, and it was easier to train a recruit to load and fire a musket. A well-trained soldier could fire four rounds per minute with a smoothbore musket, compared with one to two rounds per minute with a rifle or rifled musket. The flintlock musket fired by having a sharp piece of flint (gripped by the cocking mechanism, or cock) strike a steel frizzen. The frizzen then fell forward, and sparks ignited a "pan" of gunpowder. This powder burned through a hole in the musket's barrel and ignited the main powder charge, firing the weapon. The most commonly issued smoothbore musket used by the U.S. Army in the war was the Model 1822 Flintlock. Although the smoothbore musket's effective range was less than 100 yards, its large ball (up to .69 caliber in some models) could be deadly when fired from close formations at massed enemy troops. A major disadvantage of the flintlock weapon was that the external ignition system—with its cock, frizzen, and pan assembly— was susceptible to moisture and often malfunctioned in damp weather. The supply of muskets at the start of the war was plentiful. The U.S. arsenals at Harpers Ferry, Virginia, and Springfield, Massachusetts, had turned out sufficient muskets by the summer of 1846 to arm all of the new units authorized by Congress.

The rifled musket and rifle, both of which provided the infantryman accuracy at several hundred yards, were not widely used by U.S. regular units in Mexico. The government issued them on a limited basis, however, and they were occasionally issued by the states or ordered by wealthy officers for volunteer units. A rifled musket had the characteristics of a musket (it was loaded at the muzzle and had to be at least 53 inches long) but had rifling in the barrel. A rifle was a shoulder-fired weapon with a rifled barrel, 40 to 52 inches long, which could be muzzle or breechloaded. Most rifles used in the war were muzzle loaders, including the ones Col. Jefferson Davis (q.v.)

ordered for his famed First Regiment of Mississippi Rifles (q.v.), which distinguished itself at the battle of Buena Vista (q.v.) by employing rifle fire from a V formation. A disadvantage of the muzzle-loaded rifle was that it took longer for a soldier to ram the tightly fitting patched ball into the rifled barrels than it did to load a smoothbore musket. This problem was largely eliminated in the breech-loading rifle, which also appeared during the war years but again was not widely issued. It was further minimized with the invention after the war, in 1849, of the conical-shaped bullet with a hollow base (called the "Minié ball") by the French army officer, Capt. Claude Minié. A popular rifle in the 1840s was the muzzle-loaded U.S. Percussion Rifle, Model 1841. The effectiveness of this weapon was enhanced by its ignition system, which used a watertight percussion cap containing fulminate of mercury. It was ignited by a hammer striking it rather than by a spark from a flintlock. The Model 1841 is touted as the most accurate rifle firing a round bullet ever manufactured. By the end of the war, U.S. arsenals had manufactured thousands of rifles, although most of these never reached the hands of troops in the war zone.

Pistols were used by the U.S. Army in the war with Mexico, as they are today, as personal protection weapons, primarily by officers. The U.S. Flintlock Pistol, Model 1836, was widely issued by the army in the 1840s. Officers frequently ordered pistols made to their own specifications. These were often percussion cap pistols with barrels that equaled in technology those being developed in rifles at the time. The revolver appeared in some American units as well, notably in Col. John Coffee ("Jack") Hays's (q.v.) Regiment of Texas Rangers (q.v.). One of Hays's officers, Capt. Samuel Walker (q.v.), had worked with arms maker Samuel Colt on the design of the revolver. After the war with Mexico broke out, Colonel Hays ordered 1,000 Colt-Walker "six-shooters" and issued two to each man in the regiment.

Knives and bayonets were extensively used as personal weapons during the war. The Texas Rangers carried large knives with wide, 10-inch-long blades—knives whose prototype was designed by James Bowie in the 1830s. These "Bowie knives," which often served as coup de grace weapons, were also carried by volunteers (q.v.) in Davis's Mississippi Rifles. Bayonets were carried by most infantry soldiers in Mexico. They were detachable blades affixed to the muzzle end of muskets or rifles for use in hand-to-hand fighting. Most bayonets used during the war were the angular or socket bayonet. Some units, such as the Mississippi Rifles, were equipped with the wide-bladed sword or saber bayonet. In a war fought mostly with smoothbore muskets, fighting was commonly at close quarters, and officers and soldiers often wrote accounts of having to "go to the bayonet" during infantry assaults. When possible, commanders used artillery (q.v.) to prevent having to close with the enemy. Although Gen. Zachary Taylor (q.v.) cautioned his men constantly about the need to rely on the bayonet, his victories at Palo Alto (q.v.) and Buena Vista resulted from the effective use of artillery. *See also* ARTILLERY.

WEBSTER, DANIEL (1782–1852). A former secretary of state and powerful Whig (q.v.) senator from Massachusetts in the 1840s, Daniel Webster was a leading opponent of Pres. James Knox Polk's (q.v.) war policy. Unlike the Whig radicals, the moderate Webster voted to appropriate funds to support the army once fighting had begun. He nevertheless continued in the Senate to condemn Polk's policies on the grounds that American military action in Mexico was pure aggression. On February 15, 1848, Webster introduced in the Senate a pair of resolutions declaring that the United States would not acquire any additional territory as a result of the war. At a time when the war was won on the field of battle and an expansionist public awaited word of a favorable treaty of peace giving the nation vast new territories, Webster's proposal drew little congressional support.

WHIGS. Opposition to the war with Mexico probably came from a minority of the public in 1846, but it was a strong and vocal minority and included many substantial political figures in the country. Pro- and anti-war factions existed in both the Whig and Democratic Parties at the time. The strongest supporters of the conflict, which some critics dubbed "Mr. Polk's War" because of Pres. James Knox Polk's (q.v.) expansionist policies, came from the president's own Democratic Party. There were some dissident Democrats, however, men such as the prominent South Carolinian, John C. Calhoun (q.v.), who opposed the war. Most of the war's opponents came from various factions within the Whig Party in the northern states. The dominant group among these was the conservative Whigs, sometimes referred to as moderate Whigs, represented by political leaders such as Henry Clay (q.v.), Daniel Webster (q.v.), and former Speaker of the House Robert Charles Winthrop (q.v.). The conservative Whigs opposed Polk's war policy because, in their view, it was a policy of pure aggression, a position also taken by the Whig congressman from Illinois, Abraham Lincoln (q.v.).

The "radical" or "conscience" Whigs, politicians such as former president John Quincy Adams (q.v.) and Ohio congressman Joshua R. Giddings, condemned the war as immoral and contended that the "hidden agenda" of its supporters was the expansion of slavery. The Whig Party was thus the center of opposition during the debates about the war in Congress. When actual votes were taken on war bills, however, only the radical Whigs voted against the administration; most opponents of the war feared the political consequences of being called unpatriotic for voting against sending support to endangered troops in the field. A major irony of the war was that the two principal generals whom Polk used to prosecute the war, Winfield Scott (q.v.) and Zachary Taylor (q.v.), were both Whigs. Taylor was elected president as the Whig candidate in 1848, and Scott won the Whig nomination for president in 1852, although he was defeated in the general election.

WHITING, DANIEL POWERS. A graduate of West Point in 1832, Daniel Whiting entered the army as a second lieutenant of infantry. In the war with Mexico, Captain Whiting commanded Company K of the Seventh Infantry in the defense of Fort Brown (q.v.), fought in the battle of Monterrey (q.v.), participated in the siege of Veracruz (q.v.) and fought at Cerro Gordo (q.v.). He was brevetted major for gallantry at Cerro Gordo. During the war, Whiting used skills he developed in topographical drawing classes at West Point to sketch Gen. Zachary Taylor's (q.v.) army camp at Corpus Christi (q.v.) and other camp scenes and Mexican landscapes during the campaign in northern Mexico. Although many of his wartime sketches were lost when a steamboat sank on the Mississippi, some survived the war. Five of Whiting's sketches or watercolors—considered among the most beautiful images of Mexico to be produced during the war—were published and offered to the public as *Army Portfolio* in 1847. Whiting remained in the army after the war with Mexico and retired during the Civil War as a lieutenant colonel in 1863.

WHITING, HENRY M. (1821–1853). Henry M. Whiting was 14th in the West Point class of 1842. As a second lieutenant at the beginning of the war with Mexico, he served in Gen. Zachary

Taylor's (q.v.) army in northern Mexico. For gallantry in action at Buena Vista (q.v.), Whiting won a brevet to first lieutenant. He remained on active duty after the war and died as a first lieutenant assigned to Fort Brown (q.v.), Texas (q.v.), in 1853.

WILCOX, CADMUS MARCELLUS (1824–1890). Cadmus Marcellus Wilcox graduated along with George McClellan (q.v.) and Thomas Jackson (q.v.) in the West Point class of 1846 and served as a lieutenant in the war with Mexico. Initially, he served with Gen. Zachary Taylor's (q.v.) army but was soon transferred to the southern theater under Gen. Winfield Scott (q.v.), where he participated in the Veracruz (q.v.) operation. As aide-de-camp to Maj. Gen. John Anthony Quitman (q.v.), Wilcox fought in the attack against Chapultepec Castle (q.v.), where he earned a brevet to first lieutenant for leading a storming party. After the war, he remained in the U.S. Army until the advent of the Civil War, when he resigned his federal commission. He joined the Confederate army and rose to general officer.

During his federal service, Wilcox became a military historian, compiling a pamphlet, "Rifles and Rifle Practice," in 1859 and translating from the French "Austrian Infantry Evolutions of the Line" the same year. Wilcox's *History of the Mexican War*, published in 1892, was a detailed narrative account of the campaigns of the war. It is particularly useful to historians because it includes appendices with complete listings of all officers (regular and volunteer) of the army and navy who served in the war.

WILLIAMS, WILLIAM G. (1801–1846). As a captain in the topographical engineers (q.v.), William G. Williams, West Point graduate of 1824, was chief "topog" in Gen. Zachary Taylor's (q.v.) army from July 6, 1846, until he was killed at the battle of Monterrey (q.v.) on September 21, 1846.

WILLIAMSON, JOHN (1806–1849). John Williamson graduated from West Point in 1826 and was commissioned in the artillery (q.v.). Later serving in the Ordnance Department, Captain Williamson was assigned as an ordnance officer at Veracruz (q.v.) in the war with Mexico in 1847 and 1848. He died on active duty in 1849.

WILMOT, DAVID (1814–1868). Congressman David Wilmot, a Democrat from Pennsylvania, authored the Wilmot Proviso, which would have prohibited slavery in territory acquired from Mexico. It was tacked onto a bill authorizing a $2,000,000 payment to the Mexican government for signing a peace treaty with the United States. The entire bill was defeated in the Senate in August 1846. The Wilmot Proviso was again discussed in conjunction with the 10 Regiment Bill (q.v.), legislation authorizing the creation of 10 new regiments for the army. The bill passed in February 1847 but it did not include the Wilmot Proviso. When the United States approved the peace treaty with Mexico, the Wilmot Proviso, proposed this time by Senator Baldwin from Connecticut, again failed to pass.

WILMOT PROVISO. *See* WILMOT, DAVID.

WILSON, HENRY (d. 1872). Lt. Col. Henry Wilson led four companies of the U.S. First Infantry Regiment to Point Isabel (q.v.) on May 7, 1846, before the first major battle of the war at Palo Alto (q.v.). Later that month, he and his battalion, along with two companies of Louisiana volunteers (q.v.), crossed the Rio Grande (q.v.) to take the town of Barita (q.v.). In June 1846, Gen. Zachary Taylor (q.v.) ordered Wilson to take a contingent of four infantry companies, an artillery (q.v.) unit, and a company of Texas Rangers (q.v.) to protect the town of Reynosa (q.v.), 41 miles northwest of Matamoros (q.v.) on the right bank of the Rio Grande. He fought and was brevetted colonel at Monterrey (q.v.).

Wilson later transferred to Gen. Winfield Scott's (q.v.) army, commanding the Fourth Brigade in Brig. Gen. David Twiggs's (q.v.) First Division. He served as military commander of Veracruz (q.v.) until he was relieved by Brig. Gen. James Bankhead in December 1847.

WINSHIP, OSCAR (1817–1855). After his graduation from West Point in July 1840, Oscar Winship joined the Second Dragoons (q.v.). In the war with Mexico, he was assistant adjutant general in Brig. Gen. Gideon Pillow's (q.v.) brigade in 1846–1847 and in Brig. Gen. Franklin Pierce's (q.v.) brigade in 1847. He participated in the battles of Palo Alto (q.v.), Resaca de la Palma (q.v.), Contreras and Churubusco (q.v.), Molino del Rey (q.v.), and Mexico City (q.v.). Winship received three brevets: to captain for gallantry at Palo Alto and Resaca de la Palma; to captain for staff work, and to major for gallantry at Churubusco. After the war, he remained in the army and assisted in the translation of

Jomini's *Précis de l'Art de la Guerre* in 1853. Winship died while on active duty in 1855.

WINTHROP, ROBERT CHARLES (1809–1894). A conservative Whig, Robert Charles Winthrop of Massachusetts was a leading member of the House of Representatives during the war years. He opposed James Knox Polk's (q.v.) war policy on the grounds that it was imperialistic and against U.S. traditions of justice for other peoples. He was far from radical in his opposition to the administration, however, voting for legislation to strengthen the army and favoring Polk's diplomatic efforts to bring an early peace. Winthrop, along with Daniel Webster (q.v.) and other conservative Whigs, did not want to appear unpatriotic by opposing support for American soldiers in the field once they had been exposed to risk. Winthrop's faction of the Whig Party generally allied with the Southern Whigs, an association which earned them the name Cotton Whigs.

WOLL, ADRIAN (1795–1875). Before the war with Mexico, the French-born Adrián Woll served Gen. Antonio López de Santa Anna (q.v.) as a general in the Texas (q.v.) campaign. He led a Mexican force into Texas in a raid on San Antonio (q.v.) in the autumn of 1842. In June 1844, as commander of Santa Anna's forces on the Rio Grande (q.v.) frontier, Woll informed Sam Houston (q.v.), president of Texas, that hostilities had been resumed and warned him that any Texan found within one league of the Rio Grande would be given a summary trial and executed.

WOOD, ROBERT CROOKE (d. 1869). Robert Crooke Wood, who joined the army as an assistant surgeon in 1825, served in the war with Mexico as surgeon to the Fifth Infantry and as commander of the hospital at Point Isabel (q.v.). Toward the war's end, he took charge of the hospital at Jackson Barracks, New Orleans (q.v.), Louisiana. Wood was close to his father-in-law, Maj. Gen. Zachary Taylor (q.v.), and a constant correspondent of Taylor's during the first year of the war with Mexico. During the Civil War, in June 1862, Wood became assistant surgeon general of the army, serving in Louisville, Kentucky, where he was in charge of the Western Department for the army Medical Department until the war's end.

WOOD, THOMAS JOHN (1823–1906). After graduating from West Point as fifth in his class of 1845 where he was Ulysses S.

Grant's (q.v.) first roommate, Thomas John Wood served during the first part of the war with Mexico as a topographical engineer (q.v.); on October 19, 1846, he became an officer with the Second Dragoons. He participated in the battles of Monterrey (q.v.) and Buena Vista (q.v.) and was brevetted to first lieutenant for the latter battle. During the Civil War, he became a Union general.

WOOD, WILLIAM MAXWELL. Commo. John D. Sloat (q.v.), commander of the U.S. Navy's (q.v.) Pacific Squadron (q.v.), was under specific orders in 1846 not to commence hostile action without a formal declaration of war. Through William Maxwell Wood, the Pacific Squadron's surgeon who was en route home overland through Mexico, Sloat received word on May 17, 1846, of Capt. Seth Thornton's (q.v.) ambush (the April 25, 1846 incident along the border that would result in a Congressional declaration of war) by a courier Wood had dispatched from Guadalajara. Subsequently, Wood dispatched another message to Sloat from Mexico City (q.v.), informing the commodore of the battles of Palo Alto (q.v.) and Resaca de la Palma (q.v.). It was Wood's confirmation of these hostilities, which reached Sloat by courier on June 17, that finally convinced the naval commander that he had the authority to commence offensive operations without a formal war message from the administration. Sloat proceeded to take Monterey (q.v.), California (q.v.), on July 7, 1846.

WOOL, JOHN ELLIS (1795–1869). At the beginning of the war with Mexico, John Ellis Wool was the third-ranking officer in the army behind the only other active regular generals, Winfield Scott (q.v.) and Edmund Pendleton Gaines (q.v.). In May of 1846, Secretary of War William Marcy (q.v.) gave Wool, a veteran of the War of 1812, the mission of recruiting and training volunteers (q.v.) for deployment to Mexico. These troops, organized as the Centre Division (q.v.), were to lead an expedition to Chihuahua (q.v.), a major Mexican city 200 miles south of El Paso (q.v.). Since it was in Gen. Zachary Taylor's theater, Wool would come under his command. Wool led his division in a long and arduous march from San Antonio (q.v.) to Monclova (q.v.), where he spent the month of November 1846. During the march and stay in Monclova, the division suffered constantly from a lack of discipline among the unruly volunteers, which necessitated strong and unpopular measures from the highly professional and stern Wool. The general's firm leadership, despite opposition from some of his volunteer officers, resulted in the formation of a fighting unit that soon proved its mettle in combat.

While in Monclova, Taylor canceled Wool's orders to take Chihuahua and sent him instead to Parras (q.v.). As the Mexican forces under Gen. Antonio López de Santa Anna (q.v.) threatened the Americans south of Saltillo (q.v.), Wool was sent east to reinforce Taylor's army. As Santa Anna approached, Taylor placed Wool in charge of positioning troops and preparing the defensive battle plan at Buena Vista (q.v.). During this American victory on February 22 and 23, 1847, Wool distinguished himself in one of the major battles of the war. Continuing his army career after the war, Wool had commands on both coasts and served in major Union commands during the first two years of the Civil War. Promoted to major general in 1862, Wool retired the following year and died in 1869.

WORDEN, JOHN LORIMER (1818–1897). John Lorimer Worden, a naval officer, served aboard the storeship *Southampton* in the Pacific during the war with Mexico. During the Civil War, he commanded the USS *Monitor* in its battle with the CSS *Virginia*. This naval engagement in Hampton Roads, Virginia, was the first battle of ironclads in U.S. military history.

WORTH, WILLIAM JENKINS (1794–1849). William Jenkins Worth's army career began when he was commissioned a first lieutenant in the 23d Infantry in March 1813. In the War of 1812, Worth served under Winfield Scott (q.v.), who became a mentor for the young officer. At Lundy's Lane, where Scott's leadership brought him national acclaim, Worth received a crippling wound and a brevet promotion to major. After the war and for the next 30 years, Worth remained a close friend and professional associate of Scott. Although vain and pompous, he was widely considered one of the most professional officers in the army. Brevetted brigadier general in 1842, Worth joined Zachary Taylor's (q.v.) army in northern Mexico and distinguished himself in the critical western assault at Monterrey (q.v.). After transferring to his old chief Winfield Scott's army in the southern theater, Worth played a key role in the Veracruz (q.v.) operation, leading his division ashore in the first wave of the amphibious landing. After the fall of Veracruz, Scott appointed Worth military governor of the city, a duty he carried out in his customary professional manner. When the American army began its campaign into the interior, Scott sent Brig. Gen.

David Twiggs's (q.v.) division out first to lead the army. The decision hurt the proud Worth, who felt he had earned the honor given Twiggs, and thereafter his long-standing friendship with Scott began to cool. In reserve at Cerro Gordo (q.v.), Worth's division was the first to enter Puebla (q.v.) on May 15, 1847. Scott appointed Worth as military governor of the city while the army occupied it over the summer. During this occupation, Scott reprimanded Worth because of controversial orders he published as governor affecting Puebla's citizens. The reprimand fueled the growing estrangement between the two generals.

In the campaign in the Valley of Mexico (q.v.), Worth's division played key roles in the battles at Contreras and Churubusco (q.v.), Molino del Rey (q.v.), and the Cosmé Gate (q.v.) in the final assault on Mexico City (q.v.). Again piqued because his division was not the first to enter the central plaza when the city fell, Worth, after performing as a valiant and respected combat leader in the historic six-month campaign, became embittered when Scott wrongly accused him of giving inaccurate information to the press concerning the last battles around Mexico City. In a letter he sent through channels to Pres. James Knox Polk (q.v.), Worth accused Scott of maligning his character and military reputation. Scott, in turn, brought charges against Worth of insubordination for statements Worth made in the letter. Although the cross accusations in the Scott-Worth dispute were eventually dismissed, their relationship was never repaired. Worth returned to the United States and took command of the Department of Texas in November 1848. He lived less than a year, dying in May 1849 of cholera—the disease that took so many of the war's soldiers. Texans honored Worth when they named the city of Fort Worth.

WRIGHT, GEORGE S. (1803–1865). An 1822 West Point graduate, Capt. George S. Wright served in the Eighth Infantry Regiment during the war. He won brevets to major and lieutenant colonel for his actions at the battles of Contreras and Churubusco (q.v.), and Molino del Rey (q.v.). At Molino del Rey, Wright led a composite force of 500 men to storm the western front of the Mexican defenses. It was a costly attack. Eleven of the 14 officers in the attack fell dead or wounded, including Wright, who was severely wounded. Wright survived the war and later rose to brigadier general of U.S. Volunteers in the Civil War. He perished when a ship he was on, the steamer *Brother Jonathan*, wrecked on July 30, 1864, off the California (q.v.) coast.

WYNKOOP, FRANCIS M. (d. 1857). Col. Francis M. Wynkoop commanded the First Regiment of Pennsylvania Volunteers during the war. At the battle of Cerro Gordo (q.v.), Wynkoop's regiment came under Gen. Gideon Pillow's (q.v.) command. Pillow—widely criticized for his lack of sound judgment, dishonesty, and poor leadership—argued with Wynkoop over the placement of troops almost at the instant Pillow's command was supposed to cross the assault line to attack the Mexican right flank. When Pillow subsequently disappeared in the middle of the fighting, Colonel Wynkoop and other commanders tried desperately to contact him to receive orders for their units. This delay meant that Wynkoop was unable to effect a timely reinforcement of the main attack of Pillow's force, which resulted in considerable confusion and near disaster on the American left flank. Later Wynkoop commanded the garrison at Perote (q.v.) before being ordered by Gen. Winfield Scott (q.v.) to join the main body in Puebla (q.v.). Wynkoop survived the war and died in Pennsylvania in 1857.

X

XOCHIMILCO, LAKE. Lakes Texcoco (q.v.), Chalco (q.v.), and Xochimilco were the three lakes surrounding Mexico City (q.v.) in the Valley of Mexico (q.v.). Gen. Winfield Scott (q.v.) chose the route south around Lakes Chalco and Xochimilco for his approach to the capital.

Y

YELL, ARCHIBALD (1797–1847). Archibald Yell served as governor of Arkansas from 1840 to 1844, resigning to wage a successful campaign for the U.S. Congress. In the spring of 1845, Yell served as one of Pres. James Knox Polk's (q.v.) private agents to report on the situation in Texas (q.v.) during the time its annexation was under consideration. When the war with Mexico broke out, he left Congress, without resigning, to serve as colonel and commander of the Regiment of Arkansas Mounted Volunteers. Yell secured this position, not through the usual method of being selected by the state (the procedure for all volunteer officers below general officer rank) but through the political intervention of Secretary of War William Marcy (q.v.). His division commander, Gen. John Ellis Wool (q.v.), held him in low esteem as an officer, charging that Yell was totally incapable of training and instilling discipline in the unruly Arkansans.

Before the battle of Buena Vista (q.v.), Yell violated his orders from Wool to observe extreme caution during a scouting mission south of Saltillo (q.v.) to Encarnación (q.v.). The colonel galloped his troops as fast as he could, almost leading them into an ambush by a superior-in-numbers Mexican cavalry force. When General Taylor ordered Yell to withdraw his regiment from Encarnación to the Angostura (q.v.) Pass, Yell panicked under pressure from Mexican forces and burned valuable supply stores. Yell's panicky withdrawal, however, confused the Mexican commander. Gen. Antonio López de Santa Anna (q.v.), thinking he was facing the American main body, assumed that the withdrawing troops would not be well established at Angostura when he arrived with his army two days later. Yell's mounted troops, along with other units, had the mission of defending the American base at the Hacienda Buena Vista during the second day of the battle. When Mexican cavalry under Brig. Gen. Julián Juvera (q.v.) attacked the position, many of Yell's volunteers (q.v.) fled the scene. Yell stayed and fought, by most reports bravely, and was killed in the action.

YELLOW FEVER. Despite the many bloody engagements of the war with Mexico, the deadliest enemy of the U.S. forces in the conflict was disease. Of all the diseases to strike American soldiers during the war, yellow fever was the most dreaded. Called "the black vomit," "yellow jack," or, in Spanish, *el vómito*, yellow fever took more casualties than enemy fire. At the time, its cause (a mosquito-born infectious disease) was completely unknown, and almost as little was known about its treatment. Of the almost 14,000 men who died in the war, only about 1,500 died of combat wounds. The remainder, over 12,000 men, died of disease, and many of these fell from yellow fever. Yellow fever affected not only the men who suffered it but also Gen. Winfield Scott's (q.v.) campaign strategy (q.v.). To protect his troops and his mission, he planned his invasion of Veracruz before the start of the yellow fever season (it began in the April-May period on Mexico's Gulf coast). His strategy called for the invasion and siege to be completed in time to move his army out of the coastal zone before yellow fever struck. Delayed because of logistical problems, the operation—originally planned for January—took place in early March. Despite the delay, Scott still managed to take the city and move his army to the highlands before the advent of the dangerous season. *See also* MEDICAL AND HEALTH ISSUES.

YERBA BUENA, CALIFORNIA. The small village of Yerba Buena and its sister village, San Francisco, were merged in January 1847 to become San Francisco. *See also* SAN FRANCISCO.

YUCATAN. Because the Yucatán Peninsula had long followed a semi-independent course from the Mexican government, the United States initially exempted the region from the naval blockade (q.v.) it implemented before the war started. Although Yucatán was later included, it did not play a significant part in the war between Mexico and the United States. El Carmen Island, between the state of Tabasco and the peninsula of Yucatán, was briefly occupied by the U.S. Navy in December 1846. *See also* CASTE WAR OF YUCATAN.

Z

ZACATEPEC MOUNTAIN. Zacatepec Mountain (sometimes referred to as Zacatepec Hill) was a prominent terrain feature southwest of Mexico City (q.v.) on the western side of the pedregal (q.v.) lava field. It was used by Mexican guerrillas (q.v.) for a concealed location from which to attack American forces crossing the pedregal. Gen. Winfield Scott (q.v.) and some of his staff, including Capt. Robert E. Lee (q.v.), also used it to observe the movement of Mexican forces at Padierna (q.v.) and to make tactical plans before the battle there on August 20, 1847.

ZEILIN, JACOB. First Lt. Jacob Zeilin, the ranking marine officer on the Pacific Squadron's (q.v.) frigate *Congress* (q.v.) in 1846 and 1847, participated in the defense of Monterey (q.v.), the capture of Los Angeles (q.v.), the action at La Mesa (q.v.), the San Gabriel River (q.v.) crossing, the bombardment of Guaymas (q.v.), the fight at St. Joseph's (q.v.), and the occupation of Mazatlán (q.v.). He was promoted to captain in September 1847 and was brevetted to major for San Gabriel and La Mesa. Zeilin became the commandant of the Marine Corps in June 1864 and served in that capacity until March 1867.

ZUNI. The Zuñi was one of a number of Indian tribes that had been harassing settlements in the Rio Grande (q.v.) Valley and along the headwaters of the river before the arrival of Brig. Gen. Stephen Watts Kearny's (q.v.) army in New Mexico (q.v.). Col. Alexander Doniphan (q.v.) and his subordinates, acting on orders from Kearny, arranged peace treaties with many of these tribes, including the Zuñi, in the fall of 1846.

Bibliography

Essay

For most Americans, the conflict between the United States and Mexico is an "unknown war," overshadowed by the Civil War that followed only 13 years later. Despite the fact that material on the Civil War has far outpaced that on the conflict with Mexico, the latter has generated a vast body of primary materials and hundreds of published books, articles, and pamphlets. Many official documents printed by order of Congress are available in most research libraries and special collections. In addition, manuscript material is available in the National Archives and in several other key collections, some of which are listed in the bibliography.

In the case of Mexico, the war is far from forgotten, having had a central impact on the national experience. Primary documents in Mexico can be found in the Ministerio de Guerra y Marina (War and Navy) as well as in the Archivo Nacional in Mexico City. Another source for researchers is the Museo Nacional de las Intervenciones in Mexico City. This museum, located in the Convent of San Mateo at the site of the battle of Churubusco, has extensive displays and literature relating to the U.S. invasion of Mexico in 1846–1848, in addition to material on other interventions by foreign powers.

The war with Mexico was the first in U.S. history in which professional journalists traveled with the invading armies. Especially significant in this respect was George W. Kendall of the New Orleans *Picayune,* who accompanied both generals Taylor and Scott. His accounts, along with illustrations of key events, were sent to New Orleans and later distributed throughout the United States. In each of the major cities occupied by the invading armies, an English-language newspaper was established, in part to entertain the troops and to provide news from home but also to report events in the garrisons and on the battlefront. Mexican newspapers also published accounts of military operations and political developments.

317

Military and political figures recorded their thoughts during the conflict or later reflected on events and conditions in their memoirs. By far the most powerful and instructive of such publications is the highly detailed diary of Pres. James K. Polk, edited by Milo Milton Quaife and published in 1910 in four volumes. The president was interested in every detail of military operations but was also driven by an overpowering political suspicion that created constant conflicts with commanders in the field. Both Zachary Taylor and Winfield Scott published letters and memoirs, also with very strong political overtones. Other senior officers, including John A. Quitman and Gideon J. Pillow, gave their accounts of events. Philip St. George Cooke authored a fascinating journal describing his march west with the Mormon Battalion. Young officers who would later play key roles in the Civil War, including Ulysses S. Grant, Robert E. Lee, George B. McClellan, and George Gordon Meade, left personal accounts of their experiences in Mexico. Others, less famous in the course of history, kept journals or wrote letters that give today's reader a personal view of conditions in Mexico. Among the most interesting and entertaining of recent publications are the letters of Napoleon Jackson Tecumseh Dana, edited by Robert H. Ferrell (1990), and the journal of Capt. Franklin Smith, a member of the Mississippi Volunteers, edited by Joseph E. Chance (1991). In moving prose, Smith describes the boredom and fear of service in the eternally muddy or dusty "hellhole" of Camargo—a staging center for Taylor's northeastern campaign. It was not the enemy's bullet but impure food and water, the mosquito, and unsanitary conditions that took their deadly toll on the American army and brought such graphic descriptions from the pen of Captain Smith.

Many of the U.S. enlisted men, especially the volunteers, kept diaries or wrote letters to their friends and families back home. Often without political motive and little concerned with military tactics, many of these writings give powerful human dimension to the struggle. Several excellent, newly discovered accounts of enlisted soldiers have been brought out in recent years. One of the most graphic is the short *Mexican War Diary* of Thomas D. Tennery, an Illinois volunteer who served for one year (1846–1847). Severely wounded in the battle of Cerro Gordo, Tennery describes his experiences in a Jalapa hospital where he witnessed constant suffering and death. Eventually he recovered from his wounds, returned to Illinois, and lived a long life. One of the most recent first-hand publications (1995) is an account by Frederick Zeh, a German immigrant to Pennsylvania who, in December 1846, enlisted in a Mountain Howitzer and Rocket Company of the regular army. Zeh participated in several battles in the Valley of Mexico but gives little attention to tactics and battle plans. Instead, his matter-of-fact entries reveal complex aspects of life within an army that was composed almost one half of immigrants like himself. A truly unique publication is the diary of Susan Shelby Magoffin, a young girl who married a successful Santa Fe trader and accompanied him and the American forces on their march to Santa Fe and Chihuahua. Magoffin describes people she encountered and hardships she endured in a most proper and sophisticated manner. Firsthand accounts have been found throughout the United States, and many have been published in state or regional journals, only a few of which are listed in our bibliography. Undoubtedly many yet-to-be-discovered manuscripts of participants continue to collect dust in attics throughout the United States and Mexico.

Mexican political and military leaders recorded their interpretation of events relating to the conflict. Antonio López de Santa Anna entitled his autobiography *The Eagle* and filled it with eloquent pronouncements of self-praise. Luis Gonzaga Cuevas laments in his memoirs the harsh impact of the war on the Mexican nation. The outstanding liberal intellectual and political leader, Guillermo Prieto, wrote *Memorias de Mis Tiempos, 1828 a 1853,* which includes his views of the war. Probably the most poignant account, however, is that of José María Roa Barcena, *Recuerdos de la invasion norteamericana (1846–1848) por un joven de entonces.* A significant publication, edited by Ramón Alcaraz, *Apuntes para la historia de la guerra entre México y los Estados Unidos,* resulted from a conference of Mexican generals and other participants held in Querétaro in 1847. The work of Alcaraz was translated into English two years later by Albert C. Ramsey and published under the title, *The Other Side: or Notes for the History of the War between Mexico and the United States.* In 1989, an extensive collection of writings by Mexican participants was edited and translated by Cecil Robinson under the title *The View from Chapultepec: Mexican Writers on the Mexican-American War,* thus giving the English reader further contact with the ideas of Mexican participants and historians.

There was no Matthew Brady in 1846; photography was in its infancy. Visual images were produced by artists such as Nathaniel Currier, Carl Nebel, and numerous talented (or not-so-talented) amateurs among the ranks of the invading forces. Most illustrations reflected a romantic view of the exotic country and the battles. The lithograph came to be the most popular means of mass visual representation, with hundreds reproduced in newspapers, magazines, and a growing number of books on the war. Ronnie C. Tyler discusses the significance of illustrations in *The Mexican War: A Lithographic Record* (1973) but warns that they must be subjected to careful historical criticism. A unique and truly outstanding collection of drawings and watercolors was produced by Sam Chamberlain, an enlisted man who participated in a number of events in the course of the war. Forgotten for many years, portions of Chamberlain's *Confessions* and selected illustrations were published by *Life* magazine in 1956. Although his imagination often outpaced reality, the author-artist left a graphic impression of military events and especially of social aspects of the invasion. He did not shrink from the fact that U.S. forces often committed atrocities against the Mexican population. An outstanding collection of his sketches and watercolors can be found in William H. Goetzmann, *Sam Chamberlain's Mexican War: The San Jacinto Museum of History Paintings,* published in 1993 by the Texas State Historical Association.

Although lithographs, etchings, and watercolors were the most commonly used means to depict visual materials, a new device was in its early stages. In 1839, the daguerreotype, the earliest form of photography, was developed, and the United States–Mexican War was the first conflict to be recorded by photographers. In 1989, many of these daguerreotypes were published, along with numerous other illustrations, in an outstanding addition to the visual history of the war called *Eyewitness to War* (Sandweiss et al., 1989). The plates capture the famous correspondent George Kendall of the New Orleans *Picayune,* an aging and seemingly tormented President Polk, and young American volunteers massed in the streets of Saltillo before the bloody exchange at Buena Vista. Another excellent source of sketches, paintings, daguerreotypes, maps, and reproductions of bulletins and popular posters of the war period is Time-Life Books' *The Mexican War.*

Our bibliography presents a highly selective list of secondary works from the extensive scholarship produced on the subject. To date there is no general history of the war that equals the two-volume work by Prof. Justin Harvey Smith (1919). Smith occasionally makes provocative judgments, but his researched facts and general interpretations have stood up over time. His study is likely to remain the foremost published work on the war. The Justin Smith Transcript Collection in the Latin American Collection at the University of Texas, Austin, remains one of the important sources for research materials.

Other general works that are valuable include K. Jack Bauer, *The Mexican War 1846–1848* (1974); John S. D. Eisenhower, *So Far from God: The U.S. War with Mexico, 1846–1848* (1989); Charles L. Dufour, *The Mexican War: A Compact History: 1846–1848* (1968); and Robert Selph Henry, *The Story of the Mexican War* (1950). Of these, Bauer's is widely considered the most thoroughly researched and is probably the most valuable general work on the war after Smith's. Selected publications relating to specific military campaigns are listed in the bibliography, as are biographies of key political leaders and commanders. A number of writers have studied naval operations. Samuel Eliot Morison deals with conditions in the Gulf of Mexico in his outstanding biography of Matthew C. Perry. The most complete treatment of naval operations can be found in K. Jack Bauer's *Surfboats and Horse Marines,* published in 1969.

Finally, two citations in the bibliography are especially helpful as a guide to the literature on the war with Mexico. The volume by Seymour V. Connor and Odie B. Faulk, *North America Divided: The Mexican War, 1846–1848* (1971), has a detailed "Analytical Bibliography" categorized in a manner helpful to the researcher or general-interest reader. More recently (1981), Norman E. Tutorow published *The Mexican-American War: An Annotated Bibliography* which lists manuscript collections, government documents by source and title, National Archives record groups, and a thorough, annotated, and cross-referenced listing of published accounts of the war, both secondary and primary. Tutorow also includes a breakout by state for volunteer unit histories and appendices of maps, statistical charts, chronologies, regimental organizations, and an excellent index. A new bibliography of considerable value is Jenkins Garrett, *The Mexican–American War of 1846–1848: A Bibliography of the Holdings of the Libraries,* published by the University of Texas at Arlington in 1995.

Selected Bibliography

Manuscript Collections

National Archives (Washington, D.C.):
  Department of State (Record Group 59)
  Navy Department (Record Group 80)
  Office of the Adjutant General (Record Group 94)
  Office of the Judge Advocate General (Record Group 153)
  Office of Naval Records and Library (Record Group 45)
  Office of the Secretary of War (Record Group 107)

U. S. Army Commands (Record Group 98)
U. S. Marine Corps (Record Group 127)

Mexican Documents (Mexico City):
Archivo Nacional
Ministerio de Guerra y Marina

Selected collections containing personal papers:
Bancroft Library, University of California
Chicago Historical Society
Library of Congress
Missouri Historical Society
New York Historical Society
University of Texas Archives
U. S. Military Academy Library
Western Americana Collection, Yale University

Printed Documents

U. S. Congress: Extensive documents were published by the 28th, 29th, and 30th Congresses, by both the Senate and House of Representatives. A listing may be found in K. Jack Bauer, *The Mexican War: 1846–1848*.
Bosh García, Carlos, *Material para la historia diplomática de México (México y los Estados Unidos, 1820–1848)*. México: Escuela Nacional de Ciencias Políticas y Sociales, 1957.
García, Genaro, ed. *Documentos inéditos o muy raros para la historia de Mexico*. 36 vols. Mexico: Bouret, 1905–1911.
Manning, William Ray (ed), *The Diplomatic Correspondence of the United States, Latin American Affairs*. 21 vols. Washington, D.C.: Carnegie Endowment for International Peace, 1932–39. (vols. 8 and 9.)

Newspapers

The American Eagle (Veracruz)
The American Pioneer (Monterrey, Nuevo León)
The American Star (Mexico City)
The Anglo Saxon (Chihuahua)
Californian (Monterey, California)
The Daily American Star (Mexico City)
Daily Picayune (New Orleans)
The Flag of Freedom (Puebla)
Niles National Register (Baltimore)

Participant Accounts

Alcaraz, Ramón, et al. *Apuntes para la historia de la guerra entre México y los Estados Unidos*. México: Payno, 1848. Translated and edited by Albert C. Ramsey, with notes, and published as *The Other Side: Or Notes for the History of the War between Mexico and the United States*. New York: Wiley, 1850.

Ampudia, Pedro de. *El Ciudadano General Pedro de Ampudia ante el tribunal respectable de la opinión publica, por los primeros sucesos ocurridas en la guerra a que nos provaca, decreta y sostiene de gobierno de los Estados Unidos de America*. San Luis Potosí: Imprenta del Gobierno, 1846.

Anderson, Robert. *An Artillery Officer in the Mexican War 1846–7. Letters of Robert Anderson, Captain 3rd Artillery, U.S.A*. Edited by Eba Anderson Lawton. New York: Putnam's, 1911.

Balbontin, Manuel. *La invasión americana, 1846 a 1848, Apuntes del subteniente de artillería*. México: n.p., 1883.

Barbour, Philip Norbourne, and Martha Isabella Hopkins Barbour. *Journals of the Late Brevet Major Philip Norbourne Barbour, Captain in the 3rd Regiment, United States Infantry and his wife Martha Isabella Hopkins Barbour, Written during the War with Mexico—1846*. Edited by Rhoda van Bibber Tanner Doubleday. New York: Putnam's, 1936.

Baylies, Francis. *A Narrative of Major General Wool's Campaign in Mexico, in the Years 1846, 1847 & 1848*. Albany, NY: Little, 1851. (Reprinted Austin, TX: Jenkins, 1975).

Beauregard, P. G. T. *With Beauregard in Mexico: The Mexican War Reminiscences of P. G. T. Beauregard*. Edited by T. Harry Williams. Baton Rouge: Louisiana State University Press, 1956.

Bliss, Robert S. "The Journal of Robert S. Bliss with the Mormon Battalion." *Utah Historical Quarterly* 4 (July–October 1931): 67–96, and 110–28.

Brooks, Nathan Covington. *A Complete History of the Mexican War: Its Causes, Conduct, and Consequences: Comprising an Account of the Various Military and Naval Operations, from Its Commencement to the Treaty of Peace*. Philadelphia: Griggs, Elliot, 1849. (New edition, Chicago: Rio Grande Press, 1965.)

Brewerton, George Douglas. *Overland with Kit Carson: A Narrative of the Old Spanish Trail in '48*. Lincoln: University of Nebraska Press, 1993.

Buhoup, Jonathan W. *Narrative of the Central Division, or, Army of Chihuahua, Commanded by Brigadier General Wool*. Pittsburgh: Morse, 1847.

Carleton, James Henry. *The Battle of Buena Vista with the Operations* of the *"Army of Occupation" for One Month*. New York: Harper, 1848.

Chamberlain, Samuel E. *My Confession*. New York: Harper, 1956. (*See also* Goetzmann, *Sam Chamberlain's Mexican War*.)

Cooke, Philip St. George. *Scenes and adventures in the army; or, romance of military life*. Philadelphia: Lindsey & Blakiston, 1857.

———. *The Conquest of New Mexico and California: An Historical and Personal Narrative*. New York: Putnam's, 1878.

———. *Cooke's Journal of the March of the Mormon Battalion, 1846–1847*. In Ralph P. Bieber, ed. *Exploring Southwestern Trails: 1846–1854*. The Southwest Historical Series (volume 7, pp. 65–240). Glendale, CA: Clark, 1938.

Coulter, Richard, and Thomas Barclay, Volunteers. *The Mexican War Journals of Private Richard Coulter and Sergeant Thomas Barclay, Company E, Second Pennsylvania Infantry*. Edited by Allan Peskin. Kent, OH: Kent State University Press, 1991.

Cuevas, Luis Gonzaga. *Porvenir de Mexico*. México: Jus, 1954. (Note: Section translated by Cecil Robinson in *The View from Chapultepec*, pp. 81–90.)

Curtis, Samuel Ryan. *Mexico under Fire: Being the Diary of Samuel Ryan Curtis 3rd Ohio Volunteer Regiment during the American Military Occupation of Northern Mexico: 1846–1847*. Edited by Joseph E. Chance. Fort Worth: Texas Christian University Press, 1994.

Dana, Napoleon Jackson Tecumseh. *The Mexican War Letters of Lieutenant Dana: 1845–1847*. Edited by Robert H. Ferrell. Lexington: University Press of Kentucky, 1990.

Davis, Jefferson. *Jefferson Davis. Private Letters 1823–1889*. Edited by Hudson Strode. New York: Harcourt, Brace & World, 1966.

Donnavan, Corydon. *Adventures in Mexico: Experienced during a Captivity of Seven Months in the Interior, etc*. Cincinnati: Robinson & Jones, 1847.

Downey, Joseph T. (Ordinary Seaman, USN). *The Cruise of the Portsmouth, 1845–1847: A Sailor's View of the Naval Conquest of California*. Edited by Howard Lamar. New Haven, CT: Yale University Press, 1958.

Duncan, John. "A Morgan County Volunteer." Edited by A. J. Henderson. *Journal of the Illinois Historical Society* 41 (1948): 383–99.

DuPont, Samuel Francis. *The War with Mexico; the Cruise of the U.S.S. Cyane during the Years 1845–48*, Annapolis, MD: U. S. Naval Institute Press, VIII (September 1882), pp. 419–37.

Edwards, Frank S. *A Campaign in New Mexico with Colonel Doniphan by Frank S. Edwards, a Volunteer*. Philadelphia: Carey & Hart, 1847.

Emory, William H. *Notes of a Military Reconnaissance, from Fort Leavenworth, in Missouri, to San Diego, in California, including part of the Arkansas, Del Norte, and Gila Rivers.* Thirtieth Congress, First Session, Ex. Doc. No. 41. Washington, DC: Wendell & Van Benthuysen, 1848. (Reprinted in *The United States Conquest of California*, New York: Arno, 1976.)

Ford, John Salmon. *Rip Ford's Texas.* Edited by Stephen B. Oates. Austin: University of Texas Press, 1963.

Frémont, John Charles. "The Conquest of California." *Century Magazine* 41 (April 1891): 917–27.

Frost, John. *The Mexican War and Its Warriors; Comprising a Complete History of All the Operations of the American Armies in Mexico: with Biographical Sketches and Anecdotes of the Most Distinguished Officers in the Regular Army and Volunteer Force.* New Haven, CT: Mansfield, 1848.

Fuber, George C. *The Twelve Months Volunteer: Or, Journal of a Private in the Tennessee Regiment of Cavalry, in the Campaign, in Mexico, 1846–7.* Cincinnati: James, 1848.

General Scott and His Staff: Comprising Memoirs of Generals Scott, Twiggs, Smith, Quitman, Shields, Pillow, Lane, Cadwalader, Patterson and Pierce, etc. Freeport, NY: Books for Libraries Press, 1848. (Reprinted 1970.)

Gibson, George Rutledge. *Over the Chihuahua and Santa Fe Trails, 1847–1848, George Rutledge Gibson's Journal.* Edited by Robert W. Frazer. Albuquerque: University of New Mexico Press, 1981.

Gibson, Thomas W. *Letter Descriptive of the Battle of Buena Vista, Written upon the Ground.* Lawrenceburgh, IN: Hall, 1847.

Giddings, Luther. *Sketches of the Campaign in Northern Mexico, in Eighteen Hundred Forty-six and Seven by an Officer of the First Ohio Volunteers.* New York: Author, 1853.

Grant, Ulysses S. *Personal Memoirs of U.S. Grant.* 2 vols. Edited by E. B. Long. New York: Webster, 1885.

Gregg, Josiah. *Diary and Letters of Josiah Gregg: Southwestern Enterprises, 1840–1847.* 2 vols. Edited by Maurice Garland Fulton with an introduction by Paul Horgan. Norman: University of Oklahoma Press, 1941–1944.

Griffin, John S. *A Doctor Comes to California: The Diary of John S. Griffin, Assistant Surgeon with Kearny's Dragoons, 1846–1847.* San Francisco: California Historical Society, 1943. (Reprinted in *The United States Conquest of California.* New York: Arno, 1976.)

Hartman, George W. *A Private's Own Journal.* Greencastle, PA: Robinson, 1849.

Henry, William Seaton. *Campaign Sketches of the War with Mexico.* New York: Harper, 1847. (Reprinted by Arno Press, 1973.)

Hitchcock, Ethan Allen. *Fifty Years in Camp and Field: Diary of Major General Ethan Allen Hitchcock U.S.A.* Edited by W. A. Croffut. New York: Putnam's, 1909.

Hughes, George W. *Memoir Descriptive of the March of a Division of the United States Army, under the Command of Brigadier General John E. Wool, from San Antonio de Bexar, in Texas, to Saltillo, in Mexico.* 31st Congress, 1st Session, Senate Executive Document 32. Washington, DC.

Hughes, John T. *Doniphan's Expedition; Containing an Account of the Conquest of New Mexico: General Kearney's Overland Expedition to California; Doniphan's Campaign against the Navajos; His Unparalleled March upon Chihuahua and Durango; and the Operations of General Price at Santa Fe, with a Sketch of the life of Col. Doniphan, by John T. Hughes, A.B., of the First Regiment of Missouri Cavalry.* Cincinnati: James, 1847. (Reprint edited by William Elsey Connelley, published in 1907.)

Jay, William. *A Review of the Causes and Consequences of the Mexican War.* Boston: Mussey, 1849.

Kemper, James Lawson. "The Mexican War Diary of James Lawson Kemper." Edited by Robert R. Jones, *Virginia Magazine of History and Biography,* 74 (October 1966): 387–428.

Kendall, George Wilkins. *The War between the United States and Mexico Illustrated, Embracing Pictorial Drawings of All the Principal Conflicts, by Carl Nebel . . . with a Description of Each Battle by George Kendall.* New York: Appleton, 1851.

Kenly, John Reese. *Memoirs of a Maryland Volunteer, War with Mexico, in the Years 1846-7-8.* Philadelphia: Lippincott, 1873.

Kirby-Smith, Ephraim. *To Mexico with Scott. Letters of Captain E. Kirby Smith to His Wife.* Edited by Emma Jerome Blackwood. Cambridge, MA: Harvard University Press, 1917.

Kirkham, Ralph W. *The Mexican War Journal and Letters of Ralph W. Kirkham.* Edited by Robert Ryal Miller. College Station: Texas A&M University Press, 1991.

Lane, Henry S. "The Mexican War Journal of Henry S. Lane." Edited by Graham A. Barringer. *Indiana Magazine of History* 53 (December 1957): 383–434.

Lomard, Albert. *The "High Private" with a Full and Exciting History of the New-York Volunteers, and the "Mysteries and Miseries" of the Mexican War.* New York: n.p., 1848.

Magoffin, Susan Shelby. *Down the Santa Fe Trail and into Mexico: The Diary of Susan Shelby Magoffin, 1846–1847.* Edited by Stella M. Drumm. New Haven, CT: Yale University Press, 1963.

Mansfield, Edward D. *The Mexican War: A History of its Origin, and a Detailed Account of the Victories Which Terminated in the Surren-*

der of the Capital; with the Official Despatches of the Generals. 10th ed. New York: Barnes, 1849.

———. *Life and Services of General Winfield Scott.* New York: Barnes, 1852.

May, George S., ed. "An Iowan in the Mexican War." *Iowa Journal of History* 53 (April 1955): 167–74.

McClellan, George B. *The Mexican War Diary of George B. McClellan.* Edited by William Starr Myers. Princeton, NJ: Princeton University Press, 1917.

McNierney, Michael, ed. *Taos 1847: The Revolt in Contemporary Accounts.* Boulder, CO: Johnson, 1980.

McSherry, Richard. *El Puchero: A Mixed Dish From Mexico, embracing General Scott's Campaign, with Sketches of Military Life, in Field and Camp, of the Character of the Country, Manners and Ways of the People, Etc.* Philadelphia: Lippincott, Grambo, 1850.

Meade, George Gordon. *The Life and Letters of George Gordon Meade, Major-General United States Army.* 2 vols. New York: Scribner's, 1913.

Moore, H. Judge. *Scott's Campaign in Mexico from the Rendezvous on the Island of Lobos to the Taking of the City.* Charleston, SC: Nixon, 1849.

Oswandel, J. Jacob. *Notes of the Mexican War: 1846–47–48.* Philadelphia: Author, 1885.

Otero, Mariano. "Consideraciones sobre la situación política y social de la Republica Mexicana en el año 1847" (Diciembre de 1847). *Obras*, vol. 1. Edited by Jesus Reyes Heroles. México: Porrúa, 1967. (Note: Excerpt translated in Robinson, *The View from Chapultepec*, pp. 5–31.)

Parker, William Harwar. *Recollections of a Naval Officer, 1841–1865.* New York: Scribner's, 1883.

Peck, John James. *The Sign of the Eagle: A View of Mexico 1830–1855.* San Diego, CA: Union-Tribune, 1970.

Pillow, Gideon J. *Defence of Maj. Gen. Pillow Before the Court of Inquiry, Frederick, Maryland, against the Charges Preferred against Him by Maj. Gen. Winfield Scott.* n.p., 1848.

Polk, James Knox. *The Diary of James K. Polk during His Presidency, 1845 to 1849.* 4 vols. Edited by Milo Milton Quaife. Chicago: McClurg, 1910.

Prieto, Guillermo. *Memorias de Mis Tiempos, 1828 a 1853.* Paris: Libreria de la Vda. de C. Bouret, 1906.

Quitman, John A. *Life and Correspondence of John A. Quitman, Major-General, U.S.A., and Governor of the State of Mississippi.* 2 vols. Edited by John F. H. Claiborne. New York: Harper, 1860.

Reid, Samuel C. *The Scouting Expeditions of McCulloch's Texas Rangers*. Philadelphia: Zieber, 1847.

Reilly, Tom. "Jane McManus Storms: Letters from the Mexican War, 1846–1848." *Southwestern Historical Quarterly* 85 (July 1981): 21–44.

Rejón, Manuel Crescencio. *Manuel Crescencio Rejón, pensamiento político*. Edited by Daneil Moreno. México: Universidad Nacional Autónoma de México, 1968. (Note: Section translated in Robinson, *The View from Chapultepec*, pp. 94–100.)

Roa Barcena, José María. *Recuerdos de la invasión norteamericana (1846–1848) por un jóven de entónces*. México: Colección de Escritores Mexicanos, Porrúa, 1947. (Note: Section translated in Robinson, *The View from Chapultepec*, pp. 40–49.)

Robertson, John B. *Reminiscences of a Campaign in Mexico by a Member of the "Bloody First."* Nashville, TN: York, 1849.

Robinson, Jacob S. *A Journal of the Santa Fe Expedition under Colonel Doniphan*. Reprinted with an historical introduction and notes by Carl L. Cannon, from the edition of 1848. Princeton, NJ: Princeton University Press, 1932.

Rowan, Stephen C. "Recollections of the Mexican War, Taken from the Journals of Lieutenant Stephen C. Rowan, U.S. Navy, Executive Officer of the U.S.S. *Cyane*, Pacific Squadron, 1845–1848." (Vol. 14, pp. 530–60). Edited by George W. Tyler. Annapolis, MD: U. S. Naval Institute Press, 1888.

Sanchez Lamego, Miguel A. *El colegio militar y la defensa de Chapultepec en Septiembre de 1847*. México: n.p., 1847.

Santa Anna, Antonio López de. *The Eagle: The Autobiography of Santa Anna*. Edited by Ann Fears Crawford. Austin, TX: Pemberton, 1967.

———. *Las guerras de México con Tejas y los Estados Unidos, Documentos para la história de México*. (Documentos inéditos o muy raros para la história de México, Publicados por Genaro Garcia, Tomo 29). México: Librería de VDA de Ch. Bouret, 1910. (Note: Includes material by Santa Anna.)

Scott, Winfield. *Memoirs of Lieut. General Scott, LL.D., Written by Himself*. 2 vols. New York: Sheldon, 1864.

Scribner, Benjamin Franklin. *Camp Life of a Volunteer: A Campaign in Mexico, or a Glimpse at Life in Camp by "One Who Has Seen the Elephant."* Philadelphia: Grigg, Elliot, 1847. (Reprint, Austin, TX: Jenkins, 1975.)

Sedgwick, John. *Correspondence of J. Sedgwick*. 2 vols. New York: Battel, 1903.

Semmes, Raphael. *Service Afloat and Ashore during the Mexican War.* Cincinnati: Moore, 1851.

———. *The Campaign of General Scott in the Valley of Mexico.* Cincinnati: Moore & Anderson, 1852.

Sierra O'Reilly, Justo. *Diario de nuestro viaje a los Estados Unidos.* México: Porrúa, 1938.

Smith, Franklin. *The Mexican War Journal of Captain Franklin Smith.* Edited by Joseph E. Chance. Jackson: University Press of Mississippi, 1991.

Smith, George Winston, and Charles Judah, eds. *Chronicles of the Gringos: The U.S. Army in the Mexican War, 1846–1848: Accounts of Eyewitnesses and Combatants.* Albuquerque: University of New Mexico Press, 1968.

Standage, Henry. *The March of the Mormon Battalion from Council Bluffs to California: Taken from the Journal of Henry Standage.* Edited by Frank Alfred Golder. New York: Century, 1928.

Taylor, Zachary. *Letters of Zachary Taylor from the Battle-fields of the Mexican War.* New York: Genesee, 1908. (Reprint, Kraus, 1970.)

Tennery, Thomas D. *The Mexican War Diary of Thomas D. Tennery.* Edited and introduction by D. E. Livingston-Little. Norman: University of Oklahoma Press, 1970.

Trahern, G. W. "George Washington Trahern: Cowboy Soldier from Mier to Buena Vista." Edited by A. R. Buchanan. *Southwestern Historical Quarterly* 78 (July 1954): 60–90.

Turner, Henry Smith. *The Original Journals of Henry Smith Turner with Stephen Watts Kearny to New Mexico and California 1846–1847.* Edited by Dwight L. Clarke. Norman: University of Oklahoma Press, 1966.

Webb, James Josiah. *Adventures in the Santa Fé Trade: 1844–1847.* Edited by Ralph P. Bieber. Vol. 1 of The Southwest Historical Series. Glendale, CA: Clark, 1931.

Wise, Henry A. *Los Gringos, or, an Inside View of Mexico and California, with Wanderings in Peru, Chili, and Polynesia.* New York: Baker & Scribner, 1849.

Wislizenus, Frederick A. *Memoir of a Tour to Northern Mexico, Connected with Col. Doniphan's Expedition, in 1846 and 1847.* 30th Congress, 1st Session, 1848. (Reprint Glorieta, NM: The Rio Grande Press, 1969.)

Wool, John E. "Notes and Documents: General John E. Wool's Memoranda of the Battle of Buena Vista." Edited by K. Jack Bauer. *Southwestern Historical Quarterly* 77 (1973–1974): 111–23.

Zeh, Frederick. *An Immigrant Soldier in the Mexican War.* Translated by William J. Orr; Edited by William J. Orr and Robert Ryal Miller. College Station: Texas A & M Press, 1995.

General Works

Anderson, John Q. "Soldier Lore of the War with Mexico." *Western Humanities Review* 11 (Autumn 1951): 321–30.

Balbontin, Manuel. *La invasion americana, 1846 a 1848: Apuntes del subteniente de artillería.* México: Esteva, 1883.

Bauer, K. Jack. *The Mexican War, 1846–1848.* New York: Macmillan, 1974.

Bosch García, Carlos. "Dos diplomacias y un problema." *Historia Mexicana* 2 (Julio–Septiembre 1952): 46–65.

Bravo Ugarte, José. *Historia de México.* 3 vols. México: Jus, 1959.

Connor, Seymour V., and Odie B. Faulk. *North America Divided: The Mexican War, 1846–1848.* New York: Oxford University Press, 1971.

Cuevas, Luis G. *Porvenir de Mexico, o juicio crítico sobre su estado político en 1821 y 1851.* 3 vols. México: Cumplido, 1851–1857. (New ed., México: Jus, 1954.)

Cutler, Wayne, John S. D. Eisenhower, Miguel E. Soto, and Douglas W. Richmond. *Essays on the Mexican War.* College Station: Texas A&M University Press, 1986.

Dillon, Lester R., Jr. *American Artillery in the Mexican War 1846–1847.* Austin, TX: Presidial, 1975.

Downey, Fairfax. "Tragic Story of the San Patricio Battalion." *American Heritage* 6 (June 1955): 20–23.

Dufour, Charles L. *The Mexican War: A Compact History: 1846–1848.* New York: Hawthorn, 1968.

Eisenhower, John S. D. *So Far from God: The U.S. War with Mexico: 1846–1848.* New York: Random House, 1989.

Ellsworth, Clayton Sumner. "The American Churches and the Mexican War." *American Historical Review* 44 (January 1940): 301–46.

Faulk, Odie B., and Joseph A. Stout, Jr., eds. *The Mexican War, Changing Interpretations.* Chicago: Swallow, 1973.

Gillett, Mary C. *The Army Medical Department: 1818–1865.* Washington, DC: Center of Military History, U. S. Army, 1987.

Henry, Robert Selph. *The Story of the Mexican War.* Indianapolis: Bobbs-Merrill, 1950.

Heroles, Jesus Reyes. *Mariano Otero: Obras.* 2 vols. México: Porrúa, 1967.

Houston, Donald E. "The Role of Artillery in the Mexican War." *Journal of the West.* Vol. 2 (April 1972): 273–84.

Irey, Thomas R. "Soldiering, Suffering, and Dying in the Mexican War." *Journal of the West*. Vol. 11, no. 1 (April 1972): 285–98.

Johannsen, Robert W. *To the Halls of the Montezumas: The Mexican War in the American Imagination*. New York: Oxford University Press, 1985.

Kreidberg, Marvin A., and Merton G. Henry. *History of Military Mobilization in the United States Army 1775–1945*. Washington, DC: Department of the Army, 1955.

McCaffrey, James M. *Army of Manifest Destiny: The American Soldier in the Mexican War, 1846–1848*. New York: New York University Press, 1992.

McDonald, Archie D., ed. *The Mexican War: Crisis for American Democracy*. Lexington, MA: Heath, 1969.

McEniry, Sister Blanche Marie. *American Catholics in the War with Mexico*. Washington, DC: Catholic University, 1937.

McWhiney, Grady, and Sue McWhiney, eds. *To Mexico with Taylor and Scott 1845–1847*. Waltham, MA: Blaisdell, 1969.

Miller, Robert Ryal. *Shamrock and Sword: The Saint Patrick's Battalion in the U.S.–Mexican War*. Norman: University of Oklahoma Press, 1989.

Nevin, David. *The Mexican War*. Alexandria, VA: Time-Life Books, 1978.

Paz, Octavio. *The Labyrinth of Solitude: Life and Thought in Mexico*. Translated by Lysander Kemp. New York: Grove, 1961.

Rabasa, Emilio. *La evolución histórica de México*. México: Porrúa, 1956.

Ramírez, José Fernando. *Mexico during the War with the United States*. Translated by Elliott B. Scheer; Edited by Walter V. Scholes. Columbia: University of Missouri Press, 1950.

Ramsey, Albert C., trans. *The Other Side: Or, Notes for the History of the War Between Mexico and the United States*. New York: Wiley, 1850.

Rea, Vargas, ed. *Apuntes históricos sobre los acontecimientos notables de la guerra entre México y los Estados Unidos del Norte*. México: Biblioteca Aportación Histórica, 1945.

Risch, Erna. *Quartermaster Support of the Army. A History of the Corps 1775–1939*. Washington, DC: Quartermaster Historian's Office, 1962.

Riva Palacio, Vicente, ed. *México a través de los siglos*. 6 vols. México: Cumbre, 1940.

Rives, George Lockhart. *The United States and Mexico, 1821–1848*. 2 vols. New York: Scribner's, 1913.

Robinson, Cecil, ed. and trans. *The View from Chapultepec: Mexican*

Writers on the Mexican-American War. Tucson: University of Arizona Press, 1989.

Rodenbough, Theophilus F., and William L. Haskin, eds. *The Army of the United States: Historical Sketches of Staff and Line, with Portraits of General-in-Chief.* New York: Argonaut, 1966.

Singletary, Otis A. *The Mexican War.* Chicago: University of Chicago Press, 1960.

Smith, Gustavus W. "Company A Engineers in the Mexican War." *Military Engineer* (1964), pp. 336–40.

Smith, Justin H. *The War with Mexico.* 2 vols. New York: Macmillan, 1919. (Reprinted by Smith, 1963.)

Spell, Lota M. "The Anglo-Saxon Press in Mexico, 1846–1848." *American Historical Review* 38 (October 1932): 20–31.

Tamayo, Jorge L. "Lo que perdimos y lo que nos queda." *Cuadernos Americanos* 40 (Julio–Agosto 1948): 31–53.

Toro, Alfonso, *Compendio de historia de Mexico.* México: Patria, 1943.

Traas, Adrian George. *From the Golden Gate to Mexico City: The U.S. Army Topographical Engineers in the Mexican War, 1846–1848.* Washington, DC: Office of History, Corps of Engineers and Center of Military History, U. S. Army, 1993.

Valades, José C. *Breve historia de la guerra con los Estados Unidos.* México: Patria, 1947.

Vasconcelos, José. *Breve historia de Mexico.* México: Botas, 1944. (Note: Section translated in Robinson, *The View from Chapultepec,* pp. 134–38.)

Vázquez, Josefina Zoraida. *Mexicanos y norteamericanos ante la guerra del 47.* México: Sep–Setentas 19, Secretaría de Educación Pública, 1972. (Note: Section translated in Robinson, *The View from Chapultepec,* pp. 193–95.)

Vigil y Robles, Guillermo. *La invasión de México por los Estados Unidos en los años de 1846, 1847, y 1848.* México: Correcional, 1923.

Weems, John Edward. *To Conquer a Peace: The War between the United States and Mexico.* Garden City, NY: Doubleday, 1974.

Weigley, Russell F. *History of the United States Army.* New York: Macmillan, 1967.

Wilcox, Cadmus M. *History of the Mexican War.* Washington, DC: Church News, 1892.

Williams, Mary Wilhelmine. "Secessionist Diplomacy of Yucatán." *Hispanic American Historical Review* 9 (May 1929): 132–43.

Yáñez, Aaron P. Mahr, ed. *Proceedings of the First Annual Palo Alto Conference.* Brownsville, TX: U. S. Department of the Interior, 1994.

Zea, Leopoldo. *La filosofía como compromiso y otros ensayos*. México: Porrúa, 1965. (Note: Section translated in Robinson, *The View from Chapultepec*, pp. 142–53.)

Causes of the War and Diplomatic Relations

Brack, Gene M. *Mexico Views Manifest Destiny, 1821–1846: An Essay on the Origins of the Mexican War*. Albuquerque: University of New Mexico Press, 1975.

Carreño, Alberto María. *Mexico y los Estados Unidos de America*. México: Jus, 1962.

Fuentes Díaz, Vicente. *La intervención norteamericana en México*. México: Nuevo Mundo, 1947.

Griswold del Castillo, Richard. *The Treaty of Guadalupe Hidalgo: A Legacy of Conflict*. Norman: University of Oklahoma Press, 1990.

Hale, Charles A. "The War With the United States and the Crisis in Mexican Thought." *The Americas* 14 (October 1957): 153–74.

Jay, William. *A Review of the Causes and Consequences of the Mexican War*. Boston: Mussey, 1849.

Kohl, Clayton Charles. *Claims as a Cause of the Mexican War*. New York: New York University Press, 1914.

Lofgren, Charles A. "Force and Diplomacy, 1846–1848." *Military Affairs* 31 (Summer 1967): 57–65.

Merk, Frederick. *Manifest Destiny and Mission in American History: A Reinterpretation*. New York: Knopf, 1963.

———. *The Monroe Doctrine and American Expansionism, 1843–1849*. New York: Knopf, 1966.

Moseley, Edward H. "The United States and Mexico, 1810–1850." Edited by T. Ray Shurbutt. *United States–Latin American Relations, 1800–1850: The Formative Generations*. Tuscaloosa: University of Alabama Press, 1991.

Peña y Reyes, Antonio de la, ed. *Don Manuel Eduardo de Gorostiza y la cuestión de Texas*. México: Secretario de Relaciones Exteriores, 1924.

Price, Glenn W. *Origins of the War with Mexico: The Polk-Stockton Intrigue*. Austin: University of Texas Press, 1967.

Rejón, Manuel Crescencio. *Pensamiento politico*. México: Universidad Nacional Autónoma de México, 1968. (Note: Section translated in Robinson, *The View from Chapultepec*, pp. 94–100.)

Ruiz, Ramón Eduardo, ed. *The Mexican War: Was It Manifest Destiny?* New York: Holt, Rinehart & Winston, 1963.

Schroeder, John H. *Mr. Polk's War: American Opposition and Dissent, 1846–1848*. Madison: University of Wisconsin Press, 1973.

Sierra O'Reilly, Justo. *Diario de nuestro viaje a los Estados Unidos:*

La pretendida anexión de Yucatán, Prólogo y Notas de Héctor Pérez Martínez. Mexico: Porrúa, 1938.

———. *The Political Evolution of the Mexican People.* Translated by Charles Ramsdell. Austin: University of Texas Press, 1969.

Soto, Miguel E. "The Monarchist Conspiracy and the Mexican War." In Douglas W. Richmond, ed. *Essays on the Mexican War.* Arlington: University of Texas Press, 1986.

Stenberg, Richard R. "The Failure of Polk's Mexican War Intrigue of 1845." *Pacific Historical Review* 14 (March 1935): 36–68.

Weber, David J. *The Mexican Frontier, 1821–1846: The American Southwest Under Mexico.* Albuquerque: University of New Mexico Press, 1982.

Weinberg, Albert K. *Manifest Destiny: A Study of Nationalist Expansion in American History.* Chicago: Quadrangle, 1963.

Zorilla, Luis G. *Historia de las relaciones entre México y los Estados Unidos, 1800–1958.* México: Porrúa, 1965.

Biographies of Participants

Bauer, K. Jack. *Zachary Taylor: Soldier, Planter, Statesman of the Old Southwest.* Baton Rouge: Louisiana State University Press, 1985.

Brackett, Albert G. *General Lane's Brigade in Central Mexico.* Cincinnati: Derby, 1854.

Brown, Walter Lee. "The Mexican War Experiences of Albert Pike and the 'Mounted Devils' of Arkansas." *Arkansas Historical Quarterly* 12 (Winter 1953): 301–15.

Burke, James Wakefield. *David Crockett: Man behind the Myth.* Austin, TX: Eakin, 1984.

Calcott, Wilfrid Hardy. *Santa Anna, the Story of an Enigma Who Once Was Mexico.* Norman: University of Oklahoma Press, 1936.

Carreño, Alberto María. *Jefes del ejército méxicano en 1847: Biografías de generales de división y de brigada y de coroneles del ejército méxicano por fines del año de 1847.* México: Secretaria de Fomento, 1914.

Chance, Joseph E. *Jefferson Davis's Mexican War Regiment.* Jackson: University Press of Mississippi, 1991.

Clarke, Dwight L. *Stephen Watts Kearny, Soldier of the West.* Norman: University of Oklahoma Press, 1961.

Condon, William H. *The Life of Major-General James Shields: Hero of Three Wars and Senator from Three States.* Chicago: Blakely, 1900.

Conner, Philip Syng Physick. *The Home Squadron under Commodore Conner in the War with Mexico.* Philadelphia: n.p., 1896.

Cooling, Benjamin Franklin. "Lew Wallace and Gideon Pillow:

Enigmas and Variations on an American Military Theme." *Lincoln Herald* 84 (Summer 1981).

Cooper, Susan F. "Rear Admiral William Branford Shubrick." *Harper's New Monthly Magazine* 53 (August 1878): 400–7.

Copeland, Fayette. *Kendall of the Picayune*. Norman: University of Oklahoma Press, 1943.

Cotner, Thomas Ewing. *The Military and Political Career of José Joaquín de Herrera, 1792–1854*. Austin: University of Texas Press, 1949.

Cullum, George W. *Biographical Register of the Officers and Graduates of the U.S. Military Academy at West Point, N.Y. from Its Establishment, in 1802, to 1890, with the Early History of the United States Military Academy*. Boston: Houghton Mifflin, 1891.

De Armond, Louis. "Justo Sierra O'Reilly and Yucatán-United States Relations, 1847–1848." *Hispanic American Historical Review* 31 (August 1951): 420–36.

Dyer, Brainerd. *Zachary Taylor*. Baton Rouge: Louisiana State University Press, 1946.

Elliott, Charles Winslow. *Winfield Scott: The Soldier and the Man*. New York: Macmillan, 1937.

Farrell, John J. *James K. Polk, 1795–1849*. Dobbs Ferry, NY: Oceana, 1970.

Freeman, Douglas Southall. *R. E. Lee: A Biography*. 4 vols. New York: Scribner's, 1934–1936.

Fuentes Mares, José. *Santa Anna: Aurora y Ocaso de un Comediante*. México: Jus, 1956.

Guild, Thelma S., and Harvey L. Carter. *Kit Carson: A Pattern for Heroes*. Lincoln: University of Nebraska Press, 1984.

Hamilton, Holman. *Zachary Taylor, Soldier of the Republic*. Indianapolis: Bobbs-Merrill, 1941.

Hoyt, Edwin P. *Zachary Taylor*. Chicago: Reilly & Lee, 1966.

Kearny, Thomas. " 'Kit' Carson as Interpreted by Stanley Vestal." *New Mexico Historical Review* 5 (January 1930): 1–16.

Lewis, Lloyd. *Captain Sam Grant*. Boston: Little, Brown, 1950.

Long, David F. *Sailor-Diplomat: A Biography of Commodore James Biddle, 1783–1848*. Boston: Northeastern University Press, 1983.

McCormac, Eugene Irving. *James K. Polk. A Political Biography*. New York: Russell & Russell, 1965.

McKinley, Silas Bent, and Silas Bent. *Old Rough and Ready: The Life and Times of Zachary Taylor*. New York: Vanguard, 1946.

Morison, Samuel Eliot. *"Old Bruin" Commodore Matthew C. Perry, 1794–1858*. Boston: Little, Brown, 1967.

Muñoz, Rafael F. *Antonio López de Santa Anna*. México: México Nuevo, 1937.

Nevins, Allan. *Frémont: Pathmaker of the West.* New York: Longmans, Green, 1955.

Nichols, Edward J. *Zach Taylor's Little Army.* Garden City, NY: Doubleday, 1963.

Nichols, Roy Franklin. *Franklin Pierce: Young Hickory of the Granite Hills.* Philadelphia: University of Pennsylvania Press, 1931.

Rea, Robert R. *Sterling Price. The Lee of the West.* Little Rock, AR: Pioneer, 1959.

Reavis, L. U. *The Life and Military Services of Gen. William Selby Harney.* St. Louis: Bryan, Brand, 1878.

Robinson, Fayette. *Mexico and Her Military Chieftains.* Philadelphia: Butler, 1847.

Rose, Victor M. *The Life and Services of Gen. Ben McCulloch.* Austin, TX: Steck, 1958.

Sears, Louis Martin. *John Slidell.* Durham, NC: Duke University Press, 1925.

————. "Nicholas P. Trist, A Diplomat with Ideals." *Mississippi Valley Historical Review* 11 (June 1924): 85–98.

Smith, Arthur D. Howden. *Old Fuss and Feathers. The Life and Exploits of Lt. General Winfield Scott.* New York: Greystone, 1937.

Sobarzo, Alejandro. *Deber y conciencia: Nicolás Trist, el negociador norteamericano en la guerra del 47.* México: Diana, 1990.

Vandiver, Frank E. "The Mexican War Experience of Josiah Gorgas." *Journal of Southern History* 13 (August 1947): 373–94.

Vestal, Stanley. *Kit Carson, The Happy Warrior of the Old West.* Boston: Houghton Mifflin, 1928.

Wallace, Edward S. *General William Jenkins Worth: Monterrey's Forgotten Hero.* Dallas: Southern Methodist University Press, 1953.

————. "General William Jenkins Worth and Texas." *Southwestern Historical Quarterly* 54 (October 1950): 159–68.

Wallace, Isabel. *Life and Letters of General W. H. L. Wallace.* Chicago: Donnelley, 1909.

Waugh, John C. *The Class of 1846: From West Point to Appomattox: Stonewall Jackson, George McClellan and Their Brothers.* New York: Warner, 1994.

Zorilla, Luis G. *Historia de las relaciones entre México y los Estados Unidos de América, 1800–1858.* 2 vols. México: Porrúa, 1965.

Military Units or State Organizations

Barton, Henry W. "Five Texas Frontier Companies during the Mexican War." *Southwestern Historical Quarterly* 66 (1962): 17–30.

Brent, Robert A. "Mississippi and the Mexican War." *Journal of Mississippi History* 31 (August 1969): 202–14.

Brown, Walter Lee. "The Mexican War Experiences of Albert Pike and the 'Mounted Devils' of Arkansas." *Arkansas Historical Quarterly* 12 (1953): 301–15.

Buley, R. C. "Indiana in the Mexican War." *Indiana Magazine of History* 15 (September–December 1919): 261–326; 16 (March 1920): 48–68.

Butler, Steven R. *Alabama Volunteers in the Mexican War: 1846–1848, A History and Annotated Roster.* Richardson, TX: Descendants of Mexican War Veterans, 1996.

Clark, Francis D. *The First Regiment of New York Volunteers Commanded by Col. Jonathan D. Stevenson, in the Mexican War.* New York: Evans, 1882.

Elliott, Isaac Hughes. *Illinois Soldiers in the Mexican War.* Springfield, IL: n.p., 1882.

Fakes, Turner J., Jr. "Memphis and the Mexican War." *West Tennessee Historical Society Papers* 2 (1948): 119–44.

Greer, James K. *Colonel Jack Hays, Texas Frontier Leader and California Builder.* New York: Dutton, 1952.

Hackenburg, Randy W. *Pennsylvania in the War with Mexico.* Shippensburg, PA: White Mane, 1992.

Henderson, Alfred J. "A Morgan County Volunteer in the Mexican War." *Journal of the Illinois State Historical Society* 41 (December 1948): 383–99.

Kenley, John Reese. *Memoirs of a Maryland Volunteer: War with Mexico, in the Years 1846–47–48.* Philadelphia: Lippincott, 1873.

Kurtz, Wilbur G., Jr. "The First Regiment of Georgia Volunteers in the Mexican War." *Georgia Historical Quarterly* 27 (December 1943): 301–23.

Perry, Oran. *Indiana in the Mexican War.* Indianapolis: Burford, 1908.

Pugh, N. M. "Contemporary Comments on Texas, 1844–1847." *Southwestern Historical Quarterly* 62 (1959): 367–70.

Reid, Samuel C., Jr. *The Scouting Expeditions of McCullouch's Texas Rangers.* Philadelphia: Zieber, 1847.

Rutland, Robert. "Captain William B. Walton, Mexican War Volunteer." *Tennessee Historical Quarterly* 11 (1952): 171–79.

Ryan, Daniel J. "Ohio in the Mexican War." *Ohio Archaeological and Historical Quarterly* 21 (April–July 1912): 277–95.

Salisbury, Richard V. "Kentuckians at the Battle of Buena Vista." *Filson Club History Quarterly* 61 (January 1987): 34–53.

Smith, Isaac. *Reminiscences of a Campaign in Mexico: An Account of the Operations of the Indiana Brigade.* Indianapolis: Chapmans & Spahn, 1848.

Wallace, Lee A., Jr. "The First Regiment of Virginia Volunteers, 1846–1848." *Virginia Magazine of History and Biography* 77 (January 1969): 46–77.

———. "Raising a Volunteer Regiment for Mexico, 1846–1847." *North Carolina Historical Review* 35 (January 1958): 20–33.

Webb, Walter Prescott. *The Texas Rangers in the Mexican War.* Austin, TX: Jenkins Garrett, 1975.

Taylor's Campaign in Texas and Northeastern Mexico

Alessio Robles, Vito. *Coahuila y Texas desde la consumación de la independencia hasta el tratado de paz de Guadalupe Hidalgo.* 2 vols. México: n.p., 1945–46.

Baylies, Francis. "The March of the United States Troops, under the Command of General John E. Wool, from San Antonio, Texas to Saltillo, Mexico, in the Year 1846." *Stryker's American Register* 5 (1850): 297–312.

Ferguson, Henry N. *The Port of Brownsville, a Maritime History of the Rio Grande Valley.* Brownsville, TX: Springman-King, 1976.

Lavender, David. *Climax at Buena Vista: The American Campaigns in Northeastern Mexico, 1846–47.* Philadelphia: Lippincott, 1966.

Lea, Tom. *The King Ranch.* 2 vols. Boston: Little, Brown, 1957.

Long, Jeff. *Duel of Eagles: The Mexican and U.S. Fight for the Alamo.* New York: Morrow, 1990.

López Uraga, José. *Sumaria mandada formar a pedimento del Sr. Coronel del 4 regimiento de infantería.* México: Navarro, 1846.

Martinez, Victor. "Battle of Palo Alto." Map and text. Brownsville, TX: Walter Plitt, Palo Alto National Park Committee, 1993.

Nichols, Edward Jay. *Zach Taylor's Little Army.* New York: Doubleday, 1963.

Payne, Darwin. "Camp Life in the Army of Occupation: Corpus Christi, July 1845 to March 1846." *Southwestern Historical Quarterly* 73 (January 1970): 326–42.

Robertson, Brian. *Wild Horse Desert: The Heritage of South Texas.* Edinburg, TX: New Santander, 1985.

Salisbury, Richard V. "Kentuckians at the Battle of Buena Vista." *Filson Club History Quarterly* 61 (January 1987): 34–53.

Scott, Florence Johnson. *Old Rough and Ready on the Rio Grande.* San Antonio, TX: Naylor, 1935.

Campaigns in New Mexico and Chihuahua

Armstrong, Andrew. "The Brazito Battlefield." *New Mexico Historical Review* 35 (January 1960): 63–74.

Bancroft, Hubert Howe. *History of Arizona and New Mexico, 1530–1888.* San Francisco: History, 1889.

Beck, Warren A., and Yzez D. Haase. *Historical Atlas of New Mexico.* Norman: University of Oklahoma Press, 1969.

Bishop, W. W. *Journal of the 12 months' Campaign of General Shields's Brigade in Mexico, 1846–47.* St. Louis: n.p., 1847.

Bloom, John Porter. "New Mexico as Viewed by Americans, 1846–1849." *New Mexico Historical Review* 34 (July 1959): 165–98.

Clark, Dwight L., and George Ruhlen. "The Final Roster of the Army of the West, 1846–1847." *California Historical Society Quarterly* 44 (March 1964): 37–44.

Connelley, William Elsey. *Doniphan's Expedition and the Conquest of New Mexico and California.* Kansas City, MO: Bryant & Douglas, 1907. (Note: Includes reprint of John T. Hughes, *Doniphan's Expedition.*)

Hall, Martin Hardwick. *Sibley's New Mexico Campaign.* Austin: University of Texas Press, 1960.

Horgan, Paul. *Lamy of Santa Fe.* New York: Noonday, 1975.

Jordán, Fernando. *Crónica de un país bárbaro.* Chihuahua: Centro Librero La Prensa, 1956.

McNierney, Michael, ed. *Taos, 1847: The Revolt in Contemporary Accounts.* Boulder, CO: Johnson, 1980.

Spicer, Edward H. *Cycles of Conquest: The Impact of Spain, Mexico, and the United States on the Indians of the Southwest, 1533–1960.* Tucson: University of Arizona Press, 1962.

Twitchell, Ralph Emerson. *The Conquest of Santa Fe 1846.* Truchas, NM: Tate Gallery, 1967.

Operations in California and Arizona

Ames, George Walcott, Jr. "Horse Marines, California, 1846." *California Historical Society Quarterly* 18 (March 1939): 72–84.

Bancroft, Hubert Howe. *History of California.* Vol. 4, 1840–1845, and Vol. 5, 1846–1848. San Francisco: History, 1886.

———. *History of Arizona and New Mexico, 1530–1888.* San Francisco: History, 1889.

Bliss, Robert S. "The Journal of Robert S. Bliss, with the Mormon Battalion." *Utah Historical Quarterly* 4 (1931): 67–96, 110–28.

Coy, Owen C. *The Battle of San Pasqual*. Sacramento: California Historical Survey Commission, 1921.

Dutton, Bertha P. *American Indians of the Southwest*. Albuquerque: University of New Mexico Press, 1983.

Gerhard, Peter. "Baja California in the Mexican War, 1846–1848." *Pacific Historical Review* 14 (1945): 418–24.

Gilbert, E. W. *The Exploration of Western America: 1800–1850: An Historical Geography*. Cambridge: Cambridge University Press, 1933.

Goetzmann, William H. *Army Exploration in the American West: 1803–1863*. New Haven, CT: Yale University Press, 1959.

Golder, Frank Alfred, ed. *The March of the Mormon Battalion from Council Bluffs to California*. New York: Century, 1928.

Graebner, Norman A. *Empire on the Pacific: A Study in American Continental Expansion*. New York: Ronald, 1955.

Griffen, Helen S. "The California Battalion's Route to Los Angeles." *Journal of the West* 5 (April 1966): 207–14.

Griffin, John S. *A Doctor Comes to California: the Diary of John S. Griffin, Assistant Surgeon with Kearny's Dragoons, 1846–47*. San Francisco: California Historical Society, 1943.

Harlow, Neal. *California Conquered: War and Peace on the Pacific, 1846–1850*. Berkeley: University of California Press, 1982.

Hussey, John Adam. "Bear Flag Revolt." *American Heritage* 1 (Spring 1950): 24–27.

Marti, Werner H. *Messenger of Destiny. The California Adventures, 1846–1847 of Archibald H. Gillespie, U.S. Marine Corps*. San Francisco: Howell, 1955.

McNamee, Gregory, *Gila: The Life and Death of an American River*. New York: Orion, 1994.

Meadows, Don. *The American Occupation of La Paz (Lower California, 1847–49)*. Los Angeles: Dawson, 1955.

National Park Service, Department of the Interior. *Exploring the American West, 1803–1879*. Washington, DC: Author, 1982.

Parker, Robert J. "Secret Affairs of the Mexican War: Larkin's California Mission." *Historical Society of Southern California Quarterly* 20 (1938): 22–24.

Royce, Josiah. *California, from the Conquest in 1846 to the Second Vigilance Committee in San Francisco: A Study of American Character*. New York: Knopf, 1948.

Ruhlen, George. "Kearny's Route from the Rio Grande to the Gila." *New Mexico Historical Review* 32 (July 1957): 213–30.

Tanner, John Douglas. "Campaigns for Los Angeles—December 29, 1846 to January 10, 1847." *California Historical Society Quarterly* 48 (September 1969): 219–41.

Todd, Charles Burr. *The Battles of San Pasqual: A Study*. Pomona, CA: Progress, 1925.

Tyler, Daniel. *A Concise History of the Mormon Battalion in the Mexican War 1846–1847*. n.p., 1881.

Woodward, Arthur. *Lances at San Pascual*. San Francisco: California Historical Society, 1948.

Wyllys, Rufus Kay, *Arizona: The History of a Frontier State*. Phoenix: Hobson & Herr, 1950.

Campaign from Veracruz to Central Mexico

Bauer, K. Jack. "The Veracruz Expedition of 1847." *Military Affairs* 20 (Fall 1956): 162–69.

Clark, Paul C., Jr., and Edward H. Moseley. "D-Day Veracruz-1847." *Joint Force Quarterly* 10 (1996): 102–15.

Gordon, George H. "The Battles of Contreras and Churubusco." *Military Historical Society of Massachusetts Papers* 13 (1913): 561–98.

Lerdo de Tejada, Miguel M. *Apuntes históricos de la heróica ciudad de Veracruz*. 3 vols., México: Vicente García Torres, 1850–1858.

Lott, W. S. "The Landing of the Expedition Against Vera Cruz in 1847." *Military Service Institution of the United States* 24 (May 1899): 422–28.

Miranda, Martha Poblett. *Cien Viajeros en Veracruz: Crónicas y relatos, tomo V, 1836–1854*. Veracruz, México: Gobierno del Estado de Veracruz, 1992.

Molina, Ignacio. "El asalto al Castillo de Chapultepec el día 13 de septiembre de 1847." *Revista Positiva* 2 (Octubre 1, 1902): 444–64.

Moore, H. Judge. *Scott's Campaign in Mexico: From the Rendezvous on the Island of Lobos to the Taking of the City, Including an Account of the Siege of Puebla*. Charleston, SC: Nixon, 1849.

Museo Nacional de las Intervenciones, Coordinación Nacional de Monumentos Históricos, Exconvento de Churubusco, Coyoacán. *Churubusco, una historia*. México: Instituto Nacional de Antropología e Historia, n.d.

Pohl, James W. "The Influence of Antonine Henri de Jomini on Winfield Scott's Campaign in the Mexican War." *Southwestern Historical Quarterly* 77 (1973–1974): 85–110.

Schulz, Enrique E. "Batalla de Padierna, Agosto 16 de 1847." *Boletin de Ingenieros* 4 (1913).

Torrea, Juan Manuel. "Un héroe máximo de la intervención americana; Xicoténcatl." *Sociedad Mexicana de Geografía y Estadística* 39 (1929).

Wallace, Edward S. "The United States Army in Mexico City." *Military Affairs* 13 (Fall 1949): 158–66.

The Blockade and Naval Operations

Bauer, K. Jack. *Surfboats and Horse Marines: U.S. Naval Operations in the Mexican War, 1846–48.* Annapolis, MD: U. S. Naval Institute, 1969.

Betts, John L. "The United States Navy in the Mexican War." *Hispanic American Historical Review* 36 (1956): 370–71.

Conner, Philip Syng Physick. *The Home Squadron under Commodore Conner in the War with Mexico, Being a Synopsis of Its Services.* n.p., 1896.

Johnson, Robert Erwin. *Thence Round Cape Horn: The Story of United States Naval Forces on the Pacific Station, 1818–1923.* Annapolis, MD: U.S. Naval Institute, 1963.

Jones, Oakah L., Jr. "The Pacific Squadron and the Conquest of California." *Journal of the West* 5 (April 1966): 187–202.

Manno, Francis Joseph. "Yucatán en la guerra entre México y Estados Unidos." *Revista de la Universidad de Yucatán* 5 (July–August 1963): 51–64.

Neeser, Robert Wilden. "The Navy's part in the Acquisition of California, 1846–1848." *U.S. Naval Institute Proceedings* 34 (1908): 267–76.

Scheina, Robert L. "The Forgotten Fleet: The Mexican Navy on the Eve of War, 1845." *American Nepture* 30 (January 1970): 46–55.

———. "Seapower Misused: Mexico at War, 1846–8." *Mariner's Mirror* 57 (1971): 203–14.

Illustrations and Visual Presentation

Goetzmann, William H. *Sam Chamberlain's Mexican War: The San Jacinto Museum of History Paintings.* Austin: Texas State Historical Association, 1993.

Sandweiss, Martha A., Rick Stewart, and Ben W. Huseman. *Eyewitness to War: Prints and Daguerreotypes of the Mexican War, 1846–1848.* Fort Worth, TX: Amon Carter Museum, 1989.

Tyler, Ronnie C. *The Mexican War: A Lithographic Record.* Austin: Texas State Historical Association, 1973.

Bibliographies and Guides to Additional Material

Connor, Seymour V., and Odie B. Faulk. "Analytical Bibliography." In *North America Divided: The Mexican War, 1846–1848.* New York: Oxford University Press, 1971.

Diccionario Porrúa, de historia, biografía y geografía de México. 3d ed., 2 vols. México: Porrúa, 1971.

Garrett, Jenkins. *The Mexican-American War of 1846–1848: A Bibliography of the Holdings of the Libraries: University of Texas at Arlington.* Edited by Katherine R. Goodwin. College Station: Texas A&M Press, 1995.

Trask, David F., Michael C. Meyer, and Roger R. Trask, eds. *A Bibliography of United States–Latin American Relations since 1810: A Selected List of Eleven Thousand Published References.* Lincoln: University of Nebraska Press, 1968.

Tutorow, Norman E., comp. and ed. *The Mexican-American War: An Annotated Bibliography.* Westport, CT: Greenwood, 1981.

Yale University Library. "The Mexican War, 1846–1848: A Collection of Contemporary Materials Presented to the Yale University Library by Frederick W. Beinecke." Compiled by Jerry Patterson. *Yale University Library Gazette* 34 (1960): 94–123.

About the Authors

Edward H. Moseley, a native of Thomaston, Alabama, received his Ph.D. in Latin American history from the University of Alabama, and attended the University of Nuevo León in Monterrey, Mexico, in 1959 and 1960, through a Fulbright scholarship. Moseley served as director of the Latin American Studies Program of the University of Alabama and is presently director of the Capstone International Program Center and professor of Latin American history.

Paul C. Clark, Jr., a native of Candor, North Carolina, completed his undergraduate work at the University of North Carolina in Chapel Hill and received his Ph.D. from the University of Alabama. He is an associate professor at the Armed Forces Staff College in Norfolk, Virginia, where he teaches strategy and Latin American studies.